Flyfisher's Guide to™

CHESAPEAKE BAY

~ INCLUDES LIGHT TACKLE ~

Titles Available in This Series

Flyfisher's Guide to Colorado

Flyfisher's Guide to the Florida Keys

Flyfisher's Guide to Florida—Freshwater

Flyfisher's Guide to Idaho

Flyfisher's Guide to Montana

Flyfisher's Guide to Michigan

Flyfisher's Guide to Minnesota

Flyfisher's Guide to New York

Flyfisher's Guide to Northern California

Flyfisher's Guide to Northern New England

Flyfisher's Guide to Oregon

Flyfisher's Guide to Pennsylvania

Flyfisher's Guide to Texas

Flyfisher's Guide to Utah

Flyfisher's Guide to Virginia

Flyfisher's Guide to Washington

Flyfisher's Guide to Wyoming

On the Fly Guide to the Northwest

Saltwater Angler's Guide to the Southeast

Saltwater Angler's Guide to Southern California

Flyfisher's Guide to™

CHESAPEAKE BAY
~ INCLUDES LIGHT TACKLE ~

Ed Russell and Bill May

Wilderness
Adventures
Press, Inc.™

Belgrade, Montana

This book was made with an easy opening, lay flat binding.

Cover photograph © 2002 Lefty Kreh

Photographs contained herein © 2002 Ed Russell, Bill May and Joe Bruce

Gamefish Illustrations © 2002 Duane Raver

Information for illustrations and charts provided by Maptech:

> Maptech
> 888-839-5551
> Website: www.maptech.com
> E-mail: marinesales@maptech.com

Maps, book design and cover design © 2002 Wilderness Adventures Press, Inc.
Flyfisher's Guide to™

> *Published by Wilderness Adventures Press, Inc.*
> *45 Buckskin Road*
> *Belgrade, MT 59714*
> *800-925-3339*
> *Website: www.wildadv.com*
> *email: books@wildadv.com*

Printed in the United States of America

Library of Congress Cataloging-in-Publication Data

Russell, Ed, 1936-
 Flyfisher's and light tackle guide to Chesapeake Bay/ by Ed Russell
and Bill May.
   p. cm.
 ISBN 1-885106-94-7 (pbk. : alk. paper)
 1. Fishing--Chesapeake Bay (Md. and Va.)--Guidebooks. 2. Chesapeake
Bay (Md. and Va.)--Guidebooks. I. May, Bill, 1941- II. Title.
 SH464.C47 R87 2002
 799.1'66147--dc21

                                                              2002151123

Table of Contents

This book is dedicated to our wives, Doris and Carolyn,
for encouraging us and putting up with us.

Acknowledgments

One of the best things about living in our part of Chesapeake Country is that we're in the midst of some great people. Better yet, we're within easy driving distance of international outdoor writing and photography legends, Lefty Kreh and C. Boyd Pfeiffer, and regional legend, Gary Diamond. We've been friends with Lefty and Boyd for over 40 years and with Gary for over 25 years. All three contributed significantly to this book.

Lefty always says, "There's no better fisherman than the local expert on his home waters." We dealt with a lot of them, including, again, Gary Diamond, Joe Bruce of the Fisherman's Edge; Wayne Blottenberger, "The Sage of the Susquehanna," Captain Norm Bartlett; Captain Gary Neitzey; Captain Richie Gaines; Harry Pippin; Captain Mike Murphy, Captain Kevin Josenhans, and Captain Bo Toepfer.

From the Maryland Department of Natural Resources, we want to thank Dale Weinrcich and Rudy Lukakovick, John Surrick and Bob Lunsford. Their equally helpful counterparts at Virginia Marine Resources Commission include Claude Bain, Corey Routh, and Lewis Gillingham.

In Virginia, a lot of our information came from experts who are dedicated members of some great local clubs. From the Virginia Anglers Club, Elly Robinson, III gave us information on the CBBT and Western Shore Rivers; from the Virginia Coastal Fly Anglers, Kevin Du Bois, Jeff DuBinok, Larry Clemens, Ron Russell, and Art Greason filled us on the Tidewater area and beyond. From the Peninsula Salt Water Sport Fisherman's Association, Captain Richard Bartlett, Ron Dial, Jeff Neill, and Jeff Moss helped us learn about Tidewater and the Western Shore.

Gordon Holloway, owner of a great Fredericksburg Orvis shop, The Fall Line, was a good resource on the upper Western Shore of Virginia. John Messick of The Bait Barn and Danny Wallace of Wallace's Bait and Tackle provided information on Tidewater and Lynnhaven, and Ric Burnley helped us with Chick's Beach.

Captain Lynn Pauls shared with us his long experience in Poquoson and Virginia fishing in general as well as sharing his charts of species and times to fish Virginia waters. Richard Welton of Virginia CCA was our guide on fishing and conservation issues in Virginia waters.

Finally, thanks to Jim Casada of the Outdoor Writers Association of America who encouraged us to pursue this book.

*Flyfishing legend Lefty Kreh admires a beautiful
Chesapeake Bay striper.*

Foreword

This is a book that long needed to be written. Fly fishermen have been enjoying their sport in the Chesapeake Bay for decades. Yet, until now, no one has given it a comprehensive treatment. Ed Russell and Bill May, both lifelong residents of the Bay area, offer the fly fisherman and the light tackle angler a feast of information that will help them enjoy the sport and be more successful fishermen.

Fly fishing is the main theme of the book. But the writers recognize that at times, deep jigging, chumming, and other light-tackle methods are necessary, and these techniques are addressed as well.

The Chesapeake Bay and its tributaries are vast, nearly two hundred miles long, and it would take a lifetime to learn its mysteries. This book will supply the reader with answers to many of the Bay's secrets. More than 20 species of fish are discussed, along with many interesting fishing techniques. Valuable tips concerning each of these methods are also included.

Beginning at the head of the Bay and ending at its mouth, the writers have developed information on various areas which include species found, times of year when they appear, launch ramp sites, types of tackle, where to stay, where to eat, and other vital information.

I especially like the species charts that list the best and poorest months to seek various species in different areas of the Bay.

Ed and Bill have put together a book that is well organized and packed with invaluable information for anyone who enjoys fly or light-tackle fishing in the Chesapeake Bay.

Lefty Kreh

UNITED STATES

Introduction

THE CHESAPEAKE BAY— AN ENDANGERED TREASURE

The Chesapeake Bay, the largest estuary in North America, begins with a delta formed at the mouth the Susquehanna River. This delta, locally known as the Susquehanna Flats, lies between the towns of Havre de Grace to the west and Perryville to the east. At this point the flats are about three miles across and extend southward for about seven miles. Extremely shallow in the center, this area was a very popular duck hunting location years ago. Starting just after World War II, "body booting" was a popular hunting method. Obviously a sport for the hardy, duck hunters in chest waders were dropped off by a skiff in shallow spots with a set of decoys and a floating box on which to lay their shotgun and shells. It was an effective, if arduous, way to hunt. If a wind kicked up it could be brutal, and suppose nature called. Sadly, the decrease in the number of ducks in the Atlantic Flyway has all but ended this method of hunting.

The factor that made duck hunting so good, subaquatic vegetation (commonly referred to as SAV or simply grass) was also responsible for excellent fishing. These grasses provided nourishment and cover for many fish and forage species and were an important overall barometer of the health of the waters. Unfortunately, recent years have seen a dangerous decline in these all-important grasses, and some fish species have suffered as a result. In 1972, Hurricane Agnes ripped through and, according to the National Science Center, deposited 50 years worth of silt in the Bay. A large percentage of that amount fell on the flats area, effectively destroying most of the grasses. To date, the grasses have still not recovered fully, and may never return to their former density.

There are some bright spots however, as we've been told that the nearby Elk River, which flows into the flats on the east, saw a significant increase in the amount of native grasses in the last couple of years. Let's hope this trend continues.

Although the Susquehanna River is a free-flowing freshwater river and not a brackish tributary of the Bay, as so many area "rivers" are, the Susky is extremely important, providing the greatest volume of fresh water entering the Bay, and for that reason we will include it in the coverage of this book.

It's an odd but important legal point for anglers who fish this area to remember that the state of Maryland, for management purposes, has deemed all of the Susquehanna from the base of Conowingo Dam downstream as tidal water when, in actuality, it is not. In prior years, tidal water was considered to begin below the mouth of Deer Creek. Now, however, anyone who fishes the Susquehanna below Conowingo Dam must possess a valid Maryland Tidewater Fishing Permit (necessary to fish any of the Bay's waters or tidal tributaries) as well as a freshwater permit if they intend to fish inside the mouth of either Deer Creek or Octoraro Creek.

To properly understand the Chesapeake, you must get some idea of its size. From its beginning above Havre De Grace to its end at Hampton Roads, Virginia, the western terminus of the Chesapeake Bay Bridge Tunnel, is a distance of just under two hundred miles. The shoreline distance, not counting tributary rivers, is about two thousand miles. Adding in all the tributaries just about doubles that figure.

If you look at a map, you will notice that the Bay stays fairly narrow in its upper reaches, and the narrowest point, disregarding the uppermost part of the Susquehanna Flats, is at Annapolis where the shore-to-shore distance is only four miles. That's the main reason that the Bay Bridge was built there.

Despite its size, the Chesapeake is a shallow body of water—and getting shallower. Scientific studies indicate that the Bay is gradually filling in. Part of this is a result of silting and part is a natural process. Scientists indicate that this trend will continue.

Presently the average depth is about 22 feet. Of course, there are also many deeper holes and channels. One popular fishing spot near Crisfield, Maryland (called the Puppy Hole—we have no idea why) is over 70 feet deep. The deepest recorded spot is 174 feet, just south of Kent Island, Maryland.

The salinity of the Bay differs from shore to shore due to the amount of fresh water that the Susquehanna and other Western Shore rivers provide. This fresh water flows more heavily down the west side of the Bay (there are no true freshwater rivers on the Eastern Shore) with the result that there is a 25-mile difference in salinity between the eastern and western shores. Starting at the western side of the Bay Bridge, for example, you would have to go 25 miles farther south to reach the same salinity level as where the bridge touches land on the eastern shore.

Another interesting fact is that the average distance between waves in the Bay is approximately 18 feet. This is the reason that so many "work boats" that ply the Bay's waters are 40 feet or more in length: they can span three waves, affording a more comfortable ride.

All in all, the Bay has a rich ecosystem that is home to many species of fish; however, this ecosystem is in grave danger. Part of the problem stems from the fact that there are three separate authorities overseeing the management of the Bay—the states of Maryland and Virginia, and the Potomac River Authority. Each has its own agendas and ideas as to how the resource should be managed, and each responds more heavily to the influence of the commercial fishermen than to that of the recreational interests; facts that we will discuss later in this book.

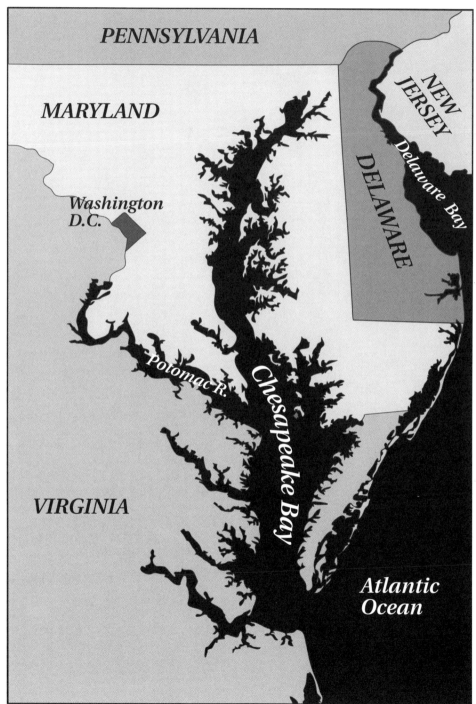

PENNSYLVANIA

MARYLAND

NEW JERSEY

DELAWARE

Delaware Bay

Washington D.C.

Potomac R.

Chesapeake Bay

VIRGINIA

Atlantic Ocean

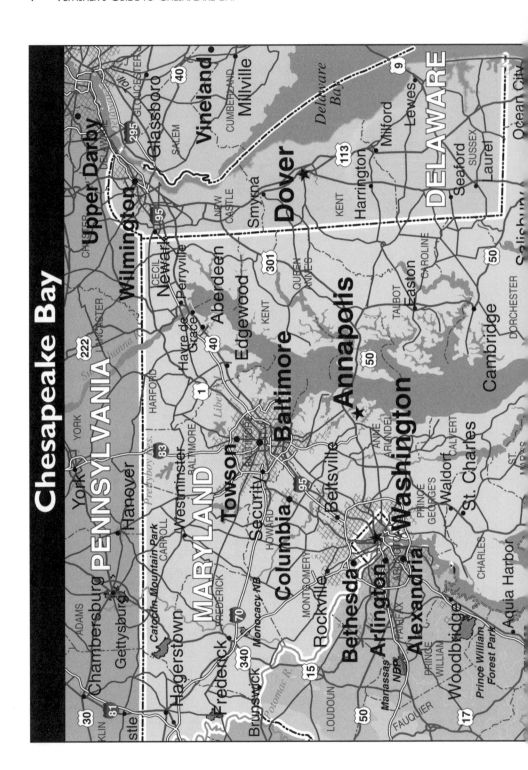

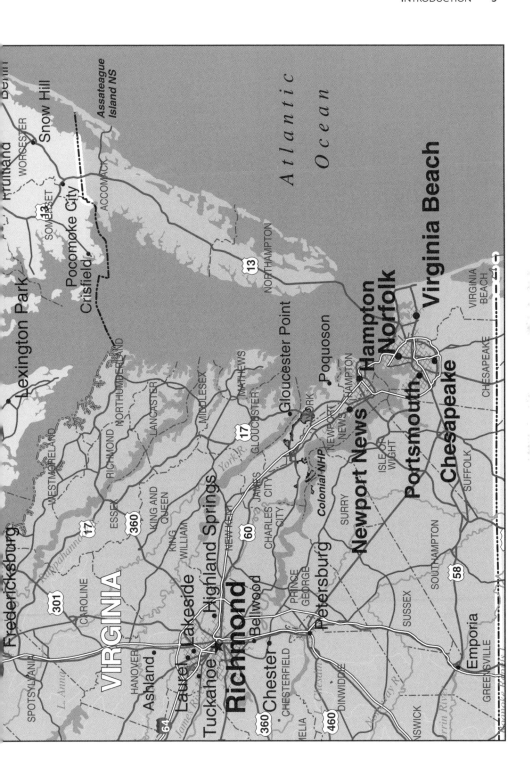

*An angler with a white shad at the base of
Conowingo Dam on the Susquehanna River.*

Chesapeake Bay Game Fish

The game fish of the Chesapeake Bay, while not as varied as those of Florida, for example, nevertheless offer the angler a chance to catch many of the popular species that inhabit mid-Atlantic coastal waters. In this book, we are dealing with species that typically swim in the Bay's waters, so we will not discuss such typically offshore species as tuna, dolphin, etc. Although these and other "blue water" species are found just offshore, they do not normally enter the Bay proper.

Some species, like Spanish mackerel, which are usually thought of as ocean-going fish, do have a large presence in the Bay, especially in late summer, so these and similar species will be discussed. Some species, such as flounder and Atlantic croaker, were previously considered bottom feeders that could only be caught in deep water on bait. However, many anglers have recently awakened to the sporting qualities of these two, and as a result, they are frequently taken on light tackle. In fact, the croakers invade the southern reaches of the Bay in early spring and can be taken by casting small jigs or soft plastic baits, as well as flies, in water that is frequently less than three feet deep.

Although striped bass and bluefish are certainly the two most sought after species in the Bay's waters, anglers are starting to realize the potential opportunities offered by other species, and they are throwing old ideas and conventions aside and catching more species on light tackle than ever before.

With this in mind, let's look at the opportunities that Chesapeake Bay provides for light-tackle anglers.

FISH SPECIES

American Shad

Hickory Shad

Striped Bass (locally called Rock)

Bluefish

Seatrout (Weakfish or Gray Trout)

Speckled Trout

Atlantic Croaker (or Hardhead)

Largemouth Bass

Smallmouth Bass (Susquehanna River)

Pickerel

Yellow Perch

White Perch

Redfish (Red Drum and Puppy Drum)

Black Drum

Flounder

Cobia

Spadefish

Tautog

Spanish Mackerel

Channel Catfish

Carp

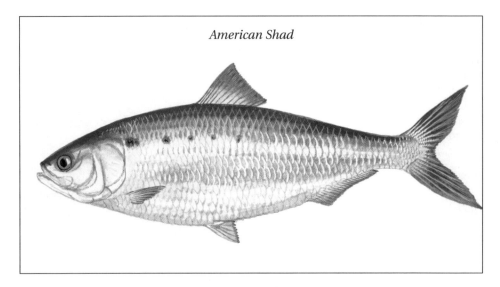

American Shad

American Shad

American shad, more commonly called white shad in this region, usually enter the Bay in late February. While not available to anglers at this time, they are nonetheless commercially netted. The fish itself is only mediocre as table fare, but the roe is considered by many to be a great delicacy and usually turns up on the menu of better local restaurants by the end of the month. Even local supermarkets will sell shad roe by March.

White shad were so important on the Susquehanna River that early landowners depended on harvesting great numbers of them to feed their servants. In fact, in Colonial America, law regulated the amount of shad that a landowner could feed his servants weekly. Like Atlantic salmon, they were often used for fertilizer in those early days of plenty.

Prior to the construction of the dams on the Susquehanna, white shad ascended this river all the way to its headwaters near Cooperstown, New York in their annual spring spawning run. This 640-mile journey was the longest of any Atlantic Coast anadromous species. (Anadromous, from the Greek language, means literally "to run uphill" and refers to a species' ascent of freshwater rivers to spawn.) Early settlers caught these fish using skills shown them by the Native Americans, and the shad numbers were so great that at times they were actually harvested with pitchforks.

In Pennsylvania, during the mid-1700s, competition for this abundance resulted in a 30-year conflict (called the "shad wars") between Connecticut Yankees laying claim to the northern tier of Pennsylvania and other settlers of that region. After the Revolutionary War, shad harvests were limited only by the amount of salt available for preservation.

Many communities along the river typically donated the catch from the first Sunday of the run to widows and orphans of the neighborhood. One documented "widow's haul" in 1790 at the Stewart Fishery, between Wilkes-Barre and Plymouth, was 10,000 fish. Think about that. Ten thousand fish in just one day from one stretch of river—kind of stretches your imagination.

In Maryland, the shad run on the Susquehanna was important both commercially and recreationally. In 1900, the commercial harvest from the Maryland portion of the Susquehanna alone was roughly two million pounds. There are photos in existence that show some of these enormous commercial net catches from the Susquehanna Flats at the turn of the century. One that we've seen shows about thirty men encircling a net that is filled to overflowing with American shad.

From that point, things went downhill fast. Dams were the principal reason for the decline. Shad, although they are strong swimmers, cannot jump obstacles, as can Pacific salmon; in fact, they cannot negotiate a barrier merely a foot high. Small dams, for various purposes, were built on virtually every tributary of the Susquehanna, so the spawning areas continually diminished. After 1900, the number of shad ascending the Susquehanna to spawn dropped precipitously. Commercial shad landings fell from two million pounds in 1900 to 33,000 pounds in 1915. In just 15 years, the commercial catch fell by 98 percent. Between 1904 and 1928 four hydroelectric dams were constructed on the main river. With the construction of the Conowingo Dam near the Maryland-Pennsylvania border in 1928, the last and largest of the four, commercial shad fishing on the Susquehanna was no more.

Recreational fishing continued, however. In the mid-fifties, fishing seemed to be quite good. In fact, a shad tournament was held every year on the Susquehanna. Quite popular with local anglers, participants and prizes were many. Shad also continued to be caught on many of the Eastern Shore rivers, such as the Tuckahoe and the Choptank, but the end was near. No one, it seemed, realized that the American shad that we sought were but a vestige of their former numbers.

Around 1974 the bottom quite literally fell out. No one was catching shad anymore. Neither whites nor their smaller cousins the hickory shad were to be found. Many theories have been advanced about their disappearance, but no one knows exactly what precipitated the disaster. Hurricane Agnes, which ripped through the Eastern Seaboard in June of 1972, is thought by many to be a principal culprit. The amount of silt carried by the floodwaters would account for the demise of that year's class of shad offspring. More importantly, the residual silt probably smothered the shad eggs for several succeeding years. Other contributing factors were poor water quality, low oxygen levels, pollution, and over-harvesting.

In all probability, no one factor caused the disappearance of the shad, but rather a combination of circumstances destroyed their numbers. Whatever the reason, stocks were so low (almost to the point of extinction) that Maryland imposed a moratorium on the taking of American shad in 1980, and on hickory shad in 1981.

Happily, although the moratorium is still in effect as of this writing, the shad are making a strong comeback. Partly as a result of extensive efforts by the state, including heavy stocking of shad fry, agreements for minimal water flow requirements from Conowingo Dam, and no harvesting of the species, American shad once more swim in the Susquehanna. For the recreational angler, what all this means is that there is once again an excellent fishery for American shad in Maryland. Although you can't keep any, you are free to catch them.

Tackle and Techniques

The white shad run occurs with fair predictability about the same time each spring. Temperature is the key, with 55 degrees the magic number. The dogwood tree, years ago called the "shad bush," is a good indicator. Usually, when the dogwood blooms, shad are in the river. Typically, early to mid-May is prime time in Maryland.

American shad like deeper, fast-flowing water that is well-oxygenated and has a gravelly bottom for spawning. They are strong, hard scrappers that tend to fight deep, unlike their cousins, the hickory shad, which tend to become airborne the moment they feel the hook. They are an excellent fly-rod fish in places where you can get the fly to them. Usually, in the Susquehanna below Conowingo Dam, this means fishing from a boat. Wading here can be described as difficult at best, and treacherous is probably a more descriptive term.

Since these fish stay deep, a sinking line is usually called for. Some anglers favor a sinking tip, but normally a full sinking line with a fast descent rate will catch more fish. Remember, these fish will be right near the bottom in pretty swift current; a sinking tip line will allow the fly to rise up on the swing. Rods of 7- or 8-weight work best as you will usually be using a weighted fly as well as a sinking line.

Small bright streamers, usually in fluorescent colors with plenty of flash, work best most of the time. A local favorite is tied on a size 6 heavy wire streamer hook. A tail of yellow hair, a bright silver or pearl body, and a red or red and yellow marabou wing completes the fly.

Overall, spinning gear is the most popular tackle for white shad by a large margin. Some anglers use ultralight outfits, which result in a prolonged fight that lessens the fish's chance of survival. At the other extreme, we've observed fishermen using surf rods, but that's ridiculous. Medium-weight rods 6 to 7½ feet in length, preferably with a fairly fast taper, are ideal, and line testing six or eight pounds is perfect.

A good reel with a smooth drag is a must. Whites don't usually make long runs, so large line capacity isn't too important, but if a large shad gets into a strong current, you will definitely have your hands full. An erratic drag will cost you fish.

Your rod should be capable of throwing two lead shad darts. These lures account for more shad than all other lures combined, several times over. You'll want your rod to be powerful enough to cast a two-dart rig. Shad darts come as small as a 32nd of an ounce, but most weigh between ⅛ to ¼ of an ounce. Which ones you choose will depend entirely on water flow—the faster the water, the heavier the darts.

These two-dart rigs can be set up a couple of ways. One way is to tie the second dart directly to the hook of the first, separating them by about 12 inches. Another way is to tie an additional 2-foot piece of mono to your line using a blood knot or a double uni-knot. When you clip the knot, leave one tag about ten inches long. Tie one dart to that and the other to the end of the line. Although any multi-lure setup is prone to tangles, if you slow down your casting rhythm you can minimize this.

What color darts to use is anybody's guess. Some folks prefer the typical yellow tail, white body, red head configuration, and our guess is that this works about as well as anything most of the time. However, shad can become quite color selective at times, and it is important to carry a variety of color combinations. No doubt, there are very good shad fishermen who will swear that a dart with a hot pink body and a purple tail is the "shad-catchinest" color ever, while others, equally good, will claim that only chartreuse with an orange tail is worthwhile. In fact, light levels, water clarity, and probably a host of other factors will determine the color *du jour*. Look at what other anglers nearby are using (if you have any illusions about shad fishing being a solitary sport, you probably also believe in the Tooth Fairy). If some anglers are enjoying more success than others, ask them what they are using. Most shad fishermen are quite willing to share information, because when a shad run is underway, there is no shortage of fish.

Sometimes, color can be a decisive factor, especially if you happen on to a bunch of shad holding in one particular area. On several occasions we've fished to shad holding in a pool and had a strike on every cast, when suddenly they stopped. Successive casts with the same color lure went untouched. Changing to a dart of a different color and casting to the same spot immediately brought a strike. This continued as before for several hookups when they again stopped biting. We repeated this procedure several times; each time, when the shad quit hitting, a color change caused a renewed interest. It was almost as if the released fish warned the others "not to grab the green thing." We've only experienced this when a good number of shad were holding in a particular spot.

Although color is important in shad fishing, presentation and position is of far more consequence. As in real estate sales, the three most important factors are location, location, and location. Shad follow precise routes and hold in specific spots in any river. Finding where these holding places are and presenting your offering in such a manner to entice the fish is all-important. Typically, a cast across and upstream will be most productive. The upstream cast allows the lure to sink to the proper level, and most hits will come as the lure makes its downstream swing.

Prime spots are the heads and tails of pools where the fish tend to congregate. The shad migrate through the faster water and then, typically, hold in the back portion of a pool until they move upstream where they again seem to hesitate prior to exiting a pool. The number-one choice is the very end of a pool just before it empties into faster water.

Depth is also an important factor. American shad like fairly deep water and will almost always be found in deeper portions of a pool or run. Take lots of shad darts or flies with you. If you aren't losing lures occasionally, you are most likely passing over the fish.

Light levels play a role, too. These fish bite best when the light is dim. Dawn and dusk are obviously the prime times, but sometimes, especially if it's overcast, they will hit all day. When light levels are high, fish the deeper, darker lies.

Hickory Shad

These smaller cousins of the American shad have also come back astonishingly well from their near extinction in the mid-'70s. Oddly enough, since they have no commercial value, the state of Maryland did little or nothing to help them recover as they did for the American shad, which do have commercial value. It appears that if a species isn't over-harvested nature will repair any decline over time.

In 1980 Maryland imposed a ban on the taking of the commercially valuable American shad. The following year, as a result of a lawsuit brought against the state by outdoor writer Joe Reynolds, hickory shad were included in the ban. The demise of the species seemed to be at hand. Most of us were convinced that we would never again see hickories in our streams.

But things improved. In the early '90s, we heard of some anglers catching a few hickories. The rumors persisted, and investigation proved that the hickories were once again in the river. By 1994, the run seemed pretty good. By 1995, they were apparently back to their old numbers. In 1996 and 1997, we participated in a study with five other anglers to see what effect, if any, catch-and-release fishing had on the species, and to do an estimate of the numbers of returning shad.

Holding tanks were set up on Deer Creek, and freshly caught shad were deposited in them. Approximately 30 fish a day went in the tank where they were held for 48 hours before being released. The conclusion: careful handling resulted in zero mortality, and the number of returning fish was at least as great as in the late '60s. Good news indeed.

As of this writing, the ban on the taking and possession of shad in Maryland is still in effect. But you may fish for them. For most anglers, this is just fine. Although the roe of the hickory is a delicacy, the fish itself is bony and soft-fleshed with no commercial value.

So, why all the recreational interest in a fish that is large at two pounds? Because they take flies readily and fight like hell. They are a flyrodder's dream fish. Their comparison to tarpon cannot be overstated. They are of the same family (herring), of which the tarpon is the largest member.

Hickory shad look and fight like miniature tarpon, but they act like Atlantic salmon, ascending fresh waters each spring to spawn. They spawn for the first time at approximately four years of age and leave fresh water after spawning to return to the salt. If not eaten by other predators, they can return to spawn two or three times.

Hickories are a fish of the Eastern Seaboard, existing from Maine to South Carolina, but their greatest concentration, by far, is in the Mid-Atlantic Region, with Maryland, Virginia, and North Carolina the best areas.

Fishing for hickories means finding them. Maryland's portion of the Chesapeake has two rivers on the Western Shore with excellent shad runs—the Susquehanna, and the Potomac. Smaller runs also occur on several Eastern Shore rivers, especially the Choptank and the Tuckahoe.

The Potomac's runs were not as decimated by Hurricane Agnes as those of the Susquehanna, and good fishing has been, and continues to be, available. However, the shad fishing in the Potomac mainly occurs in a stretch of a few miles near Chain Bridge and is terminated by the Great Falls of the Potomac. This is true fresh water and is outside the coverage of this book.

In Virginia, the Rappahannock River, near Fredericksburg, gets top billing, but again, the principal fishing area is well upriver from tidewater. Another stream to try is the Gunpowder. It's well known as a trout stream in its upper reaches, but nearer the mouth, hickories have been caught. Although we've not tried this area personally, we've gotten some good reports. Two problems, though, are access and parking. Both are limited.

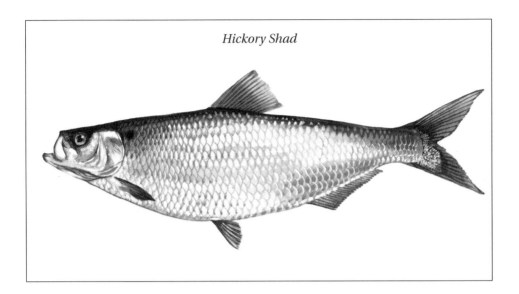

Hickory Shad

Tackle and Techniques

Fishing for hickories is fairly simple, but more success will come to those who learn a few basic things. First, hickories like white shad, are extremely light sensitive, and bite best at dawn and dusk. An exception to this rule is if you can locate a pod of fish holding in a deeply shaded spot. If you can get a fly or a dart to them, you should be able to take some.

Morning and evening are when shad move upstream. At this time, they become aggressive and will attack flies that either threaten or annoy them. Our experience indicates that the single best spot to entice hickories, like white shad, is at the tail of a pool. Typically, they move upstream from pool to pool, holding in the quiet water at the tail, ostensibly to rest.

Most times, a hi-density sink tip and a short leader will draw far more strikes than a floating line. Since you will seldom be fishing in water more than four feet deep, a short sink tip, such as the Teeny mini-tip, which is only five feet long, works well and is fairly easy to cast. In the evening, shad move up in the water column as they travel upstream. Then, a floating line shines. For this reason, unweighted flies are desirable. Carrying both lines will facilitate fishing deep with the sink tip and shallow with the floating line.

Tackle is what you would typically use for trout. A 4- to 6-weight rod and a 6-pound tippet are about ideal. Some people use lighter rods and finer tippets, but they are unnecessary and the use of such ultralight rods combined with frail tippets prolongs the fight and places undue stress on the fish. There is little reason to go lighter than a 6-pound tippet. A reel with a click drag is adequate. Unless you hook a large female in fast current, a velvety drag is unnecessary.

Flies can be almost anything bright and fairly small. Little streamers tied on size 6 to 10, 2X long hooks are perfect. Colors and patterns vary enormously, but needn't be complex. A favorite pattern for many years has been a bright silver tinsel body and a fluorescent red marabou wing on a size 8 hook. That's all. No tail, no beard, no nothing.

When the fish are deep, this color combination tied Clouser style is quite effective. Some friends who are very successful with shad like the wing to be a combination of red and yellow, and chartreuse is almost always good. This last color is a bit of a puzzle in that nothing in nature, save for some exotic amphibians, is chartreuse. However, studies have shown that this is one of the most visible colors to the human eye, and apparently to that of fish as well. There's a saying among fishermen: "If it ain't chartreuse, it ain't no use."

Although many anglers have favorite patterns, choices are frequently based more on confidence in a particular pattern, which translates to more frequent use. All things being equal, presentation is far more important than color.

When fishing for hickories, timing is of the utmost importance. Since they are migratory, they are in the streams for only a short while when conditions are right. The most critical component is water temperature. Fifty-five degrees Fahrenheit is the magic number. A little below that and you may catch a few but not many. Sixty to sixty-five degrees will see the fish at their most active, and when that occurs in a stream with a good run, catching more than 50 fish an evening is normal. Cold weather will put the fish down, though. Sometimes they will move downstream to deeper water or even the main river. It is common to experience excellent fishing one day only to do almost nothing the next, due to an overnight cold snap. Warming temperatures brings them back.

Light levels are also important. Longer periods of daylight are another migratory trigger and may move fish into streams when other factors have conspired to keep the water temperature too low. When this happens, it is entirely possible to find a stream filled with fish that won't bite. A warm rain that raises the temperature a little and clouds the water slightly usually fixes things. Incidentally, hickories will still hit in pretty muddy water. We don't know how they see the fly, but they do.

As mentioned earlier, the dogwood tree is supposedly a good indicator of a shad run. When it blooms, the shad are in the river. However, this indicator is really keyed to the larger white shad, which enter the river a little later than hickories. I've found that the apple and cherry trees, which bloom a little earlier than dogwoods, are better barometers.

In the Chesapeake tributaries a few shad first show up in late March. This is not the main run, but seems almost like a scouting party. The main runs start in early April in Virginia waters and about two weeks later in Maryland. The run usually peaks the first week in May and is over by the fifteenth. Obviously, the time of the runs vary with their north/south location.

Hickories are not difficult fish to catch. They don't require much in the way of stealth, but location is everything. We have seen countless examples of two anglers fishing close together where one takes fish after fish and the other only occasionally catches one. The difference is that one is reaching a lie and the other is not. The fly must be out in front of the fish. Careful observation will reveal holding spots. Look for the "V" formed where a pool empties into a run. Just above this area is almost always a good spot. Obstructions that create deep eddies are another hotspot. But we cannot overemphasize the importance of putting the fly right on the fish's nose.

The fishing can be crowded at times. Often, there is almost a party atmosphere. But we'll let you in on a little secret: the very best fishing comes just before dark, and all but the well informed will have left the stream.

Shad do not feed during the spawning run, and even if they did, we can't imagine what you could tie to imitate their food, since they are plankton feeders. They are thought to strike flies out of annoyance or anger. The only important fact is that they do strike. The more shad in the stream, the more strikes you will get, not only because of greater numbers, but because competition seems to make them more aggressive.

Hook a hickory, especially in a current, and you will gain a new appreciation for their capabilities. Since they are a saltwater fish, they are much stronger and faster than similarly sized freshwater species. Not only that, when conditions are right, they are most willing to take a fly. Sometimes, the fishing can actually get too good. If they were present in the streams year-round, we would probably ignore them.

Nonetheless, shad are an excellent spring tonic, eagerly anticipated by many fly fishermen. It is the first serious fishing that many of us do each year, and if it does become too easy, the fact that they don't stay around for too long is a blessing.

Chuck Edghill, a longtime friend and outstanding fly fisherman, summed it up best years ago: "I'm always glad to see them come, and I'm always glad to see them go."

*Fly rods, shad flies, and cherry blossoms
go together on the Susquehanna.*

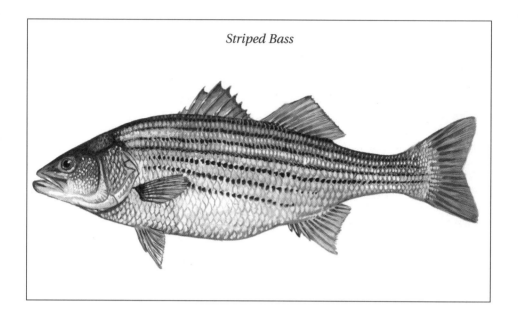

Striped Bass

Striped Bass

Striped bass, locally called "rock" or "rockfish" (maybe because of their fondness for structure or because the second part of their Latin name, *Morone saxatilis*, means rock dweller), are certainly the premier game fish of the Chesapeake. More money is spent and more time expended in the pursuit of stripers, both by recreational anglers and commercial fishermen, than any other species that inhabits the Chesapeake. Catchable across the Bay from late March to mid-November, and into December and early January in the lower reaches of the Bay, they can also be found in the warmwater discharges of several power plants. Baltimore Harbor also offers excellent fishing during the coldest months, making striper fishing almost a year-round sport.

They can be caught by just about any means possible, as their food preferences are quite eclectic. They will eat small crabs, perch, small shad, herring, croaker, spot, juvenile bluefish, eels, spot, grass shrimp, and, like most fish, smaller members of their own family. Basically, stripers will eat anything that doesn't eat them first, but their overwhelming favorite food fish is the Atlantic menhaden, closely followed by the so-called bay anchovy. As a result of that preference, a host of lures and flies are manufactured that imitate both of these two species.

A shortage of menhaden in the Bay in recent years, primarily caused by the "Menhaden Fleet" that operates out of the Reedville, Virginia area, has had far-reaching consequences. This fleet of boats nets virtually all the menhaden that enter the Bay and then sells them for fertilizer and chicken food. As a result, the stripers are denied their primary food fish, and must feed on bay anchovies and other baitfish. A big problem with this is that menhaden are far more nourishing than other foods, and in recent years a large number of "skinny" stripers have been reported.

Stripers are a semi-migratory species. We say semi-migratory because until fairly recently, biologists thought all the Bay stripers left the Chesapeake and moved south and off the coast somewhere for the winter. According to Maryland Fisheries Biologist Eric Durell, recent studies have shown that this is not true. It now appears that some stripers do indeed move down the Bay, but then move into the deep holes and mini-canyons that exist near the mouth where they are joined by large females that have moved south from farther up the coast. Other members of the family simply move into deep water wherever they please.

The stripers will remain in these deep locations until the water begins to warm in the spring. A soon as the water temperature approaches the mid-40s, these large fish will begin to move up the Bay to stage near the mouths of their natal rivers until the water temperature gets to about 55 degrees, when spawning begins.

The greatest numbers of fish move all the way to the Bay's headwaters at the Susquehanna Flats. Originally, biologists thought that this was where these stripers spawned, but they now believe that the actual spawning takes place in most of the Upper Bay tributaries, with the Susquehanna proper getting the lion's share.

Once spawning concludes, the stripers fan out. Some of the smaller fish remain in the Susquehanna until the fall, while the larger fish, about 90 percent of which are female, move down and out of the Bay and migrate northward, ending up in New England where they spend the summer. The balance of the smaller stripers, those under about 10 pounds, spread out all over the Bay. Usually, the larger fish stay south of the Bay Bridge. When the waters cool in the fall, the process is repeated.

While stripers can be found in substantial schools, especially in late summer and fall when they target large schools of baitfish, they can also be somewhat solitary and will frequently be found hiding out by rock piles, downed timber, and underwater stumps. This preference for differing habitat gives anglers opportunities to fish for them with different methods.

Tackle and Techniques

Striped bass are caught by just about any angling technique you can imagine. Trolling, especially for the big stripers that move down the Bay after spawning, is popular with some folks. We don't consider this light-tackle angling, since the typical rig consists of a heavy boat rod with an equally heavy reel (sometimes spooled with wire line to go deep) and dragging either a very big spoon or an umbrella rig with multiple lures. Since this method employs what we deem "heavy tackle," that's all we'll say about this method.

Chumming may be the most popular method of striper fishing in the Bay. Extremely effective, it is also quite controversial. Years ago, anglers chummed with ground up soft-shell clams. Today, with the collapse of the clamming industry because of extreme over-harvesting, the favorite chum is ground menhaden. Typically, the ground fish is ladled over the transom of an anchored boat. This establishes a long "slick" of fish pieces and fish oil, which attracts stripers from long distances. Once actively feeding, the fish may come to within a few feet of the boat.

Anglers bait hooks with pieces of menhaden and allow the bait to drift back with the chum. Usually, there's little trouble getting the stripers to hit.

Several problems exist with this method, however. First, the use of menhaden for bait contributes to the diminishment of an already stressed resource. Second, the amount of boats that use this method, and this method only, throughout the summer is staggering. No one knows for sure how much ground menhaden goes into the Bay's waters, but some top guides feel that the chum contributes to the pollution of the Bay and also conditions the stripers to feed behind the army of chumming boats, much like hogs at a feeding trough. They feel that this is keeping the stripers from moving farther up the Bay in search of food, as they would do normally. Whether or not this is really the case is open to conjecture, but it does give one pause.

Yet another problem exists with the use of bait that involves undersized fish. Although various conservation groups and Maryland and Virginia fisheries departments extol the use of circle hooks for chumming, there's little indication that many anglers are paying attention. Trouble comes when an undersized fish swallows the bait. Then, a normal hook may lodge in the gills or stomach. Since undersized fish must be released, usually the fish dies—especially, during the warmer months when the water temperatures can top 80 degrees in the Lower Bay. Mortality rates for these "released" fish are off the charts. Using circle hooks, which almost always hook the fish in the mouth, would help tremendously, but even a carefully handled and released fish is a stressed fish, and they may still die when the water temperature is high. Thus, so-called catch-and-release fishing, when the chumming method is employed, especially in warm weather, might better be termed catch, release, and kill. It is imperative that anglers who chum use circle hooks and fight and land the fish as quickly as possible. Many scientific studies show that fishing with very light tackle, and thus playing a fish for a long time, while fun for the angler, decreases the fish's chances for survival.

There are better ways. Probably the most exciting form of striper fishing is to chase them as they tear through huge schools of baitfish on the surface. This is sight fishing at its best, and it can be done with fly, spinning, or casting gear. This activity starts as early as July, and simply gets better as you move into the fall. During this early period, breaking stripers can be found all over, from Bloody Point to locations north of the Bay Bridge. Points and bars near river mouths are excellent spots, as are the Upper Bay lumps north of the bridge. Usually, it's an afternoon to evening proposition. One point to consider: larger stripers, and seatrout as well, can often be found beneath the breaking fish feeding on the "fallout." If you use a heavy lure or weighted fly on a fast-sinking fly line, you can reach these fish, and they hit with abandon.

As the season progresses and the water cools surface action moves farther down the Bay, and the schools of stripers get larger. October and early November provides the best surface activity, and the action can be found anywhere south of the Bay Bridge. The colder it gets, the farther south the best fishing will be.

Some really exciting fishing can be had by working many of the undercut sod banks and submerged stump fields near Crisfield and around Smith and Tangier Islands in the Lower Bay. This is just like fishing for largemouth bass, except the fish are bigger. Flies or lures are cast right into the stumps and will draw explosive strikes from lurking fish. This is one of our favorite ways to seek stripers.

Late fall and early winter, the stripers will be concentrated at the Chesapeake Bay Bridge Tunnel. This 18-mile long structure acts like a fish magnet, and some of the largest stripers can be taken on light tackle by fishing the pilings and man-made rock islands during that period. We'll get into specifics for stripers and other game fish as we address each section of the Bay.

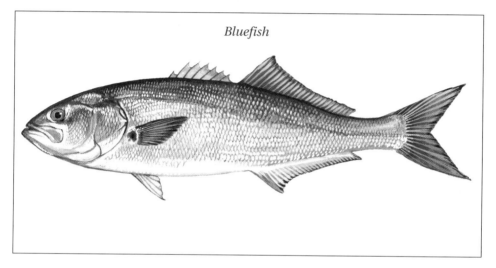

Bluefish

Bluefish

Bluefish like higher salinity levels than stripers and are therefore found primarily in the waters of the Lower Bay. Usually, this means well south of the Bay Bridge, especially for larger specimens. But if there's been a dry summer, they will move north of the bridge, and they have been caught on the Upper Bay lumps and even in Baltimore Harbor. On several occasions, during especially dry summers, anglers have caught small blues right from the walkways along Baltimore's "touristy" Inner Harbor complex. Usually, though, due to the differing salinity levels of the shores of the Bay, they will most frequently be on the eastern side.

Blues that come this far up the Bay are normally small, under three pounds, but there have been times when bruisers moved into the Upper Bay. Throughout the 1970s, big bluefish, many topping 16 pounds, moved into the shallows of the Eastern Shore from Bloody Point south of the bridge, all the way to Tolchester well to the north. Small numbers of these fish arrived in late April, and by mid-May the fishing was fantastic. Slowly and quietly working the shoreline in depths of two to three feet provided heart-stopping excitement.

The typical method was to prospect along the shoreline throwing large surface poppers with spinning or casting rods. Once a pod of blues was located, many anglers would switch to a fly rod and a popping bug. When the big blues hit, the strike was like someone dropping a cinder block into the water from a height of 20 feet. A lot of times, the fish would miss the bug and re-attack or lose out to one of its brethren. The fishing was really fantastic. By early June the blues would move out and it would all be over.

By the early 1980s, it was over in its entirety. The phenomenon of big blues in shallow water hasn't occurred again as of this writing. No one knows why the fish were there in the first place. Prior to the '70s, no one that we knew of had ever experienced such fishing. Perhaps they were there all along, but there simply weren't any light-tackle anglers looking for them. Perhaps it was due to an overabundance of menhaden that happened during those years, causing the blues to follow the bait. Perhaps it was a cyclical overabundance of bluefish. No one knows, but one thing is certain. If the commercial over-harvesting of menhaden continues, the sight of a huge bluefish crashing a surface plug in a couple of feet of water in the Upper Bay, will never be experienced again.

Tackle and Techniques

What size rods, flies, or lures that you use for bluefish varies considerably depending on the size of the fish and on what they are feeding. Basically, match the rod to the size of fish expected. For larger blues, those over 10 pounds, I'd suggest a 10-weight fly rod or a spinning or casting rod of 6 to 7 feet that can handle lures from ¾ ounce to 1½ ounce. For smaller fish, typically what you will find as breaking schools, a 7- or 8-weight fly rod is ample, as is similarly downsized conventional tackle. Fairly stiff actions are desirable. Choose artificials that match the prevalent bait. If blues are feeding on 2-inch silversides, a 6-inch fly or lure may well be ignored.

Normally, bluefish are caught in deeper, more open water, and in water with high salinity. Therefore, the farther south you go in the Bay, the greater number of bluefish will be found. However, bluefish have periodic booms and busts. Currently, we are in a period of low population numbers, so when you find breaking schools of fish, they will more likely be stripers, although sometimes the schools will be mixed. If that's the case, you will probably lose some flies or lures until you add a short wire leader to the end of your line. Bluefish have fearsome teeth. Unlike most toothy fish, blue-fish dentures, while short, are sharp and serrated on the sides. Even a small one can cause a nasty gash. A truly big one might conceivably sever a finger. And bluefish are malevolent. They actually try to bite. Handle with care.

But, boy, are they fun to catch. They strike hard and fight ferociously. They are much stronger than a striper, and a two-pounder easily fights as hard as a five-pound striper.

Sometimes, when they are on a feeding spree, anything that you throw may draw a strike. Put a hook on a file handle, and you can catch a blue. Other times, however, like stripers, they can be maddeningly selective, and the fly or lure had best match the size, shape and color of the prevalent bait.

Although fall is usually the best time to find breaking bluefish, and the Lower Bay the best place to find these schools of fish, there are other alternatives. One is to fish the rocky structures around the Chesapeake Bay Bridge Tunnel. Frequently, bluefish will take refuge in one of the many rocky hiding places and lie in wait for suitable prey. In this, they act just like striped bass, or even largemouth bass. Casting a surface lure right up into the rocks can draw a strike from either a blue or a striper, so be prepared with a short wire leader.

Many people feel that bluefish are poor table fare. Not so. With a little care they are very good to eat, but proper care is very important. For one thing, they should be cleaned and iced down as soon as possible. Bluefish have very strong digestive systems, and, if left uncleaned and not chilled, their digestive juices will begin attacking the meat of the fish. Because the flesh is oily they don't last very long in the freezer. Three months is about as long as you would want to keep them.

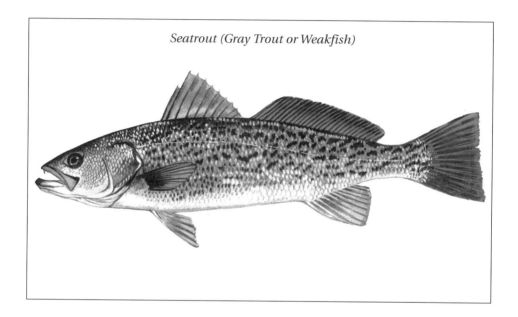

Seatrout (Gray Trout or Weakfish)

Seatrout

Two species of seatrout have overlapping ranges in the Chesapeake. The gray trout, or weakfish, is a very important fish in the Chesapeake. The range of the weakfish is mostly more to the north, but good numbers are found in the Chesapeake, especially in early spring. A pretty fish (only the speckled trout can compare in beauty), they are willing takers of flies and lures and are fairly good fighters. Belonging to the same family as the red drum, they are sought after more for their eating qualities than their fighting ability. Still, on appropriate tackle, they give a decent account of themselves.

Recent years have seen a strong comeback in both of these species. Most experts feel that the principal reason for the increase is the mandatory use of "Turtle Escape Devices" (TED), whose use has been mandated for trawlers. These devices, primarily aimed at reducing death to sea turtles that get caught up in the nets, also allow juvenile seatrout to escape. The number of juvenile game fish thus saved numbers in the millions.

Early in the year, they can be found is waters as shallow as a foot or so, but they retreat to deeper water as soon as the waters begin to warm. From about mid-May to mid-June, the shallow grassy areas of the Lower Bay and the stump-filled shorelines of many of the Bay's islands are prime locations. As they move into deeper water, structure is the key, and any of the many wrecked ships in the Bay's waters are prime spots. By the end of June, they will be in water as deep as 70 feet, and there they will remain until they begin their southerly migration in the fall.

Tackle and Techniques

Forget surface activity; seatrout usually don't look up for their food. Look at the structure of their mouth—it's towards the bottom of the fish's head and is ideally suited for picking up shrimp, crabs, or other bottom-dwelling critters. One exception to that may be in the spring when the fish are in very shallow water; then, a small popper can trigger an explosive strike.

For the flyrodder, an 8- or 9-weight rod and sinking lines will be needed. When the fish are in shallow water, an intermediate sinking line or a sinking tip line are perfect. When the "trout" go deeper, a fast-sinking line is called for. Lefty's Deceivers or the Clouser Deep Minnows are the most popular flies, and chartreuse is a popular color. Other colors, often including mixes of gold and copper flash materials, also work. Effective colors will vary depending on water depth, clarity, the preponderance of bait, and even water temperature. Local knowledge is very valuable. If you are new to the area, consider hiring a guide. Failing that, the next best option is to talk to a local tackle shop. Usually, they will know what's going on, where the action is, and what flies or lures are "hot."

For spinning or casting tackle, a fast action rod that will throw ½-ounce to 1-ounce lures is ideal when the fish are shallow. Several lures stand out—Bill Lewis's Slap-Stick, a floater/diver, is a great choice for water up to about six feet deep over submerged grass beds, and many soft plastic lures work well. A particular favorite is a 4-inch Bass-Assassin (or similar lure) rigged to be weedless. Bass Assassin has a color that they call "Limetreuse," which is an intense chartreuse color. It's been a favorite for fishing structure in all but the clearest water. Gold or silver fleck also works well.

With either type of tackle, cast right up to the cover and use a slow "twitchy" retrieve, as seatrout hang close. If your lure isn't "weedless" you'll lose a lot of them if you are fishing properly.

One time you can catch seatrout in open water is when there are large schools of breaking stripers in the area. Frequently, seatrout will suspend below the breaking fish feeding on the fallout. A Bass Assassin, rigged on a 1-ounce jighead is ideal. You'll need a fairly stiff rod to properly work the jig, and one of the new low (or no) stretch lines helps detect the strike.

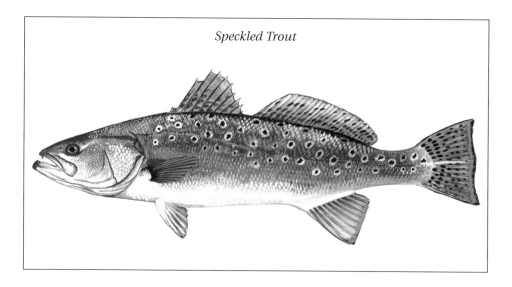

Speckled Trout

Speckled Trout

Speckled trout, locally called specks, are a southerly fish, and as a consequence, are normally found in the lower reaches of the Chesapeake. From below a line roughly across the Bay from about the Honga River on the east to the Patuxent River on the Western Shore is where you will find speckled trout, and the farther south you go, the more numerous they become. The waters of Lynnhaven Bay near Virginia Beach on the Western Shore are a top spot. On the east, Cape Charles, with a shoreline that features many cuts and inlets, is a popular destination; in fact, the world record speckled trout was caught just to the north near the Maryland/Virginia line.

Tackle and Techniques

Quite similar in their habits to the gray trout, they'll be found in the same locations and take the same artificials as their larger cousins. Usually, just scale down the size of the tackle that you use. For example, a 6-weight fly rod is regarded by many as ideal for specks.

One interesting and important difference between speckled trout and weakfish is the way they feed. Weakfish feed facing into the tide, and as a result they will usually be found on the downtide side of any structure looking for baitfish swept along by the tide. To be successful, an angler must present his offering in such a way that it moves naturally with the water flow. A streamer or lure retrieved against the tide will be ignored. Speckled trout, on the other hand, appear to be less finicky and will hit an artificial that's moving in any direction.

If you wish to use bait for either species, nothing, absolutely nothing, beats a small piece of soft crab. Some anglers use peeler crab, but if you choose soft crabs instead, and keep them on ice, you can eat what bait is left over. Basically, today's bait is tomorrow's blue plate special. If you can't find soft crabs, or don't want to spend the money, fresh chicken breasts have become quite popular as a substitute.

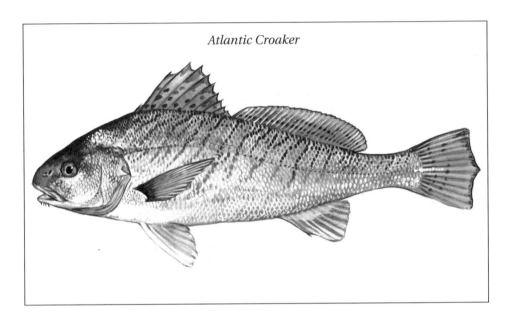

Atlantic Croaker

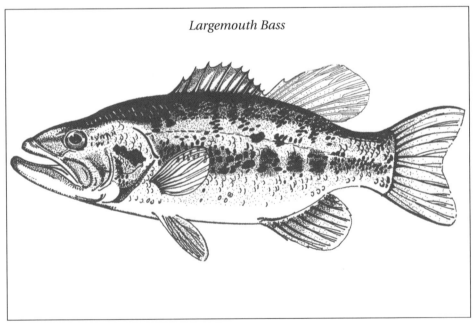

Largemouth Bass

Atlantic Croaker

The last ten years has seen a dramatic increase in the numbers of croaker in the Chesapeake. The primary reason for this (like the increase in seatrout) is most likely the mandatory "Turtle Escape Devices" (TEDs) that are now required by law on all nets used to trawl for shrimp. These devices, primarily aimed at allowing sea turtles that became caught up in the nets to escape, also allow juvenile seatrout, of both species, and croaker to swim free of the shrimp nets. These juvenile fish, previously part of the so-called by-catch, now survive, causing a rebound in the numbers of these fish in the Chesapeake.

Although most fishermen equate fishing for croaker with squid strips and bottom rigs (and that's still how the vast majority of this species is harvested) the fact is that these are active predators, and anytime you can locate them in moderate depths, they are excellent quarry for the light-tackle angler.

Tackle and Techniques

The best time to find these fish in the shallows is in the spring when they are mixed with weakfish or speckled trout in grassy areas of less than five feet. At that time, a chartreuse and white Clouser Minnow or a chartreuse and gold Bass Assassin or similar soft plastic lure is a good choice. So-called "natural" patterns can be even more effective at times. For example, local fly shop owner and innovative fly tier Joe Bruce has developed a bay anchovy pattern that is extremely effective. D. L. Goddard's Glass Minnow is also quite good.

For lures, small soft plastic lures behind lead heads work quite well. Small Bass Assassins, Sassy Shads, or various curly-tail grubs are all effective. Small crankbaits, like the ¼-ounce Rat-L-Trap can work, but because you must be right on the bottom to score, they hang up frequently. A jig is a better choice, and it's even better if it's rigged to be weedless.

Medium-weight tackle, a 7- or 8-weight fly rod or medium spinning or casting gear with 8-pound line, is about right. Best results will come on a moving tide, and some locations work best on an outgoing tide, while others will be better with incoming water. Prospecting is a requirement to finding these fish.

Light levels are also extremely important. Best results will almost always be early morning or from late afternoon to just before dark. Night fishing with bait is extremely effective, but artificials don't seem to work after dark.

Largemouth Bass

Although largemouth bass are typically a freshwater fish, large numbers of them exist in the brackish waters of the Bay's tributaries. The rivers of the Upper Bay are probably the best spots, and places like the mouths of the Bush, Seneca, and Gunpowder Rivers on the upper Western Shore and the mouths of the Sassafras, Elk, Chester, or Corsica on the Eastern Shore are all popular areas. Unfortunately, many of these areas are not what they used to be because of the loss of a large percentage of sub-aquatic vegetation.

Tackle and Techniques

Fishing for largemouths in brackish water is similar to fishing for them in fresh water, with one important distinction. Brackish bass are just as tide-oriented as any true saltwater fish. And since they are just as structure-oriented and light sensitive as freshwater fish, the best fishing will occur around piers, docks, and any other structure, whether natural or man-made, during periods of low light and with a moving tide. The mouth of the Gunpowder, for example, is always best when a high tide occurs a little before dawn.

One very effective technique is to fish under boat docks. This is a favored hangout for largemouths, and fishing there can be effective when the sun is too bright elsewhere. Of course, you'll have to seek out times and places where there is little human activity. The trick is to get your offering under the structure. This can be accomplished with a skip cast—a very useful technique for either fly rods or spinning or casting gear. It takes a little practice, especially with casting gear, but learning the technique will pay dividends.

Often, night fishing can be quite effective around docks and piers that are lighted. Bass will hold in the shadowed areas and strike at baitfish (or artificials) in the lighted areas.

Tackle should match the conditions. Eight-weight fly rods and fairly powerful spinning or casting rods are the best choice. In fly rods, we favor fairly stiff, fast-action rods. The Loomis FR1088-GLX is an excellent choice as is the Sage 890 RPLXI. As far as casting and spinning rods go, although there is an enormous number of these rods on the market from which to choose, we feel the Loomis rods are, by far, the best. Yes, they are expensive, but the difference between this line of spinning and casting rods and everything else is astounding.

If you are casting into heavy cover, it's prudent to use line or leader heavy enough to free a fly or lure that hangs up. Twenty pound is a good choice. Many anglers favor one of the "super braids" that combine strength with small diameter for this fishing. For the flyrodder, choose a leader material that features high abrasion resistance like Berkley Big Game. You needn't worry about visibility since tidal bass aren't particularly leader-shy.

The choice of fly or lure for tidal bass is wide open. Bass eat most anything, so anything that appears edible is likely to draw a strike. Of course, every angler has a favorite, and we are no exception. For subsurface lures, especially in dingy water, a noisy lure is our first choice. There's probably nothing better than an appropriately sized Rat-L-Trap, although the Berkley Frenzy series is also an excellent choice.

Excellent top-water choices include Rat-L-Trap's Spitfire, Storm Lures' Chug Bug, and Rebel's Pop-Rs.

Any well-designed fly-rod popper (one with adequate hook gap) will work. Color seems unimportant in a surface lure except that, if you are fishing at or near dark, a black lure shows up best.

One thing to keep in mind when buying flies or lures for tidal bass fishing—buy models that feature either stainless (preferred) or saltwater-resistant, plated hooks. Remember, you will be fishing in brackish water, and that means some salt content. Salt corrodes regular hooks very quickly. When possible, our preference is to buy lures with "salt-safe" hooks (many companies produce saltwater versions of their freshwater lures that are equipped with corrosion resistant hooks). That way, we aren't concerned over which lures we use in salt water, and which we use in fresh.

If you must use a fly or lure without saltwater hooks in brackish water, take along a small wide-mouthed jug filled with fresh water. Whenever you change lures or flies, drop the used one into the jug and retrieve and dry it when you get home. This simple trick will keep hooks from rusting.

Eastern Chain Pickerel

To say that pickerel are an overlooked species is a huge understatement. Few anglers target pickerel. They are usually an incidental catch made by bass fishermen. Sometimes, however, they are the salvation of a fishing trip. Willing pickerel have saved many an otherwise unproductive bass expedition.

This small member of the pike family shares many of the same characteristics of its larger cousins. It is an active predator, feeding entirely by sight, and usually during daylight. Like all members of the family, pickerel are "ambushers," preferring to hold motionless in heavy cover. Look for them suspended amid underwater grasses and lurking in downed timber waiting for a meal to swim by.

Pickerel are an excellent target for fly fishermen. Since they are principally minnow feeders, they are made-to-order for a streamer. Yellow, white, and chartreuse are especially good colors, and flash materials add to their effectiveness.

A pickerel's favorite food is a shiner, but it's a highly opportunistic feeder that will attack anything it thinks it can swallow. Alan Heft, Eastern Regional Fisheries Manager for Maryland's Department of Natural Resources, has received numerous reports of large pickerel consuming ducklings and even small turtles.

Pickerel are most active when the water temperature is between 50 and 60

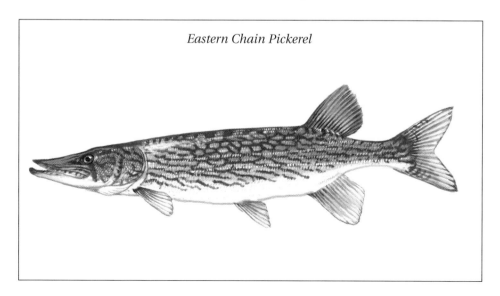

Eastern Chain Pickerel

degrees. As a result, the best times to fish for them is when the water is too cold for most other species. October and November can be excellent, but once the water temperature reaches the 40s, pickerel become sluggish.

The best time of all is probably February through March, when there is little other fishing to be had; pickerel can provide a "spring tonic." There's a pre-spawn "bite" that occurs when the water temperature gets in the low 40s. Typically, hardy bait fishermen will bundle up and drift large shiners to catch some of the largest pickerel of the season, but a big flashy artificial will draw lots of strikes, too.

Tackle and Techniques

Finding the fish is the key. Most surface weed cover will not be visible during the colder months, so look for downed timber or underwater weed beds. Seek out the warmer spots. A shoreline with a southern exposure (the north side of a river) will warm earliest, and shallows along this shoreline warm fastest of all.

The shorelines of many tidal creeks feature a distinct "shelf" of shallow water (usually two or three feet deep) that extends out from shore for several feet, then drops abruptly into water maybe six feet deep. Pickerel frequently cruise this edge, and this is a very good spot to look for them.

If you can locate beds of underwater weeds, pickerel will often be lurking right among them. Here, a fly fisherman has a distinct advantage. Using a slow sinking line or a 10-foot sinking head and employing the countdown method, one can present a streamer just above the weeds. This gets the fly close enough to be seen, yet avoids getting tangled in the bottom growth. Further, since the fly can usually be kept at pretty much the same depth, you can keep your offering in the strike zone far longer than with other methods.

The retrieve is quite important. Gary Neitzey, one of the area's top light-tackle guides, has some very definite ideas on that score. According to Gary, the trick is to allow the fly to sink to the desired depth, and then retrieve it with a few long strips followed by a long pause. Continue with the strip-pause, strip-pause cadence until you either get a hit or you have to pick up the line. Most anglers, says Gary, used to fishing for stripers, tend to make both the strip and the pause too short. The long pause is the key, and most strikes will occur with the fly motionless and slowly sinking.

The back ends of coves or backwaters will often collect a mat of debris. This is an especially good spot. Sometimes, pickerel will lie so far back in this cover, that you will literally have to throw your lure into the "brush" to draw strikes. A basic rule of thumb is that the more difficult a spot is to fish, the more likely pickerel will be hiding there.

Soft plastic lures are a good bet because they can be rigged to be weedless. Any soft plastic minnow imitation is a good bet. There is a product called a "Hitch-Hiker" marketed by Diachii Hook Company that is very useful for this type of fishing. It's a little brass coil that attaches to the eye of a jighead. To use it, screw the coil into the front of a soft plastic lure like a Bass Assassin or a Fin-S-Fish and insert the hook point into the body of the lure, leaving the hook point covered. You can throw that right into the "stuff" and retrieve it slowly. It's deadly. Drawback? Pickerel are well equipped with teeth, and the soft plastics don't last long; but that's a small price to pay.

Gary Neitzey's favorite soft plastic lure is a 5-inch Kalin Grub in either white or chartreuse. He's not sure why the Kalin Grub is so effective, but as far as he's concerned, it's the best.

Also, no matter which lure you choose, fish it slowly. In late February and early March, the average water temperature will be well below 50 degrees, and the fish will not be as active as when the water warms as spring progresses.

Good pickerel water is not difficult to find; almost any brackish creek like the Severn and Magothy on the western side and the Wye and Nanticoke on the Eastern Shore are pickerel hotspots.

Any fly rod from a 5-weight to an 8-weight will do the job, and a medium-weight spinning or casting rod works just fine. You can go lighter if you wish since the tackle will vary more according to the cover being fished than the expected size of the quarry. If you are fishing right into heavy weed cover or brush, you'll need fairly stout tackle and tough line. For conventional tackle, any one of the so?called super braids is a good choice. For the flyrodder, use a heavy leader and attach a tippet of abrasion resistant mono. (All major manufacturers market abrasion resistant mono.)

A quiet approach is a must. Because pickerel are ambushers, lurking in a safe spot awaiting a passing meal, a lot of commotion will spook them. They may not run for cover the way a startled trout would, but they will simply lie low and ignore your best offerings.

Yellow Perch

Yellow perch are another predominately freshwater fish that adapts well to brackish environs. In past years, the yellow perch was one of the most sought-after fish in the Bay because of their excellent eating qualities. Unfortunately, this fact has led to over-fishing both by commercial netters and recreational fishermen. This, combined with diminished underwater vegetation and pollution, has taken a toll on the population. Still, in some locales, and at certain times of the year, the fishing can be quite good. All of the Upper Bay tributaries hold yellow perch, but the best ones are probably the Bush River and Dundee Creek on the west side and the Wye River on the east. The Wye is especially good in the fall.

Tackle and Techniques

Yellow perch feed primarily on smaller baitfish, so any fly or lure that imitates one of the predominate forage species will work. Small grubs, little bucktails, and ultralight crankbaits will work, as will the ever-popular Clouser Minnow or other small flashy streamers. Work any of these along shoreline drop-offs for best results. If you are fishing a streamer, you will score more consistently if you use a sinking tip fly line. A full sinker isn't required since the depths that are most productive will usually be less than six feet. Fly rods of about 4- or 5-weight are fine as long as you use small, lightly-weighted flies. A light or ultralight spinning or casting outfit with 4- to 6-pound test line is ideal.

Not known as a super fighting fish, yellow perch, like their freshwater cousin the walleye, strike hard but do their best work in a frying pan.

Yellow Perch

White Perch

The white perch is not a true perch at all, but is a member of the bass family and a cousin to the striped bass. It is another fish that lives comfortably in either fresh or brackish water. Look for them in river mouths and tidal creeks, mostly in the upper portions of the Bay.

Probably the best early spring destination is the Susquehanna River near where it enters the Susquehanna Flats. White perch ascend fresh water to spawn, and the Susquehanna has one of the largest numbers of spawning white perch of any Chesapeake tributary.

Usually beginning in early April, large female white perch move into the rocky upstream waters first. Some of these females can reach two pounds and give quite a good account of themselves, especially in the faster currents.

Other Bay tributaries also have good populations of this tasty fish. The Severn and the Magothy on the west side, and the Choptank and the Wye on the Eastern Shore provide excellent fishing for white perch most of the year. In fact, white perch may be one of the most widespread species in the Bay. Just don't expect them to be prominent in the lower reaches of the Bay—the salinity is too high.

Tackle and Techniques

White perch are made to order for light to ultralight tackle. Since one of their principal foods is smaller fish, a fly or lure that imitates these fish is called for. For the fly-rodder, small white or yellow and white Clousers are probably as good as anything, and the addition of a small inline spinner will up your odds. A 4- to 6-weight fly rod is ideal. A sinking tip line, or even a full sinking head, may be necessary depending on the water's depth and speed.

For spinning tackle, small spoons like the little Huntington Drones (if you can find them) or other small spoons or spinners work quite well, as will a "safety pin" spinner/grub. But probably the all-time favorite, especially when fishing spots where hang-ups are frequent, is a $1/8$- to $1/4$-ounce shad dart or any similar small, inexpensive lead jig. Depending on where you are fishing, cost can be a critical factor. White perch often school up near heavy cover and you can lose a lot of flies or lures. If you wish to use bait, nothing beats grass shrimp.

One other pleasant aspect of white perch is that they are excellent table fare. Dipped in batter and deep fried, they are one of the better eating fish you can catch, and since their population numbers are high, there is no harm in bringing home a full stringer.

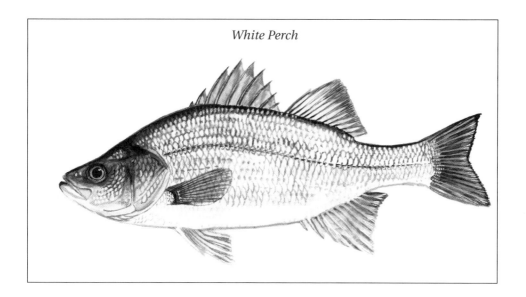

White Perch

Redfish (or Red Drum)

Redfish are found most often in the lower reaches of the Bay, typically near the mouth. In the spring, they can be found in several hotspots in deeper areas where they are often caught by fishing clam baits on the bottom. Since this really doesn't fall under the guise of light-tackle fishing, that's all we'll say about this method. However, they also venture into very shallow water where they can be caught by light-tackle anglers, and one of the best spots is in the waters of Lynnhaven Bay. Redfish invade the shallow areas and can often be spotted by seeing their distinctive spotted tails above the water surface as they grub for edibles.

Unfortunately, this is usually a catch-as-catch-can proposition since the fish move in and out on their own schedule, and predicting their presence is closer to witchcraft than science. Typically, in this region, they will usually be an incidental catch, commonly caught by anglers who spot them while targeting speckled trout.

Other good locations include the mouth of the Honga River and occasionally over any of the Lower Bay lumps. Normally, these fish will show up in late July through early September, but they are usually caught while fishing for trout or stripers.

Tackle and Techniques

Redfish, often called puppy drum, are strong, determined fighters. Although their initial run can be impressive, after that they tend to be sluggers rather than speedsters. They can be very spooky and difficult to approach in shallow water, sometimes flushing at the sight of the line in the air. Stealth is the watchword for catching this species.

Eight-weight fly rods and medium spinning rods capable of throwing a ¼-ounce lure are ideal for fish up to about 10 pounds. Casting tackle isn't well suited to these fish as you need a rod that can cast a small lure, yet still have the backbone necessary to handle the fish. Small coppery flies (Clouser-style flies are very popular) and small gold spoons are the overwhelming favorites. Since these lures must be fished right on the bottom, weedless versions are preferred.

Poppers are also effective in drawing strikes at times, but hooking-up is difficult. Just look at the mouth of a redfish and you'll see why. The mouth is low down, much like a bonefish or a carp, and is ideally suited to picking food off the bottom. In order for a redfish to take a surface offering, it must go through some gyrations and misses the target a lot. Still, it's exciting to watch.

Black Drum

Black Drum are found in the Lower Bay fairly early in the spring. From mid-April to mid-May is the prime time, and the waters near Cape Charles the prime location. As the season progresses, black drum will move up the Bay, sometimes as far as Chesapeake Beach. This member of the drum family grows quite large, but the fight is more of a standoff than a battle. They are simply not as sporting a fish as their copper-hued cousins.

Tackle and Techniques

This is a species that usually is caught in deeper water using heavy tackle and clam baits. They may take artificials at times, but deepwater bait fishing is the norm. Since this falls outside the scope of this book, we mention black drum simply because they are found in the Bay's waters.

Redfish (or Red Drum)

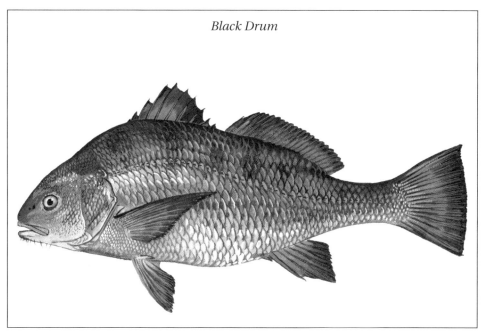

Black Drum

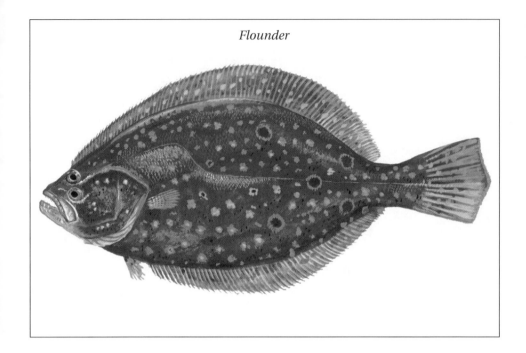

Flounder

Flounder

Flounder are found throughout the Bay, from about Mid-Bay south. Since flounder are a true saltwater species, you will generally find the largest fish, as well as the greatest numbers, in the saltier southern reaches of the Bay. The Lower Chesapeake gives up some truly exceptional fish and the area around the Chesapeake Bay Bridge Tunnel (CBBT) is a real hotspot. "Drifting the tubes" at the CBBT (working over the underwater humps formed by the submerged tunnel) during a running tide, is one of the best techniques. Flounder over eight pounds are not uncommon.

Although flounder lie camouflaged on the bottom and mount a sudden quick attack at any passing baitfish, they are also an active sight-feeding predator and will take flies and lures willingly, often following an artificial for quite a distance before striking.

Tackle and Techniques

Although flounder fishing is most closely associated with minnow and squid baits drifted along the bottom, anglers using flies and lures can score as well. The biggest trick (in addition to locating the fish in the first place) is keeping your offering on the bottom—flounder simply don't move very far up in the water column unless they are chasing something. Then they will follow a fly or lure for quite a distance (sometimes almost to the boat) before striking. Still, full fast-sinking lines for the flyrodder, and fast-sinking lures for other tackle choices are needed to interest the fish. Bucktails are probably the most popular lure, but we especially like a 5-inch Bass Assassin in chartreuse with silver flecks on a 1-ounce or heavier head. Some version of a Clouser Deep Minnow is undoubtedly the most popular fly. Chartreuse and/or white with some flash is the most popular color.

Natural colors also work well, especially if the water is unusually clear. Since flounder depend on both their sense of sight and smell, a scented lure, or a fly dipped in an attractant can be more effective than a "bare" offering. Just remember, for fly-rodders who might be seeking a record, adding scent to a fly would disqualify the catch for record consideration.

Cobia

Mark Sosin calls cobia "the man in the brown suit." Local names include ling cod, lemon fish, and crab eater. These incredibly strong fish are a bit of a mystery as far as their presence in the Chesapeake is concerned. In this region, cobia are found almost exclusively right near the mouth of the Bay, and their habits seem to have changed in recent years. It used to be that the best fishing for cobia occurred in August and September in the vicinity of the Bridge Tunnel. This made sense because, despite the fact that they migrate as far north as Cape Cod, cobia are basically a warmwater fish and August and September would be when the Bay's waters are at their warmest. However, in recent years, spring and early summer have seen better numbers of cobia in the Lower Bay. No one knows why.

Cobia are also different in the fact that (like bluefish) they are a species unto themselves; they have no known relatives.

They are tough fish, not only on the line, but after being boated as well. Many an unknowing angler has suffered injury or broken tackle from the thrashing a large cobia did after he was boated. If you plan to keep your fish, some anglers suggest a blow to the head (the cobia's) with a ball peen hammer instead of the more commonly used club. Reason? The hammer concentrates the blow. We have found that covering the fish's eyes with a towel works better, since they seem to immediately calm down when this technique is used.

By the way, cobia are excellent table fare. They are very firm-fleshed and bear some resemblance to a pork chop.

Tackle and Techniques

Despite their elusiveness in this area, cobia are a sought-after species. They frequent various types of structure, and buoys are an especial favorite. Larger specimens will usually be solitary, while smaller fish tend to swim in small groups. Frequently, they will swim just under the surface, offering an excellent sight-fishing opportunity. They attack lures with a vengeance, and your reel had best have a smooth drag since their initial run is quite powerful. Forget light leaders or mono of less than 12 pounds.

Light rods are equally inappropriate for these fish. Fly rods of about 10- or 11-weight and equivalent spinning or casting rods are needed. Since these fish feed heavily or crabs, a fly or lure sporting green and dull copper colors is a good idea, although almost any swimming plug or streamer will probably draw a strike if properly presented. Your offering should land close enough for the fish to see it and not

Cobia

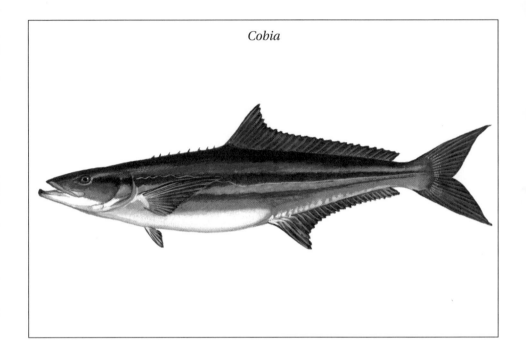

Spadefish

close enough to frighten it. Further, as with most all predators, the lure should be retrieved so as to swim away from the quarry. No baitfish swims towards something that may eat it.

Flies or lures should employ very strong hooks. Like all fish that feed heavily on crabs or other crustaceans, Cobia have very powerful crushing jaws and will easily destroy light hooks.

Spadefish

Slab-sided and tall, built quite similar to an angelfish, here's a sport fish that looks like it just escaped from someone's saltwater aquarium. Spadefish are a fairly recent phenomenon in the Bay. Ten years ago, practically no one was catching them. It's unsure whether they weren't present, or if they've been here all the time but anglers were unaware of them or did not know how to catch them. Whatever the case, spadefish are now a very popular summer species in the Lower Bay. They're strong dogged fighters, sort of like an enormous bluegill, and are excellent eating.

Spadefish are available near the CBBT from about mid-May until September, but the biggest ones are caught in June when specimens topping eight pounds are caught regularly.

Tackle and Techniques

Spadefish feed principally on "cannonball" jellyfish, and some anglers fish for them using pieces jellyfish as bait. A couple of jellyfish are netted and one is suspended from an anchored boat over a spot known to harbor spadefish. This is done by attaching a length of monofilament line to the rubbery mouth of the jellyfish and attaching another length of line with a two-ounce sinker on the end, also to the mouth. (Don't worry; cannonballs do not have stinging nettles.) The whole contraption is then lowered to the desired depth, and the line tied off to a cleat. The other jellyfish is cut into small pieces and used as chum and bait. Small pieces are put on about size 4 hooks and a small split shot is affixed to the line well up from the hook. This is then drifted with the chum. Many anglers have been quite successful with this method.

A much simpler plan is to purchase a supply of clams and use them as chum and bait. Anchor up in an appropriate spot and start a chum line by crushing the clams and ladling shells and all over the stern. The rig is constructed by tying the line from the rod to one side of a bobber. Six to eight feet of line is tied to the other side of the bobber, a small slip sinker added, and the line is then tied to a swivel. A couple more feet of line is tied to the other end of the swivel, and a size two hook is tied to the end. A small chunk of clam is used for bait and the rig is allowed to drift well back from the boat on a moving tide. It might not be as effective as the jellyfish routine, but it's a lot easier to do, and it works quite well.

Since spadefish rely principally on their sense of smell to locate food, taking one on a fly is difficult. Supposedly, when they are actively feeding in a chum slick, they'll hit flies that look like a piece of clam or jellyfish (depending on which chum is being used) and some anglers claim to have taken spadefish on flies. This happens more often when chumming with clams. A fly that looks like a piece of jellyfish has proven difficult to construct, but one that resembles a bit of clam is easily created.

Nothing special is needed in the way of tackle; just use a strong enough setup for the expected size of the fish. No matter how they are hooked, however, be prepared for a substantial fight. They run hardly at all, but turn their flat sides to the direction of pull and resist being landed. A sizeable specimen will provide quite a tussle.

Tautog

Although tautog (also called tog or blackfish) are more commonly a fish of the ocean, good populations of these tough, stubborn fighters are found in the lower reaches of the Bay when the waters are cold. For this reason, tog are caught most readily in early spring and again in late fall. Tog are strictly bottom dwellers and feed principally on crustaceans such as crabs and shrimp. They have sharp, protruding teeth designed to crush crab shells. They can also crush an unwary finger, so be very careful when handling these guys.

Tog are surprisingly strong fighters that live right amid the worst underwater structure possible, so you'll need fairly stout tackle to land one of these fish.

Tog are one of the very best eating fish in the Bay, but they are quite difficult to clean. Their skin is tough and covered with a slippery coating. An electric fillet knife helps, as does a Kevlar fish-handling glove. If you have some means of clamping the fish to a board of some sort, your task will be easier. One trick we use, if no clamping device is at hand, is to employ a stout fork to aid holding the fish. Remember the Kevlar glove—we've seen all too many anglers cut themselves when cleaning a tog.

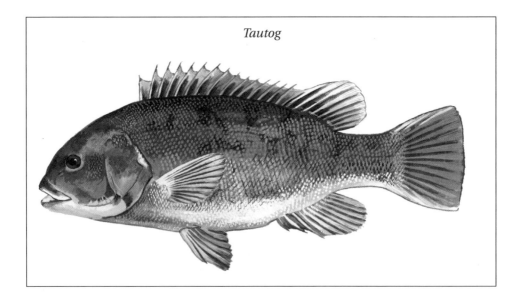

Tautog

Tackle and Techniques

As mentioned, tog live right among the rocks or inside of any kind of wreck. Their bite can be described as tentative at best; an old tog fisherman's advice is to set the hook just before they bite. When they are hooked, they immediately head to the bottom and whatever obstruction is available. Larger models are hard to turn. This presents a dichotomy—you need tackle sensitive enough for you to feel the take, yet stout enough to move the fish away from its lair. For this reason, light but stiff graphite rods and one of the no-stretch braids like Berkley's Fireline are perfect for tog fishing.

As far as we know, tautog are caught exclusively on bait. Considering where they live, it would be difficult indeed to get a lure within range without hanging up. The preferred baits are peeler crab, parts of hard crabs, small green crabs or "sand fleas." The only real trick to tog fishing is to drop the bait right among the rocks with as light a weight as possible. At the slightest nibble, set the hook.

Spanish Mackerel

Spanish mackerel, also called Atlantic mackerel, are a prominent game fish in the Lower Chesapeake. One of the smaller members of the mackerel family, averaging about 2 to 3 pounds, these quick slender gamesters enter the Lower Bay once the water temperature goes above 68 degrees. Although they usually prefer the higher salinity levels of the Lower Bay and are found in greatest numbers near the Bridge Tunnel at the mouth of the Bay, in dry years they will range farther up the Bay and can be caught as far north as the Bay Bridge. We know of one specimen that was taken at the mouth of Bush River a few years ago. Since this is near the uppermost reaches of the Bay, this individual obviously was lost. An excellent table fish, Spanish mackerel are a much sought-after species.

Tackle and Techniques

Quite a lot of anglers troll small spoons on fairly heavy tackle for these fish. Although effective, this is not exactly a sporting (or fun) way to catch them. When conditions are right, usually a fast running tide over underwater lumps, large schools of Spanish can be found breaking the surface chasing bait, and the action can be frantic. If you get into a large school driving bait to the surface, you won't soon forget the experience.

This situation is ideal for the light-tackle angler. Small silvery spoons, like a Stingsilver or a Hopkins, or small flashy streamers are deadly. Sometimes, when they are feeding frenziedly, they'll hit most anything. We've actually taken them on 4-inch blue-backed Wind Cheaters. Most times, however, your offering should closely match the bait (in most cases this will be small silversides or bay anchovies).

Mackerel are noted for their keen eyesight, and they can be extremely boat-shy—to the point that, in calm water, it can be difficult to get within casting range of a school. An exception to this is when the schools are chasing bait in turbulent water like that which occurs over the tubes at the CBBT during a fast running tide. Then, seemingly, you can almost net them at the boat.

Their keen eyesight also makes them leader-shy, and they will frequently ignore a lure with a wire leader attached. However, this is not as big a problem as might be imagined since, despite the fact that Spanish mackerel have substantial dentures, their teeth are conical and not sharp on the sides like those of a bluefish. Because of that, a moderately heavy monofilament leader will usually work. We tend to favor 20-pound test mono with good abrasion resistance. Berkley Trilene Big-Game is a good choice.

Because these are usually not big fish, you can, within reason, use as light a rod as you like. The strike of the Spanish mackerel is harder than their size would indicate, and their initial run is quick, but after that, they come to boat rather easily.

Channel Catfish

Several species of catfish inhabit Bay waters, but the channel catfish is the only one considered a game fish. Despite the fact that these are predominately bottom feeders that rely heavily on their sense of smell to locate food, they are also active predators that will take a small lure or streamer that gets close enough for them to notice. Although classed as a freshwater fish, channel cats can be found in the brackish estuaries at the mouth of freshwater Bay tributaries, such as those at the mouth of the Gunpowder and Bush Rivers on the Western Shore. The Susquehanna River below Conowingo Dam probably has the best population. Because the rivers of the Eastern Shore are simply brackish arms of the Bay and not freshwater rivers, channel cats are less common on that side.

Tackle and Techniques

Nothing special is needed to fish for catfish. By far, more cats are taken bottom fishing with bait (chicken livers are a favorite) than any other way. However, flies, crankbaits, jigs, and spinners will all work for channel cats, and recent developments in scented soft plastic lures make them a top choice for an artificial. Usually, though, channel cats will be an ancillary species caught while fishing for other fish. They put up a strong fight, but they do not make runs of any length, so elaborate tackle is unnecessary.

Carp

For many years, carp have been viewed with disdain by most anglers in this country. In Europe, it's a different story. There, they are regarded as excellent game fish and fine table fare. We can agree on their sporting qualities, but there are far better eating fish. As far as we are concerned, they are the piscatorial equivalent of a groundhog—edible, but not desirable. Recent years have seen a substantial increase in the number of anglers actively fishing for carp.

Carp are hardy fish, tolerating a wide range of conditions, and they grow quickly so large specimens are common. They are also one of the most intelligent fish, and catching one requires stealth on the part of the angler.

Spanish Mackerel

Channel Catfish

Tackle and Techniques

Although carp are quite suspicious and leader/line-shy, ultralight tackle has no place in this endeavor. Carp are strong, and their runs, while not terribly fast, can be long and powerful. Many anglers have learned about sight fishing for carp in freshwater streams using small nymphs. The same type of activity can be found in the shallow brackish areas of the Bay. Carp can tolerate a moderate amount of salinity, but usually they will be found near where freshwater streams meet the Bay.

Carp spawn in late May or early June, and this is a prime time to seek them in shallow water. Look for them in locations like the Susquehanna Flats or the mouths of Bush and Bird Rivers. An 8-weight fly rod or equivalent spinning/casting rod is ideal. Stalking and casting to carp in shallow water has been likened to bonefishing. Try to see which way the fish is moving and cast well ahead of its path. Use a small dark streamer or small bucktail, and let the lure sink to the bottom. When the carp is within a foot or so, give a short gentle jerk to your offering. If you don't spook the fish, he'll most likely take the offering. Then, if it's a big one—hold on.

Carp

Basic Tackle

TO GET STARTED, USE WHAT YOU HAVE

Fly tackle on the Chesapeake ranges from 5- to 10-weights and sometimes even heavier. Many saltwater flyfishers in the Chesapeake area have some experience with fly fishing in fresh water for trout, panfish, or bass. You can probably start fly fishing in salt water with this same tackle—if you pick the right species and places, and if you have—or will get—the right lines and leaders.

As an experiment, our crack(ed) research staff (the authors) dug out a pair of vintage mid-1960s fiberglass rods intended for bass, a Fenwick FF98, a 9-foot rod rated for a 9-weight line and a Fenwick Ferralite FF85, an 8½-foot rod rated for an 8-weight line. We were surprised by their performance. The small diameter guides on these rods made casting thick, modern floating lines like a Wulff Triangle Taper 9- or 10-weight difficult to impossible. But with thin and dense sinking lines and with shooting heads, it was a different story. Using the 9-weight, we could cast a Teeny 350 and a heavy Clouser Deep Minnow pattern 80 feet with comfort. We did nearly as well with the 8-weight and a Teeny 300. Undoubtedly, an expert like Joe Bruce or Lefty Kreh would do considerably better.

These are fish-catching distances with sinking lines, the most productive in the saltwater flyfisher's arsenal. We're not advocating buying these old rods, though. Their casting characteristics are simply inferior to rods developed in the last five years that deliver better performance with a lot less effort, and their hardware won't stand up to the saltwater environment as well. But if you have them, you can try your hand at saltwater fly fishing as long as you use the right lines and leaders. (Make sure to take extra care of such rods, or they won't last long in the salt.)

LIGHT-TACKLE APPROACHES

Light tackle is appropriate for certain Chesapeake species under certain conditions. A 5-, 6-, or 7-weight rod can be a good choice for such smaller species as hickory shad; Spanish mackerel; chain or grass pickerel; possibly flounder; and such panfish species as white perch, yellow perch, hardhead and spot. It can also handle the occasional 12- to 16-inch striper, blue, or trout that may be mixed in with these species.

The light-tackle rod must be matched with a single action reel that has a decent drag system and holds at least 100 yards of 20-pound test backing. Two types of lines may be used: a sink-tip line with a 10-foot sinking head section in a weight matching the rod will suffice for shallow water situations. For deeper waters, use a fast-sinking line like a Teeny T-150 for a 5-weight rod or a Teeny T-200 for a 6- or 7-weight rod. A level 3- to 4-foot leader of 16- to 20-pound monofilament, with any of these lines, completes this rig.

These rigs will allow you to cast unweighted streamer fly patterns like a Lefty's Deceiver or Bruce's Bay Anchovy and lightly weighted versions of such flies as a Clouser Deep Minnow or a Half-and-Half pattern. However, this is best done only in light wind conditions and in places—and at times—when you are not as likely to encounter a double-digit striper or bluefish or have to horse a fish from tight cover.

Some of the more open waters of Upper Bay rivers (the Wye, the Choptank, Baltimore Harbor, the Patapsco, and the Severn) are examples of such locations.

The disadvantages to light fly tackle are obvious: It does not allow the angler to fish poppers or large and/or heavily weighted flies, and it presents the problem of losing large fish or, worse, playing them to death. And the angler can't control what takes his fly. About 10 years ago, we were fly fishing the Susquehanna River near Conowingo Dam, using 9-weight rods and floating lines. Giving up on stripers, we began casting size 8 Zonkers for white perch and the occasional smallmouth bass slashing into small perch and minnows feeding on a caddis hatch. On the first swing into a new area, a striper estimated at 12 to 15 pounds greyhounded across the surface, fell on a Zonker, and was hooked. Only slack-jawed surprise prevented a fierce reaction strike that would've popped the leader. It took a while, but the striper was safely landed and released. If we had been using a 5-weight for the perch and smallmouth, that striper likely would have ended up miles downriver at Port Deposit, probably floating dead with the entire line and backing.

RECOMMENDED FLY TACKLE

An 8-weight rod is the choice of many Chesapeake anglers. It will handle a good sinking line, like a Teeny 300, and an intermediate line. It will also handle a bass-sized popper—under ideal conditions. But most fly fishing experts agree that the ideal Chesapeake Bay fly rod is a 9-foot, 9-weight. The major reason for this choice is that this rod has enough backbone to cast the bulky poppers or weighted streamers, such as Clouser, Half-and-Half, and Whistler patterns. It is light enough to cast all day and still gives the pleasure of a deep bend on the 16- to 22-inch striper, bluefish, or trout typical of the Bay, and it even lets you know that such species as hardhead, perch, or Spanish mackerel are gamesters, too. It also has the muscle to dispatch double-digit stripers and blues, horse fish from such hazards as rock jetties and barnacle-encrusted pilings, and lets you fly cast safely and effectively in the gusting winds often encountered on the Bay.

Some excellent rods are available in the $200 to $300 range, such as the St. Croix Avid and Ultra Legend rods. You can pay twice as much for a top-of-the-line Sage or Loomis GLX. Whether it's worth the difference depends on how much you fish. To us it is worth the difference. With any rod, we suggest paying a bit more and getting a travel version, which casts and plays fish just as well. When you travel, you can take it on the plane and store it in the overhead compartment. Otherwise, you will sooner or later have your own missing rod disaster story.

This rod should be matched with a single action, saltwater fly reel with a good drag system and a capacity of 150 yards of 20-pound test backing, or better yet, 200 yards of 30-pound backing. When considering reels, also consider the price of extra spools—you need at least one—and they're usually half the price of the reel. Reels stamped from sheet metal will be adequate for most Chesapeake situations. We have landed stripers in the 15-pound range, like the fish in the above incident, on a 30-

year old Pfleuger 1498. You can still get stamped reels, like the Pfeulger 1598 RC, that will do the job. But for about $150 you can get a quality machined reel, like the Scientific Angler System II, that will not fail on the Chesapeake or anywhere else unless you hook a nuclear sub.

There are at least three approaches to saving money on extra reel spools. First, purchase reels that use plastic cassettes instead of spare spools, such as those manufactured by STH or Orvis. Second, you may make use of interchangeable shooting heads as described below and in the appendix, "Making Shooting Heads and Add-Ons." Third, in a fairly recent development, you may purchase a multi-tip line that can match, to some degree, the performance qualities of floating, sink-tip, intermediate, and fast-sinking lines. Airflo, Orvis, and Scientific Anglers make such lines now and more are sure to follow.

The fly line used 80 to 90 percent of the time in the Chesapeake is a fast-sinking

An assortment of typical striper flies.

line, preferably a shooting head type, with the head weighing between 250 and 400 grains. (A shooting head is simply a fly line with the casting weight very condensed in the forward portion of the line, usually the first 20 to 30 feet.) Teeny lines at present are almost synonymous on the Chesapeake with fast-sinking lines, but Scientific Angler, Cortland, Orvis, and other companies make comparably fine lines.

You have a choice for a 9-weight rod. Many experts prefer the Teeny TS 350, a 30-foot head on a 105-foot line. Others prefer the Teeny 300, a 24-foot head on an 82-foot line that's a dream to cast. Its slightly slower sink rate of 6 inches per second is adequate to plumb depths to roughly 20 feet. Try these or comparable lines and decide for yourself. Use the level leaders suggested above. This is the rig for fishing streamers, shrimp patterns, eel patterns, crab patterns, and similar flies.

The other fly line needed, stored on an interchangeable spool of the same reel, is a floating line, which is used mostly for fishing poppers. (They can also be used with streamers and other sinking flies.) Poppers are generally only effective in low-light situations, usually in early morning before the sun has fully risen on the horizon. But poppers offer two great advantages. First, they produce spectacular surface strikes. Second, they are big-fish flies, and not just for stripers but also for blues, trout, and redfish.

Experts differ in their preferences on floating lines. Some prefer a full fly line in a weight-forward or saltwater taper; others prefer floating shooting heads. There are some great full floating lines made today, such as the Scientific Anglers' weight-forward lines with AST finish. We still lean toward the shooting head camp. Wulff's Triangle Taper is a great casting, 30-foot, floating shooting head that maintains its flexibility even in cold weather. Another great line is Cortland's XRL floater, which is also a commercial shooting head. Like many anglers, we recommend a floating shooting head be sized one line weight over the rod manufacturer's rating. So, a 10-weight floating head would be the choice for a 9-weight rod.

The leader on a floating or intermediate line is much more critical. There are some commercial tapered leaders on the market, but we've had better results with hand-tied leaders. (See "Leaders and Knots" below.)

An intermediate or slow-sinking line is a specialty line used far less than the other two, but it's the line of choice when a carefully controlled sink rate and/or slow retrieve is called for. Two prime examples are when drifting flies in chum lines and when working in shallow, colder water, such as near the warmwater discharges around Baltimore Harbor in winter. It's also good for spooky fish in shallow, clear water situations. Scientific Anglers' Stillwater Line, a clear line that does not become stiff in cold water, has performed admirably and produced some very big fish for us. This is a full tapered line, so the weight usually should match the rod maker's recommendation (such as a 9-weight line for a 9-weight rod as on a floating line). Prepare a loop at each end of this line, attach a leader, and keep it stored and readily available on the plastic spool it comes with so you can switch off with one of the other lines as the need arises. In clear-water conditions, we usually use the same full leader as on floating lines.

Two other excellent intermediate lines are Cortland's Striper Line, a commercial head, so you should use one size heavier than the rod's line rating, and Scientific Anglers' Uniform Sink—Type II with an AST finish, a full line.

Other Lines and Options

While floating, fast-sinking, and intermediate lines are the three basic choices, there are some other options. Sink-tip lines, which are floating lines with a 5- or 10-foot sinking tip of varying densities, can be very effective in shallow water. Designed for freshwater fishing, we have found them very effective in the shallow waters of Bay rivers for such species as pickerel, bass, and white and yellow perch, as well as for stripers. Most of the major line companies make sink-tips in full fly line and 30-foot head modes.

We use these in the lighter 5- to 8-weight range. They tend to offer a subtlety of retrieve that can make a big difference. Several years ago while fishing the Baltimore Harbor with Bill Kehring, we watched him take a number of good stripers on a slowly-retrieved Bruce's Bay Anchovy worked over a sunken barge hull while our Clouser patterns fished on fast-sinking lines requiring faster retrieves were less successful.

Add-ons are short pieces of sinking line that are quickly and easily added as a way of tuning a fly line to run deeper. Like shooting heads, they are commercially available from Orvis, Gudebrod, and others, or you can make them yourself. One simple way to make an add-on is to use a short section of 27-pound test lead core line or Cortland's CR-13 material and add a loop to each end. (Use the loop techniques described in the appendix "Making Shooting Heads and Add-ons.")

An add-on may be used on any line, converting a floating line to a sink-tip and enhancing the sink rate of any sink-tip or sinking line. We generally put the add-on between the end of the fly line and the leader (assuming a loop-to-loop set up). As stated, the casting performance of the line, especially a floating line, usually deteriorates some, but you can get away with it on the heavier lines like 8- to 11-weights.

Multi-tip lines are relatively new on the market. They keep improving and appear to be a trend that's here to stay. As stated, they are versatile, can save money by replacing several different lines, and reduce the need for extra reel spools and/or shooting heads. Fly lines are a very dynamic and rapidly improving field. However, at this point, the consensus of most experts is that multi-tip lines do not perform as well as the lines designed solely to be floating, intermediate sinking, sink-tip, fast-sinking, or extra-fast-sinking. This could change as line technology continues to improve.

Leaders and Knots

As stated, our leaders on fast-sinking lines and sink-tip lines are usually a level section of 16- to 20-pound test monofilament or fluorocarbon. It is attached to the fly line via a loop-to-loop connection, with a braided or whipped loop in the end of the fly line. The loop for the butt of the leader is a surgeon's knot.

Leaders for floating and intermediate lines are longer and much more critical. There are a number of commercial leaders available with saltwater tapers and tippet strengths. Most have the advantage of being knotless, which is helpful in weedy situations. But we have generally not found them nearly as satisfactory as leaders we make ourselves.

The leaders we use now are a Joe Bruce adaptation of a standard leader formula. Joe uses Berkley Big Game monofilament leaders and ties two versions. His long leader has a butt of 4 feet of 50-pound test, next is a 2-foot section of 40-pound test, then a 1-foot section of 30-pound test. The loop at the end of the 4-foot butt section and the 1-foot terminal section is made with a surgeon's knot. Then Joe adds a 3- to 4-foot leader of 16- to 20-pound test. The loop in the leader is made with a Bimini knot, then doubled over to form a loop-to-loop connection with the 30-pound section. Joe's shorter leader uses the same weight lines and knots. The butt is 30 to 34 inches of 50-pound test, then 18 inches of 40-pound test, then 9 inches of 30-pound test. The same 3- to 4-foot leader of 16- to 20-pound test is used.

These heavy leaders provide positive turnover at the end of the cast for large poppers and weighted flies. If you find your casts with such flies "dying," not unrolling at the end of the cast, the problem may be the leader more than your casting technique. So we recommend you try these leaders.

We use the 100 percent loop knot for tying on flies. The loop allows the fly plenty of movement on a heavy leader. Properly tied, this knot lives up to its name for strength.

THE TWO FLY ROD SYSTEM

While a 9-foot, 9-weight is the ideal Chesapeake fly rod, one fly rod is not the ideal choice. Many veterans carry two rods, a 10-weight equipped with a floating line and a popper, and a 9-weight equipped with a sinking line and a streamer (usually weighted). So, as you begin to buy tackle, plan accordingly. If you go this route, the best approach is to get two matching reels with an extra spool for each. Should one of the reels become damaged on a trip, you can still have access to your full range of spools and lines.

The 10-weight would be equipped with similar lines—a 10-weight, weight-forward floating line or 11-weight floating head, a fast-sinking line of 350 to 450 grains, such as a Teeny TS-350 or 450, and an intermediate 10-weight line or 11-weight head stored on a plastic spool.

SHOOTING HEADS

Like tapered leaders, there are two types of shooting heads, those made by manufacturers and those made by anglers. As stated above, many line companies produce floating, intermediate, sink-tip and fast-sinking lines that are shooting heads. Most use a running line that is a much thinner version of the head; one line, Cortland's XRL, uses a coated braid for a running line.

While making your own shooting heads may seem unnecessary with so many good commercial versions on the market, it does have its advantages. You can "tune" the head to your individual rod and casting style by adjusting the length of the head. For those of us who are not casting immortals, you can add even more distance to your casts with a head you make. And heads can save money in at least two ways: Some companies, like Cortland and Scientific Anglers, sell shooting head lines with no attached running line. These heads are significantly cheaper than full lines. Also, you can buy some floating lines in double taper, cut them roughly in two, and make two floating heads. Finally, and most importantly, you can save money and storage space with heads by eliminating extra reel spools, which aren't cheap.

Having said all this, shooting heads do have disadvantages in some situations. First, you must retrieve the line all the way back at least to the head before making another cast. In some kinds of fishing, like casting to bonefish on the flats or dropping bass bugs along a shoreline, a shooting head is a poor choice because you want the ability to pick up the line and cast again after a short retrieve. Second, you may surrender a bit of delicacy, since a heavier fly line will be hitting the water. However, in fly fishing the Chesapeake, long casts and long retrieves are the rule, and delicacy is rarely a factor. A third disadvantage, if you use braid as the running line, is that you must use some kind of finger guard with this abrasive material. Braid is also a bit delicate, so it doesn't tolerate being stepped on continually. It's also a bit light and prone to blow around in the wind. Using a shooting basket, which we recommend for most fly fishing situations with any line, solves these problems. There are other alternatives to braid as discussed in the back of this book.

TRY BEFORE YOU BUY

Fly tackle in a highly individualized choice. Not only must the rod, reel, line, and fly be in balance, they must suit the casting style of the individual fishermen. Simply selecting the most expensive equipment is no shortcut, since sometimes the higher priced rods are more difficult to use for beginners, who are better served by cheaper, slower-action rods. Our best advice is to get recommendations and try out a variety of tackle at a shop that specializes in fly fishing. Ideally this shop should also teach fly casting.

You can also get some idea of appropriate tackle by using the equipment provided by guides. You should be aware, however, that the guide's choice of equipment may be dictated by his or her casting style or by which manufacturers offer the best deals. We always prefer to use our tackle, since we have tuned it to our needs over the years. (Again, having travel rods is a big help.) We will often try out the tackle provided by the guide, but this is just research. Your own properly tuned tackle is a joy to use.

CONVENTIONAL TACKLE

Despite the fact that we love to fly fish, we almost always take along a conventional rod on our forays on the Chesapeake. The first reason is wind. Once winds get above 20 knots fly fishing can be difficult, and, in a small boat, dangerous. There are some tricks to beating the wind, but there are limits. We've also hit occasions of severe roughness, due to the wind and tide being in opposition, where it was more difficult to maintain one's footing while fly casting.

Another reason is depth. It's true you can fire out a long cast with a sinking line and let is sink far down before beginning the retrieve. But there are practical limits to this approach, and it begins to transition from fun to a chore or a stunt. While we've

This bluefish fell to a Rat-L-Trap.

taken fish down to 35 feet with fly tackle, often we use 20 to 25 feet as a transition point. Plus, deep jigging is such a fun and effective way to work deep water.

Exploring the water is also something for which to consider conventional tackle. It can be faster to explore an area by fan casting a section of water with a jig or Rat-L-Trap just to see what the bottom is like and if any game fish are home.

The last consideration is age or condition. Conventional tackle is often easier to use. If you're out all day, it may be the "better part of valor" to switch off occasionally.

Casting Versus Spinning

Each has its advantages, and we use both. Casting tackle arguably offers more accuracy and definitely provides better fish-fighting capability. It also seems that casting reels hold up better under heavy use, and we prefer them for deep jigging. So for cranking fish out of cover or off the bottom, casting tackle is our choice.

But it's a tradeoff, because spinning gear has two great advantages: It offers easily replaceable spools, allowing you to cast with lines of differing test, which in turn allows you to cast lures in a wide range of weights. Also, it's not only foolproof, it's angler-proof. No matter how educated your thumb or how good the anti-reverse on the reel, when the boat takes an unexpected bounce and your thumb comes off the spool of a casting reel in the middle of a heave toward the horizon, it's backlash time.

So if we know we're going to be running the boat or stuck in the middle of some tight, run-and-gun situations, where a backlash could be fatal to the lure, we'll often opt for spinning tackle.

RODS, REELS AND LINES

Generally, we like two-piece rods, since we feel their survival rate in cars and boats is much higher. In recent years, several manufactures have developed three-piece travel casting and spinning rods in weights ranging from light to heavy. Again, these provide the same good action at a bit more cost, and they are a boon to the angler who needs to take tackle aboard planes.

A longer rod generally casts farther, but 6 to 7 feet is a reasonable rod length, especially considering that some people in a boat take umbrage when you bounce a lure off their heads (if they're lucky enough not to get impaled). We recommend rods with a medium range of graphite content, a somewhat soft tip, and the ability to cast a good range of weights. We also like a rod that will throw a lure a long way with a flat, line-drive cast; one that cheats both the wind and circling gulls looking for an easy meal. There are a lot of good rods on the market. On the high end, Loomis makes wonderful casting and spinning rods. On the low end, the Lunkerstick Light series delivers surprising good performance. In the middle, St. Croix makes great rods at very reasonable prices.

Reels are critical in saltwater fishing, and cheap ones will not hold up. For the medium and medium/heavy tackle, look for a reel with a capacity of at least 150 yards of 15-pound test monofilament, and 200 yards is better. The reels should be extremely well made and feature a smooth, rugged drag system. For casting, the Abu Garcia Morrum, Model 5600, is a delight for mid-range equipment.

You can learn a lot by observing the equipment the professional guides use and questioning their choices. They will quickly steer you away from failure-prone equipment. While their choices are sometimes dictated by the company that offers the best terms, few guides will tolerate inadequate gear. Plus, there can be other reasons worth considering. Fishing with veteran guide Mike Murphy recently, we noticed all his spinning reels were Shimano 4000s. When we asked him why, he responded that they held up extremely well fishing day after day in the Chesapeake.

Lighter Tackle

One favorite rig for fishing for pickerel and panfish in some of the Bay tributaries, such as the Dundee, Wye or the Magothy, is a 6-foot, light spinning rod and a Spidercast SC 30 reel loaded with 12- to 20-pound test Gorilla Braid, with a 12- to 18-inch leader of 12- to 15-pound monofilament. This rig can toss $1/8$-ounce jigheads and grubs attached to "safety pin" spinners and catch white and yellow perch all day. Yet, should the occasional big largemouth bass or striper grab your offering, you can handle the bigger fish with this rig.

Medium Tackle

Spinning rods 6 to 7 feet long, casting ¼- to ⅝-ounce lures are probably the most popular light-tackle choice on the Bay. For medium spinning tackle, 10-pound test monofilament is probably the all-around choice, with an extra spool of 8- or 12-pound test monofilament. There are a number of good spinning reels on the market in this category.

Rods for casting should have the same specifications as the medium spinning rods above. Lines can be monofilament or braid and in slightly heavier tests, with 12- to 16-pound test a good range for monofilament and 20-pound test for braid.

Medium/Heavy Tackle

Medium/heavy casting and spinning tackle is extremely versatile, often handling lures in the range of ½ to 2 ounces, so it can be used with a variety of baits and rigs. These rods are often longer, in the 6½- to 7½-foot range. We recommend 12- to 17-pound monofilament for spinning, 12- to 20-pound test for casting. Braid for casting can be 20- to 30-pound test.

Striper taken on a heavy Clouser.

NOTES ON LINES AND LEADERS

There are plenty of good choices of monofilament lines. In our opinion, any major brand will do. Chesapeake guides and experts are divided on clear versus light green colored monofilament, though the majority lean toward green. The verdict is also split on fluorocarbon leader material, though the majority avoid it.

There are some great new "knotable wire" products available for dealing with toothy critters like bluefish. Surflon-Micro Ultra is one such brand. However, a lot of Chesapeake fish—Spanish mackerel being an extreme example—are put off by wire. A "bite leader," consisting of a 12- to 18-inch piece of abrasion-resistant monofilament can be a better choice unless you're dealing with bluefish of five pounds or more.

Braided lines definitely have a place, though as fly line backing isn't one of them. We like braid for deep jigging, chumming, bottom fishing, and other such baitfishing applications as livelining and eeling. The sensitive feel and positive hook-setting qualities make braid a great choice for these applications. Braid can also be a great choice for light-tackle panfishing in 12- to 20-pound test as described above. For medium tackle, we recommend 20-pound test, for heavy, 30-pound test.

Again, there are a lot of good brands of braided lines. Braided lines demand special knots. In our experience, the best way of adding a monofilament (or fluorocarbon) leader to braid is with a pair of uni-knots. First tie a uni-knot in the braided line around the butt of the monofilament leader. Then pull about a foot of the monofilament butt past this knot and use it to tie a uni-knot around the braid above the first knot. Pull on both lines until the two knots butt up against each other. Trim the ends. This knot does not fail.

In tying braid directly to hardware, such as a swivel, the Trilene knot (double improved clinch knot) works well. But, to make sure, add another overhand knot above it and, perhaps, a drop of knot glue.

Braided lines also require special techniques in breaking off when your lure or bait is snagged. You want to avoid cranking down on the reel and burying the braid in the other wraps, thus requiring the whole spool of line to be cut off. You also want to avoid yanking on the heavy test line and having a hook or set of hooks catapulted back in your face. The standard approach is to carry a short section of broom handle. When the line becomes snagged wrap several turns around the handle just above the reel and pull in a direction away from yourself until the hook frees or the line and/or leader breaks. Obviously, this technique can also be used for monofilament.

KNOTS

Knots are critical, and we've listed a couple of knot books in "Resources" in the appendices. To keep things simple, we use mostly the Trilene knot or the Palomar knot to attach lures to monofilament or fluorocarbon lines or leaders. For casting very light lures on heavy line, such as when casting unweighted plastics, we may use the 100 percent loop knot.

We use a pair of uni-knots, as discussed above, to attach braided line to a monofilament or fluorocarbon line of leader. The Bimini knot or spider hitch is used for creating double lines.

CLOTHING AND ACCESSORIES

We're hardly fashion plates, but clothing is important, mostly for safety reasons. We recommend a brimmed cap of some kind and polarized sunglasses, both for better vision and protection from the sun and from errant casts. We recommend long-sleeved shirts and long pants for the same reason.

For footgear, we like boating shoes or some kind of crepe-soled boots. We always carry good raingear; we've found weather forecasters about as reliable as stockbrokers. Raingear is also a great way to block wind and is part of our layering strategy in cold weather. Remember: the best fishing on the Chesapeake is usually in the colder months.

Use of sunblock cannot be over-emphasized. Apply it before you go out and renew it throughout the day. Sun gloves to protect the hands are also a good idea; in cold weather use the fingerless wool gloves popular with steelhead fishermen. Finally, make sure to apply lip balm.

We recommend that a small first-aid kit also be carried. Antacids, antihistamines, seasick tablets, aspirin, and bandages are minimal requirements. Bug repellent can also prevent an unpleasant day on the water.

A good pair of long-nosed pliers/wire cutters is the first tool to have. We also strongly recommend a Boga Grip in the 30# size. This is a great fish-handling device, and it also includes a built-in scale. It prevents injuries to the fish when landing them and facilitates quick unhooking and release; it also protects the fisherman from hooks and from the teeth of bluefish, pickerel, and other toothy species. If you have this device, you really don't need a net. It's much less damaging to fish and it takes up little room. On the minus side, it's not cheap and it doesn't float; make sure you use the wrist thong every time.

There are a number of effective deep hook removers on the market, and we recommend carrying some kind, even if you never fish bait. We've seen many types of game fish absolutely inhale flies on occasions. The Dehooker, by Dehooker, Inc. of Palm Coast, Florida (800-772-5804) has proven so effective that it's endorsed by the Maryland Department of Natural Resources (MDNR).

We recommend using a stripping basket. If you don't want to use one, carrying a weighted net, like a minnow seine that can be draped over clutter in the boat, can save a lot of headaches.

Some kind of towel helps keep your hands from getting too slippery and dropping things overboard—like rods and reels; we've seen it happen.

A wireless phone, protected by some kind of waterproof case, is not a replacement for a VHF radio in case of emergencies, but it is handy and private. Upper Bay guides are big fans of these devices. (On the other hand, if you're out on the water with some big important fellow who is on the phone all day because he can't be out of reach of the office for a minute, we feel you are justified in suggesting he put the phone away someplace where only a proctologist can find it.)

Finally, you should carry a good set of navigational charts, again in some kind of waterproofed case.

(See the "Travel/Boating Checklist" in the appendices for a more complete list of recommended gear.)

Basic Chesapeake Bay Flies and Lures

NOTES ON FLIES

A review of our Chesapeake fly boxes reveals mainly variations of three basic patterns: Lefty's Deceivers, Clouser Deep Minnows, and combinations of Half-and-Half patterns. There are two major reasons for this: Our friendships with Lefty Kreh, Bob Clouser, and Joe Bruce (one could do worse), and more importantly, that's basically all that are needed. Throw in a popper pattern for top-water action, bendback versions for weedy shallows, and Bruce's Bay Anchovy to match the predominant Chesapeake baitfish in summer, and you're set. In fact, in discussing this section with Lefty, he said that if you added Bob Popovich's Surf Candy to this list, you could fish anywhere in the world.

But all of the above flies are styles of tying. A wide range of sizes, colors, and the amount of flash materials are needed to meet the conditions of the Chesapeake, especially for stripers, which can be maddeningly selective at times in regard to size. And within these styles are some specific patterns that have proven effective over years. Fortunately, all of these flies are easy to tie and all are durable.

Like Joe Bruce, we usually tie our Clouser Deep Minnow and Half-and-Half patterns with all materials on top of the hook and somewhat full. We use Mustad 34007 hooks, sharpened and with the barbs mashed down, for most patterns. We use Mustad 34011 hooks for the bendbacks, and humped hooks for popper and sliders. As circle fly hooks are perfected, we expect to begin using them.

Most of the patterns shown may be found in Lefty Kreh's *Saltwater Fly Patterns*, which is widely available. Specific Joe Bruce patterns may be found in his books, *The Fisherman's Edge's Striper Fly Patterns* and *Fly Design Theory and Practice*, and ordered through The Fisherman's Edge at 410-719-7999.

MUST-HAVE FLIES

Bruce's Nite and Day Popper—This simple, foam-body popper with a black bucktail tail is all you need for top-water striper action. It's best fished at dawn. The black bottom, providing better visibility for fish, is made with a waterproof felt tip marker.

Chartreuse over White Clouser Deep Minnow—Tied in a variety of sizes, this is arguably the most popular saltwater fly pattern around the world.

Bruce's Crab-Colored Clouser—Let's put it this way: This fly is so good Lefty Kreh bummed some from us when he saw how well we were doing with them on a trip to Hooper Island with Lefty, Bob Clouser, and Joe Bruce a few years ago. We tie these in 2- to 4-inch lengths. From the top down, this fly has a layer of olive bucktail, a thick layer of copper Flashabou, a layer of tan bucktail, a few strands of gold Krystal Flash, and a bottom layer of white bucktail. Joe claims the secret to this fly's success is the pattern of natural color; others think it's that copper Flashabou. The stripers just blast it. The smaller sizes are very effective for white perch and hardheads, as well.

Bruce's Crystal Bugger—Originally developed for smallmouth bass, this is a versatile saltwater pattern, which we always tie with saltwater hooks in 2- to 4-inch lengths in pearl, chartreuse, or black.

Chartreuse or Yellow Over White Perch Clouser—These basic chartreuse over white or yellow over white Clouser patterns, both with a bit of flash material, in 1- to 2½-inch lengths are ideal flies for white and yellow perch.

All Black Lefty's Deceiver—This is a great night pattern in shallow water.

White Half-and-Half—This fly has done well in the winter and early spring months. We tie it in a range of sizes.

Chartreuse Over White Half-and-Half—This is a standard big fly for big fish and is usually 5 to 7 inches long. We've done well fishing with this pattern around bridges and pilings, day and night. It also does well during the catch-and-release season on Susquehanna Flats.

Chartreuse Over White Lefty's Deceiver—This is a classic Lefty's Deceiver that is tied in a wide range of sizes and works for all major Bay game fish.

Fisherman's Edge's Lefty's Deceiver—The blue and pink layers of this fly combine to give off a purplish flash that imitates menhaden. Joe Bruce, Billy Zeller, and Walt Knapp used this pattern one day in the late fall of 2001 to take 10 stripers over 30 pounds, including two over 40 pounds. We tie these from 2 to 6 inches.

Chartreuse Over White Bendback Deceiver—This is just a bendback version of a standard Deceiver and is used for shallow, snaggy waters.

Lefty's Bloody Chum Fly—This is the fly to use when fly fishing in a cut chum line. Use white and red or brown and red patterns. Some fishermen use red over orange Clouser patterns. Whatever the fly, use an intermediate sinking line, cast across or upcurrent to achieve a natural drift, and strike quickly.

Bruce's Bay Anchovy—This small fly is often the pattern of choice in summer when all game fish feed on bay anchovies. This fly can also be tied Clouser Deep Minnow style. Sometimes when schools of bluefish are chewing these up, we substitute the Albieclouser.

FLIES FOR PANFISH

White perch, yellow perch, hardheads, and pickerel all readily take streamers, particularly Clouser patterns with their up-and-down action. We've found scaled-down versions of the patterns we use for stripers, trout, etc. to be very effective tied on a size 2 hook for panfish. In specific patterns, we like Joe Bruce's Crab-Colored Clouser, Bull Minner, Bay Anchovy, and Crystal Bugger. In generic patterns, we like all white and yellow or chartreuse over white. Panfish, especially white perch and pickerel, love spinners. One easy way to make a spinner fly is to tie the above patterns Clouser-style on a jig hook and clip on a small, inline or "safety pin" spinner to the hook eye. (You need to cast these rigs with a more open loop.) Of course, the spinners will be quick victims to the corrosion of salt water, but they increase the fun while they last.

While we have been drawing parallels between fishing streamers and fishing a variety of underwater lures and especially bucktails and plastics, there is one vital difference. In retrieving a fly, all retrieve actions are created by the line hand; the reel and rod are rarely, if ever, used. When using conventional tackle, reeling and often twitching the rod tip are the primary means of creating action to a lure or enhancing built-in action.

NOTES ON LURES

You don't need a great variety of lures to be successful in Chesapeake Bay waters. But within these types, size, color, and the amount of flash, plus strength of construction are the key considerations. If you look at our list, you'll see only three surface lures, one metal jig, one "any depth" lure, and five jig and/or plastic lures marked as indispensable and discussed in some detail below.

Big lures and flies match the predominant baitfish in the spring (herring and white perch) and fall (menhaden). But in summer, especially in the Upper Bay, bay anchovies are the predominant bait, and game fish often "lock in" on one- to three-inch baits.

Size doesn't seem as critical with surface lures, which are usually retrieved quickly, and the surface commotion is the primary attraction. Once you drop off the surface, however, size may be critical. You may want sizes from one to nine inches—or more.

This range of sizes is easy for many plastics. Most of the lures listed come in multiple sizes and colors. So it's better to have, for example, the full range of sizes of Rat-L-Traps than to have six different brands of similar sizes and colors.

Most anglers agree that white/pearl and chartreuse are the preferred primary colors for lures (and flies) including bucktails and plastics. Usually lures have dark backs of blue or black and at least some flashy silver sections.

Many serious gray and speckled trout fishermen insist color is critical and recommend dark green, smoke, root beer, chartreuse, and pearl. Others insist that color isn't that critical.

The major construction features are hook strength, hook hangers, and body strength. Some are tougher than others, but you can break any hard plastic lure or unpaint any jighead with a hard, errant cast against riprap or concrete. (We speak from experience.) A lot of good freshwater lures work well in saltwater. Fortunately, many top lure makers are now producing successful freshwater lures with saltwater hooks and hangers. The Rebel Pop-R, now available with saltwater Excalibur hooks, is a good example. The penalty for using standard freshwater lures is having trophy fish open the hooks or—worse yet—rip them out of the plug (experience again).

Stripers seem to possess a special genius, which improves with age and size, for bulling into the nearest barnacle-encrusted object when hooked. When you clamp down on the reel spool to stop such a trophy, a quality saltwater lure will rarely fail. Anything less probably will.

MUST-HAVE LURES

Stillwater Popper—This new popper floats tail down at rest. Tough, with beautiful finishes and available in two sizes and several finishes, this is the popper of choice for many Upper Bay guides.

Creek Chub Striper Strike—We always carry this old favorite for two reasons: First, it's a proven, effective popper that casts well. Second, it sinks when not retrieved, an invaluable feature when birds are diving on bait. Stop the retrieve and let the lure flutter down, an action causing birds to turn off and often triggering strikes from fish.

Top Dog—A guides' favorite for "walk the dog" retrieves, weaving the lure from side to side with downward twitches of the rod tip. Other anglers will prefer the old classic Zara Spook with saltwater hooks.

Jighead and Bass Assassin—This is the indispensable lure for Upper Bay guides fishing for stripers. Make sure you use jigheads with quality, saltwater hooks with plenty of hook gap, such as those made by Bigmouth Lures, Got-Cha or Offshore Angler. In our opinion, long-shanked hooks, as featured on the brands listed, tend to give the lure a fluttering, dying minnow action on the "drop," the pause between pumps or twitches, which is when most strikes occur. The jigheads should be in ¼-, ⅜-, ½-, ¾-, and 1-ounce sizes, with ⅜ being the most versatile. White and chartreuse are the recommended jighead colors. The guides' favorite colors for Bass Assassins are Albino Shad, Opening Night, and chartreuse in 5-inch lengths, although 4-inch and 7-inch versions are sometimes used.

Stingsilver—Another "must have" lure and arguably the best lure on the Bay, it can be cast or deep jigged. We clip one barb from the treble and mash down the other two barbs for easy releasing. The 1¹/₈- and 1¼-ounce sizes are the most popular on the Upper Bay; the 2- and 3-ounce sizes are the choices in the Chesapeake Bay Bridge Tunnel area. The Stingsilver is a killer for such game fish as stripers, trout, blues, and redfish. Adorned with a strip of squid, it is also deadly on hardheads, flounder, and sea bass.

Rat-L-Trap—This is a foolproof and effective lure for all Bay species. Simply cast it out, allow it to sink to the proper depth, then crank back with a steady fast retrieve. While the ½- and ¾-ounce sizes are the most popular, don't be afraid to drop down to the ¼- and ⅛-ounce models when you need to match small baitfish. We recommend silvery, natural finishes. As good as the Rat-L-Trap is, we talked with a number of Lower Bay experts who strongly prefer the MirrOlure.

Fin-S Fish—The Fin-S can be fished unweighted for great shallow water action or on a jighead or on a Carolina rig. Fished unweighted, Fin-S patterns are best slowly twitched to imitate crippled minnows. In all cases, it is critical to use a saltwater hook; using a standard, offset shank bass hook may well result in that hook being opened by a large striper, bluefish, or redfish. Fin-S Fish come in six sizes between 2½ and 10 inches, and it's not a bad idea to have them all. Alewife and Blue Ice are two of many effective colors.

Offset ("Safety Pin") Spinner Grub—This is a great lure for perch and hardheads. We prefer white or chartreuse Power Grubs. If a large striper grabs this lure, with the inherently weak hook of most commercial jigheads this size, your fish-playing skills will be tested. We like to cast our own small jigheads on stronger jig hooks.

Jighead and Grub—This is another good, all-around pattern to match smaller baitfish. The jigheads can be white, red, or chartreuse with grubs in matching colors. The best sizes are ¼- and ⅜-ounce.

Billy Zeller's forty-plus-pound striper was a true trophy.

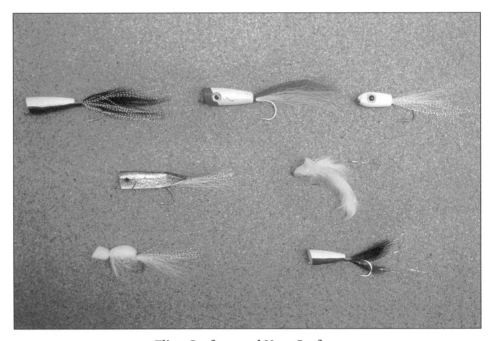

Flies, Surface and Near Surface

Top row, left to right:
   Bruce's Nite and Day Popper, Jackson Cardinal Popper, Foam Slider

Second row, left to right:
   Blados' Crease Fly, Saltwater Dahlberg Diver

Third row, left to right:
   Gartside Gurgler, smaller Bruce's Nite and Day Popper

Clouser Deep Minnow and Clouser-Type Patterns

Top row, left to right:
Chartreuse over White Clouser, Bruce's Crab-Colored Clouser,
Bruce's Bull Minner

Second row, left to right:
Bruce's Pickerel Fly, Cactus Striper Fly, Red over Orange Chum Fly

Third row, left to right:
Bruce's Crystal Bugger, Tom Earnhardt's Albieclouser, Chartreuse or
Yellow over White Perch Clouser

Deceivers, Half-and-Half Patterns, Bendbacks

Top row, left to right:
    All Black Deceiver, White Half-and-Half, Chartreuse and White
    Half-and-Half

Second row, left to right:
    Chartreuse over White Deceiver, Bruce's Fisherman's Edge's Lefty's Deceiver,
    White Deceiver

Third row, left to right:
    White Deceiver, Chartreuse over White Bendback with weedguard,
    Chartreuse over White Bendback Deceiver

Various Other Important Patterns

Top row, left to right:
   Lefty's Bloody Chum Fly, Bruce's Bay Anchovy, Del Brown's Crab Fly

Second row, left to right:
   Bruce's Crystal Shrimp, Whistler, Bruce's Spoon Fly

Third row, left to right:
   White Shad Fly, Hickory Shad Fly, Josenhans' Worm Fly

Fourth row, left to right:
   Lefty's Red and White, Pfeiffer's Invincible

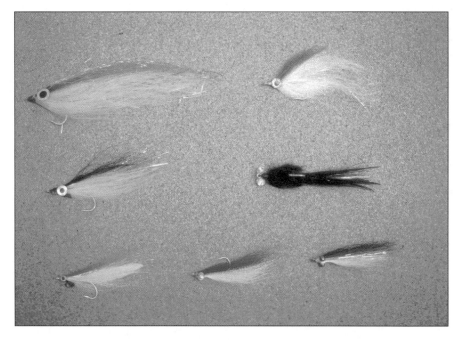

A Selection of Flies of the Virginia Coastal Fly Anglers

Top row, left to right:
    Two sizes of Art's Yak Attack

Second row, left to right:
    Larry's Yak Deceiver, Dolly Parton

Third row, left to right:
    Glass Minnow, Blue over White Clouser, Black over White Clouser

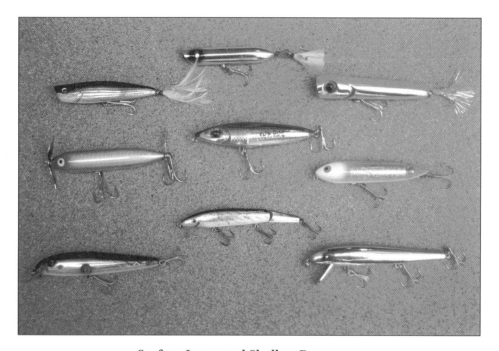

Surface Lures and Shallow Runners

Top row, left to right:
   Stillwater Popper, Creek Chub Striper Strike, Rattlin' Chug Bug

Second row, left to right:
   Zara Wounded Spook, Top Dog, Zara Spook

Third row, left to right:
   Windcheater, Jointed Rebel, Red Fin

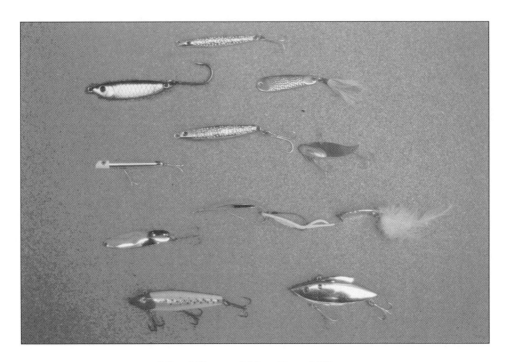

Metal Jigs and "Any Depth" Lures

Top row, left to right:
  Crippled Herring, Stingsilver, Hopkins Shorty

Second row, left to right:
  Got-Cha Plug, 2-ounce Stingsilver, Silver Buddy

Third row, left to right:
  Gator Spoon, Johnson Silver Minnow with stinger weedless hook and split chamois strip, Tony Accetta Pet Spoon

Fourth row, left to right:
  MirrOlure, Rat-L-Trap

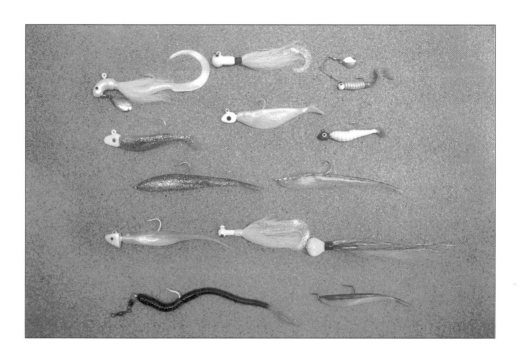

Jigs and Plastics

Top row, left to right:
   Road Runner Bucktail with plastic curlytail, Commercial bucktail with
   plastic curlytail, Safety pin spinner grub

Second row, left to right:
   Three Got-Cha jigheads with various plastic minnow/grub bodies

Third row, left to right:
   Two Fin-S Fish rigged weightless on open, long-shanked saltwater hooks

Fourth row, left to right:
   Got-Cha jighead with Albino Bass Assassin, Chartreuse $^3\!/_8$ ounce Bucktail
   and chartreuse plastic curlytail, Art Greason homemade jig with yak hair tail

Fifth row, left to right:
   Florida-rigged swimming plastic worm, smaller Fin-S Fish

How to Fish Flies and Lures in Chesapeake Bay

Many anglers use considerably different approaches for fly fishing versus conventional tackle. While techniques with these two types of tackle are not identical, we suggest that there are basic principles in presentation and in such factors as sizes and colors that should be common to both approaches.

One good feature of flies is their single hook, which can be made barbless for easy catch-and-release fishing. To the degree possible, we like to apply this principle when using conventional tackle, preferring to use single hook lures and to limit the number of hooks and barbs on multi-hook lures.

Fly tackle and conventional tackle have different capabilities. Conventional tackle can be more effective in windy and rough conditions and fishing depths over 30 feet. Likewise, fly tackle is often more effective in other situations, such as quiet and skinny water. We'll highlight some of these differences below. But honestly, the major appeal of saltwater fly fishing, in our view, is that it's just more challenging, more satisfying, more fun.

FISHING THE SURFACE

Fly Fishing

As mentioned earlier, our usual starting fly fishing rigs consist of a 10-weight rod rigged with a floating line and a popper and a 9-weight rigged with a fast-sinking line like a Teeny TS 350 and some kind of streamer. In our experience, poppers are effective mainly in early morning low-light situations and in shallow water. So poppers are used in a relatively small percentage of a fishing day. But we love to fish them because they produce spectacular, visual strikes and seem to produce big fish.

And poppers are not just for stripers and blues, either. In shallow water, poppers and other surface lures and flies are the top choice for big seatrout and redfish. In the rivers feeding the Bay, where one cast may produce largemouth or smallmouth bass or pickerel and the next a striper, blue, or trout, poppers are often the most effective choice. Again, this is particularly true in waters of less than five feet, especially in weedy waters. The Susquehanna River, Susquehanna Flats, Gunpowder, Dundee, and Northeast are just a few examples. We've also taken white perch, yellow perch, channel catfish, crappie, bluegill/sunfish, even walleye and flounder on surface lures and flies fished for the species named above, but such catches are more chance than anything else.

Chesapeake poppers should be simple. One favorite for stripers, Joe Bruce's Nite and Day Popper, has a round, tapered flat-faced, a 1½-inch Styrofoam body, and a tail nearly twice that length, creating a fly 4 to 4½ inches long. The long-shanked, humped, 2/0 hook is nearly 3 inches long, and as a result, it provides plenty of clearance from the body for efficient hooking. We also carry smaller versions of this basic popper, as short as 2½ inches.

Generally, the best retrieve for stripers and blues is fast, steady, and splashy. For seatrout, redfish, and pickerel, a slightly slower version of this approach is usually best. Creating a loud "bloop" with a cupped popper may be the best choice for large-mouth bass, and sometimes for the major saltwater species. There was one day at the Calvert Cliffs Power Plant when the deliberate bass-type retrieve was the ticket. But this was memorable because it was such an exception; we've had many more days that produced consistent strikes only when we were retrieving so fast it seemed like we were trying to take the popper away from stripers.

Soft foam poppers and sliders are also effective and can be especially good in brackish water, where a variety of species may be attracted to these flies. These produce quieter surface disturbances and can be fished fast or slow. These flies can also be fished on sink-tip, intermediate, or fast-sinking lines to mimic the action of struggling baitfish, swimming erratically and trying to dive to the bottom against forces pushing them toward the surface. In other words, you can mimic the action of a shallow crankbait like a Rebel, Redfin, or Rapala.

Just at dawn, a large popper or slider crawled slowly and steadily across an oily surface to create a rippling wake can ignite serious surface action. This is the fly rod version of the technique described below as "wake me in the morning." Frankly, we think this technique works better with conventional tackle, but it's worth a try when you're fishing with a fly rod, too.

Conventional Tackle

Poppers are our top surface choice for conventional tackle, too—fished with the same fast and splashy retrieve. We generally carry two kinds: floating poppers like the Stillwater, Super Pop-R with saltwater Excalibur hooks or the saltwater Rattlin' Chug Bug and sinking poppers like the Creek Chub Striper Strike. The floating lures are good for keeping the hooks above snags, such as the weed beds of the Susquehanna Flats or from rock crevices off the islands of the Chesapeake Bay Bridge Tunnel.

Sinking poppers are our choice when birds are blitzing bait. When you see a gull (or, worse, a pelican) target your popper, simply stop retrieving and let it flutter below the surface; nine times out of ten the bird will turn off. (Good luck on that tenth one.) As stated, this fluttering action often triggers strikes from some of the bigger fish, too.

Most of the above lures have their belly trebles attached via split rings. If we get into smaller fish, we'll often temporarily remove the belly hook to avoid having the extra treble snag a hooked fish elsewhere along the head or body. You will miss some strikes this way; it's a price we're willing to pay.

Stick lures, fished with the "walking the dog" retrieve are also effective for stripers and are a good choice in those brackish water situations where bass and stripers are possibilities. Walking the dog is achieved by a rhythmic series of downward strokes and pauses during the retrieve, causing the lure to dart first to one side then the other in a Z-shaped pattern. Heddon's Zara Spook is the classic lure for this; make sure to get the models with saltwater hooks, with or without the rattles. Top Dog is a new favorite. They're also good for working over weeds, particularly when the trebles are converted to double hooks with both barbs curving up toward the body of the lure. You can do this either by clipping one tine off the treble, which may also require repositioning the hook in the hook hanger, or replacing trebles with double hooks.

Propeller lures are also very effective in saltwater. In our experience, bluefish try to kill them, and they're also dynamite on shallow-water trout. Our most productive retrieve with this type of lure is two short, quick strips followed by a pause before repeating the pattern. But it pays to experiment. The classic Heddon Tiny Torpedo, Baby Torpedo, and Heddon Wounded Spook, a cross between a stick bait and prop bait, are three top baits. As with stick baits, these lures are also good for bass and can be rigged with double hooks.

But some days prop baits can be frustrating. Bass and/or stripers will climb all over them or knock them flying through the air—and not be hooked. This can happen to a lesser degree with poppers, too. Our best advice on these days is to switch to shallow running lures or flies.

Finally, there's the "wake me in the morning" approach, which the guys on southern reservoirs think they invented. Cast a large floating crankbait, like a seven-inch Cotton Cordell Red Fin, to a shallow area near a drop-off just at daybreak on a calm morning, let the rings disappear, then crawl it back across the surface so that the lip creates a V-wake. This is a big bait, big fish technique for stripers, blues, and trout. This approach is popular among some regulars on the Susquehanna River and Flats.

Not-So-Stupid Popper Tricks

The Pop and Drop—This old killer rig can be fished with either fly or conventional tackle. It consists of tying a 12- to 24-inch piece of monofilament off the end of a popper and then tying a sinking fly or jig to the end of this line. With a fly rod, tie the line to the bend of the fly rod popper hook and use a lightly weighted Clouser Deep Minnow as the dropper. With a conventional popping lure, tie the monofilament leader off the loop or off one bend of the tail hook and use a light jig or Clouser Minnow as the dropper.

Fish are attracted to the noise of the popper, but sometimes they won't take it. Often in these situations they will take the dropper fly or lure. Obviously, with fly tackle, you must cast this rig carefully with a rather open loop.

The Pop and Switch—This is another old trick that still works and is a favorite of Bay guide Norm Bartlett. It requires two anglers. One uses conventional tackle to make a long cast to a promising shallow water area with a large, hookless surface plug. He brings it back to the boat with a fast and splashy retrieve. Excited stripers or blues follow the plug back toward the boat to within easy casting distance of a second angler using a fly rod. The second angler drops his fly rod popper or streamer in the path of the charging fish, retrieves it more slowly than the first, and allows the fish to take it.

This is a great technique under difficult casting conditions or for less than heroic fly casters, since it draws fish in closer. Obviously, the angler with the "real" lure can use conventional tackle also.

The Pop and Pop—This is probably an old technique, but it's new to us—at least in salt water. (Most freshwater trout fishermen can attest to the effectiveness of a pair of wet flies or a pair of dry flies.) Guide Gary Neitzey has been using this rig in recent years. It's rigged the same as the Pop and Drop except that the second lure is also a popper or at least a floating lure. This can be an ungainly rig to cast with fly or conventional tackle, but the two lures seem to excite fish into striking readily.

*Joe Bruce with a white perch taken on a small
Bruce's Crab-Colored Clouser.*

FISHING SHALLOW TO MID-DEPTH

Fly Fishing

There are times, usually in shallow and/or weedy tributaries off the main Bay, when we will fish a streamer with a floating line, but we usually prefer a 10-foot sink-tip with a 3- to 5-foot leader. This combination with a 5- or 6-weight outfit is our choice for chain pickerel, white and yellow perch, and hickory shad. Using an 8- or 9-weight outfit for largemouth bass and stripers, we will use either a floating line or a floating line with an add-on to sink the tip of the line.

But as stated earlier, once we transition from floating lines, our usual choice is a fast-sinking line. We were among guide Kevin Josenhans' early fly fishing clients at Crisfield, and when we set up our tackle he was skeptical of our fast-sinking lines. He gently pointed out that we would start at Fox Island in water two to five feet deep and loaded with stumps. The first cast with the Teeny 300 and large Lefty's Deceiver produced a striper. This set the pace for the next nine hours in a variety of spots throughout the area.

Fishing the typical shallow water situation throughout the Chesapeake usually involves casting up against a shoreline, bar, or riprap and working the fly along a shallow bottom to a breakpoint to deeper water, letting the fly drop down that and then retrieving along that more deeply sloping bottom. Very often casting to the deeper spot will not do the trick; the fly must come from the shallows to the deeper area.

An extreme example is sometimes encountered in Baltimore Harbor, where the perfect cast puts the fly right on the crest of a wave as it hits the shore, whereupon the fly is raced back to the breakpoint, dropped to deeper water and the quick retrieve resumed. Strikes may come 5 to 20 feet from the bank, near the breakpoint. The angler executing this retrieve will outfish the angler casting within three feet of the bank by a ratio of two or three to one.

If all of this sounds like an angler with conventional tackle fishing a jig or a crankbait, we say, "You're catching on."

As we'll discuss on the section of fishing jigs, Captain Mike Murphy said with some exasperation recently: "You're always asking me how I fish a jig. I try a bunch of different retrieves until I find the one the fish want. Then I use that one."

Bingo! And the same is true for fishing streamers and other subsurface flies.

Retrieves with Subsurface Flies

The Dead Drop—Contrary to popular belief, saltwater fly fishing is not all poppers and Clouser Deep Minnows (although mostly it is). One overlooked, highly effective retrieve, if you can call it that, is the dead drop. This is especially effective in water less than five feet deep. Use a floating or sink-tip line and a fly with a very slow sink rate, such as a saltwater Muddler Minnow, Clouser Crippled Minnow, Tabory Slab Fly, or our favorite, a Bendback tied with a bit of deer hair or strip of foam at the head. Cast against a piling, riprap or into a hole in the weed and let the fly simply drift down, while watching it intently. Game fish will dart seemly out of nowhere to grab the fly.

The Drift or Swing—As Lefty Kreh constantly preaches, "Flies don't attack fish." Most fly fishing in the Bay consists of presently a fly to a game fish lurking downcurrent off structure to ambush bait. (Chumming and breaking fish are obvious exceptions.) So, in many situations, the fly (or lure) needs to be swung to the fish using the current, not dropped on their heads. A classic case we encountered was at the ripraps protecting Smithfield Harbor. Stripers were stacked in the quiet water at the end of the jetty, picking off bait as it was washed past them. A Lefty's Deceiver or Clouser cast to the end of the jetty—right to the fish—produced nothing. The same flies cast five feet upcurrent of the end of the jetty and swept to the fish by the current were taken with confidence. Likewise, a fly can be swung upcurrent or downcurrent to fish lurking behind rock jetties or bridge pilings.

The Strip and Pause—This is the most frequently used and productive retrieve for subsurface flies. It is used with any line and almost infinite variations are possible depending on the sink rate (if any) of the line, the sink rate of the fly, the speed and length of the strips, and the length of the pauses.

Probably the most frequently used retrieve is a strip of about one foot, a pause of a count of "one," then a repetition of this pattern. Another variation is two strips, a pause, then a repetition.

Fast swimming retrieves can be achieved by a series of fast, long strips with no discernable pause. Some anglers make this retrieve by locking the rod under one arm and using each hand alternately to retrieve the line; others lock the rod between their legs and use the hands as above. We're not big fans of either approach: With the first you could risk losing the rod on a heroic strike; with the latter you could lose your—er—dignity as well.

Walt Knapp caught this 35-pound striper on Mike Murphy's boat, "Tiderunner."

The Clouser Flip—As part of our "stealing from the best" philosophy we learned this trick from Joe Bruce, who observed Bob Clouser using this retrieve. (Yes, that Bob Clouser, the creator of the Clouser Deep Minnow flies.) Bob grabs the line with the same thumb-on-top-and-fingers-underneath grip used to hold the rod, then pulls the line sharply downward. At the end of this stroke, just as the stripping arm is straight down, he sharply snaps his wrist back. This causes the fly to quickly accelerate, dart spasmodically upward, then flutter down like a wounded baitfish (or also, to be honest, a plastic jerkbait). This retrieve is particularly good on active fish.

Conventional Tackle

Once you drop off the surface, most guides prefer that their clients fish single hook lures for two reasons. First, they are generally less injurious to the fish. Second, they are generally less injurious to the fishermen and guides. We tend to agree. However, some multi-hook lures are fun to fish.

There are a numerous floating crankbaits designed specifically (or mostly) for salt water. Some of our favorites are the Cotton Cordell Red Fin in 5- and 7-inch sizes,

Ed Russell with a striper taken on a Windcheater.

the Rebel Windcheater (a favorite of the Chesapeake Bay Bridge Tunnel regulars), the Rebel Jointed Minnow in sizes from 3½ to 5½ inches (a favorite of Susquehanna River regulars at Conowingo Dam and throughout the river, where it takes largemouth and smallmouth bass in addition to stripers), the Rebel Spoonbill Minnow and saltwater Rapalas.

These can be fished with a variety of retrieves. We already described the V-wake method under surface lures. Cranking the lure under a few feet, pausing, and letting it rise to the surface, then repeating will imitate the action of a crippled baitfish and is often effective in the shallows. It is the retrieve of choice with the Jointed Rebels. But most often a steady fast retrieve invoking each lure's built-in action seems more effective in most situations.

Unweighted soft plastic jerkbaits are deadly for freshwater and saltwater species in shallow waters. Our favorites are Fin-S Fish, Zoom Salty Super Flukes, and Bass Assassins in 3½- to 5-inch lengths. These are fished in a series of twitches, which give the plastics the spasmodic action of an injured baitfish. You can also fish these baits deep on Carolina rigs, just like freshwater bass fishermen do.

It is important to use strong hooks for plastics. We have had freshwater worm hooks opened up by big saltwater fish. You do not necessarily need to use a worm hook for an unweighted plastic; it's more important to use a strong hook with a big enough gap for hook setting.

These plastic baits should be stung along the hook shank with the dark or flat side up, with plenty of hook gap, and with the body of the lure straight and parallel to the hook shank, not bent.

The Rat-L-Trap is probably the best known of a host of sinking crankbaits. All you need do is cast, count it down to the desired depth, and crank it back. Simple but effective.

Fishing Jigs

This covers leadheads with skirts of bucktail, nylon, feathers, or various plastics. All the plastics mentioned above can also be fished with jigheads. As with conventional lures, we want our leadheads made with strong, saltwater hooks, if possible, and with a large enough hook so that it presents a good hook gap when a plastic is added.

Jigs are probably the most versatile and effective lures fished with conventional tackle in salt water. With their single hook they are a good choice for catch-and-release fishing. With their relatively cheap price you can also fish them "in harm's way," the kind of cover you may not dare venture into with expensive, multi-hooked lures.

For perch and pickerel fishing, it's hard to beat a $1/8$-ounce jighead attached to a safety pin spinner with a size 0 or 1 blade and a white or chartreuse curlytail grub 2 to 3 inches long. A curlytail grub should always be added so that the tail curls up. A steady, medium-speed retrieve usually works best.

For large game fish, most guides use ¼- to ½-ounce jigheads or bucktails unless the fish are extremely deep. Probably $3/8$ ounce is the most popular all around size, but jigheads can be as heavy as 1 to 3 ounces or more. White, pearl, shad, and chartreuse are the most popular colors for most game fish. Trout can be a lot more demanding, and color can be critical. As stated, dark green is often the choice for trout, with chartreuse, smoke, and root beer other popular choices. Adding a plastic curlytail or a piece of white, red, or yellow pork strip enhances the appeal of most bucktails. We like to thread the plastic all the way up the hook shank so that it flares out the bucktail and creates a pulsing action on retrieve.

Leadheads can be fished with the same variations described above for streamers—swung crosscurrent or downcurrent, cast upcurrent and allowed to drop, swum at differing speeds at various levels in the water column, fished in a "yo-yo" pattern with a pump and crank retrieve, bounced along the bottom, skipped along bottom, ripped just under the surface, and so on. Fishing jigs, like fishing streamers, is an art, and most guides are masters of this technique, having learned from long hours on the water.

Guides we've fished with have their own preferences for heads. With bucktails, a bullet, globe, or bulb-headed shape is the choice of many guides. When fishing with soft plastics like the Bass Assassin, some prefer a flat sided, triangular head to give added flutter when the lure is twitched.

Jigs can also be "sweetened" by adding a strip of squid, a strip of fish belly, a live or dead minnow, or a piece of shrimp or crab. On some slow days, this makes a big difference.

Stripers, and sometimes bluefish and trout, can be notoriously selective and sometimes lock in on baits of a certain length. This often happens in summer when bay anchovies, one to two inches long, fill the Bay. For this reason guides usually carry plastics in 1- to 3-inch sizes as well as the traditional larger baits. They'll string these tiny plastics on standard ¼-ounce heads or fish tandem rigs with a small lure above a standard size lure or fish two small lures in tandem.

For fishing above a snaggy, shallow bottom, they'll use a popping cork above a jig or use the Pop-and-Drop rig mentioned earlier.

Fishing Deep Water
Fly Fishing

We fly fish in the conventional manner up to depth of about 20 to 25 feet using fast-sinking lines. We have fished water over 35 feet by making long casts, letting the line drop all the way to bottom, then crawling it back. This is a rather tedious approach and one that should not be tried in a snaggy environment. However, once we get past 20 feet, we usually resort to the deadly techniques of deep jigging with conventional tackle.

Conventional Tackle—Deep Jigging

You can use standard casting or spinning tackle with this technique. However, since it often involves fishing fairly heavy lures slowly at depths over 20 feet, we like medium/heavy casting tackle for handling the weight and braided line for detecting delicate takes and for setting the hook(s). A clear monofilament leader is used with most rigs, often with a swivel as discussed below.

Metal Jigs—The Stingsilver, Hopkins Shorty, Crippled Herring, and Silver Buddy are our favorite lures for this type of fishing. The Stingsilver has become a Bay favorite in recent years and is almost synonymous with deep jigging in many parts of the Bay. The 1⅛-ounce and 1¼-ounce sizes are the standard in the Upper Bay; 2 or 3 ounces is often the standard in the swifter waters of the Lower Bay.

Since all these lures twist, although this is minimal with the Stingsilver, some sort of swivel is recommended. We often simply tie on a black snap swivel to the end of the monofilament line or leader and attach the lure directly to that. Some guides feel the snap swivel looks unnatural with the lure and recommend tying a black swivel about 12 to 18 inches above the lure and attaching the lure with a loop knot. Guide Mike Murphy, as described below, uses a Bimini Twist and Palomar knot. (If you're using braid, the swivel makes a handy transition point; tie the braid on one end and monofilament to the other.)

Murphy, who plies the deep waters between Hooper Island and Solomons, is a master of the deep jigging technique. The 1¼-ounce Stingsilver in green and white, blue and white, or chartreuse and white has become Mike's lure of choice for stripers, trout, bluefish, and Spanish mackerel in recent years—and not just in deep water. "In the fall I'll fish it from the surface down to 80 feet," he relates. But again, there are a few distinctive Murphy touches. First, he clips off one barb from the lure's 3X Mustad hook. (We do the same for the Hopkins Shorty and other treble hooked metal jigs; the Crippled Herring and some Hopkins lures come in a single hook version.) This provides the same effective hooking action but makes it much easier to release fish. Second, he doubles the terminal 1½ to 2 feet of line or leader with a Bimini Twist and attaches the Stingsilver with a Palomar knot. (A snap swivel between the main line and the leader avoids line twist.) "I've seen lots of times when one of the loops becomes cut, and I figure this Bimini trick has saved me another Stingsilver," says Murphy. He'll also use the small-lure-above-the-main-lure trick with the Stingsilver.

Stripers, and to a lesser degree blues and trout, can lock into a certain size of bait and refuse to hit anything else. In summer the bait is usually bay anchovies, often barely an inch long. To match this size Captain Mike Murphy adds a dropper loop above the Bimini and ties on a small Glass Minnow fly of his design. A small grub or Fin-S Fish, either on a jighead or plain hook, may be substituted. Some days Murphy finds almost all the fish are taken on the smaller lure.

Fish in the Mid-Bay are often suspended and can be spotted in distinct bands on the depthfinder. One rough but effective technique for reaching a desired depth, say, 40 feet, is to use a spinning rod with the reel's bail open or a casting rod with the reel in free spool and the tip of the rod and the Stingsilver lowered to the water's surface. Then lift the rod directly overhead and quickly return it to the water's surface. The lure will have dropped about 10 feet. Repeat three more times to reach 40 feet.

But often the Stingsilver is dropped straight to the bottom, quickly lifted off 3 or 4 feet, then dropped again. Or you can "stair-step" the lure—crank it up a few feet, pause, then crank up again—all the way back to the surface. Or just drop it to the bottom and crank it back quickly to the top. Strikes may come at any time in these routes, including the drop to the bottom, so it's critical to watch the line and strike at any indicative movement.

Metal jigs are also effective on breaking fish. One good retrieve is a shallower version of the stair-step retrieve. Let the lure drop 5 to 10 feet below the surface, crank it back to the surface, and—if a fish hasn't hit yet—repeat the action.

Metal jigs can also be sweetened by adding a strip of squid, fish belly, crab, shrimp, etc. On a number of occasions, we have seriously outfished baitfishermen using standard bottom rigs and bait for hardheads, trout, and other species by simply deep jigging a Stingsilver with a strip of squid.

Guide Richie Gaines believes that adding bucktail to the hook of any metal jig greatly increases the hookup percentage.

Heavy Leadhead Jigs—These can be fished in the same manner as metal jigs. They are single hook lures to begin with, and since twist is not a factor, no swivel is needed. Again, you can add pork rind, plastics (for bucktails), and various bait sweeteners. The downside of these lures is that they are expensive and big. Large size sometimes is an attraction and sometimes not when game fish are locked in on smaller baits.

The Bunky Conner Trout Rig—This is simply a version of a bottom rig made out of 60-pound test monofilament. We first discovered it about five years ago on a hectic fall morning's fishing aboard Conner's *Kathy C* out of Solomons. Our party of writers quickly limited out on stripers and we headed for deeper water for trout. But we couldn't get our flies and lures past the layers of 18- to 22-inch stripers to reach the trout below. (Life is full of troubles sometimes.) Conner's rig solved that problem.

He makes a loop at the top of the rig using a perfection loop or double surgeon's knot, then a monofilament loop about 8 inches below that, followed by another about 8 inches below that, and a terminal dropper loop, again using a perfection loop or double surgeon's knot, about 8 inches below that. The terminal loop is about three inches in diameter, and a ½- to 4-ounce Dipsey sinker is attached via the loop-to-loop method. The line is tied to the top loop. Size 1/0 spinner hooks are attached to the middle two loops, again using the loop-to-loop method, and a 3- to 4-inch curytail grub is added to each hook.

This whole rig can be fished as described above with metal jigs, but the simple drop, short lift, drop method is usually best.

The Richie Gaines Feather Jig Rig—This rig uses a $^{1}/_{8}$-ounce, large-eyed feather jig, with a tail consisting of from four to six hackle feathers in yellow, white, or chartreuse. The entire jig is about three inches long. Plastics, pork rind, squid, or minnow sweetening may be added. The rig is built around a 3-way swivel. The line is tied to the top arm, and a snap is attached to the bottom arm. This snap attaches to a Dipsey sinker weighing from ½ to 3 ounces depending on depth and current encountered. The jig is tied to a 36-inch leader of stiff, 20-pound test monofilament and the leader attached to the side loop of the 3-way swivel. The sinker hangs directly below the main line, and the light jig on the stiff leader will wave, dart, and dive as the rig is worked.

This rig can be cast and retrieved or deep jigged in any of the ways described above, but it is particularly deadly in fishing bridge pilings, like the Chesapeake Bay Bridge, which is part of Richie's home water. Richie describes it this way:

"In the summer and early fall stripers will hold on bridge pilings and steep drop-offs and suspend, especially if there is a good current flow. These areas are difficult to fish as the current starts to wash your lure away from the structure as soon as it enters the water. By increasing the weight on your feather jig you can ease up to a bridge piling and drop the jig right next to it and fish vertically.

"In September and October bridge pilings and stone piles hold good numbers of stripers. They are usually suspended tight to the structure between 12 and 25 feet deep and feeding on bay anchovies and silversides. A 2-ounce sinker will let you fish tight against the pilings even at full tide flow. This has proven to be a deadly technique, and we often outfish other anglers casting bucktails because we are better able to present the lure tight to the cover where the fish are holding."

Gaines also uses this rig for fishing stone piles and humps by simply deep jigging or walking this rig up or down the slope of the hump or stone pile with a snap lift and drop retrieve.

When fishing bridge pilings or other vertical structure, Richie recommends a straight drop next to the structure until the rig hits bottom, then reeling and snapping the jig up sharply as you reel, taking three cranks on the reel handle between each snap until the jig reaches the surface. This is a variation on the stair-step retrieve.

Excalibur Ghost Minnow, Swim'n Image,
Suspending Spot.

SPECIAL TECHNIQUES

Chumming

If you read the Chesapeake fishing reports from June through the end of the year, chumming is the method most often mentioned for taking such game fish as stripers, blues, and trout and such bottom species as hardheads (croakers), spot, and white perch. There's a bit more to chumming than simply grinding up bait and tossing it over to lure fish (although sometimes not much), and there are several ways to go about it. The major advantage of chumming is that it can provide fast fishing on light tackle unencumbered by any weights or other rigging.

The first step is to select an area. Some areas are good chumming grounds year after year, such as Pooles Island in the Upper Bay, the Thomas Point Light area south of the Bay Bridge, the tip of Hooper Island where the Honga River empties into the Bay, the old gas dock area off Solomons Island or—the all-time champ—the Southwest Middle Grounds out of Point Lookout.

Then pick an area you want to try—and that your boat can handle. Many of the spots named, like the Middle Grounds, are big waters calling for a big boat, usually 19 to 21 feet or more. However, there are several ways of chumming. What you're really looking for are areas with big concentrations of fish, whether they are being taken by chumming, bottom fishing or even jigging (but not trolling).

Once you arrive at the fishing grounds, you need to get set up in a good position. At such areas as the Middle Grounds or Pooles Island, you will often see a line of boats. If you note they're into fish you may want to select an open spot; however,

White perch are plentiful in the Upper Bay and make excellent table fare.

crowding other boats or breaking into their chum lines is not only unsporting, it can lead to violence. We have seen this happen.

With or without a fleet, look for an area providing a breakline into significantly deeper water, like the edge of a channel, end or slope of a sandbar or edge of a hole. An ideal length of anchor rope is generally 5 to 10 times the depth of the water. So, for example, if you want to hold the boat at a spot where the bottom drops quickly from 20 to 40 feet of water, you would ease the anchor over about 150 to 200 feet uptide of that breakline, dig it in, then play out anchor line until the bow of the boat is several boat lengths uptide of the breakline, then tie off the anchor rope. Obviously, this requires a depthfinder and good boat handling skills. The idea is to drift the chum down the breakline slope.

The Standard Chumming Method—This method calls for whole menhaden (bunker), the freshest you can get. The menhaden is ground and ladled directly into the water to attract fish and get them feeding, and the anglers drift cut pieces as bait or cast flies or lures in the chum slick.

On a recent trip with Captain Bruce Scheible, of Scheible's Fishing Center in Wynne, Maryland, he demonstrated his approach at the Southwest Middle Grounds. As we motored out, mate Joe Owens, prepared roughly 1-inch cubes from a strip cut along the top of the menhaden then made a slit about an inch aft of the gill plate, reached in with his forefinger and removed the gizzard. When Captain Scheible anchored up, he created the chum slick by running the remainder of the bunker through a 5-horsepower grinder and slowly ladling the ground menhaden over the side. Various less powerful electric, gas, or hand grinders are available to the amateur angler.

Generally, you do not need to drop prodigious amounts of ground menhaden over, especially once the fish start appearing, usually within about 15 minutes of the beginning of chumming, but you do need to keep feeding small amounts over to keep the fish interested. A good rule of thumb is that a five-gallon bucket of menhaden is good for three hours of chumming.

The Maryland DNR strongly recommends circle hooks be used for chumming with bait, since their studies show much less chance of killing fish by deep hooking with circle hooks compared with conventional hooks. While circle hook sizes vary considerably, and they're made much differently than conventional hooks, a wire circle hook, size 4/0 is about right. Captain Scheible feels fish view brightly tinned hooks in the chum line as unnatural, and fish will not strike if the bright metal is not covered by bait. He prefers bronzed hooks; others prefer hooks coated in a red finish, arguing this color hook is actually an attractant. (Coating a tinned hook with a red waterproof felt-tip pen produces this effect, though it wears off after a while.)

Unless a very heavy monofilament line or leader is used, 30-pound test or more, I like to create about a 2-foot loop in the end of the line with a Bimini Twist or spider hitch, then attach the hook via a Palomar knot. This greatly lessens the chance the hook will be bitten off by a bluefish or trout, plus it gives a leader to let an angler swing the fish aboard.

For bait fishing, Scheible recommends a small bait, a one-inch cube of menhaden topped by a menhaden gizzard so that only the very tip of the hook is exposed. Simply drop the baited hook into the slick and let it drift naturally. If you're using circle hooks and a fish hits the bait, simply begin reeling as soon as you feel a fish; the hook will set itself in the corner of the fish's jaw. If you're using a conventional hook, take up slack and strike before reeling.

The standard approach is effective, but messy. One way around it is to find a shop where you can buy some whole menhaden that can be cut into bait chunks and have the shop grind up the rest. All this is done off the boat and brought aboard in plastic bags and buckets you keep iced down for use.

When you hit the fishing grounds, slowly ladle out small amounts of ground chum, then bait up or begin fishing as described above.

You can fish with lures, or, more effectively, with flies using the ground chum method. Fly fishermen need to tune their lines and their flies to the actions of the fish in the chum line. Use the Bay standard 9-foot, 9-weight fly rod. Usually, the most effective line is an intermediate sinking line with a 3- to 4-foot level leader of 16- to 20-pound monofilament. If you need to get the fly deeper, either because the current is particularly fast or fading and the fish have dropped down, you may attach an add-on between the fly line and leader or switch to a full sinking line like a Teeny T-300 or TS-350.

There are two approaches to your choice of flies: Match the chum or match the smaller fish attracted to the chum that the game fish may feed on. For matching the chum, perhaps the most effective pattern is Lefty's Chum Bloody Fly, which consists of a 1/0 to 3/0 hook (preferably bronzed or red), lead wire wrapped on the shank, with chenille wrapped over it as an option, and thick bunches of 1½- to 2-inch brown or white marabou, with some red marabou mixed in, tied in at the head or behind the chenille. Use roughly 4 to 15 wraps of .030 lead wire to achieve different sink rates. This is cast into the chum slick and allowed to drift like natural bait. But you must be quick with the hook-set, since fish hit and quickly reject the fly.

Flies imitating baitfish should generally also be small, such as Joe Bruce's Bay Anchovy or Silverside patterns or Clouser Minnows in red over orange, blue over white, or chartreuse over white. These flies should likewise be cast into the chum line and allowed to drift naturally, with only an occasional twitch.

Sometimes the fish prefer the chum flies, sometimes they prefer the streamers. You can also try medium conventional tackle with such lures as metal jigs, bucktails, or grubs. Again, just allow the lure to drift naturally in the chum slick with an occasional twitch.

The Ground Frozen Chum Method—There's another chumming method that's simpler, cheaper, arguably more sporting, and—perhaps—a bit less effective. It's used with the same conditions of tide, holding water, and so forth. With this method, ground, frozen chum is placed in a fine mesh bag that is lowered over the side or stern, sometimes with internal weights to hold the bag in place part way to the bottom. The melting chum, mostly fine pieces and liquids, is swept through the bag by the current to create a game fish and baitfish-attracting slick. The stripers and other game fish are attracted to the slick and to the baitfish.

Sometimes this method is used to supplement the standard method to keep the chum line going while everyone aboard is too busy playing fish to keep releasing fresh-ground chum.

But more typically it used as a way of "priming the pump," since you're not really presenting much, if anything, for the target fish to feed on, but just getting them in a feeding mood. Sometimes more aggressive priming, known variously as "chum bombs " or "depth charges" are also used. The former method calls for wrapping a fistful of frozen chum in sand and dropping it over the side; the latter calls for dropping a paper bag full of frozen chum. It's the same idea of slowly feeding small bits of bait to the fish.

These techniques can be employed in any fish-holding area—points, wrecks, docks, rock piles—even in shallow water. But again, typically the best areas are drop-offs to deeper water such as the edges of shipping channels in 20 feet of water or deeper.

Fly anglers cast streamers and anglers with conventional gear cast metal jigs, bucktails, grubs, Rat-L-Traps, and other swimming lures into the slick to take the turned-on fish. Since there are no edibles in the slick, other than the baitfish, the game fish hit the phony offerings. You can use the slow-drifting approaches with these lures and flies as described above, but often a more aggressive retrieve is better. This is much more like actually fishing with an artificial.

We have seen occasions where the game fish "lock in on" the baitfish attracted to the slick. Two years ago, Mike Murphy was using frozen chum over a drop-off in the Honga River area. Lefty Kreh, Joe Bruce, and Bob Clouser cast streamer patterns from Mike's boat, and we did the same from Ed's boat. While a number of flies took stripers, we discovered that Joe Bruce's Bay Anchovy, a 2-inch close imitation of the small fish that are the major game fish food source in the Bay during the summer, was far more effective. We concluded that the stripers may have been attracted to the slick and more especially to the anchovies attracted to the slick.

The Liquid or Powdered Chum Method—A variation of this method involves the use of powdered chum material, such as "dry chum," that's released from a perforated PVC holder or with pellets that dissolve through a mesh bag. Again, this is a "prime the pump" approach. The big advantage is that it takes virtually no advance preparation. We carry the holder, loaded with a dry chum cartridge, aboard our boats for use when things are slow, especially for those situations where we can spot fish hanging off a breakline but can't get them to hit. Dry chum can make a difference. A disadvantage is that it's a bit on the expensive side, but that's offset by the fact that you only use it once in a while. The newer pellet chums are more reasonable and easier to use. Some of our expert fly fishing friends swear by this stuff. Fishing methods are the same as described above for using frozen chum.

Besides being a lot more sporting, these alternative chumming methods are much less likely to injure fish with deep hookups.

Eeling

Fishing with eels is not our favorite way to fish, but it can be an extremely effective big-fish technique, especially in the fall. We prefer medium/heavy casting tackle with braided line and a 3-foot leader of 20- to 25-pound test monofilament for this type if fishing. Eels can be fished with light trolling methods, and this has been a standard method on the Susquehanna River and such other Upper Bay spots as Poole's Island and the Bay Bridge. In the Susquehanna, a typical rig is a pencil eel (usually 6 to 9 inches long) lip-hooked on a bucktail. A clamp-on or trolling sinker may be added 2 to 3 feet above the bucktail/eel combination as necessary to achieve extra depth.

Eels can also be fished below a float, another popular technique for Susquehanna shoreline fishermen.

But more typically, throughout the Bay large eels of 9 to 15 inches are drifted just off the bottom. One rig is the classic "fish finder" rig, where the main line is run through a plastic sleeve, known as a fish finder, holding a clip for a Dipsey sinker weighing from ½ to 4 ounces or more as needed. The line is tied to a #1 swivel. The 30- to 36-inch monofilament leader is tied to the other end of the swivel and a 5/0 circle hook is tied to the other end with the eel lip-hooked. An alternative is simply tying the main line to one ear of a trolling sinker and the leader with the hook and eel to the other ear. Most anglers find the latter rig preferable when drifting; some like the fish finder rig when fishing from an anchored boat.

With either rig the approach is to drop it straight to the bottom, lift it slightly and let the weight tick along the bottom or just above it. When a strike is felt, usually as a distinct "thump," but sometimes just as added resistance, you briefly freespool the line then throw the reel in gear and tighten up. With a conventional hook, you then set the hook; with a circle hook, you simply start reeling and the hook sets itself.

Eels can be difficult to handle. We like to store them in a refrigerator in plastic bucket lined with wet newspaper. On the boat a few ice cubes on top of the newspaper keep the eels from getting too lively. To hook the eel grasp it near the head using a rag in your hand, quickly lip hook it and get the eel overboard as soon as possible before it starts tying knots in your rig.

Livelining

This is probably the best big-fish technique, other than trolling parachute rigs, on the Bay. The tackle and rigs are the same as used for eeling. The best bait is a live spot 4 to 8 inches long; a white perch this size is a second choice. The bait can be lip-hooked and trolled or drifted weighted or unweighted. For still fishing the fish can be either lip-hooked or, more effectively, hooked in front of the dorsal fin and fished weighted, unweighted or below a float. Guide Richie Gaines recommends tail hooking the bait when fishing humps, wrecks, pilings, or other deep structure. With this arrangement, the baitfish tends to dive toward the bottom or toward structure, hopefully into harm's way.

Bottom Fishing

We do very little of this, sometimes for hardheads or white perch, more commonly for spot for bait. We use medium tackle. In deep water, braid is superior because of its sensitivity and low stretch.

A standard "bottom rig" or "high/low rig," with appropriately sized hooks (#2 is a good, all-around size) and enough weight to get it to bottom is all that's needed. Many Eastern Shore captains make their own rigs. One common variations calls for taking a 30-inch piece of 30-pound (or heavier) test monofilament and tying a loop or swivel at the top to attach to the main line. Then add a dropper loop about 12 inches down and another dropper loop another 12 inches down. A hook is tied to the end of the line, a bank or Dipsey sinker added to the bottom loop via the loop-to-loop method, and the second hook added to the loop above the sinker, also using the loop-to-loop method. Another version has the same arrangement of loops, but the sinker is tied to the end of the line (or attached via a terminal loop) and the hooks are added to each of the dropper loops above. Most captains disdain commercial high/low rigs with snelled hooks as too hardware-intensive and feel they provide too much slack for efficient hook-setting.

Bloodworms are probably the top bait, but they're expensive. Grass shrimp, squid, and fish belly are more reasonably priced choices.

Breaking Fish

Schools of breaking fish are a frequent occurrence in the Bay from early summer into early winter, with the fall months being the prime time for size and numbers of fish. Breaking fish in the Upper Chesapeake are predominantly stripers, and usually in the summer these groups are made up of smaller fish, 12 to 18 inches. Sometimes bluefish are mixed in.

But the Mid-Chesapeake from roughly Solomons on the west to Hooper Island on the east and south all the way past the Middle Grounds is renowned for breaking fish in schools of up to 20 acres. The schools are predominantly stripers, 16 to 28 inches, with blues, usually smaller, mixed in and often with gray trout up to 24 inches below and Spanish mackerel, in the 12- to 20-inch range, on the fringes of these schools. Just to make this situation as near a sure thing as you're likely to encounter in fishing, schools of 16- to 20-inch hardheads cover the bottom in 30 to 40 feet of water in many areas.

As the weather turns in late September, menhaden are often added to the game fish diet of bay anchovies and the feeding spree intensifies. Stripers and trout are the main species, as other game species migrate south. But even with this abundance, technique is critical in taking good numbers and especially in taking good sizes of fish.

The first piece of advice is don't go barging up to the center of the school. The second is to consider something other than a surface fly or lure.

In a typical Mid-Bay school—if there is such a thing—smaller stripers are at the top, often mixed with smaller blues; trout are below, often in a distinct layer on the depthfinder. Larger stripers may be found below as well, sometimes mixed in with the trout, and they may be feeding on trout and smaller stripers. So, obviously, you want to try for these deeper fish.

Fly fishers should use standard Bay fly tackle—a 9-foot, 8- or 9-weight rod casting a fast-sinking line, like a Teeny T-300 or TS-350 respectively, a 3- to 4-foot level leader of 16- to 20-pound test, with the fly attached via a 100 percent loop knot. If blues are mixed in, Micro Ultra wire can be added as a bite leader. Recommended flies include Glass Minnow patterns, Clousers, Albieclousers and other streamer patterns, and Joe Bruce's Bay Anchovy or Silverside patterns, about 2 to 3½ inches in length.

For conventional tackle, the lure of choice is a 1¼-ounce Stingsilver or other metal jig or the tandem metal jig and small lure or fly rig or the feather jig rig all described in the section "Deep Jigging."

The boat must approach the fish quietly, by getting upwind or uptide of the school and drifting to the fish with the motor off. As the boat approaches the breaking schools, anglers need to avoid the temptation to cast into the school as they first approach. Anglers with conventional tackle should drop their metal jig rigs off the bow, stern, or gunwale upwind or uptide of the school and let the rig go all the way to bottom. As the boat gets to the school, anglers employ the deep jigging retrieves and hang on. In the unlikely event of no hookup, the action is repeated.

Fly fishers should likewise cast their fast-sinking lines off the bow, stern, or upschool gunwale, let their flies sink while paying out line with occasional twitches, then rip the flies back on the retrieve. (Speed of retrieve triggers strikes. If a fly fisher casts toward the school, he or she cannot retrieve a fly fast enough with the boat drifting toward the fly.)

Light Trolling

We use light trolling to explore, usually when fishing from a small boat in a fairly shallow area, like Susquehanna Flats. Trolling can mean simply tossing a lure behind the boat and trolling a breakline or likely area. Jigs, plastic eels, and crankbaits are the choice here. Another good rig is a double rig formed by using a 3-way swivel, with a heavier lure, usually a jig, on the short bottom arm and a lighter lure, a spoon or jig, on the longer top arm.

We occasionally take a more methodical approach, using trolling planers to work specific depths. The lures of choice with this approach are spreader rigs trailed by jig and plastic rigs. The trolling plane trips up when a fish hits or the planer hits bottom, allowing the use of comparatively light tackle for trolling.

This is another type of fishing where our preferred tackle is medium/heavy casting tackle with braided main line.

Fishing the Chesapeake Bay

The Chesapeake Bay is roughly two hundred miles long with close to two thousand miles of shoreline, if you don't count the tributaries—a tremendous amount of water to fish. For the uninitiated, this would seem to be an easy place to catch fish. It isn't. Although a fertile body of water, like most saltwater environs, much of it isn't frequented by fish. To be successful fishing the Bay, one must know where the targeted species is most likely to be at any given time. Our purpose in writing this book is to help you locate the most promising fishing spots. Also, since out-of-towners especially need this advice, wherever possible, we will include information on where you can launch a boat, buy gas, eat a meal, book guides, buy tackle or find lodging.

Given the size of the Bay, we thought it best to divide it into sections from the uppermost reaches to the mouth of the Bay near Virginia Beach, and also longitudinally by eastern and western shores. We'll start at the top of the Bay in Maryland and work our way down.

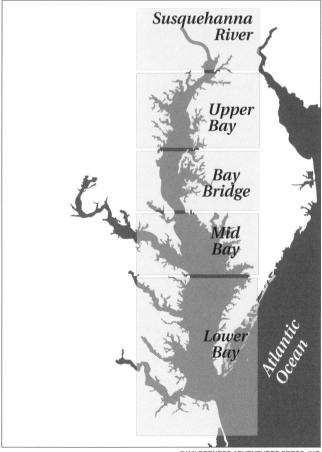

© WILDERNESS ADVENTURES PRESS, INC.

An Introduction to Maryland Waters

The following seasonal fishing charts for the Upper and Mid-Bay regions of Maryland are based on the format that veteran fishing guide Captain Lynn Pauls uses on his excellent website, www.tideflyer.com, for Virginia's portion of the Bay.

This information is very broad, and serves only as a guideline. Conditions change year to year depending on water temperature, salinity, baitfish movements, cyclical gamefish populations, etc. All charts reflect fishing conditions, not regulations for catch-and-release fishing or for keeping fish. Check your yearly fishing regulations—which also change.

RATINGS:	E = Excellent	G = Good	F = Fair	N = Not Available

Conowingo Dam to End of Susquehanna Flats at Turkey Point

	JAN	FEB	MAR	APR	MAY	JUN	JUL	AUG	SEP	OCT	NOV	DEC
Hickory Shad*	N	N	F	E	E	N	N	N	N	N	N	N
White Shad	N	N	N	G	E	G	N	N	N	N	N	N
Striper**	N	N	F	E	F	F	F	F	G	G	G	G
White Perch	N	N	F	E	E	G	G	G	G	G	F	N
Smallmouth Bass*	N	N	F	G	G	G	G	G	G	G	F	N
Largemouth Bass	N	N	N	N	F	G	G	G	G	G	N	N
Channel Catfish	N	N	F	G	G	G	G	G	G	G	N	N
Carp	N	N	G	G	G	G	G	G	G	G	G	N

*Rivers Only
**Includes catch-and-release season and closed season in spring

End of Susquehanna Flats to Pooles Island

	JAN	FEB	MAR	APR	MAY	JUN	JUL	AUG	SEP	OCT	NOV	DEC
Striper	N	N	N	N	F	G	F	F	G	G	N	N
White Perch	N	N	G	G	E	G	G	F	F	G	G	N
Bluefish*	N	N	N	N	N	N	F	F	F	F	N	N
Largemouth Bass	N	N	N	N	F	G	G	G	G	G	N	N
Channel Catfish	N	N	F	G	G	G	G	G	G	G	N	N

*Mostly in southern part of range during dry years

Pooles Island to Choptank River

	JAN	FEB	MAR	APR	MAY	JUN	JUL	AUG	SEP	OCT	NOV	DEC
Striper	N	N	N	F	F	G	F	F	G	E	G	N
Bluefish	N	N	N	N	F	G	G	G	G	G	N	N
Gray Trout	N	N	N	N	N	N	N	N	F	E	G	N
Spanish Mackerel	N	N	N	N	N	F	F	F	F	N	N	N
White Perch	N	N	N	F	E	E	E	E	E	E	F	N
Croaker	N	N	N	F	G	G	F	F	N	N	N	N
Pickerel*	G	G	G	F	N	N	N	N	F	G	G	G
Flounder	N	N	N	N	F	G	G	G	G	F	N	N

*Magothy and Severn Rivers only

Choptank River to Virginia Line

	JAN	FEB	MAR	APR	MAY	JUN	JUL	AUG	SEP	OCT	NOV	DEC
Bluefish	N	N	N	F	G	G	E	E	E	G	N	N
Cobia*	N	N	N	N	F	F	F	F	N	N	N	N
Croaker	N	N	N	F	E	E	E	G	N	N	N	N
Flounder	N	N	N	F	G	G	G	G	G	F	N	N
Red Drum*	N	N	N	F	F	N	N	N	N	N	N	N
Spanish Mackerel	N	N	N	N	F	G	E	E	G	F	N	N
Speckled Trout	N	N	N	G	G	G	G	G	G	G	F	N
Striper	F	N	F	G	E	E	F	F	G	E	E	E
Gray Trout	N	N	N	F	G	G	G	G	E	E	G	N
Spot	N	N	N	F	G	G	G	G	G	G	N	N
White Perch	N	N	F	G	G	G	G	G	G	G	F	N

*More of an occasional bonus than a targeted species

Maryland Launch Ramps

Most of the ramps we have recommended in Maryland are public ramps. The Maryland DNR has an excellent website, www.dnr.state.md.us. Under "Fisheries," along the left margin is a listing, "Atlas of Boat Ramps," which provides—by county—locations, directions and listings of facilities at each ramp and whether there is a fee. This information is accurate. You can also call 800-688-FINS for a free publication, *A Fisherman's Guide to Maryland Boat Ramps*, a state map listing all ramps.

Typical shad flies.

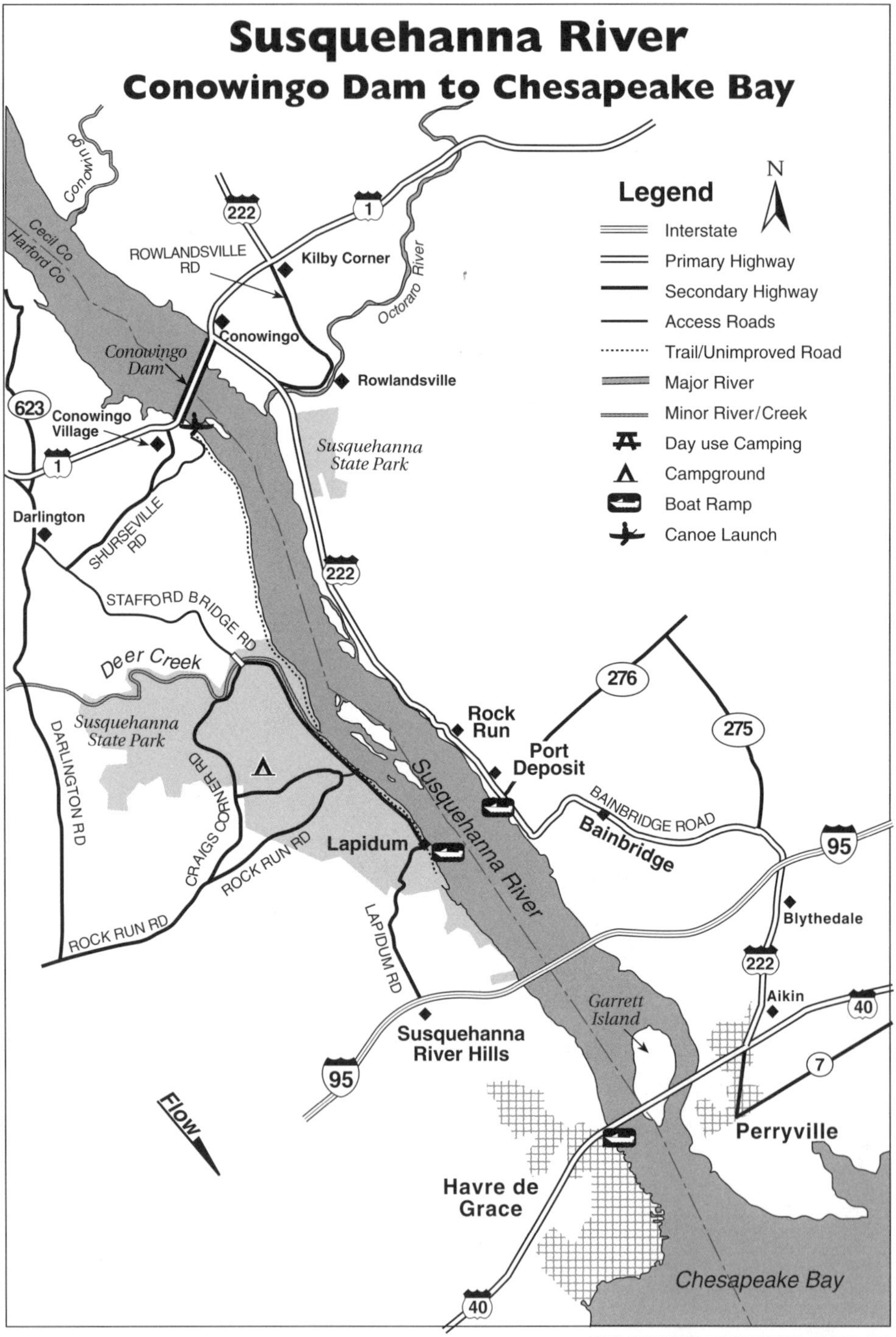

Susquehanna River
Conowingo Dam to Chesapeake Bay

Legend

N

═══	Interstate
══	Primary Highway
▬	Secondary Highway
▬	Access Roads
········	Trail/Unimproved Road
▬	Major River
▬	Minor River/Creek
⊼	Day use Camping
⋀	Campground
⊟	Boat Ramp
✈	Canoe Launch

Conowingo Co

222

1

ROWLANDSVILLE RD

Kilby Corner

Octoraro River

Cecil Co
Harford Co

Conowingo

Conowingo Dam

Rowlandsville

623

Conowingo Village

1

Susquehanna State Park

Darlington

SHURSEVILLE RD

STAFFORD BRIDGE RD

222

Deer Creek

Susquehanna State Park

DARLINGTON RD

CRAIGS CORNER RD

ROCK RUN RD

Lapidum

ROCK RUN RD

LAPIDUM RD

Rock Run

276

275

Port Deposit

BAINBRIDGE ROAD

Bainbridge

95

Susquehanna River

Blythedale

222

Garrett Island

Aikin

40

7

Perryville

Susquehanna River Hills

95

Flow

Havre de Grace

40

Chesapeake Bay

© WILDERNESS ADVENTURES PRESS, INC.

The Susquehanna River

When Conowingo Dam, the dam farthest downstream on the Susquehanna River, was completed in 1929 it stopped the upstream migration of several species of fish. Affecting principally American and hickory shad, which previously had run upstream as far as New York, it also affected the spawning run of striped bass, but to a lesser extent. Until just a few years ago, the shad runs decreased dramatically every year until they were just about non-existent. Fortunately, this decline reversed, and both species of shad are thriving, with the number of spawning fish now increasing every year. In fact, shad are now moving over Conowingo by means of an elaborate fish ladder and continuing into Pennsylvania. What this means, of course, is that an excellent springtime angling opportunity once again exists.

Beginning in April, both the American (or white) shad and the smaller, but more acrobatic hickory shad enter the river. Word spreads quickly when the fish arrive, and water temperature is the key to success. Shad rarely strike a lure when the water is below 55 degrees. Sixty degrees is much better and 65 to 69 ideal.

Fishing for shad is pretty simple. The overwhelming choice of lure is a lead shad dart. Ranging from about $1/16$-to ¼ ounce and available in many color choices, these lures are available from many mail-order houses, such as Cabela's, and any tackle store within 50 miles of the river, will have a good supply of darts when the shad run is on.

Different anglers have distinct favorite color combinations, but proper presentation is probably far more important than color. You'll need to prospect to find where shad are holding. A good choice is at the tail end of a pool just before the beginning of the fast water. Migrating shad tend to move into a pool and rest at the first bit of calm water.

When the Susquehanna is running hard, these locations are difficult to spot. The good news is that once you locate a productive spot, it will usually produce throughout the run. Although the low-light levels of early morning and evening are usually the best times to fish, shad can be caught midday, but you'll have to probe the deepest, darkest holding spots.

A typical technique is to cast quartering upstream and allow the lure to sink before beginning the retrieve. This takes some experimentation. If the lure doesn't get deep enough, you won't get any strikes. Too deep, however, and you'll hang bottom. Most accomplished shad fishermen will adjust both the size and the number of lures they use depending on the amount of water being released by the dam. Two shad darts tied in tandem is common.

Most strikes come "on the swing." Typical procedure is to cast quartering upstream, allowing the line to sink. It should then be adjusted to swing across a

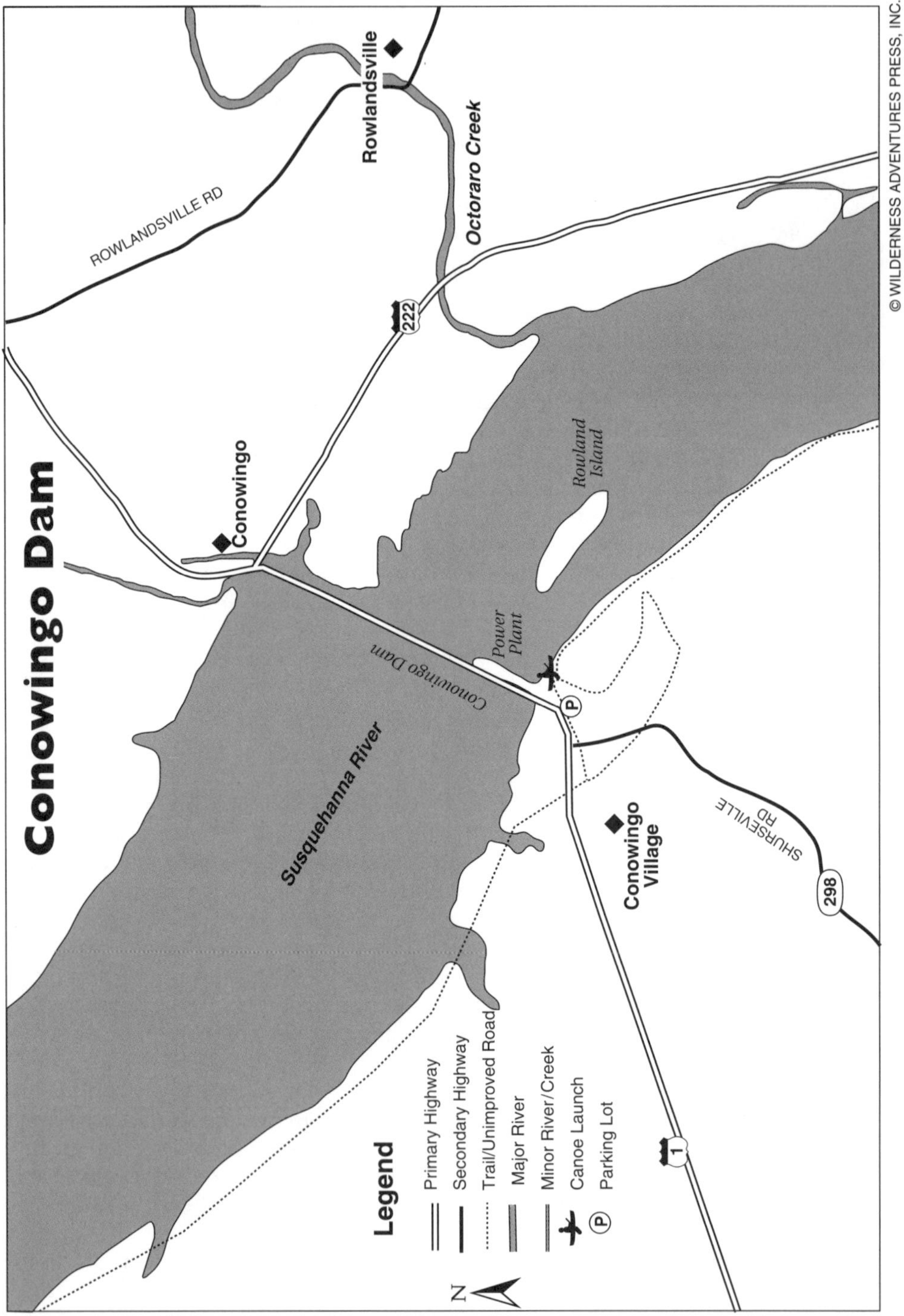

Conowingo Dam

Rowlandsville

Octoraro Creek

ROWLANDSVILLE RD

222

Conowingo

Rowland
Island

Conowingo Dam

Power
Plant

Susquehanna River

P

Conowingo
Village

SHURSEVILLE RD

298

1

Legend

Primary Highway
Secondary Highway
Trail/Unimproved Road
Major River
Minor River/Creek
Canoe Launch
P Parking Lot

N

holding lie at the end of the drift. Don't be too quick to retrieve. Very often, a streamer simply dangling in the current will draw a strike.

In fact, this author (Ed Russell) almost lost a good fly rod that way years ago. I had placed my rod on a large rock while I was searching through my fly vest. Stupidly, I had left the small streamer dangling in the water. You guessed it, a hickory struck, and he and my rod and reel started downstream. Fortunately, a friend wading nearby saw what happened and grabbed the rod. Unfortunately, he slipped while doing so and belly flopped into the water, getting completely soaked. No matter. The rod and reel were saved, and he would get dry eventually.

For the shore-bound angler, the easiest access is on the Harford County side of the river (the west side). From the base of the dam downstream to the town of Lapidum, there are loads of spots where an angler can get to the river. There is a large parking area by the dam, where one can access the river right below the spillways, move farther downstream, and clamber over the rocky banks anywhere. The prime spots are quite near the dam. Drive into the parking lot, climb the steps to the old railroad bed and just observe. When the run is in full swing, you'll see fish being caught constantly.

*Shad fishing near Conowingo Dam on the Susquehanna
River is rarely a private affair.*

Just below the parking lot, a hiking/biking trail parallels the river and goes for about two miles downstream where it crosses the mouth of Deer Creek and continues through part of Susquehanna State Park. You can access the river anywhere along here, but the overhanging tree branches present some difficulty. If the water flow is not too great, you can wade out a little way to get clear. Be careful, though. The water levels can and do fluctuate and you must watch for that. When the sirens sound and the red lights flash, be prepared. These warnings are sounded whenever the water flow is to change either more or less.

Fly fishermen can fish for shad in the main Susquehanna, but the big problem with using a fly rod below the dam is space. Unless you are adept with a spey rod and can roll cast 60 feet or more, a fly rod is ill advised. The banks are steep and rocky. Most of the area is covered with a tangle of brush and trees. A normal cast, including the backcast, is difficult to achieve. During normal water flows, wading out from shore any distance is suicidal. The bottom drops of quite quickly in most places and is covered with large slippery rocks.

An exception to this is when water flow is low. Since Conowingo Dam is a hydroelectric dam, water flow varies considerably. When only a small amount of electricity is being generated, you can safely wade out far enough from shore to fly fish effectively. The problem is often in getting back. A release from the dam will cause the water level to rise rather quickly. Plenty of warning is given, however, and if you heed these warnings and take appropriate steps, you'll be okay. But most years include the drowning of foolhardy people.

As an illustration, years ago, my friend Jim Heim and I (Ed Russell) were fishing the river early on a Saturday morning—a time of typically low water. Around nine

Anglers lined up on the Susquehanna fishing for white shad.

A hiking-biking trail allows easy access to the Susquehanna River.

o'clock, we heard the sirens and knew the water would be coming up, but since we were in my canoe, we were little concerned. As the water began to rise, we heard cries for help. About a quarter-mile above us, four young men were in trouble. They had waded out early on, and the little channel they had crossed now had several feet of rushing water in it and it was getting deeper by the minute. Fortunately, we were able to reach them. Two of them couldn't swim and were literally "scared green." We put those two in the canoe with an admonishment to sit on the bottom and not move and put the other two on a large rock that had a tree growing on it. Two "ferries" later, all four were safe on shore. We were exhausted. They were lucky. There wasn't another boat anywhere in sight.

If you fish this river, be aware of the dangers. Pay attention to the warnings and you shouldn't experience any trouble. Know the water release schedules. Falling water, while not the danger of rising, can also cause problems, leaving you stranded on the rocks for many hours. Call 410-457-4076 for water release schedules and 410-457-2409 for fishing information. Also, it is important to note that none of the information regarding water releases is 100 percent accurate. If customer demands for electricity are greater than anticipated, additional water will be released.

Although the main rivers can be "stuffed with fish," the best location for fly fishermen is often in the tributaries. Two streams that feed the Susquehanna below Conowingo Dam are Octoraro Creek on the eastern side and Deer Creek on the west. Both are moderately sized, with easy wading. A road parallels each, and you can be fishing within 50 yards from your car. Almost anywhere there are holding lies will produce fish at the peak of the run.

In Deer Creek, you will encounter only hickory shad—and loads of anglers. Hickories are a favorite quarry for fly fishermen, and Deer Creek is a Mecca. From the mouth all the way up to the dam above Route 161, fly fishermen and anglers using ultralight spinning gear will be seeking these high-jumping beauties.

Fly fishermen will be using anything from a 2-weight to a 7-weight, but a 4 or 5 is ideal. Almost without exception they will be using small, brightly colored streamers. A simple size 6 streamer hook with a flashy body and a fluorescent red wing is probably most popular. Since shad are quite light sensitive, the best fishing occurs early and late in the day. Some evenings, you might not get a strike until 7:30, and then hook 40 fish in the next hour and a half. It can be wild.

Another tributary with an excellent shad run is Octoraro Creek, about a mile below the dam on the eastern side of the river. This stream is quite similar in size and makeup to Deer Creek, but suffers from an access problem; parking is quite limited, and one landowner, who owns a substantial stretch of shoreline, has posted his land against trespassing. Years ago, this wasn't a problem, but some bad experiences with people other than fishermen has caused this restriction.

Although the shad run is a huge draw in the early spring, there are other species to be sought; big smallmouth bass, for example, are available throughout the river, but an especially good spot is as close to the face of the dam as possible. Anglers cast live white perch or large broken-back Rebels upcurrent as far as possible and frequently score with smallies over three pounds. The best time to fish is from about an hour before dawn to maybe two hours after.

Ed Russell with a Deer Creek hickory shad.

Remember, the bass season is closed in Maryland from March 1 to June 15, but catch-and-release is permitted.

Spawning striped bass will also be in the river in large numbers. Be advised, that this species is totally protected in the spawning rivers (the Susquehanna is one) from March 1 to May 31 and, with the exception of a special one-month catch-and-release season specific to the Susquehanna Flats (more on that later), may not be targeted.

The game wardens know full well that an angler may catch a striper accidentally while fishing for another species. However, if they observe an individual slinging 6-inch long flies or lures and catching stripers repeatedly, they are not likely to believe that the angler was fishing for shad or white perch. Of course, any angler seen with a striper in possession will be fined. Once the spawning season is officially over, you can fish for stripers in the river, and the fishing can be excellent. Oddly enough, not many anglers fish the Susquehanna for stripers during the summer.

The chief difficulty to fishing the Susquehanna is the widely varying water flows. In years past, the power company that controls the flow of the river would hoard water behind the dam during dry periods, releasing only enough water to provide the required electricity for its customers. As might be expected, this sometimes resulted in virtually no water release at all, and was responsible for a number of fish kills. Now, the dam operators are required by law to provide minimal flows adequate for the survival of fish at all times.

Still, the flows vary a lot. You should call the dam office for water release schedules (410-457-4076) but be advised—these are subject to change. The only actual requirement is that there be adequate warnings via flashing lights and sirens when any change in water flows, whether an increase or decrease, is about to happen. Therefore, it is imperative to know the proposed schedules and to be attentive at all times to the warning signals.

The best areas to prospect for stripers are in the rocky upper reaches of the river upstream from Lapidum. The river is full of rocks and ledges, shallow fast water, and deep slower pools. Any of these may hold stripers. In the warmer months, the fast water will likely fish best due to its higher oxygen content.

Morning and evenings are the best times, and just after dawn and again in late evening make sure to prospect in the slow pools. Stripers will move into them to forage at these times. The best time of all is at night, but I would advise against fishing then. The river is difficult enough when you can see well.

A favorite summertime method with some anglers is to float the river from the dam down to Deer Creek using belly boats. The problem with this is that your legs can get quite banged-up. A few fishermen that we know resorted to using shin guards, like those worn by soccer or lacrosse players, to protect their legs. A much better idea is to use an inflatable pontoon boat. Since you sit above the water in one of these, your legs aren't in any danger. Also, oars are used for propulsion with these craft, making them much faster and more maneuverable than a float tube. So far, inflatable pontoon boats are far more popular on the rivers of the western states than here in the east, but this is gradually changing. Because of their ease of use, stability, and the ability to bounce off rocks without damage, they may well be the best means of float fishing this river.

This is good water for the flyrodder. A 7- or 8-weight rod, a floating line or a sinking-tip line, and any reel with a decent drag will work fine. Surface poppers are ideal early and late in the day. Best bets are ones that are fairly long and that can raise a lot of commotion. Sometimes, when the water is very low, a noisy popper will scare the fish; at these times, a slider will be the best choice.

Streamers need not be elaborate. Because of the rocky nature of the river, you'll lose lots of flies, so try to keep your selection to simply tied flies. Losing several of these is less traumatic than losing a gorgeous replica that took an hour to tie. Lefty's Deceivers, Clousers, and the old Joe Brooks Blonde series will all take their share of fish. Streamers with white or chartreuse hair or hackle combined with some flash material like Crystal Flash are popular combinations. Try to determine what the predominant baitfish is and try to match its size. We find that size makes more of a difference in this fishing, as in most, than color. In this river, especially in the warmer months, the bait will be fairly small.

For spinning or casting gear, try a Creek Chub Striker Strike in ½-ounce or ¾-ounce size, or a Storm Lures' Rattlin' Chug-Bug in $3/8$-ounce size. When less disturbance is needed, a walk-the-dog type of lure is a good choice. A Zara Spook is good, and an Excalibur Spit'n Image is excellent, especially in a shad finish. Another lure ideally suited to this fishing is Rat-L-Trap's Slap-Stick. This lure floats vertically but moves up and forward with a side-to-side motion when retrieved—offering a good imitation of a floundering baitfish.

A float tube is one way to fish the Susquehanna.

For subsurface fishing, typical crankbaits like the extremely popular Rat-L-Trap will work well, but because most varieties are equipped with two sets of treble hooks, they'll frequently hang up in the rocks. A better choice is a soft plastic lure on a jig-head. These are readily taken by stripers, but snag much less frequently than a crankbait. Many varieties are available, but our favorite is a 4-inch Bass Assassin. Try a pearl or silvery color to match the juvenile shad that will be present in the river.

If smallmouth bass are the target, much of what we've already said about striped bass applies except for fly or lure selection. For smallmouths, you'll want smaller baits to imitate hellgrammites and crayfish as well as baitfish imitations. A dark brown or black weighted Woolly Bugger will do for the hellgrammite imitation and any simple crayfish pattern can be quite effective, as will most of the same choices used for stripers, just in smaller sizes.

For the angler using spinning or casting gear, it's hard to beat a tube lure on a ¼-ounce weedless jighead. Different colors work at different times, but if we were limited to one color, it would be green pumpkin. This is really more of a dingy brown, and its effectiveness is directly tied to the fact that it closely matches the color of the native crayfish. Work the lure very slowly right on the bottom; it's a deadly technique.

Another very effective method is to fish a 4-inch white or pearl Assassin or Zoom lure, rigged with no weight. Cast the lure out and let it sit. It will sink very slowly. When it gets down about a foot, raise hell with it. Jerk the line and vibrate the rod. Attempt to make the lure jerk, skitter, and jump violently while retrieving as little as possible. Then stop abruptly, let the lure sit for a good while and repeat. It sounds (and appears) bizarre, but this retrieve really excites bass. It will probably work on stripers, as well.

The Susquehanna also has enormous caddisfly hatches many evenings. When caddisflies come off, just about every species in the river gets interested. Perch, cat-fish, and especially smallmouth bass really key in on them, so be prepared with some appropriate flies. A simple Elk Hair Caddis works just fine as a dry and an equally simple soft hackle in tan or brown is a good choice for a wet fly.

White perch are another species that invades the Susquehanna in large numbers in the spring. The biggest white perch (almost exclusively gravid females) enter the river first. They usually show up about the last week in March or the first week in April. Shortly thereafter, the males move in and for about a month and a half, you can hardly miss fishing for perch.

Although some spots may be better than others, almost any deeper spot in the river will yield good catches when the run is underway. Many anglers fish for white perch from shore and do fairly well, but for the best fishing, especially for the larger early fish, you'll need a boat and a depthfinder. Look for water depths from 18 to 25 feet. Two excellent spots are just above the I-95 Bridge, one on the east side, the other on the west. Big perch stack up here, but be prepared to hook a striper now and then.

To catch these fish, you'll most often need to get your offering near the bottom. Small shad darts on ultralight spinning tackle are a favorite lure, as are tiny spoons less than an inch in length. You can find these in local tackle shops, as well as mail-order houses, but they'll probably be called ice-fishing lures in the catalogs. For a fly, either a white or chartreuse marabou streamer is all you'll need. One tied with dumbbell eyes like a Clouser or with a conehead will work best. So-called crappie jigs also work.

One exception to this is when the caddisflies hatch as previously described. When this happens, you can catch all the perch you want using a lightweight fly rod, a floating line, and caddis imitations.

For the bait fisherman, there's nothing better than a couple of grass shrimp impaled on a size 6 hook. Grass shrimp are normally available in local tackle shops, but during the peak of the run they may be hard to find. If that's the case, you can use worms, but they aren't as effective.

After the females spawn, they move out, but hordes of smaller males remain well into the summer. They'll take artificials readily, and catching 40 or more in a morning is not uncommon. What they lack in size, they make up for in numbers.

Catfish are another possibility. Good-sized channel cats are most numerous near the dam where the turbines used to generate electricity also serve up a good supply of chopped bait. Most "cats" will be taken as an incidental catch, but if you wish to target this species, then the fishing catwalk along the dam face is the place to go. You'll need pretty stout tackle to haul up a 10-pounder from a height of 50 feet or more.

Walleye are another species you may encounter. The best fishing for walleye occurs in the early spring when the water is still pretty cold. You'll need to fish deep to score with these fish, and actually, few angler target this species in the Susquehanna. They can be caught, but their numbers are not great.

Be advised that the state of Maryland has declared the Susquehanna River tidal water from the base of the dam downriver, so you must have a Maryland Chesapeake Bay Sport Fishing License (which is good for the rest of the Bay). In addition, if you want to fish either of the aforementioned tributaries, you'll need a Maryland freshwater license, as well.

Getting There

US Route 40, Interstate 95, and US Route 1 are the three routes crossing the Susquehanna in Maryland. Route 1 runs right across the top of the dam. To reach the fishing area below Conowingo Dam coming from the east side, follow Route 1 to Shuresville Road, about a half-mile from the western side of the dam. Turn onto Shuresville Road and proceed about a half-mile to a very sharp left-hand turn onto Shures Landing Road. This will wind down some steep terrain and you'll come into a large parking lot. You can park here and work upstream or down or drive upriver to the parking area near the dam.

To get to Deer Creek from the east, follow Shuresville Road to Stafford Bridge Road. Turn left and that will take you to Stafford Bridge, which crosses Deer Creek. From there you can go upstream or down, but parking upstream is quite limited. Downstream there is significantly more parking available including an actual parking lot.

To reach Deer Creek and Susquehanna State Park from the west, exit Route 1 at Darlington. Go into the town and turn left at the first main intersection—Shuresville Road. Follow this to Stafford Bridge Road and proceed as before.

A nice catch of spawning white perch.

From I-95 or Route 40, exit at Route 155 and proceed to Route 161. From 161, exit at Rock Run Road, which will take you to the state park in the Deer Creek area or continue on 161 into Darlington, then proceed as above to reach either Stafford Bridge or Shures Landing Road.

To reach Octoraro Creek, follow Route 222 north from I-95 or Route 40 or south from Route 1. The stream runs under the road about a mile and a half below the dam. Vehicle access is only upstream.

Launch Ramps

There is an excellent launch ramp in Susquehanna State Park at the village of Lapidum, and another called Rock Run Landing across the river at Port Deposit, right on Route 222. There is also a small, ramp near the downstream end of the parking lot for Conowingo Dam. It's not much—suitable only for cartop boats or canoes. A trailered boat will get stuck.

Be warned that upstream from Lapidum, the river is very rocky. Outboards with pitchfork rigs to protect the propellers or jet drives are the only way to go. Negotiating the river is tricky at best, and an unprotected propeller will likely be destroyed.

Local Services

The only thing in the immediate area is an extensive camping facility at Susquehanna State Park. Beyond that, there are some small independently owned motels along Route 1 near Darlington. The best option is to stay at one of the motels on Route 22 just a mile or so from the Aberdeen exit from I-95. At least four major motel chains have units there. Another option would be to stay at one of the Perryville locations described at the end of the next section.

There are very few sporting goods store near the upper river. One that we know of is called Ann's Bait and Tackle, located on Shuresville Road right by the turn onto Shures Landing Road. Tackle-wise, it's not much, but they do have a good selection of lures and flies common to the area. It is a good spot to stock up on shad darts.

Lefty Kreh's grandson, Larry, with a hefty Susquehanna striper.

Fly shop owner Joe Bruce with an excellent spring striper from the Susquehanna Flats.

The Susquehanna Flats

The Susquehanna Flats begin just below where the I-95 Bridge crosses the river and extend downstream to a line between Turkey Point on the east and Sandy Point on the west. Shaped like an inverted bowl, the center is quite shallow, less than a foot in many places, and is an area where the uninitiated or unwary can easily run aground. As a result, the flats seem difficult to fish, but if you look at a good chart and pay attention you'll quickly see that if you simply follow the well marked channel and watch your depthfinder, it's easy to fish most all of the worthwhile areas. Just don't try to cut across the middle. To cross the flats, you'll usually need to go south following the western channel, around the bottom of the flats, and up the eastern channel. There is an unmarked channel across the top end, and you can get almost all the way across without much difficulty. It's the last half-mile that's a problem. Better to go the long way than run aground. We would seriously recommend getting a good chart of the area. ADC Maps, in Alexandria, Virginia publishes a very detailed *Chesapeake Bay Chart Book*, as well as individual charts of the upper, central, and lower portions of the Chesapeake Bay. You can reach them at 703-750-0510.

The flats are the staging ground for the spring spawning stripers. The big fish move onto the flats in March and stay until about mid-May when they begin their migration down the Bay. With one exception, however, it is illegal to fish for these fish during the spawning season, which ends (officially) in June. The exception is

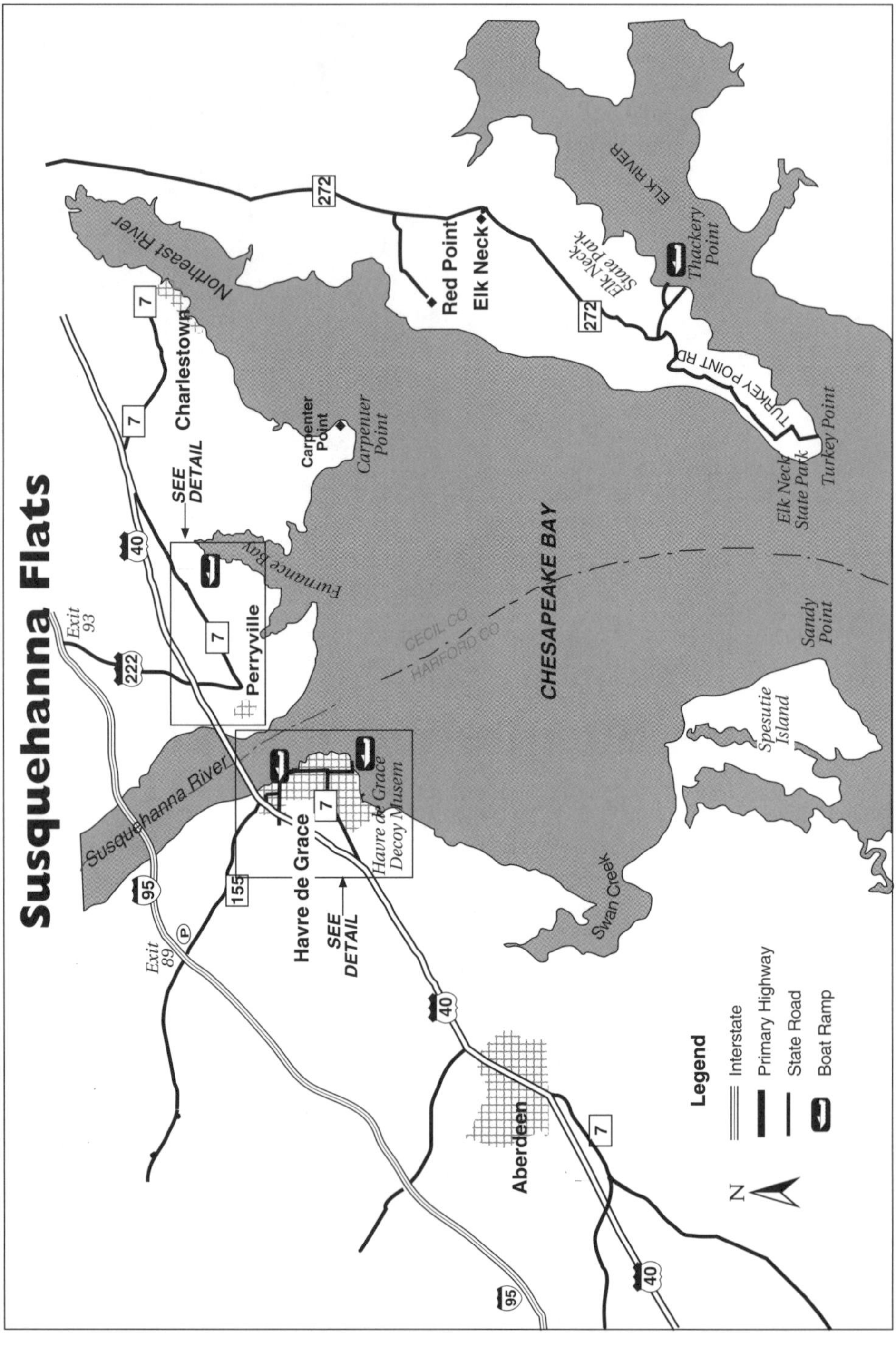
Susquehanna Flats
Northeast River
Charlestown
Red Point
Elk Neck
Elk Neck State Park
ELK RIVER
Thackery Point
TURKEY POINT RD
Turkey Point
Carpenter Point
SEE DETAIL
Furnance Bay
Perryville
Exit 93
CECIL CO
HARFORD CO
CHESAPEAKE BAY
Sandy Point
Spesutie Island
Susquehanna River
Havre de Grace
Havre de Grace Decoy Musem
Swan Creek
Exit 89
Aberdeen
Legend
Interstate
Primary Highway
State Road
Boat Ramp
N

that the state of Maryland has established a catch-and-release season that extends for about four weeks in April. During this period, you are allowed to fish for the big stripers using artificial lures or flies only. Although barbless hooks are not required, their use is recommend. Concerned anglers also remove the treble hooks on their lures and exchange them for single hooks, as well. It can be quite difficult to release a fish unharmed that has two trebles in its mouth. Actually, knowledgeable flats anglers seldom use multi-hooked crankbaits.

A selection of streamers that are useful on the Susquehanna Flats.

Tackle and Techniques

Two methods account for the majority of fish caught. The first is to use a fly rod capable of casting and working a large streamer fly (six inches is a common size) on a fast-sinking fly line. Something on the order of a Teeny 300 or better will work. Blind casting is the norm, and it can be tiring. If a wind is blowing or there is much of a tide, you can cast, let the line sink, then retrieve very slowly while drifting. This covers a lot more territory per retrieve and is a favored method.

The second technique uses either spinning or casting tackle and one of two lures—either a large bucktail that has some flash material mixed in with the hair and perhaps a trailer of a white or chartreuse plastic worm or a soft plastic bait on a ½-ounce or heavier head. Two versions of soft plastic lures are most popular—a 4- or 6-inch Sassy Shad in either pearl or in white with a blue back or a 4- or 6-inch Bass Assassin in either albino or chartreuse.

Wayne Blottenberger with a spring striper caught on the Flats during the April catch-and-release season.

A new color we tried for the first time this spring is bone shad, produced by Bass Assassin, and possibly others. We've always had mixed feelings about how much difference color makes in a lure, but an incident that occurred one evening on the flats really made us believers. We had been fishing with only moderate success, when Ed decided to try one of the aforementioned bone shad Assassins that he had received as a trial. The first cast brought a strike, as did roughly every other cast thereafter. It was unbelievable, and we were convinced that key was the color. There were thousands of herring and small shad present, and the stripers were apparently homing in on them. The bone shad closely matched the coloration of the baitfish. This color will always be in our tackle bags from now on.

Since there is a very real possibility of catching a striper in excess of 20 pounds, we suggest you use fairly heavy tackle. An 8-weight fly rod would be an absolute minimum, and a 9 or 10 much better. You'll need two lines—a fast-sinking line will get the most use, and for those times when the fish are in very shallow water, either a floater or a slow sinker.

Any reel with a capacity to hold the fly line and 100 yards of backing will do, as long as it has a decent drag. Stripers are stubborn fighters and may make quick dashes, but they don't make long runs.

A spinning or casting reel with a similar capacity of 12- to 14-pound test line is fine. The best rod is a fairly stiff graphite one around 7 feet in length. One suited to casting lures from ½-ounce to 1½-ounce is about right.

The legal fishing area extends from the Route 40 Bridge at the upper end to a line between Turkey Point and Sandy Point at the lower end, a distance of about nine miles. Fishing for stripers either above or below these lines is prohibited.

Most anglers will spread out over the deeper water just below the shallow flats proper. A good starting point is Red Buoy Number 2. From there south to the legal line and all the way up the deeper water on the eastern side is generally where most of the fish will be caught. Sometimes, the best fishing will be in deeper cuts in very shallow water, but these are difficult to find and require a very shallow-draft boat. Actually, the entire eastern channel, from the mouth of the Northeast River down to the "A" (which is actually a little below the legal line of demarcation) is six plus miles of prime water.

Although the April season is the best time to catch large stripers on the flats, fishing for this species diminishes greatly as the water temperature rises. After June 15, when it becomes legal to fish for stripers, they will mostly have left the flats. From then on, largemouth bass dominate. Water temperature is the key to good fishing. As long as the water temperature stays moderate, fishing can be good. When it climbs past about 80 degrees, however, fishing will be quite slow until the waters cool in the fall. Because of the shallow nature of the flats, warm summer water temperatures are to be expected. Then, the best spot on the flats is probably the mouth of the Northeast River. Years ago, this was considered one of the best largemouth bass spots in Maryland. However, due to pollution in recent years, coupled with the disappearance of most of the indigenous aquatic grasses, the Northeast River isn't as good as it once was. Still, if you are fishing the flats, and not doing well, the Northeast River is well worth a shot.

Getting There

The north end of the Susquehanna Flats is best accessed from the town of Havre de Grace on the west shore or Perryville on the east. Havre de Grace is reachable from Exit #89 off I-95 or Route 155 from Route 40. Perryville is reached by taking Exit #93 from I-95 or Route 275 from Route 40.

If time permits, visit the decoy museum in Havre de Grace. It ranks as one of the best in the country. Since the area was a hotspot of waterfowl hunting, both recreationally and commercially, this is no surprise. Some of the best-known decoy carvers in the country are represented here. As an aside, the museum also has a very good selection of fish carvings. It's worth a visit.

Launch Ramps

Havre de Grace sports several launch ramps, the best being at the City Yacht Basin at the foot of Commerce Street. To reach the ramp, take Exit #89 from I-95 (Route 155). Go southeast to Otsego Street. Turn right (east) to Union Avenue, then south to Commerce Street. The ramp is in Tydings Park. The second ramp is in the Jean Roberts Memorial Park. Follow the above instructions to Otsego Street, but follow Otsego to the end. The park is on the right.

To reach the ramp at Perryville, take Exit #93 from I-95 (Route 275 south). Follow that towards the river. The ramp is on Aiken Avenue, just off Route 40.

The only ramp within a reasonable distance from the flats at the lower end is in Elk Neck State Park near the mouth of the Elk River. You can launch there, and run right around Turkey Point and be fishing the lower end of the flats. The ramp is on Route 272 about ten miles south of the town of Northeast. A Cecil County Permit is required to launch at this ramp.

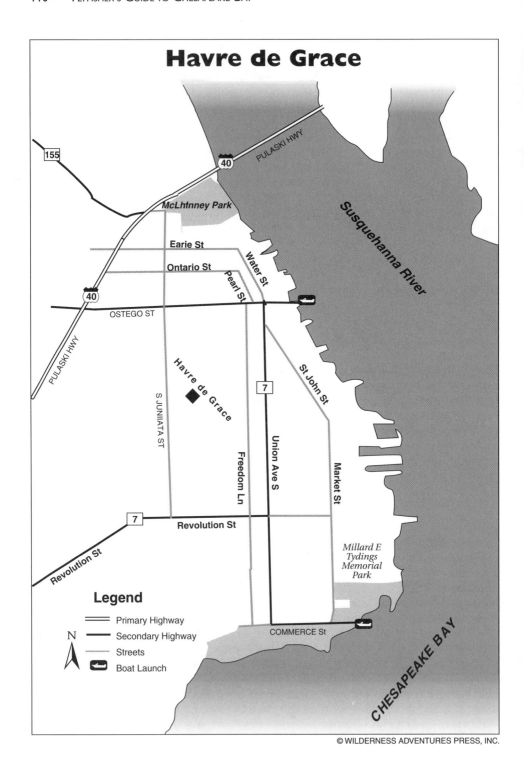

Havre de Grace

Legend

Primary Highway
Secondary Highway
Streets
Boat Launch

N

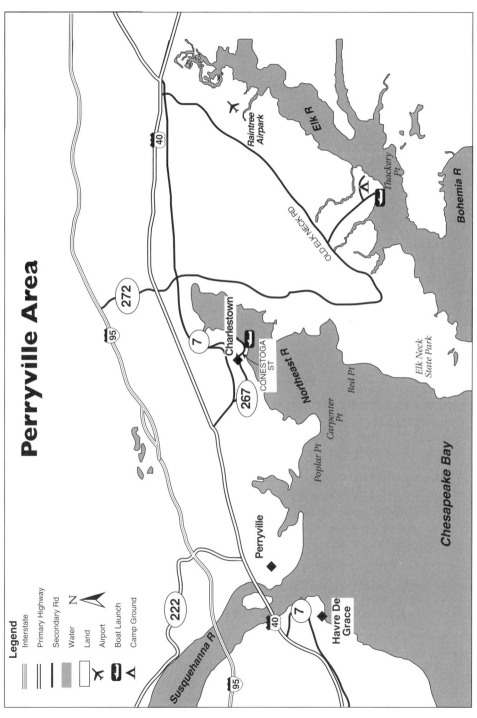

Perryville Area

Legend
Interstate
Primary Highway
Secondary Rd
Water
Land
Airport
Boat Launch
Camp Ground

N

Raintree Airpark

Elk R

Thackery Pt

Bohemia R

OLD ELK NECK RD

Charlestown

CONESTOGA ST

Northeast R

Elk Neck State Park

Red Pt

Carpenter Pt

Poplar Pt

Chesapeake Bay

Perryville

Havre De Grace

Susquehanna R

222

95

40

7

95

40

7

267

272

Hub Cities for the Susquehanna River and Flats

Havre de Grace

Population—11,331

Havre de Grace is French for Harbor of Grace. Much of the town's history is centered around the war of 1812. The British burned Washington D.C. then proceeded to Baltimore where they were stopped at the battle of North Point. As they were retreating, they moved to Havre de Grace and burned the town. Only three buildings were left standing. One is currently in use as a bed and breakfast.

One thing there is no shortage of in Havre de Grace is restaurants. A few that are especially good are MacGregor's, The Crazy Swede, and The Tidewater Grille. MacGregor's has excellent food. We've been there for lunch (try the French Dip) and dinner and were well pleased. The Crazy Swede doesn't look like much from the outside, but inside it's a different story-elegant but not overdone. We've sampled the Chicken Chesapeake, a chicken breast stuffed with crabmeat in a sherry sauce, and it is fantastic. A similar dish, utilizing halibut instead of chicken, was better than any halibut we've had in Alaska. The Tidewater Grill overlooks the Susquehanna Flats and specializes in fine seafood. Although we've not been there ourselves, friends claim it's excellent.

ACCOMMODATIONS
Super 8 Motel, 929 Pulaski Highway; 410-939-1880
Vandiver Inn, 41 South Union Street; 800-245-1655
Spencer Silver Mansion B&B, 200 South Union Street; 410-939-1097
Currier House B&B, 800 South Market Street; 800-827-2889

CAMPGROUNDS AND STATE PARKS
Susquehanna State Park, Lapidum, three miles northwest of Havre de Grace, off RT. 155; 69 sites, 6 with electric, 6 cabins; pets welcome but must be leashed; reservations usually necessary, 888-432-2267

RESTAURANTS
The Crazy Swede, 400 N. Union Avenue; 410-939-5440
Macgregor's, 331 St. John's Street; 410-939-3003
The Bayou Restaurant, 927 Pulaski Highway; 410-939-3313
Tidewater Grill, 300 Foot of Franklin Street; 410-939-313

FLY SHOPS, TACKLE STORES, AND SPORTING GOODS
Penn's Beach Marina, foot of Lewis Street; 410-939-2060
Ann's Sporting Goods, Shuresville Road, Darlington; 410-457-5182

LAUNCH RAMPS AND MARINAS
Havre de Grace City Marina, adjacent to Tydings Park, foot of Commerce Street; 410-939-0015

Penn's Beach Marina, foot of Lewis Street; 410-939-2060

BOAT EQUIPMENT AND REPAIR
Boat Services Unlimited, 1353 Old Post Road; 410-939-4795

Mark's Marine, foot of Bourbon Street; 410-939-4801

AUTO REPAIR
Adams Chevrolet, 1517 Pulaski Highway; 410-939-2255

Atlantic Automotive Service Center, 933 Pulaski Hwy # B; 410-939-5033

HOSPITALS
Harford Memorial Hospital, 501 S. Union Street; 410-939-2400

FOR FURTHER INFORMATION
The Havre de Grace Tourism Commission, 224 North Washington Street, P.O. Box 339, Havre de Grace, Maryland 21078; 800-851-7756 or 410-939-3303

Wayne Blottenberger hoists a big spring striper from some productive Chesapeake Bay water.

Aberdeen

Population—13,842

Aberdeen is best known for two things. It is the site of Aberdeen Proving Ground, which includes the U.S. Army Test and Evaluation Command and the U.S. Army Research Laboratory and other Army high technology organizations, and it is the home of former Baltimore Orioles ballplayer Cal Ripken.

ACCOMMODATIONS

Days Inn Aberdeen, 783 W. Bel Air Avenue; 410-272-8500

Econo Lodge of Aberdeen, 820 W. Bel Air Avenue; 410-272-5500

Four Points Hotel by Sheraton, 980 Hospitality Way; 410-273-6300

Holiday Inn, 1007 Beards Hill Road; 410-272-8100

Quality Inn, 793 W. Bel Air Avenue; 410-272-6000

Red Roof Inn, 988 Hospitality Way; 410-273-7800

Super 8 Motel, 1008 Beards Hill Road; 410-272-5420

CAMPGROUNDS

See Havre de Grace.

RESTAURANTS

Gabler's Shore Restaurant, 2200 Perryman; 410-272-0626

Smittys Pub, 1007 Beards Hill Road; 410-272-8100

The Bull Pen, US Rt. 40 & Carol Avenue; 410-272-6500

Bob Evans Farm Restaurant, 1024 Beards Hill Road; 410- 272-9046

The Olive Tree, 1005 Beards Hill Road; 410-272-6217

FLY SHOPS, TACKLE STORES, AND SPORTING GOODS

See Havre De Grace.

LAUNCH RAMPS

See Havre de Grace.

BOAT REPAIR

Otter Creek Marina, end of Otter Point Road at the tip of Bush River, east of Route 40 between Edgewood and Aberdeen; 410-676-0994

AUTO REPAIR

Anderson Automotive, 1615 Perryman Road; 410-273-2580

F.C. Automotive, 13 Bush Chapel Road; 410-575-6863

HOSPITALS

See Havre de Grace.

FOR FURTHER INFORMATION

Aberdeen Chamber of Commerce, 115 North Parke Street, Aberdeen, MD 21001; 410-272-2580

Perryville

Population—4,678

During the Revolutionary War, Perryville served as a staging area for the Continental Army. Colonel John Rodgers, who operated the ferry and tavern in Perryville, raised the 5th Company of the Maryland Militia. During the 1800s, Perryville was the central point for the Wilmington to Baltimore Rail Line. Perryville is the home of the Perry Point Veterans Hospital, the Perryville Travel Plaza, and the Perryville Outlet Center.

ACCOMMODATIONS

Douglass Motor Inn, 224 Blythedale Road; 410-378-2191
Perryville Motel, 5288 Pulaski Highway; 410-642-2044
Relax Inn, Route 40; 410-642-2282
Rendezvous Inn/Bar & Restaurant, 362 Front Street; 410-642-0045
Comfort Inn Perryville, 61 Heather Lane (Exit 93 off I-95 at SR 222); 410-642-2866 or 800-228-5150

CAMPGROUNDS AND STATE PARKS

Elk Neck State Park, Turkey Pt. Rd., North East; 410-287-5333
Riverside Ponderosa Pines, Carpenter's Pt.; 410-642-3431
Riverview Campground, 1200 Frenchtown Road; 410-642-6200

RESTAURANTS

Backer's Family Restaurant, 5293 Pulaski Highway; 410-642-3414
Bob's Place, 5256 Pulaski Highway; 410-642-6456
Caldwells Family Restaurant, Rts. 40 & 222; 410-642-2470
Denny's Restaurant, 41 Heather Lane; 410-642-6701
Ercole's Pizza and Pasta, 641 Broad Street; 410-642-3200
Island Inn Restaurant, 648 Broad Street; 410-642-3448
Rendezvous Inn/Bar & Restaurant, 362 Front Street; 410-642-0045

FLY SHOPS, TACKLE STORES, AND SPORTING GOODS

The Bait Shack, 1039 Round House Drive; 410-642-9166
Herb's Tackle Shop, 203 South Main Street, North East MD; 410-287-5490

LAUNCH RAMPS AND MARINAS

Perryville Launch Ramp, Aiken Avenue off Route 40 east of Perry Point, VA
Chestnut Point Marina, 85 Chestnut Pt. Road; 410-642-6639
Craft Haven Marina, 900 Carpenters Pt. Road; 410-642-2515

BOAT REPAIR

See Havre de Grace.

AUTO REPAIR

Clayton Auto Park, 1424 Clayton Street; 410-642-6821

HOSPITALS

Union Hospital, (Cecil County) 106 Singerly Avenue, Elkton MD, 410-398-4000
Harford Memorial, (Havre de Grace, Harford County) 501 S. Union St. Havre de Grace; 410-939-2400

FOR FURTHER INFORMATION

Perryville Town Hall, 515 Broad Street, P.O. Box 773, Perryville, MD 21903; 410-642-6066

Two of author Ed Russell's grandsons with a first striper.

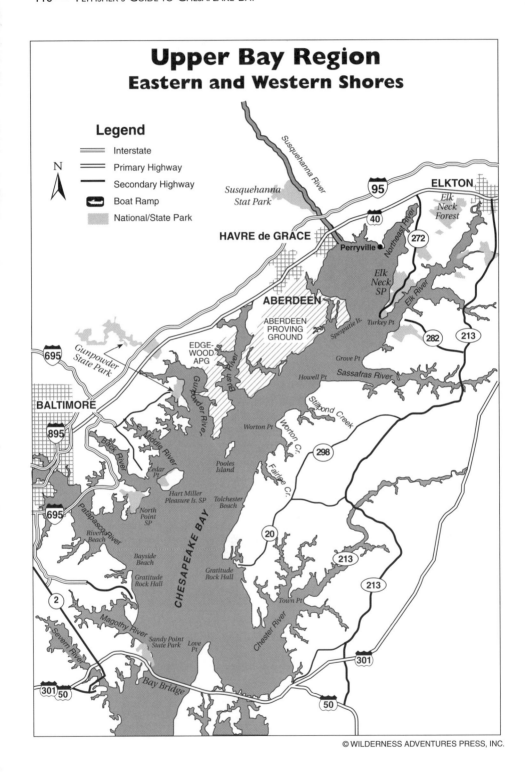

Upper Bay Region
Eastern and Western Shores

Legend

=== Interstate
=== Primary Highway
— Secondary Highway
Boat Ramp
National/State Park

N

Susquehanna River

95

40

272

ELKTON

Elk Neck Forest

Susquehanna Stat Park

HAVRE de GRACE

Perryville

Northeast River

Elk Neck SP

Elk River

ABERDEEN

ABERDEEN PROVING GROUND

Spesputie Is.

Turkey Pt

282

213

EDGE-WOOD APG

Grove Pt

695

Gunpowder State Park

Bush River

Howell Pt

Sassafras River

BALTIMORE

895

Gunpowder River

Worton Pt

Worton Cr.

Stillpond Creek

Middle River

298

Back River

Cedar Pt

Pooles Island

Fairlee Cr.

695

Hart Miller Pleasure Is. SP

Tolchester Beach

North Point SP

Patapsco River

20

Riverdale Beach

Bayside Beach

Gratitude Rock Hall

Gratitude Rock Hall

213

Town Pt

213

2

CHESAPEAKE BAY

Magothy River

Sandy Point State Park

Love Pt

Chester River

Severn River

301

301 50

Bay Bridge

50

301

Upper Bay, Eastern Shore

The rivers of the Upper Bay are not what they once were. Agricultural pollution, acid rain, and diminished freshwater flows due to increased use by an ever-increasing human population have taken their toll on the subaquatic vegetation that once was so abundant in this area. As a result, there is much less food and cover for baitfish and small fish and, thus, less reason for the larger predators to frequent the area. Still, some decent fishing can be found, some in the spring, but most in the fall. Light-tackle guide Gary Neitzey, who fishes the Upper Bay quite a lot, told us that he concentrates his efforts on areas like the mouth of the Gunpowder or the mouth of the Chester and points south most of the time. In the fall, however, Gary will take clients to many Upper Bay locations, especially if he launches his boat from a ramp reasonably close by. The reason—these Upper Bay rivers see little pressure, and although there may not be great quantities of fish, in the fall, there are enough unpressured fish to make working the best spots worthwhile.

A significant point that Neitzey makes is that moving tide is vital to this fishing (as it is to just about any saltwater fishing) and an outgoing tide is best for virtually every Upper Bay hotspot. He reasons that a falling tide moves and concentrates baitfish near the river mouths where stripers and other predators can lurk in the security of deeper water and wait for a meal to be presented to them.

Although there are better spots to seek stripers (most of the area is off limits to fishing for this species until June 1 and after that the waters warm excessively) there is still some decent largemouth bass fishing in the spring. When the waters cool in the fall, the river mouths can offer good fishing for stripers, largemouth bass, and white perch.

A nice white perch taken on a Stingsilver.

Wayne Blottenberger about to release a big striper.

NORTHEAST RIVER

Years ago, Cara Cove in the Northeast River at the head of the Bay was an extremely popular bass fishing hotspot. Unless the grasses that once blanketed much of this cove return, its glory days are over, but some fishing still exists. Red Point, on the south side of the river just below Cara Cove, is a good spot for striped bass. In years when there is some grass present, stripers will cruise the edges of the grass as well as the point itself. You may find breaking stripers any time from early afternoon on in the fall, but the fish will likely be fairly small.

Carpenter Point, on the north side of the river's mouth, can be good for large-mouth bass as well as stripers. Grasses are again a key element. If there is grass, it's likely that largemouth bass will be there, as well. You may catch a largemouth on one cast and a striper on the next. Both locations are best in the spring and fall, although summer can also be good for largemouths, but the best action will be early or late in the day. The absolute best time is the first two hours of the outgoing tide at dawn.

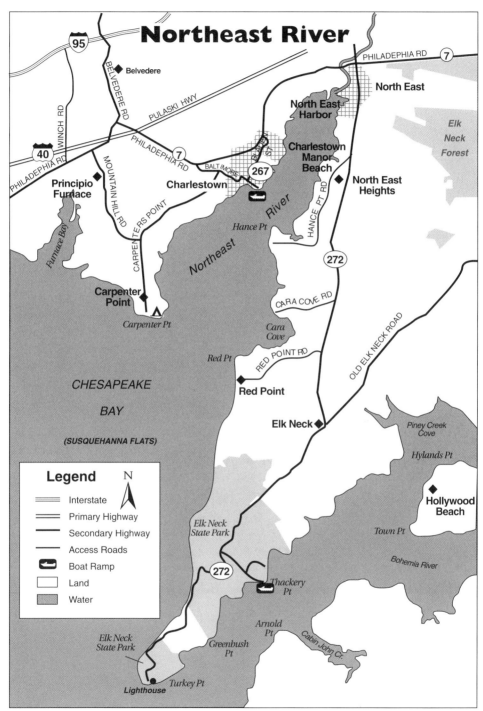

Northeast River

95

Belvedere

BELVEDERE RD

PULASKI HWY

PHILADEPHIA RD

7

North East

WINCH RD

North East Harbor

Elk Neck Forest

40

MOUNTAIN HILL RD

PHILADEPHIA RD

7

BALTIMORE

267

ST

Charlestown Manor Beach

HANCE PT RD

North East Heights

PHILADEPHIA RD

Principio Furnace

CARPENTERS POINT

Charlestown

Hance Pt

272

Furnace Bay

Carpenter Point

CARA COVE RD

Cara Cove

OLD ELK NECK ROAD

Carpenter Pt

Red Pt

RED POINT RD

Piney Creek Cove

CHESAPEAKE

Red Point

Hylands Pt

BAY

Elk Neck

(SUSQUEHANNA FLATS)

Hollywood Beach

Legend   N

Town Pt

Interstate

Primary Highway

Secondary Highway

Access Roads

Boat Ramp

Land

Water

Bohemia River

Elk Neck State Park

272

Thackery Pt

Elk Neck State Park

Arnold Pt

Cabin John Cr.

Greenbush Pt

Turkey Pt

Lighthouse

© WILDERNESS ADVENTURES PRESS, INC.

Getting There

There is a launch ramp at Charlestown inside the mouth of the Northeast River. It can be reached by taking Route 40 to Route 7 (Old Philadelphia Road) east to Route 67 east to Market Street; go to the end. You can also launch at Perryville. It's a short run from there. You'll need a Cecil County permit for either ramp.

RED POINT TO TURKEY POINT

This area is actually the eastern side of the Susquehanna Flats. A deep channel runs all along this side, and both the channel and the adjacent shallows are some of the best areas for stripers during the spring catch-and-release season. Except for that one-month season, this area is closed to striped bass fishing until June 1. You can, however, fish for largemouth bass, and there is a lot of structure, including rock piles, riprap, and downed timber along the shoreline. It's not the best place in the Bay, but if you are in the area, it is probably worth investigating.

Access would be from one of the ramps previously mentioned.

TURKEY POINT TO STILLPOND

This stretch of shoreline encompasses several river mouths and a creek or two. Turkey Point is on the north side of the Elk River. This river mouth is only fair for stripers, but there is some decent bass fishing farther upriver. If you launch a boat at Elk Neck State Park, you can start out at the mouth of Cabin John Creek directly across from the ramp, and the mouth of the Bohemia River is about a mile and a half to the northeast. There is a lot of structure in this area, but really good bass fishing is dependent on the presence of underwater vegetation.

During a good year, especially very early in the spring, you can find some nice bass up in the grass. A favorite method shown to us years ago is to fasten a large bull minnow behind a big Mepps spinner and throw it well up into the grasses. We'd dredge up a lot of grass, but we'd also catch some 4-pound-plus bass. I suspect a weedless soft plastic, especially a larger Bass Assassin, rigged to be weedless would be deadly.

Wroth Point to the south of Turkey Point marks the southern side of the Elk River. Moving south along the shoreline to Grove Point the area is fairly featureless, and few anglers bother with this portion. Grove Point to the north and Howell Point to the south form the mouth of the next river—the Sassafras. Much of what was said about the Elk and the Bohemia applies to the Sassafras, except that, of the upper Eastern Shore rivers, the Sassafras probably offers the best spring bass fishing. There are more and better grass beds in the Sassafras, and there is a launch ramp well up the river that puts you right into the best areas. Turner Creek, where the ramp is located, offers some good largemouth fishing.

Turning west from the Turner Creek Ramp, heading towards the mouth of the river, you will see Lloyds Creek on the south shore. There is a very small opening into what looks more like a lake than a creek. On an outgoing tide, Gary Neitzey says that this is one of the better spots to fish and one of his favorite spots to work a surface

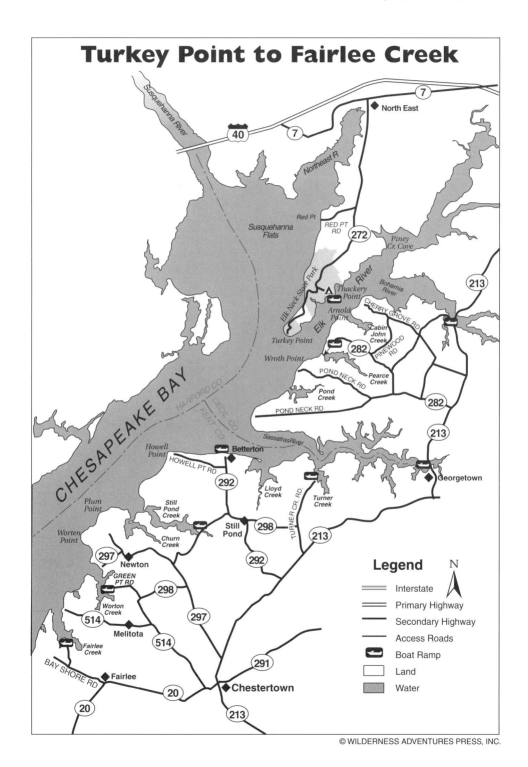

Turkey Point to Fairlee Creek

Susquehanna River

40

7

7

North East

Northeast R.

Red Pt

RED PT RD

272

Piney Cr. Cove

Susquehanna Flats

213

Bohemia River

Elk Neck State Park

Thackery Point

Arnold Point

CHERRY GROVE RD

Elk River

Cabin John Creek

PINEWOOD RD

282

Turkey Point

282

Wroth Point

POND NECK RD

Pearce Creek

Pond Creek

POND NECK RD

213

SassafrasRiver

282

Howell Point

Betterton

213

HOWELL PT RD

292

Lloyd Creek

Turner Creek

Georgetown

Plum Point

Still Pond Creek

TURNER CR. RD.

CHESAPEAKE BAY

HARFORD CO.

KENT CO.

CECIL CO.

Worten Point

Still Pond

298

213

Churn Creek

292

297

Newton

GREEN PT RD

298

Worton Creek

297

514

514

Fairlee Creek

Melitota

291

BAY SHORE RD

Fairlee

20

Chestertown

20

213

Legend

N

═══ Interstate

═══ Primary Highway

── Secondary Highway

── Access Roads

Boat Ramp

☐ Land

▨ Water

© WILDERNESS ADVENTURES PRESS, INC.

Turkey Point to Sassafras River

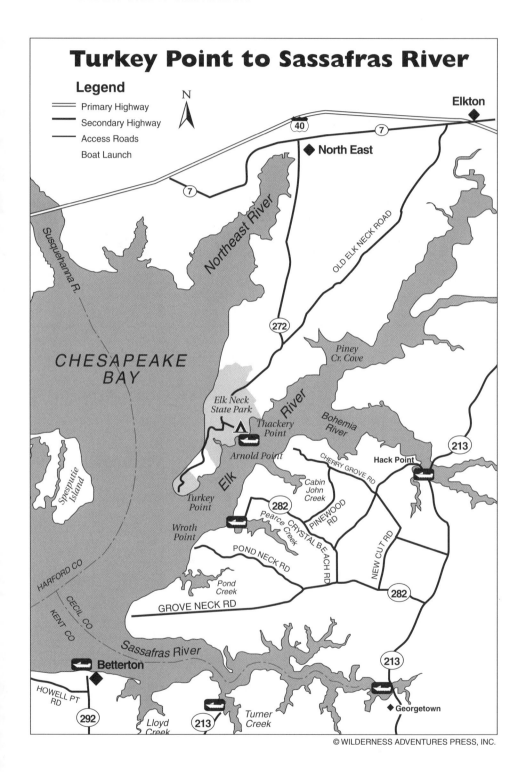

© WILDERNESS ADVENTURES PRESS, INC.

lure. Since the opening is small, there is quite a funneling effect when the tide flows out, and the tidal flow is quite strong. Expect vicious strikes to a lure in the fast current. The incoming tide, while not as good as the outgoing, is still worth trying.

Stick close to the shore when trying to enter the creek. There are a couple of sandbars out from the mouth and the water is actually deeper closer to shore. Average depth inside the creek runs from a little over two feet to about six.

Just inside the mouth of the Sassafras, in front of the town of Betterton, there is quite a large pile of concrete rubble about 150 yards from shore. Whether from an old dock or some other structure, the debris provides good cover. It's not a spectacular spot, but worth a few casts.

Howell Point forms the southern end of the Sassafras, and despite looking fishy it seldom produces, and the shoreline between there and Stillpond to the south is only marginal.

Launch Ramps

There is a launch ramp at Turner Creek. To get there, follow Route 213 to Route 298 West to Turner Creek Road. The ramp is at the end.

Another ramp is in the town of Betterton. To reach it, take Route 213 to Route 292 West—follow 292 to end. A Kent County permit is required for either ramp.

STILLPOND TO FAIRLEE CREEK

Stillpond is just north of Plum Point. Formed by the confluence of Stillpond Creek and Churn Creek, this has always been a favorite largemouth spot. The south shoreline of Churn Creek for about the first two hundred yards is especially good. Stillpond Creek is better for stripers, and unlike most areas, is best on an incoming tide, probably because there is deeper water on the inside of the creek. There are a couple of rocky points on the shoreline outside the south shore of Churn Creek that are good striper spots. This is one spot where you might run into a sizeable striper, especially in the fall. A 30-incher is possible from October until the water temperature reaches the high 40s. Breaking fish also show up outside the mouth in the fall.

Plum Point is a bit of a sleeper. It doesn't look like much because most of the structure is underwater, but when the tide is running well, there is a well-defined tidal rip, and stripers frequent the area. Sometimes there will be breaking fish, but this point is worth fishing any time a tide is running whether or not breaking fish are evident.

Worton Point and Worton Creek are next. Offshore about 300 yards from the point there is a series of underwater humps that hold fish most of the time. This is a spot that is always worth trying on any moving tide. The top of one of these humps is only six feet deep at low tide, and there is 25 feet of water on one side and 35 on the other. The tidal action here is very strong on either incoming or outgoing water. According to Neitzey, this is one of the most reliable spots in the Upper Bay to encounter breaking fish, although they tend to be somewhat small. Still, with a light outfit, you can have a ball. If it has been a dry year, you may well catch bluefish and Spanish mackerel in addition to stripers.

Author Ed Russell with an early fall striper taken near Worton Point.

The shoreline around Worton Point is also good. Since it's fairly shallow, 3 to 4 feet, a fly fisherman can use a slow or intermediate line and fish either streamers or poppers. A person fishing spinning or casting gear should use lightweight bucktails or soft plastics or shallow running crankbaits, as well as any type of surface lure. For whatever reason, the bottom structure around Worton Point seems particularly attractive to striped bass.

Inside the mouth of Worton Creek, the shoreline opens up to form a mini-bay. There's lots of structure, including an old breakwater and the remains of old docks or piers, a grass bed, and a sunken barge. The grass bed usually holds largemouth, while everything else holds both stripers and bass. This area is best from midsummer on, usually at low light. Surface fishing for largemouths is especially good here, most often on a moving tide, regardless of whether incoming or outgoing. According to Neitzey, he and clients have caught a largemouth bass, followed by a striper, followed by a white perch, and then a yellow perch on sequential casts. Not bad. This is a "must fish" spot in the Upper Bay.

Fairlee Creek is about three miles south of Worton Creek and is another striper hotspot. The shoreline configuration is such that an outgoing tide flows north into the Bay proper, and since the opening to the creek is quite restricted, the term tidal

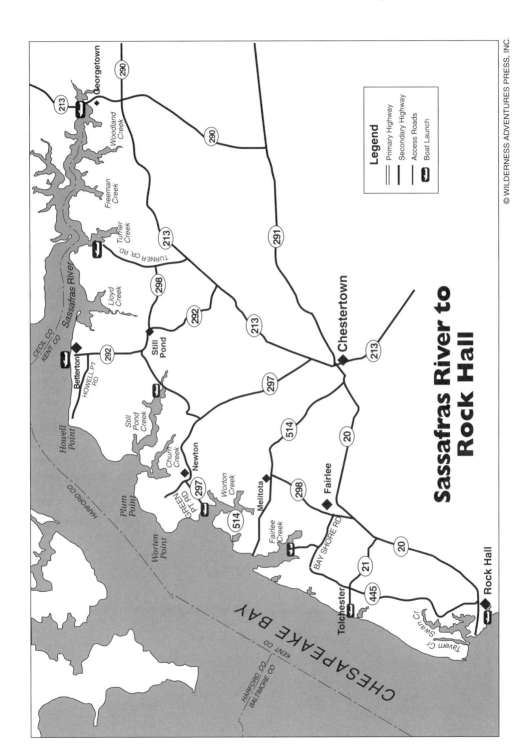

Sassafras River to Rock Hall

Legend
Primary Highway
Secondary Highway
Access Roads
Boat Launch

rip really applies. The outgoing tide is much better than the incoming, and the best place to fish is the shoreline to the north of the creek from the shore out for about 50 yards.

Inside the creek on the south side there frequently are heavy grass beds. If these are present, it's a good spot for bass. Try working a buzz-bait right along the surface. Fly-rod poppers may also work, but they had best be weedless.

A disadvantage to this spot is the fact that Great Oaks Resort and Yacht Basin lies inside the creek's mouth, and weekend boat traffic is substantial. Late fall, it's not much of a problem, but during moderate weather, avoid this area on weekends except at first light.

Launch Ramps

There are several launch ramps that serve this general area. Green Point Launch Ramp is on Worton Creek. To get there, take Route 213 to Route 297 North to Route 298 West to St. James Newton Road North to Green Point Road West. The nearest town of any size is Chestertown.

Fairlee Public Landing is on Fairlee Creek. To get there, take Route 213 to Route 291 West to Route 20 West to Route 298 North to Bay Shore Road West to Fairlee Landing Road. Chestertown is again the nearest town for a reference point. Both ramps require a Kent County permit.

FAIRLEE CREEK TO ROCK HALL

South of Fairlee Creek, all the way to Rock Hall, which is our defining point for the Upper Bay, there's only one spot along the shoreline that is much good, and that's at the Tolchester Marina. The concrete riprap marking the entrance to the marina holds both stripers and bass at times. South of that the shoreline is sandy, shallow, and rather featureless. All of this shoreline, in fact most of the shoreline of the entire Bay, is in private hands. There are no public access points along this 10-mile length, and most of the fishing that's any good will be well out from shore on the lumps described later in this book.

Guide Gary Neitzey with a striper from Fairlee Creek.

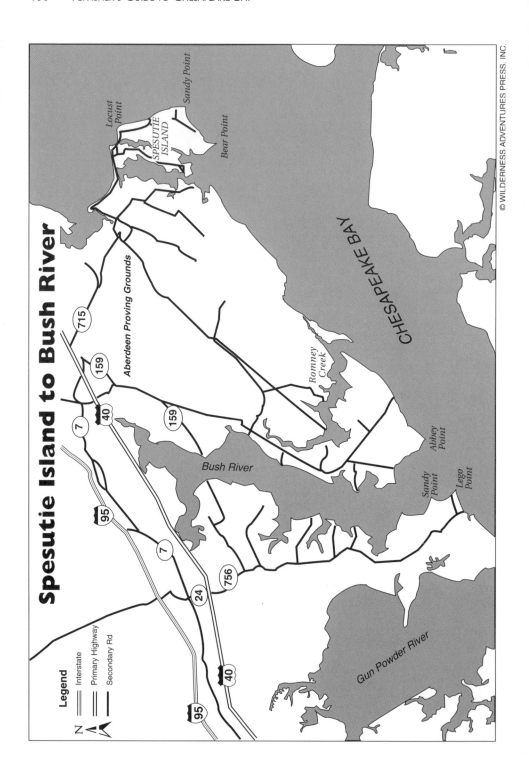

Spesutie Island to Bush River

Locust Point

Sandy Point

SPESUTIE ISLAND

Bear Point

Aberdeen Proving Grounds

CHESAPEAKE BAY

Romney Creek

715

159

40

7

159

Bush River

Abbey Point

Sandy Point

Lego Point

95

7

756

24

40

Gun Powder River

95

Legend

N

Interstate
Primary Highway
Secondary Rd

© WILDERNESS ADVENTURES PRESS, INC.

Harry Pippin with a nice striper taken on a popper from the Upper Bay.

The Upper Bay, Western Shore

SPESUTIE ISLAND TO BUSH RIVER

The first thing to know about fishing this area is that sometimes you can't. The entire shoreline, indeed all of Spesutie Island itself, is part of the military reservation—Aberdeen Proving Grounds. You can fish all around the island, but you may not go ashore. There are some interesting spots with downed timber and riprap here and there. Locust Point, at the north end of the island, is good for both stripers and bass. The best times are during low-light levels with an outgoing tide during the fall.

Sandy Point, towards the lower end of the island, is quite good in the spring. In fact, during the catch-and-release season on the flats, this is one of the best spots to try top-water offerings. Noisy crankbaits also produce well. We had one of our most productive days ever throwing Rat-L-Traps right up against the shoreline in this spot two years ago.

The best spot is probably Bear Point at the southern tip of Spesutie Island. There are lots of rocks right off the point. They are seldom visible, but they provide good cover for bass or stripers—as well as being a hazard to propellers. Fish with care.

Below Spesutie Island all the way down to the Bush River, the near-shore waters are part of the downrange terminus of an artillery firing range. There is a line of yellow can buoys that mark the edge of the prohibited waters. When there will be gunnery activity, the Army stations picket boats along this perimeter to warn boaters away. There is actually little danger, but the possibility of an errant round does exist. Romney Creek empties into the Bay about seven miles below the tip of Spesutie Island. Although you can fish the shoreline in the area, including the mouth of the creek (as long as there is no artillery action) entering Romney Creek proper is prohibited at all times.

A little farther south, at the mouth of the Bush River, is Abbey Point—one of the best and most reliable spots on the upper Western Shore. This is one of the few places in the Upper Bay where the incoming tide is much better than the outgoing, probably because the shoreline blunts the incoming water and causes it to flow faster around the outside of the point.

Inside the mouth of the river, on the north shore, there are rockpiles around Bush Point, and this is a good spot for both striped bass and largemouths. Stripers will hit almost exclusively during the low-light periods of early morning and evening. Largemouths, however, don't seem to care, and for some reason will hit all day as long as the tide is moving. It's a wonderful spot for a fly rod and a popping bug.

On the south side of the river mouth, Lego Point has submerged pilings and stumps and looks good, but it is dangerous. There is a large, unmarked rock pile just under the surface about 300 yards offshore. About a dozen boats a year hit these rocks. Gary Neitzey has the location plugged into his GPS as a waypoint with the name "Widow Maker."

Another problem occurs if a fisherman moves into the mouth of the river and is unaware that artillery firing is scheduled for the day. Should he be inside when the firing begins, he may well be forced to remain inside until the exercise is over. Sometimes there will be a scheduled lull in the firing, and when that occurs, the patrol boats will generally allow anyone caught literally "up the creek" to get out. Should you find yourself in this situation, the best bet is to motor up to the picket boat and ask if and when there will be a break. If you are told there will be a pause in the firing, there will be only a small window of opportunity to get out. Use it. You can call the firing range at 410-278-2250 (weekdays) or 410-306-0564 (weekends) to find out the schedule, but the time frame is short—not for more than one day in advance.

BUSH RIVER TO THE GUNPOWDER RIVER

The shoreline south of Bush River is unremarkable until you get to Robins Point at the bottom east end of the peninsula that forms the mouth of the Gunpowder River. This fishes just like Abbey Point as previously described, and for the same reasons. The topography makes an incoming tide by far the best time to fish. Striped bass are pretty much the main event. Largemouth bass are infrequently caught here. Rickett Point, which is on the west side, looks good on a chart but is actually much too shallow to fish.

Carroll Point is a good spot on the west side of the river. The shallow gut between Carroll Point (actually a small island) and the main shoreline is another good spot for stripers. It takes some care to fish as there are some very shallow spots, but it can be quite productive, again, principally in the fall.

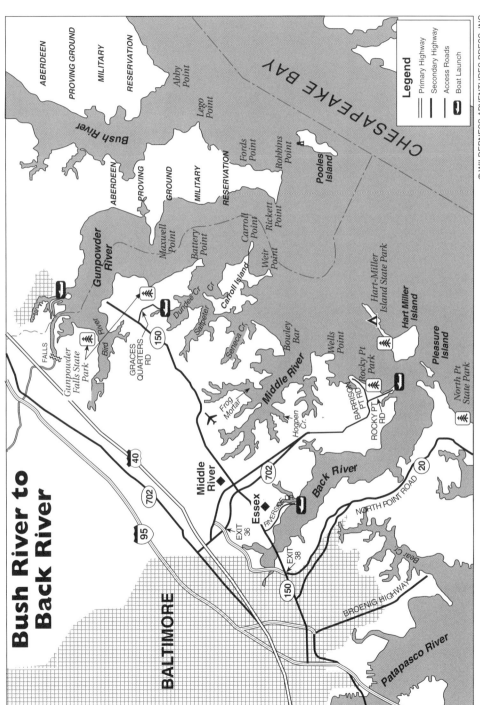

Bush River to Back River

BALTIMORE

Legend
- Primary Highway
- Secondary Highway
- Access Roads
- Boat Launch

CHESAPEAKE BAY

ABERDEEN PROVING GROUND MILITARY RESERVATION

Bush River

Abby Point

Lego Point

Fords Point

Robbins Point

Pooles Island

ABERDEEN PROVING GROUND MILITARY RESERVATION

Gunpowder River

Maxwell Point

Battery Point

Carroll Point

Rickett Point

Weir Point

Carroll Island

Durdee Cr.

Saltpeter Cr.

Seneca Cr.

Bowley Bar

Wells Point

Rocky Pt Park

Hart-Miller Island State Park

Hart Miller Island

Pleasure Island

North Pt State Park

FALLS

Bird River

Gunpowder Falls State Park

GRACES QUARTERS RD

150

40

95

702

Middle River

Frog Mortar

Middle River

Hogpen Cr.

BARRISON PT RD

ROCKY PT RD

Back River

Essex

RIVERSIDE DR

EXIT 36

EXIT 38

150

702

20

NORTH POINT ROAD

BROENIG HIGHWAY

Bear Cr.

Patapasco River

© WILDERNESS ADVENTURES PRESS, INC.

Maxwell Point, about three miles inside the mouth of the Gunpowder, is a well-known striper hotspot. There is a fairly deep hole (8 to 10 feet) right off the point that isn't shown on the charts. It's best in the evening, and either tide is good.

Dundee Creek, just inside the mouth of the Gunpowder on the west side, is home to some excellent largemouth fishing. Structure consists of loads of docks, pilings, piers, and in good years, grass beds. Although the bass are plentiful, they are well educated since they receive heavy pressure. The best time to fish is the last half of the outgoing tide. This is a departure from what is considered normal, but the end of the tide seems to pull the baitfish, which the bass relish, out of the shoreline grasses.

Weedbeds like these were once thick around the mouth of the Gunpowder River as well as at many other locations. While they are scarce now, there are some signs of recovery.

GUNPOWDER RIVER TO BACK RIVER

Pooles Island is about a mile and a half southeast of Abbey Point, just outside the mouth of the Gunpowder. The south half of the island is usually best, but the shoreline and bottom are quite rocky, and the rocks extend well out from shore. There is one large boulder that is visible, but many more lie just beneath the surface. This provides excellent fish habitat, but use caution as the rocky shallows extend out from shore as much as 200 yards in some places. A shallow-draft boat is really best. Fishermen with bass boats frequent this area.

The fishing can be good all summer long, and it gets better as fall arrives. Late afternoon to dark is the prime time, and like most of the Upper Bay spots, an outgoing tide is, by far, the best. Mornings are good too, but the action occurs at first light and is typically short-lived. This is a very good spot to catch sizeable stripers in shallow water. Don't fool with a light rod or line when fishing here.

Below the Gunpowder, there are some interesting looking spots right near the mouth of Seneca Creek, and the Seneca itself can be good for largemouth bass when grasses are present. The shoreline of the Bay proper in this location is shallow, sandy, and the site of at least one public swimming beach. Few people fish this area.

Middle River, less than two miles south of the Seneca, was once a prime largemouth destination, and the little tributaries like Hog Pen Creek on the south side of the river and Frog Mortar on the north side were literally choked with vegetation. Frog Mortar, in fact, was once considered one of the absolute best largemouth spots in Maryland.

As a young teenager, I remember standing on a pier and looking in wonder at the bass finning among the eelgrass and duckwort in Hog Pen Creek. The grasses were so thick in the upper end of the creek that it was difficult to row a boat through them. Sadly, this is no longer the case. Most of the grasses have fallen victim to pollution, siltation, and disease. The bass fishing isn't as good as it once was, but it's still worthwhile. You simply need to fish different structure. And there's an immense amount of that in the form of docks and piers. Any structure that affords shade and cover will be places that largemouth bass key on. Work any pier carefully. There's a premium placed on casting ability since you will often have to cast a fly or lure under a pier to connect. Occasionally, in the fall, school stripers invade the river and you may well catch both species during an outing. If you get a year where there is any amount of grass, the fishing will be better.

From Middle River to the mouth of Back River, a distance of about three miles, fishing is spotty at best. However, just off the mouth of Back River, right across from Rocky Point State Park are Hart and Miller Islands. The shoreline all around these two islands offers good fishing for both striped bass and white perch. The shoreline on the Bay side is riprap, while the inside shoreline is in its natural state. Usually, the Bay side is more productive, but on a moving tide the fish can literally be anywhere around the island.

Typical Upper Bay streamers: Conehead, two Clousers, and a Crystal Bugger.

Tackle and Techniques

Tackle for fishing all of the Upper Bay river mouths will be much the same. Since the fish will seldom be much over five pounds, fly, spinning, or casting tackle suitable for largemouth bass will be fine. Some anglers use fly rods as light as a 5-weight. If your abilities are such that you can cast this outfit in the almost ever-present Bay winds, more power to you. Personally, we feel that an 8-weight is the minimum size fly rod for fishing the Bay. Likewise, we discourage the use of very light line when using spinning or casting tackle. There are a lot of underwater obstructions, and both largemouth bass and stripers favor such locations. To be successful, you must put your offering where the fish live, and that means hanging up frequently. Too light a line means losing lures. Gear your line choice to the expected size of the fish. For smaller fish, 6-pound line is probably okay, but 8 is better, and 10-pound test is about the minimum if there is any possibility of larger fish. One option, of course, is to choose a no-stretch "super-line" like Berkley's Fireline. This allows the use of smaller diameter line (for casting smaller lures) with greater strength. Also, since much of this fishing may be catch-and-release, the use of tackle that is too light results in a protracted battle, which, though it might be fun for the angler, often results in a fish that is released but dies shortly thereafter. Use common sense.

Flies and lures for all of these Upper Bay river mouths will be similar. Only size or color may change to match existing baitfish. Fly choices are fairly simple. Smaller

Lefty's Deceivers or Clouser Deep Minnows, in white, chartreuse, or combinations thereof, are excellent choices. When the Bay anchovies are the predominant bait, any of the semi-transparent patterns tied to represent them are a good choice. If the fish are working the top, a simple foam popper to match the size of the bait is all you need. Typically, we use white or yellow bodies with hair tails. We seldom use feather tails since they tend to foul around the hook too much.

For lures, ½-ounce Rat-L-Traps, Berkley's Frenzy series, or similar noisy lures are very effective. Baitfish imitations like the Excalibur Saltwater Swim'n Image, the Excalibur Ghost Minnow, the Rebel Minnow, or the Rapala are all excellent. For noisy top-water lures, our favorites include the Excalibur Saltwater Super Pop-R, the Excalibur Saltwater Pop-n Image, Bill Lewis's Spit Fire, the Creek Chub Striker Strike, and Storm Lures' Saltwater Chug Bug. When less commotion is desired, an Excalibur Saltwater Super Spook, Jr, a Creek Chub Darter or Bill Lewis' Slap-Stik or Walkin'-Stik fill the bill. All of the lures mentioned feature saltwater-proof hooks and come in smaller sizes suitable for the smaller fish of the Upper Bay.

Gary Neitzey's favorite lure is a spinnerbait. He feels that day in and day out, a spinnerbait will out-produce any other fly or lure in the Upper Bay river mouths. But for the most fun, he likes to use a buzz-bait. When there are grass beds present, his favorite technique is to cast a buzz-bait deep into the cover and retrieve it fast enough to skim along on top of the grass. An explosive strike is often the result—usually from a largemouth, but occasionally a striper will slam one of these, as well.

Of course, bucktails and soft plastics are always a good choice. Again, smaller sizes (about four inches) are ideal. Bass Assassin, Berkley, and others feature a huge selection.

Although you can use most any fly or lure suitable for bass to fish this area, if they do not feature stainless or saltwater-proof hooks, you'll need to take some precautions or the hooks will quickly rust.

Launch Ramps

One difficulty in fishing this area is the lack of launch ramps. Most of the shoreline from Havre de Grace to the mouth of Back River, a distance of about 30 miles, is a military reservation with no public access permitted. The only ramp with direct access to the Bay is at Rocky Point State Park at the mouth of Back River. To reach this ramp, take Interstate 695 to Exit #36 to Route 702 east. Follow 702 to Barrison Point Road east then go south on Rocky Point. Unfortunately, this ramp is small and the water quite shallow; it's marginal for larger boats.

The overall best ramp is on Dundee Creek within Gunpowder Falls State Park. From the ramp to the mouth of the Gunpowder is about an eight-mile run. To reach this ramp, follow Interstate 695 to Exit #38 to Route 150 east. Follow 150 east to Graces Quarters Road east. You'll see the signs for the park.

There is another ramp on the Gunpowder, but it's well up the river and there is a long 6-mph speed zone. The one at Dundee is a better choice.

Upper Bay Islands, Lumps, Holes, and Channels

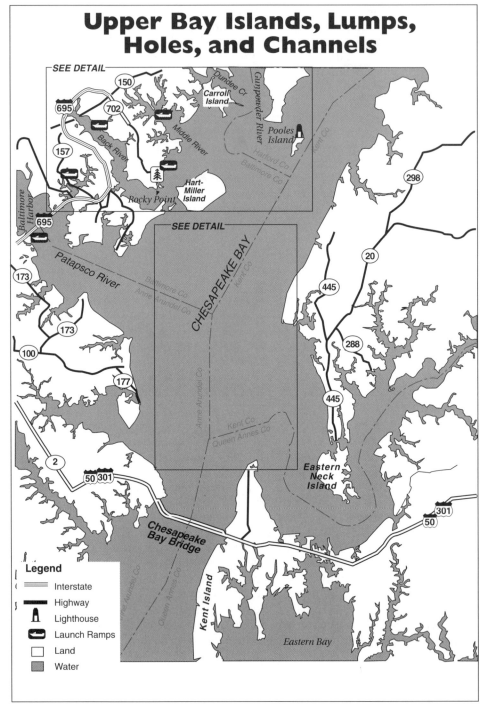

© WILDERNESS ADVENTURES PRESS, INC.

An early catch.

Upper Bay Islands, Lumps, Holes, and Channels

A glance at a fishing map of the greater Upper Bay area from roughly Pooles Island south to the Chesapeake Bay Bridge area tells the story. In addition to the island structures of Pooles Island and the Hart-Miller Island complex, which includes a state-provided reef, this area is loaded with a host of underwater fish-attracting structure; including "The Lumps," "Teakettle Shoals," "Gales Lumps," and farther south, "Man O' War Shoals," Brewerton Shipping Channel, Craighill Channel, "Seven-Foot Knoll," "Nine-Foot Knoll," and "Belvedere Shoals."

Trolling has long been the most popular way of working these lumps and chan-nels, and veteran charter captains and recreational fishermen continue this tradi-tion. But in recent years fly and light-tackle approaches have become increasingly popular and are being employed by guides and individual fishermen.

Top Upper Chesapeake fly fishing and light-tackle guides, including Gary Neitzey, Norm Bartlett, and Richie Gaines, among others, find consistent success in these waters from early summer through the end of December. Not only are these waters desirable areas in their own right, but, as a bonus, they are near some other prime areas, such as Baltimore Harbor, the Chesapeake Bay Bridge, Kent Island, and even the brackish waters of the Gunpowder and Dundee Rivers. So they also offer a terrific "Plan B" if fishing in the above areas should be poor—provided the anglers have enough boat and motor for runs of about 10 to 15 miles or more.

Fishing begins in May with stripers migrating up and down the Bay and white perch moving in. (When fishing these waters early in the year, check the regulations: Craighill Channel is one of several boundaries in this area where various regulations apply, including the no-fishing season, catch-and-release-season, trophy season, and open season.) By July, bluefish are usually in and some hardheads and flounder have migrated this far north. Usually some channel catfish and carp from the brackish waters are mixed in, too, and in some years Spanish mackerel may join the party. The trout usually arrive by late August.

The prime fishing in this area for all these species is August through November. Fishing for stripers and perch can last as late as the end of the year.

The basic approach is, to quote the old football coach's cliché, "Hit 'em high and hit 'em low." As soon as you launch your boat from any of the locations listed at the end of this chapter, keep scanning the sky and water surface for bird, fish, and boat activity and keep scanning the depthfinder for fish on the breaklines.

Recommended tackle is the Bay standard 9-weight and/or 10-weight fly rod casting a floating line with a large popper or streamer or casting a fast-sinking line, such as the Teeny 300 or TS-350, with streamers. As has been the case in most of the

Guide Gary Neitzey with an early December-caught white perch from the Upper Bay Lumps.

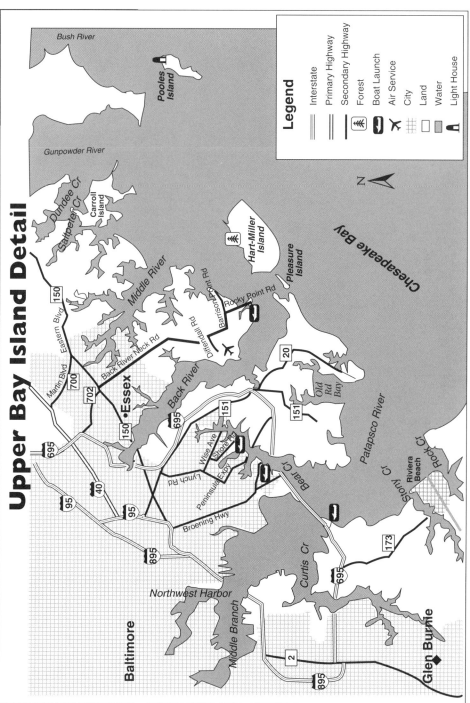

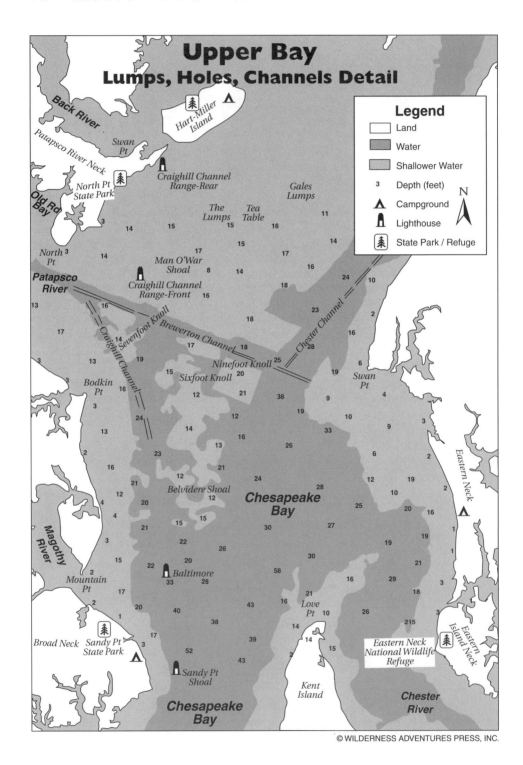

Upper Bay
Lumps, Holes, Channels Detail

Back River

Patapsco River Neck

Swan Pt

Hart-Miller Island

Old Rd Bay

North Pt State Park

Craighill Channel Range-Rear

Gales Lumps

The Lumps   Tea Table

Legend

	Land
	Water
	Shallower Water
3	Depth (feet)
⛰	Campground
⛯	Lighthouse
⛩	State Park / Refuge

N

14   15   15   16   11

North Pt   3

15   14

Man O'War Shoal   17

Patapsco River

14   17

8   16

Craighill Channel Range-Front   16

18   24   10

16

13   16   Sevenfoot Knoll   Brewerton Channel   18   23   16   2

17   14   17   18   Chester Channel   28

13   19   Ninefoot Knoll   25   6

Bodkin Pt   15   Sixfoot Knoll   20   19   Swan Pt   4

3   16   12   21   38   9

24   12   19   10   9

13   14   16   33

2   13   26   6   2

16   23   21

Belvidere Shoal   24   28   12   19   2

21   12   Chesapeake Bay   25   10   20   16

12   20   15   15   30   27   19   1

Magothy River   3   22   26   30   19   1

15   22   20   58   21

2   Mountain Pt   33   Baltimore   28   16   29   3

17   16   18

2   20   40   43   16   Love Pt   10   26   215

1   38   14

17   39   14   15   Eastern Neck National Wildlife Refuge

Broad Neck   Sandy Pt State Park   52   43   2

Sandy Pt Shoal   Kent Island   Chester River

Chesapeake Bay

© WILDERNESS ADVENTURES PRESS, INC.

Upper Bay the last few years, the best streamer pattern has been Joe Bruce's Crab-Colored Clouser, tied on a 2/0 hook about 3½ to 4½ inches long. The classic chartreuse-over-white Clouser Minnow the same size and a slightly smaller Bruce's Pickerel Fly have also done well.

Large Half-and-Half patterns do well at times, tied on 2/0 or 3/0 long-shanked hooks, with $1/24$- or $1/32$-ounce eyes and in the colors of all white, all chartreuse, chartreuse and white, or Crab Clouser colors.

Recommended conventional tackle includes medium casting or spinning tackle using good quality poppers about four inches long, jig and grub combinations, and metal jigs. Gary Neitzey favors a ¾-ounce jighead with a Silver Phantom, 5-inch Bass Assassin; Richie Gaines favors the same rig with a 5-inch Albino Bass Assassin. Another favorite color among guides and everyday fishermen is chartreuse.

Among the metal lures, the ¾-ounce Hopkins Shorty in silver, the $1^1/8$-ounce Stingsilver in silver or chartreuse-and-white, and the silver ¾-ounce Silver Buddy have all done well.

Breaking fish are common in this area. While there are often bigger fish below the breaking schools, this is not always the case. It seems characteristic of this general area, and particularly the lumps, for some very large stripers to be mixed in with smaller fish. Guide Richie Gaines has frequently noticed this phenomenon and advises anglers to look for extra large swirls or splashes in schools of breaking fish and to listen for any kind of feeding activity that looks or sounds different.

Harry Pippin applied this principle last fall near Sixfoot Knoll. We were all casting poppers into a school of breaking fish and taking stripers in the 16- to 22-inch range. But Harry heard a heavy slurping strike behind him, turned, fired a popper, and took a 32-inch striper, our best fish of the day.

As in so many other areas of the Bay, fish can stack in layers in these waters. Even when stripers and/or blues are breaking, you can get some real lunker stripers below a working school feeding on the smaller fish. Often a layer of larger stripers will lay below small breaking stripers, with seatrout mixed with some jumbo white perch hanging below the stripers.

These layers of fish or fish hanging off the breaklines of the lumps or channels can be effectively worked with fly rods and fast-sinking lines at depths of up to 20 feet. Make long casts to the fish-holding areas; let the fly sink in a controlled drop, watching the line for subtle signs of a strike; then begin working the fly back with a swimming or strip-pause-strip retrieve. Experiment with retrieves until the fish tell you what they want.

For conventional tackle, use similar swimming or hopping retrieves at these depths. But often the best technique, and by far the best technique for depths over 20 feet, is deep jigging using leadhead jigs, metal jigs, or the feather jig rig described in the section "Fishing Deep Water."

Whatever the tackle, it is quite common to catch small white perch. Because there are often large fish mixed in, this is a good opportunity to set up a livelining rig with a small white perch, spot, or legal-sized bluefish in hopes of taking a lunker striper or trout.

This striper was taken on a live eel.

Besides paying attention to fish and bird activity, it's also important to pay attention to boat activity. Caution is called for in these waters. Commercial and pleasure boat traffic is often heavy on weekends in summer and fall months. Moreover many of these structures lie near or between shipping channels, where cargo ships and barges moving at full speed create very large wakes that can build to dangerous waves as the displaced water hits the shelves. The unwary small boater can be swamped or flipped over, as veteran author Keith Walters relates in *Chesapeake Stripers.*

Within a few hours on a fall afternoon, we witnessed two near misses. In the first case, a party of trollers was busy watching their lines instead of where they were going—which was straight at a huge container ship going full speed on an easterly course across Brewerton Channel before turning north. When the container ship captain finally gave the warning of five short blasts, the captain of the troller barely had time to run to the wheel and turn off. As it was, his boat slid off the wake of the container ship in a near 45-degree angle. Later, returning to Baltimore Harbor, we watched the captain of a small boat run out of gas on one six-gallon tank and fumble around in the stern switching over to another. The problem was that this happened right at the junction of the Brewerton and Craighill Channels and the boat was bobbing around unpowered dangerously close to a large barge coming east across Brewerton Channel.

But these are not big waters, and they can be fished in good weather in relatively small boats. We have fished this area on calm fall weekdays in Harry Pippin's 17-foot Key West, launched from Dundee Creek or from Rocky Point. But generally a 19-foot or larger boat is preferable, especially when rougher weather or longer runs are involved.

The closest ramp for accessing the area is Rocky Point Park. This park provides free launching from a pair of double ramps that are in good condition, if somewhat shallow in slope. As soon as you clear the narrow cove of the ramp, you should begin to look around for signs of fish and boat activity, especially in the fall. Rocky Point is right at the junction of Back River and Middle River and behind the Hart-Miller Island complex. In the last few years, some very large stripers have been taken in these waters in the fall by trollers using shallow running lures, bucktails, plastics and spoons. Likewise, breaking fish are often seen in this area. Another advantage to the Rocky Point area is that the protected waters and closeness to the ramp provide ideal small boat opportunities.

Usually, we, like the guides, bypass this area unless we see signs of active fish and instead head straight out through the narrow channel south of Hart-Miller, getting into the area of the lumps within a few miles.

Launch Ramps

There are numerous ramps in Back River, Bear Creek, Middle River, Baltimore Harbor, or even Dundee Creek. The ramp we strongly recommend is Rocky Point Park, a free, 4-ramp facility sheltered behind Hart-Miller Island that provides great access to the heart of this area. (See the Baltimore hub city for further information on ramps and services.)

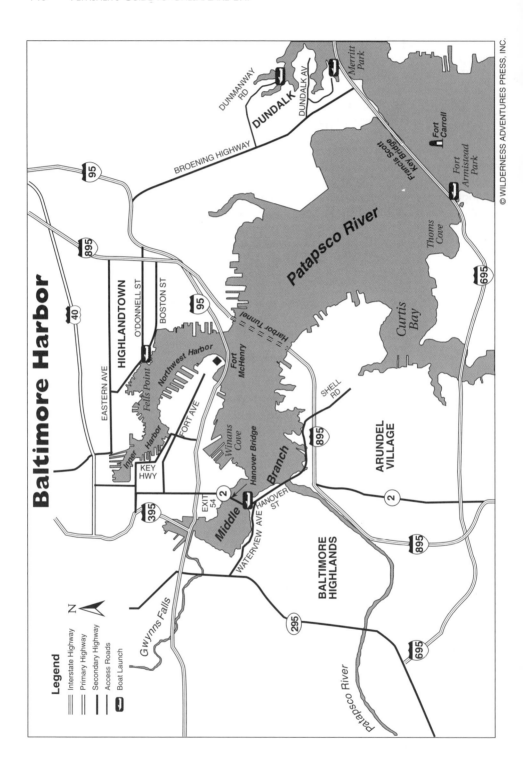

Baltimore Harbor

Fishing structure in Baltimore Harbor.

Baltimore Harbor

The six-mile stretch of the Patapsco River from Baltimore Harbor to the Key Bridge provides a tour of Baltimore history from the modern, revitalized Inner Harbor with its office buildings, major league baseball (Orioles) and football (Ravens) stadiums, and other tourist attractions on the northwest branch of the river to Baltimore's blue collar roots in shipping facilities, coal piers, and steel mills on the middle branch and farther south. At the junction of these branches lies Fort McHenry, "The birthplace of the Star Spangled Banner," and, perhaps of more importance to fishermen, the center of the striper fishery. While this is not the most scenic area, unless you're fond of shipyard cranes, loading docks, container ships, steel mills, and abandoned piers and warehouses, it provides plenty of stripers.

The striped bass range from 12 inches up to 12 pounds, with 16- to 24-inch fish predominating. White perch are also abundant, and some are quite large. We've taken white perch up to 15 inches on Clouser patterns intended for stripers. Gray trout arrive in early summer and linger until mid-fall. Bluefish, usually of the snapper variety, but in the 3- to 5-pound range some years, arrive in mid-summer and depart in early fall, as do small numbers of hardheads and spot. Channel catfish are year-round residents, as are pickerel, carp, and even an occasional largemouth bass in some of the feeder creeks like Marleys Creek. But stripers are the big attraction.

Good fishing begins in late June, peaks in October and November with more big fish and breaking fish, and remains good through December or January. From then through late March the stripers may hold near any of the several warmwater discharges above and below the Hanover Street Bridge.

Spring and early summer fishing is often hit or miss. Other than the concentrations at the warmwater discharges in winter, the fish appear to move often in the harbor area in response to the schools of bait; because of this, it is more fruitful to check out types of cover by casting and reading a depthfinder rather than seeking specific spots. However, much of the good fishing occurs in certain kinds of areas.

Finding structure in this area is not the problem; there's a ton of structure. The problem is finding fish-holding structure and, more importantly, active fish. You'll need to use your depthfinder as well as your eyes. The most productive pattern is fan casting against rocky shorelines and at points on the main branches and points within bays on a moving tide, especially an incoming tide. Look for shallows that taper off into deeper water. Prime targets are shipping berths in narrow bays with shallow flats and ripraps, jetties, rocky shorelines, or areas with broken chunks of concrete to attract and hold baitfish and stripers. Lesser targets are the tips of some piers and seawalls in shallow water with deeper waters nearby. Stripers trap the bait up against such shorelines and man-made objects and rip into baitfish, blue crabs, and grass shrimp.

Joe Bruce (right) displays a striper taken by Alan Feikin (left) on a Deceiver at Baltimore. The destroyers are no longer there, but the stripers still are.

The waters around the peninsula of Fort McHenry typify productive Baltimore Harbor structure. The waters are shallow, averaging about three feet deep against the seawall on all three sides. On the south side is a large hole six to nine feet deep that often holds good numbers of fish; farther out are a series of breaklines. Farther down that shore (west) toward the Hanover Street Bridge are a series of deep holes and humps by the piers of the South Locust Point Marine Terminal. Stair-step breaklines, holes, and mounds provide ambush points on the east and north sides.

Sunken boats and barges are other forms of productive structure found particularly on the southwest side of the Middle Branch. Several outlet pipes also attract bait and game fish along this shore. The northeast shore provides plenty of structure, such as the coal piers, and there is fish-holding structure scattered along this shore all the way into the Boston Street Ramp. (Shoreline fishermen do well, on occasions, from all three ramps.) Finally, look for currents and eddies that trap bait, particularly along abandoned piers.

Moving down the harbor toward the Bay, you'll encounter Fort Carroll (designed by Robert E. Lee while he was still with the U.S. Army) just past Key Bridge. While it's an inviting piece of structure, we've had little success here, and most regulars have had similar experiences.

But farther down on the southwest side lies Curtis Bay, which provides a repeat of the patterns described above: piers; shallow, rocky points; channels and drop-offs. You can continue south into Marleys Creek, where you'll encounter more freshwater species, including pickerel, perch, channel catfish, carp, and bass. Points and piers along the southwest side just as you enter Curtis Bay of the Patapsco have proven particularly productive.

Breaking fish are frequently seen in the shipping channels in the summer, including the channels at the mouth of Curtis Bay, usually stripers with bluefish mixed in, but these schools rarely hold sizeable stripers until late fall and winter. However, breaking fish working bait against shorelines and structure are always a good bet.

Tides are critical. The ideal period is about 3½ to 1½ hours before either high or low tide. If you can combine this with morning or evening low-light conditions, so much the better. Slack tides, cold fronts, and slack waters created by opposite pulls of tides and winds all shut down the fishing. Though tidal variances are minor, often less than a foot, if the water is not moving, fishing is generally poor.

Standard Bay fly tackle is the best choice, a 9-foot, 9-weight fly rod casting a fast-sinking line with a 4-foot leader of 16- to 20-pound monofilament, and a streamer and a 9-foot, 10-weight rod casting a floating line and an 8-foot leader tapering to 16 pounds with a popper. Reels need only sufficient capacity for the line and perhaps 100 yards of backing plus a dependable drag. While some anglers use lighter tackle, suited to the typical 16- to 24-inch fish, this strategy is questionable. Every year we take a good number of fish over 30 inches, often in the midst of barnacle-encrusted pilings and riprap. When one of these lunkers hits, you'll want enough rod and leader to lead him (or her) out of harm's way.

You only need a few streamer patterns to fish on the sinking lines, but size is important. Clouser Minnows, size 2/0 and 3 to 4 inches long for stripers and about 2

Baltimore Harbor to Marley Creek

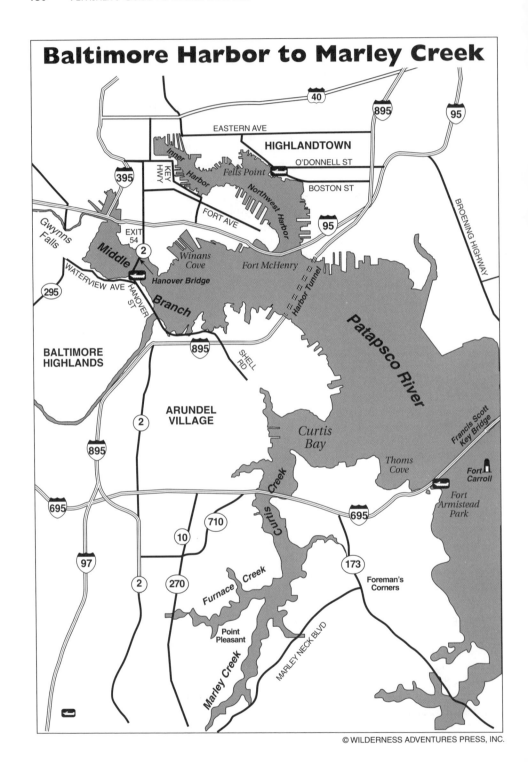

inches long on size 4 hooks for white perch, are the most effective patterns most of the time. Bruce's Crab Clouser, chartreuse over white and yellow over white are the top Clouser patterns. In the last few years Bruce's Bay Anchovy patterns tied on size 2 hooks, in streamer or Clouser-style, have often been the fly of choice in the summer. In late fall and winter, menhaden and white perch are often the stripers' menu choice. The 5- to 6-inch Lefty's Deceivers tied on size 2/0 hooks in Fisherman's Edge Lefty's Deceiver, chartreuse over white, or all white with a black topping are the flies of choice.

Typically, flies should be cast on fast-sinking lines right up against the structure or right up against the shoreline and retrieved fast; in fact, the ideal shoreline cast is right on top of a wave as it breaks against the shore or structure. The strike may come several yards out or even right at the boat, but you'll get far more strikes with presentations tight to cover.

Poppers fished on floating lines have been the best big striper lures when fished at dawn. The ideal situation is to be on the water before sunrise, especially in the fall, with an outgoing tide. Every year it seems the biggest fish are taken on poppers during this magic period. An overcast sky can prolong this time. We once pounded stripers up to 12 pounds for almost two hours on an overcast fall morning with Harry Pippin. Then fishing abruptly stopped. (We found fish suspended over a breakline in 15 to 20 feet of water, but they simply wouldn't hit.)

The Nite and Day Popper is the choice of most regulars, but any large popper can work. Make it look big with a splashy and fairly fast retrieve. Again throw it right up against the structure or the shoreline. While strikes may come 10 feet out, you need to put it in tight to trigger a strike.

For conventional tackle, we recommend medium-heavy 6- to 7-foot rods and 12- to 15-pound monofilament, preferably with a 2-foot section of 20-pound "bite leader." Since you can find yourself hauling large stripers from nasty cover, as described above, casting tackle is our first choice in these waters. Again, poppers fished at dawn and in overcast conditions have produced our best fish. Dropping down from the surface, shallow and intermediate running lures are the ticket. Jointed Rebels in the 3½- to 5½-inch sizes can be fished as surface and near-surface lures. The 4½-inch Windcheater is another effective shallow runner. The choices for intermediate running lures are ½- and ¾-ounce Rat-L-Traps, Bass Assasins, Fin-S-Fish, and other plastics fished on 3/8 and larger jigheads. Metal jigs have done well when dropped below breaking fish, especially in the fall. But for some reason we have not consistently done well in the harbor deep jigging when fish are not breaking, even when clearly over fish.

NIGHT FISHING

But there's another side to the fishery that's lesser known, even—until recently—to regulars, like us, who fish and write about this area: It's an excellent night fishery, with a kind of surreal "industrial beauty." (Okay, the harbor does look better at night.)

The tackle, lures, and flies are mostly the same at night in the harbor, but the

Author Bill May with a striper in Baltimore Harbor.

tactics change. However, most guides and experienced fishermen will tell you surface lures, with whatever tackle, are almost never effective for nighttime striper fishing.

Structure also changes at night. The number-one structure is lights—piers, docked ships, Maryland Port Authority cranes, streetlights, whatever; the more the better. If the lights coincide with ideal daytime structure like points or rocky shallows near deep water so much the better. But look for lights first; they draw the silversides, bay anchovies, baby hardheads, and white perch that the stripers and seatrout will feed on. (Bluefish and white perch may also be taken, but stripers and trout are the predominant night species.) However, don't go barging into the brightest spot right away. Often the largest game fish will be hanging on the faint edge of the light to ambush the baitfish from semi-darkness. Start at the edge and work your way into the brighter areas. Very often you will see the baitfish, and likewise you will see a striper rise to take your fly or lure. Casting into complete darkness near a bright area, such as in the dark area between the pilings of a brightly-lit pier, usually doesn't work, however.

Night fishing success calls for additional stealth, organization, and casting ability. Approach a fishing area quietly. Drifting is better than an electric motor, if possible, and try to avoid banging around in the boat or shining a flashlight on the water. Retrieves should be smooth—steady retrieves for conventional tackle, 1- to 1½-foot strips for flies. Fly casters should cast "on the oval." (Make the backcast wide of the body and the forward cast more overhand, and generally concentrate on smooth mechanics to avoid tangles.) Likewise, it's a good practice to have several flies already rigged on leaders with large loops at the end opposite the fly so a fly change can be made with a simple loop-to-loop connection rather than extensive retying. You may want to have several rods rigged, as well.

There's also a premium on safety. The Boston Street and Harbor Hospital ramps provide good launching facilities. The harbor always demands vigilance because of frequent floating debris, unlighted hazards, and the wakes of large ships. Although the harbor is fairly well lit at night, be aware of these obstacles, be observant, and moderate your pace, so you have time to avoid obstacles. Two particular threats are unlighted nun buoys marking the shipping channels and head-high cables mooring large shops to pilings away from a main pier.

Make sure you have warm enough clothing for the fall and winter fishery. We also recommend wearing the required life vest for night fishing.

You must also take care to be seen. In addition to the required nightlights on the boat and flares for emergencies, we also carry a powerful searchlight beam that can operate off one of the boat batteries.

We would never recommend you fish the harbor—or any other area—at night if you aren't familiar with it by day. Fishing a few hours late in the afternoon before an evening's fishing, even for veterans, makes night navigation easier.

Like freshwater bass, stripers seem to need about an hour to acclimate to the darkness and move to the new feeding grounds. So after dusk settles into night, we usually stow the daytime tackle, enjoy coffee and a sandwich, and leisurely motor to one of the lighted hotspots.

Maryland regulations allow for nighttime striper fishing, but even during periods when stripers may be kept, you may not come in after 9 p.m. with a striper in your possession. Fortunately for the catch-and-release crowd of regulars, that regulation represents no change.

WINTER FISHING

Winter fishing is wonderful some years and a non-event other years. While theories abound, most relate to the presence of baitfish or a "thermal barrier" being created by fast-dropping temperatures in early winter, no one really seems to know why winter fisheries are so variable. But like the little girl with the curl, when it's good, it's very good.

The Brandon Shores Power Plant, just southwest of the Key Bridge, is the best known and usually most productive of several warmwater discharges in the harbor. (Two of the others include the American Sugar refinery and one above and west of the Hanover Street Bridge.) Stripers, including some very large specimens, will often congregate in very shallow water in this area.

The fly tackle of choice is still the 9-foot rod in either a 9- or 10-weight, and the best line is usually an intermediate with a 4- to 8-foot leader. Big flies, 5- to 6-inch Lefty's Deceivers, white with a dark topping, are the flies of choice, but the Deceivers and Clousers used during the July through November period also work. Generally, a moderate speed retrieve works better than the fast retrieve of the regular season.

Conventional tackle is the same with the same shallow-running and intermediate lures. Shallow-running crankbaits and plastics on light jigheads are particularly good.

Safety is a prime concern in winter. Waters are often rough and water temperatures may drop into the thirties. These conditions call for substantial boats of at least 18 feet or more, and lend themselves to fishing with a partner—preferably with other boats around and while exercising the greatest caution. The nearest ramp to this area is the recently-improved Fort Armistead Park ramp, but we continue to hear problems of vandalism here.

Buildings and docks aren't the only structure you will find in Baltimore Harbor.

SAFE NAVIGATION

In good weather and calm conditions any stable 15- to 20-foot boat open for fly casting and with enough motor for short runs will do. (Larger boats can continue down the Patapsco to the main stem of Chesapeake Bay, near to such excellent areas as the Upper Bay lumps, holes, and channels and the Bay Bridge. The smaller the boat, the less the range.) Since fish in this area move around a lot, a good depthfinder is extremely helpful, and one with a temperature sensor is even better, since it helps you find outlet pipes. Use this tool to find fish to work but also to find patterns: what kind of structure the baitfish and predators are relating to. A suitably powerful electric motor is almost mandatory for moving into the shallows, working in among the piers, and holding boat position.

A number of jagged obstacles and the large wakes of container ships call for cautious boat handling, but the harbor is not really a dangerous area. (Once boats clear Key Bridge, they crank up and wakes are a more serious consideration.) However, there can be large amounts of floating debris, especially after heavy rains. Even when running in the channels, keep a sharp lookout and moderate your speed.

WADING

There are places in this area where you can wade and fish. We don't recommend it, though. The first reason is that in many areas there are a lot of things you don't want to step on, including such industrial remnants as sharp pieces of broken concrete, glass, rebar, boards with nails, and so on. The second reason is that some fishermen who have waded parts of the harbor have noticed that their waders deteriorated shortly afterwards; it seems the seam sealers tend to dissolve.

CATCH-AND-RELEASE

While we often recommend catch-and-release for the sake of the fish, here it's also recommended for the sake of the fishermen. The harbor waters are much cleaner than they were 20 years ago. Nevertheless, the Fairfield (Westport) area on the south shore is lined with chemical plants, and it appears there may be significant land, water, and air pollution problems. Admittedly, most of the fish in these waters move in and out from the main body of the Bay, but we do not recommend eating any fish from these waters.

GETTING THERE

Baltimore is a major tourist attraction, worthy of a book in its own right. If you're in town for business, tourism, or attending a sporting event, staying in the Inner Harbor area, with its easy walking access to a variety of attractions, is the best bet. The guides in this area offer full-day, half-day and evening trips, so harbor area fishing could be a good way to round out a visit.

If you do want to bring your own boat and engage in some of the other activities listed above, staying in the Inner Harbor or downtown areas is probably not an option, since you'd have a difficult to impossible task in finding parking. However, you could find accommodations outside this immediate area where you could bring a boat. Fortunately, there are several excellent guides fishing Baltimore Harbor regularly.

Fishing in this area can be outstanding at times, and the area is accessible via major interstates. Whether you visit the area for fishing only or for the whole tourist bit, it's worth the trip.

Bill May gets ready to release a small striper.

Hub City for Baltimore Harbor
Baltimore
Population of Baltimore—651,154
Population of greater Baltimore area—2,552,994

Baltimore Inner Harbor Shopping and Tourist Areas, Science Museum, National Aquarium, Major League Baseball and Football Stadiums, Fort McHenry, and many other historic sites.

ACCOMMODATIONS

Admiral Fell Inn, 888 S. Broadway; 410-522-7377
Baltimore Marriott Inner Harbor, 110 S. Eutaw Street; 800-228-9280
Brookshire Inner Harbor Suite Hotel, 120 E. Lombard Street; 410-625-1300
Days Inn Inner Harbor, 100 Hopkins Place; 800-942-7543
Pier 5 Hotel, 711 Eastern Avenue; 866-226-9330
Henderson's Wharf Inn & Marina, 1000 Fell Street; 800-522-2088
OMNI Inner Harbor Hotel, 101 W. Fayette Street; 800-THE-OMNI
Sheraton Inner Harbor Hotel, 300 S. Charles Street; 800-325-3535
Stouffer Harborplace Hotel, 202 E. Pratt Street; 800-HOTELS-1
The Inn at Fell's Point, 1718 Thames Street; 410-276-8252
Radisson Plaza Hotel Baltimore Inner Harbor, 20 W. Baltimore Street; 410-539-8400
Harbor Court Hotel, 550 Light Street; 410-234-0550
Marriott Baltimore Waterfront, 700 Aliceanna Street; 410-385-3000
Marriott Baltimore Inner Harbor, 110 S. Eutaw Street; 410-962-0202
Courtyard Baltimore Downtown, 1000 Aliceanna Street; 410-923-4000
Tremont Plaza Hotel, 222 St. Paul Place; 410-727-2222
Wyndham Baltimore Inner Harbor, 101 W. Fayette Street; 410-727-2000
Hilton Baltimore and Towers/Radisson Plaza, 20 West Baltimore Street; 410-539-8400
Renaissance Harborplace Hotel, 202 E. Pratt Street; 410-547-1200
Holiday Inn Baltimore-Inner Harbor Hotel, 301 W. Lombard Street; 410-685-3500

CAMPGROUNDS AND STATE PARKS

There are no campgrounds or state parks in the immediate Baltimore area. However, the following are reasonably close by. The best bet for camping is Patapsco.

Gunpowder Falls State Park, offers some very limited camping and cabin rental; Mill Pond Cottage is worth asking about; contact Gunpowder Falls State Park, P.O. Box 480, 2813 Jerusalem Road, Kingsville, MD, 21087; 410-592-2897; call 888-432-CAMP(2267) for reservations
Patapsco Valley State Park ,offers camping in several park areas; contact Patapsco Valley State Park, 8020 Baltimore National Pike, Ellicott City, MD 21043; 410-461-5005; call 888-432-CAMP(2267) for reservations

RESTAURANTS

McCormick & Schmick's, 711 Eastern Avenue; 410-234-1300
Phillips, Light Street Pavilion; 410-685-6600
Pisces, 300 Light Street; 410-605-2835
Rusty Scupper, 402 Key Highway; 410-727-3678
O'Brycikis Crab House, 1727 East Pratt Street; 410-732-6399
Bohager's Bar and Grill, 515 South Eden Street; 410-563-7220
Chiapparelli's, 237 S. High Street; 410-837-0309
Della Notte, 801 Eastern Avenue; 410-837-5500
Dalesio's of Little Italy, 829 Eastern Avenue; 410-539-1965
Tio Pepe, 10 E. Franklin Street; 410-539-4675
Admiral Fell Inn, 888 South Broadway; 410- 522-7377
Aldo's Ristorante, 306 South High Street; 410-727-0700
Atlantic Restaurant, 2400 Boston Street; 410-675-4565
The Brass Elephant, 924 N. Charles Street; 410-547-8485
Caesars Den, 223 South High Street Little Italy; 410-547-0820
Cafe Bombay, 114 East Lombard Street; 410-381-7111
The Cheesecake Factory, 201 East Pratt Street; 410-234-0990
J. Paul's, Harborplace, Light Street Pavilion, 1st Level; 410-659-1889
Morton's, 300 S. Charles Street; 410-547-8255
The Prime Rib, 1101 N. Calvert Street; 410-539-1804

FLY SHOPS, TACKLE STORES, AND SPORTING GOODS

Fisherman's Edge, 1719-1/2 Edmondson Avenue; 410-719-7999
Tochterman's Fishing Tackle, 1925 Eastern Avenue; 410-327-6942
Fishin' Shop, 9026 C Pulaski Highway; 410-391-0101
Upstream Angler, 9191 Baltimore National Pike; 410-465-1112
Clyde's Sport Shop, 2307 Hammonds Ferry Road; 410-242-6108
Set's Sport Shop, 509 York Road, Towson; 410-823-1367
Dick's Sporting Goods, 5220 Campbell Blvd.; 410-933-0134
Sports Authority, 6510 Baltimore National Pike; 410-788-9650

FLY AND LIGHT-TACKLE GUIDES

Norm Bartlett, 410-679-8790
Gary Neitzey, 410-557-8801
Tom Hughes, 410-747-9431

MARINAS (BALTIMORE AND SURROUNDING BALTIMORE COUNTY)

Baltimore Marine Center, 2701 Boston Street; 410-675-8888
Bowley's Quarter Marina, 1700 Bowleys Quarters Road, Middle River; 410-335-3553
Swann's Wharf Marina, 1001 Fell Street; 410-342-1111
Anchor Bay East Marina, 8500 Cove Road; 410-284-1044
Anchorage Marina, 2501 Boston Street; 410-522-7200
Anderson Bros. Boat Sales, 2434 Holley Neck Road; 410-574-8281
Boating Center of Baltimore, 2015 Turkey Point Road; 410-687-2000

Buedel's Marina & Boatyard, 1907 Old Eastern Avenue, Essex; 410-687-3577
Center Dock Marina, 802 S. Caroline Street; 410-685-9055
Baltimore Yacht Basin, 2600 Insulator Drive; 410-539-8895
Cutter Marine Yacht Basin, 1900 Old Eastern Avenue; 410-391-6482
Deckelman's Boat Yard, 201 Oak Avenue, Essex; 410-391-6482
Essex Marina Boat Yard, 1755 Hilltop Avenue, Essex; 410-687-6149
Harborview Marina, 500 Harborview Drive; 410-752-1122
Henderson's Wharf Inn & Marina, 1000 Fell Street; 410-522-7900
Long Beach Marina, 800 Chester Road, Middle River; 410-335-8602
Lynch Cove Marina, 1915 Willis Road; 410-288-1332
Maryland Marina, Bowleys Quarter Road, Chase; 410-335-8722
Markel's Boat Yard, 7745 N. Point Creek Road; 410-477-3445
Markley's Marina, 233 Nanticoke Road, Essex; 410-687-5575
Middle Branch Marina, 3101 Waterview Avenue; 410-539-2628
Norman Creek Marina, 2229 Corsica Road, Essex; 410-686-9343
Porter's Seneca Park Marina, 918 Seneca Park Road; 410-335-6563
Riley's Marina, 1901 Old Eastern Avenue, Essex; 410-686-0771
Riverside Inn & Marina, 1106 E Riverside Drive, Essex; 410-574-5292
River Watch Restaurant/Marina, 207 Nanticoke Road, Essex; 410-687-1422
Rudy's Marina, Wise Ave. Ext.; 410-477-3276
Sheltered Harbor Marina, 8100 Stansbury Road; 410-288-4100
Sparrows Point Country Club, 919 Wise Avenue; 410-477-1500
Sunset Harbor Marina, 1651 Browns Road; 410-687-7290
Stansbury Yacht Basin, 1600 Martin Blvd.; 410-686-3909
Tradewinds Marina, 412 Armstrong Road; 410-335-7000
Weaver's Marine Service, 730 Riverside Drive; 410-686-4944
West Shore Yacht Center, 1100 E. Riverside Avenue, Essex; 410-686-6998

BOAT EQUIPMENT AND REPAIR
BOAT-US Marine Supply, 6863 Loch Raven Blvd.; 410-296-0451
E & B Marine Supply, 8302 Pulaski Hwy, Rosedale; 410-574-7770
Marine Venture Enterprises, 4520 O'Donnell St.; 410-563-3885
Marle Industries, P.O. Box 878, Jessup; 410-799-7739

RECOMMENDED LAUNCH RAMPS
Upper Bay Lumps: There are numerous ramps on Back River, Bear Creek, Middle River, Baltimore Harbor, or even Dundee Creek. The ramp we strongly recommend is Rocky Point Park, a free, 4-ramp facility sheltered behind Hart-Miller Island that provides great access to the heart of this area. The ramp is reached by taking the Baltimore Beltway, I-695, to Maryland Rt. 702, which merges into Back River Neck Road, then left at the sign on Barrison Point Road, and right at the sign on Rocky Point Road.

RECOMMENDED LAUNCH RAMPS, CONTINUED

Baltimore Harbor—Harbor Hospital Ramp (Middlebranch-Broening Park): The Harbor area is easily accessible via several good ramps. Two double ramps are found at the base of the Hanover Street Bridge, next to Harbor Hospital. The state of Maryland refers to this area as Middlebranch-Broening Park; everyone else refers to this ramp as Harbor Hospital ramp. (This hospital adjoins the parking area.) This ramp can be accessed from I-95 North by taking Exit 54, crossing the bridge, and taking an immediate left or by taking I-895, the Harbor Tunnel Throughway, south through the tunnel to Exit 7 to Route 2 north and turning right into the launch area just before crossing the bridge.

Baltimore Harbor—Boston Street: Another excellent ramp is located at Boston Street in the Fells Point area, just at the foot of East Street, site of the Korean War Memorial. (Officially, it's Canton Waterfront Park.) Taking the Eastern Avenue or O'Donnell Street Exits east off I-95, I-895, or I-695 will put you on East Street. Both ramps are free and open 24 hours.

Baltimore Harbor—Other: Ramps with more limited hours can be located off I-695 at the foot of the Key Bridge at Fort Armistead Park and at Merritt Park off Merritt Boulevard. While we have never experienced any problems, we have heard reports of vandalism at the Harbor Hospital Ramp. However, with the hospital nearby, police and other vehicles are often in the area, problems are rare. The Boston Street Ramp is likewise frequently patrolled. There have also been some problems reported at the Fort Armistead Ramp. But this ramp is much closer to the Brandon Shores Power Plant and can save you eight miles of running through the cold weather.

AIRPORTS

Baltimore-Washington International Airport, P.O. Box 8766, BWI Airport, Baltimore; 800-I-FLY-BWI

Washington Dulles International Airport, Washington; 703-572-2700, fax: 703-572-6817

Ronald Reagan Washington National Airport, Washington; 703-417-3500

AUTO REPAIR

A-1 Automotive & Light Truck Repair, 3041 Frederick Avenue; 410-566-5878

AAA Auto Care & Diagnostic Center, 1316 Ingleside Ave.; 410-944-4357

D & J Auto Care, 1100 W. 41st Street; 410-889-6536

Fells Point Auto Repair, 1500 Eastern Avenue; 410-675-1525

HOSPITALS

(Baltimore is a major medical center featuring several world-renowned medical institutions.)

Bon Secours Hospital, 2000 West Baltimore Street; 410-362-3000

Franklin Square Hospital, 9000 Franklin Square Drive; 410-682-7000

Good Samaritan Hospital, 5601 Loch Raven Blvd.; 410-532-8000

Harbor Hospital Center, 3001 S. Hanover Street

Johns Hopkins Medical Center, 600 N. Wolfe Street; 410-955-5000

Maryland General Hospital, 827 Linden Avenue; 410-225-8000
St. Agnes Hospital, 900 Canton Avenue; 410-368-6000
Sinai Hospital, 2401 W. Belvedere Avenue; 410-601-9000
Union Memorial Hospital, 201 E. University Pkwy.; 410-554-2000

MAPS

Charts of the Chesapeake, produced by the editors of *Chesapeake Bay Magazine*, provides particularly detailed maps of this area on pages 31-33; this book is the bible of most harbor regulars. It's available at most tackle shops.

OTHER ATTRACTIONS

UPPER BAY LUMPS—This area is more a fishing area than a destination stop, but there are some amenities:

Rocky Point Park and Beach, 410-887-0338; office, 410-887-3873 to reserve facilities; this is just past the ramp entrance; there is a fee during the summer season; offers swimming, playgrounds, picnic grounds, sailing instructions, pavilions and tent areas.

Rocky Point Golf Course, 410-887-0215, is an 18-hole county course off Back River Neck Road

Ballestone Manor, 410-887-0217 or 410-887-0218, is an 18th century farm manor, also on Back River Neck Road

BALTIMORE—The Baltimore Inner Harbor is a great place to explore by foot, shuttle bus, or harbor water taxi or shuttle.

Harbor Shuttle (water), 410-675-2900
Water Taxi, Harbor Boating, Inc. (water) 410-563-3901 or 800-658-8947; www.thewatertaxi.com
Maryland Tours, shuttle bus with narrator, 410-685-4288
Maryland Science Center and Davis Planetarium, 601 Light St.; 410-685-5225
The National Aquarium, Pier 3, 501 E. Pratt St.; 410-576-3800; www.aqua.org
U. S. Frigate Constellation, Pier 1, Pratt St.; 410-539-1797
Baltimore Maritime Museum, Piers 3 &5 Pratt St.; 410-396-3453; www.baltomaritimemuseum.org
Fort McHenry, end of E. Fort St.; 410-962-4290; www.nps.gov/fomc
B & O Railroad Museum, 901 W. Pratt St.; 410-752-2490; www.borail.org

FOR FURTHER INFORMATION

Baltimore Guide Services and Tourist Information, 301 East Pratt Street, Baltimore, MD 21201; 410-837-4636 or 800-282-6632

Baltimore Area Convention and Visitors Association, 100 Light Street, Baltimore, MD 21201; 800-343-3468 or 410-659-7300

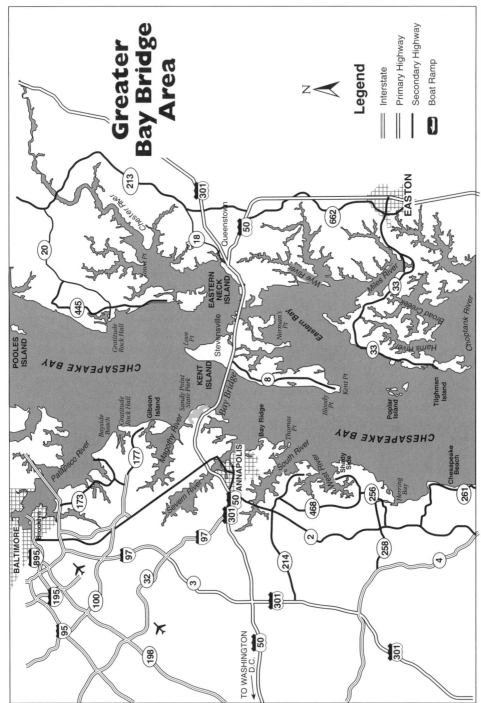

Greater
Bay Bridge
Area

Legend
Interstate
Primary Highway
Secondary Highway
Boat Ramp

Greater Bay Bridge Area

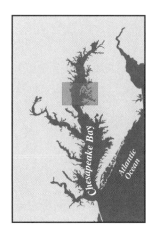

The Chesapeake Bay Bridge, a pair of parallel 4-mile spans connecting the Western Shore with Kent Island on the Eastern Shore, provides fish-attracting and holding structure from early May through the end of the year. Though not as intensively fished as it was from the mid-1960s through the late 80s before the moratorium, when the concentration of chummers, jiggers, and, unfortunately, snaggers was sometimes so dense it seemed possible to cross the Bay by jumping from boat to boat, it still is a popular and productive piece of structure.

Fishing generally begins in May, with school-sized stripers migrating up the Bay to join similarly sized stripers plus solitary, large stripers dropping down the Bay from such spawning grounds as the Susquehanna and Chester Rivers. White perch are usually right behind the striper migrations.

These early fish will often be in the warmer waters of the top 15 feet of the water column but could be at any depth. Since they're roaming and feeding, the first task is to locate them. Eastern Shore fly and light-tackle guide Richie Gaines relates that his first approach is to head directly to the Eastern Shore Rock Pile (Piling #28, on the southern span), which sits in about 50 feet of water. If he spots bay anchovies, visually or on the depthfinder, his confidence soars. But in any case, he works this structure from top to bottom, paying special attention to the corners of the pile.

In the old days mentioned above, dropping large, big-eyed bucktail jigs, some 2 to 4 ounces and often up to a foot long with large pork rinds or such plastics as Sassy Shads attached, was the preferred method. Such tactics are still used with some success. But with the prevalence of small bait in the Bay, Gaines prefers his custom feather jig rig described earlier in the "Deep Jigging" section. As described there, this rig allows an angler to explore the entire water column from bottom to top. (You could do similar explorations with a standard deep jigging approach; single hook, and homemade versions may be the choice in this snaggy environment.) Gaines will also use a jighead and plastic, such as a Bass Assassin, for exploring structure 20 feet deep or less.

But as Gaines points out, the stripers aren't always hanging right against the pilings waiting for you to come by and drop them a lure—although that's usually the first and highest percentage approach. The fish can still be relating to the structure but be located well away from the pilings. Nor are they always deep. Besides the tendency to hang in the top 15 feet of the water in early spring, they will also tend to be near the surface at predawn, dawn, and dusk in summer through fall.

Shade is another form of cover and always one worth exploring. One classic example is the wooden overhang about three feet above the water on a number of pilings between the Eastern Shore Stone Pile and the Western Shore Stone Pile.

Fishing between the spans of the Chesapeake Bay Bridge.

Stripers often suspend just beneath the surface all along this structure, and you can actually see them. Making an uptide cast with a streamer on a sinking line or a bucktail or jig and plastic on conventional tackle and swinging the fly or lure to the fish is the winning technique for these areas.

Besides noting the presence and activities of other boats, looking for fish and bait in the water or on the depthfinder, looking for temperature differences on an electronic sensor, and looking for light and shadow, the pattern of current around the pilings also gives indications of possible holding areas. Note the way the currents rip and swirl around the pilings and take special note of large, flat, slick areas downcurrent that often indicate prime fish holding water. The classic advice of "the last two hours before high tide and the last two hours of low tide" often applies, and some anglers feel ebbing tides are preferable at the Bay Bridge.

Since he's coming from the Eastern Shore side, Gaines will usually hit the Eastern Shore Stone Pile, work his way over to the Western Shore Stone Pile, then return to the Eastern Shore Stone Pile and begin working his way in along the pilings toward the Eastern Shore (Kent Island). He'll study the depthfinder for fish, bait, breaklines (like channel edges), and he'll scan the surface for bait, fish, and patterns of current. Gaines recommends pilings on the north span of the Bay Bridge on the Eastern Shore side, particularly pilings with the most current on breaklines.

Just north of the bridge and coming off the Eastern Shore is a rock-covered outlet pipe that forms, in effect, an underwater jetty, with a depth of 12 to 20 feet. The edges of this pipe are marked by a pair of buoys. This area almost always holds fish.

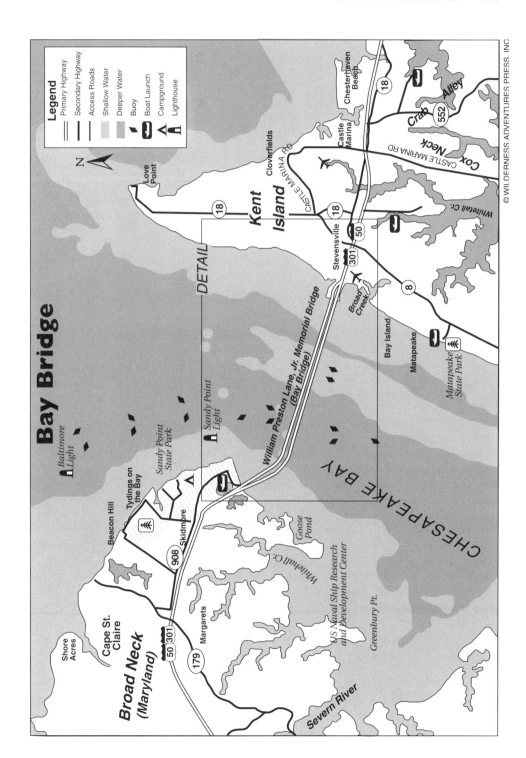

Bay Bridge

Legend
Primary Highway
Secondary Highway
Access Roads
Shallow Water
Deeper Water
Buoy
Boat Launch
Campground
Lighthouse

N

Love Point

Kent Island

Cloverfields

Castle Marina

Chesterhaven Beach

18

552

Crab Alley

Cox Neck

CASTLE MARINA RD

Whitetail Cr.

18

Stevensville

50

301

8

DETAIL

Broad Creek

Bay Island

Matapeake

Matapeake State Park

William Preston Lane, Jr. Memorial Bridge (Bay Bridge)

CHESAPEAKE BAY

Baltimore Light

Sandy Point State Park

Sandy Point Light

Beacon Hill

Tydings on the Bay

Skidmore

908

Goose Pond

Whitetall Cr.

US Naval Ship Research and Development Center

Greenbury Pt.

Shore Acres

Cape St. Claire

Broad Neck (Maryland)

50 301

Margarets

179

Severn River

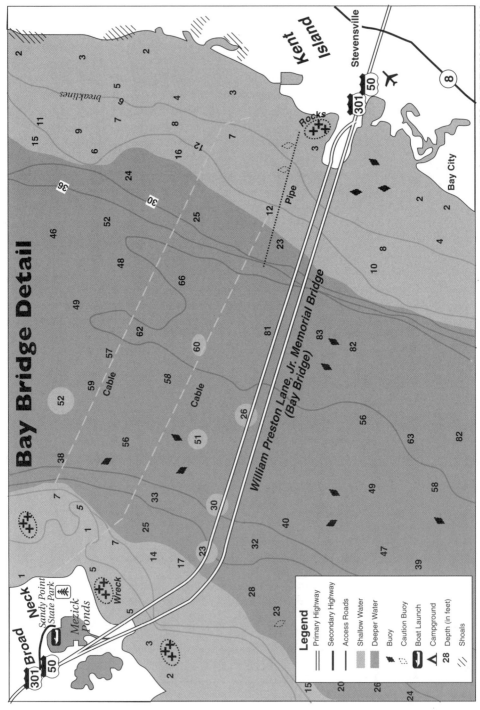

Again, this is best fished with an upcurrent presentation that swings the fly or lure to the fish.

Anglers coming from the Western Shore, usually launching at Sandy Point State Park, may and often do follow a reverse process: starting at the Western Shore Stone Pile and working their way over to the Eastern Shore Stone Pile, then returning to the Western Shore Stone Pile and working their way back in along the pilings to the Western Shore.

Since the fish are often moving, returning to either of the major stone piles is worth trying; you may strike out one time and strike it rich the next. Of course, because there will be other anglers at the bridges, you will need to modify your approaches accordingly. One could easily spend a full day working the Bay Bridge area.

Some Bay Bridge regulars work this area from May through the end of the year, usually aiming to work the predawn bite, which can include surface action on poppers at times.

Richie Gaines recommends the Bay Bridge area from early May through the third week of June, then again from August to November or December. He offers this rough chronology for the latter part of the year: In August and September, school-sized stripers, plus white perch, hardheads, and bluefish are in the area. Most fishing is deep except for dawn and dusk. By October the blues will be moving out, the gray trout will be moving in. Bigger stripers of 6- to 10-pounds will appear, and they can be caught in shallower water. By November the blues and hardheads are gone, trout will be schooled up solid and can be targeted, and some big, solitary stripers will be found. By Thanksgiving, the trout and small and medium stripers depart, but groups

Fishing the Chesapeake Bay Bridge.

Working the rocks near the Bay Bridge.

of big (36 inches and more) ocean-run stripers arrive for a brief stay. These fish appear to be feeding on large bay anchovies and the remnants of the smaller stripers and trout. They often travel in "rat packs" of 15 to 20 fish, and their presence may be indicated by small groups of birds and by surface swirls.

The feather jig rig and other deep jigging approaches are probably the best way to find fish, and offer one of the most effective ways to fish the bridges. Once fish are located, as long as they're not glued to the bottom in deep water, they may also be fished for successfully by upcurrent or downcurrent swinging techniques with fly, spin, or casting tackle. Boat handling is critical with either approach.

There are a number of wild theories about multiple tides in this area. Most guides feel the explanation is simpler: There's a lot of water moving through this "necked down" area of the Bay in roughly north and south directions. When the tide changes, the water doesn't simply stop and reverse course; there's usually a delay of up to two hours. (We're not counting the wind and other unusual weather conditions here.) So, for example, if a low tide is listed at noon at the Bay Bridge, the tide would begin coming in and the water rising, but the current would continue running south for as much as two hours, losing force as time passes before switching north.

In the upcurrent approach, the boat is held behind and slightly to the side of the second piling downcurrent and the lure cast above and just to the side of the first piling upcurrent and swum along both pilings and the underwater structure back to the boat. The fly or lure should be swung along the pilings, not directly attacking the fish. Count down different drops (5, 10, 15, 20 seconds) in successive casts until you locate fish and then retrieve with a slightly jigging, twitching retrieve, though sometimes a near dead drift is better. Always maintain enough tension on the fly or lure to be able to detect strikes and set the hook. With conventional tackle, spinning may have a slight advantage here, because of the constant retrieving.

The downcurrent approach is a parallel but opposite technique. The boat is held upcurrent and to the side of the first piling downcurrent. The fly or lure is cast nearly against the first piling and allowed to swing downcurrent along both pilings and the connecting structures by playing out line while the lure swings and sinks. With conventional tackle, casting is preferred, with the rod held in the non-dominant hand (the hand that you do not reel with) with the thumb resting lightly on the spool and line freelspooled to create the drift. When a fish hits, the reel is instantly engaged, and the hook set with the rod.

With fly tackle, sufficient line is stripped off the reel to allow the farthest end of the drift retrieve, not the cast. Once the cast is made, loose line is released by shaking the rod tip, if necessary, while letting the line slip through the circle created by the thumb and forefinger of the line hand. When a fish hits, grasp the free line and strike with the rod.

Because Bay Bridge fishing may involve some hefty fish and will definitely involve yanking fish from cover and through crowded conditions, we lean toward heavier tackle here. For fly fishing, the 10-weight with the 350- to 450-grain fast-sinking line is the choice. A 9-weight with a 300- to 350-grain sinker is the minimum. Standard flies to match the prevalent baits, such as Bay Anchovy and Silverside and Glass Minnow patterns and Clouser and Deceiver patterns in 2- to 6-inch lengths and shrimp patterns, are the best choices. Eel patterns may be considered from midsummer on.

For conventional tackle, we recommend medium, or better yet, medium-heavy casting and spinning tackle with reels with good drags and fish-fighting characteristics and lines of 14- to 20-pound test. Metal deep jigging lures, bucktails, jighead and plastic combinations, poppers and swimmers should all be in the angler's arsenal.

If you care for baitfishing this area, the same medium-heavy casting or spinning tackle is the choice. Eeling and livelining can be very effective at times, especially toward dusk. Chunking with cut menhaden, spot, bluefish, and the like can be effective. You can also fish various bottom rigs baited with shrimp, squid, or bloodworms for abundant white perch throughout the season and for croaker from dusk through midnight in midsummer.

ADJACENT AREAS

There are a number of other fish-holding structures in the general area of the Bay Bridge that provide fly and light-tackle opportunities. North of the bridge on the Western Shore, Baltimore Light, outside Gibson Island and Sandy Point Light offer rocky structure with adjacent deep water. South of the bridge on the same side lies Thomas Point Light, offering the same kind of structure. North of Thomas Point, Tolly Bar, at the mouth of the Severn River is a classic bar structure. South of Thomas Point, off the mouth of the West River is a large flat, known as the "Wild Grounds." This 20- to 30-foot channel edge holds big stripers in May and June many years, and it can be successfully fished by drifting and deep jigging or it can be fished with drifting and chunking bait methods.

Farther south below Kent Island on the Eastern Shore side Poplar Island and Poplar Island Flats offers large expanses of rocky riprap that attract and hold game fish and panfish.

SAFETY CONSIDERATIONS

This whole area is big water, with a lot of boat traffic and a lot of things to hit. While all right-thinking anglers know bridge pilings and channels are meant for our use and to attract fish, some of your fellow boaters—including supertankers and charter boats on trolling runs—may have other ideas. While we have crossed the Bay in a 15-foot aluminum boat, we do not recommend it. These waters call for boats of at least 18 feet and over 20 feet is preferable. As mentioned earlier, boat-handling skills and knowledge of the boating "rules of the road" are at a premium, and courtesy and safety should be the first order. There are plenty of people doing stupid things in boats near the Bay Bridge; we feel their ranks need no further additions.

LAUNCH RAMPS

The Chesapeake Bay Bridge can be accessed from a number of ramps on the Western Shore. The closest ramp, which also provides the best facilities, is Sandy Point State Park, which features 22 ramps and over 900 parking spaces. It also provides fishing and crabbing licenses, restrooms, ice, bait, tackle, boat rentals, and fuel. The ramps put you on well-protected Mezick Pond, a marsh pond just northwest of the bridge. Once you clear the rock jetty at the mouth of the pond, you are right at the western side of the bridge. Sandy Point State Park is reached by taking Exit #32 North off Maryland Rt. 50. There is an entry fee to the launch ramp, but once you enter the park, you have access to all facilities. This also includes picnic tables, grills, and a beach on Chesapeake Bay that has lifeguards on duty from Memorial Day through Labor Day.

A number of ramps on Kent Island provide access to the Chesapeake Bay Bridge from the east side. Use of these ramps requires purchase of an annual Queen Anne County Boat Ramp Permit. The exception is the closest ramp, Matapeake State Park. A drop box system is in place here. Matapeake provides a single ramp, 50 parking spaces, ice, bait, fuel, and restrooms. Matapeake State Park is reached by taking Maryland Rt. 8 south off Rt 50/301, then turning right into the park.

BOAT RENTALS

This is one of the few areas of Maryland's portion of the Chesapeake Bay offering rental boats. Sandy Point has a fleet of 18 rentals: 16-foot skiffs powered by 7.5-horsepower motors. They're available on a first come, first served basis from April 15 through October 31. Persons born after July 1, 1972 must have and display a certificate of having passed a boating safety course. Call the Marine Manager at 410-974-2149 for further details.

Bay Bridge Area Rivers, Eastern Shore

Kent Narrows and the Chester River

Kent Narrows is a narrow channel between the Chester River on the north and Eastern Bay on the south that separates Kent Island from the mainland of the Eastern Shore of Maryland. All of these waters provide the fly and light-tackle fisherman outstanding opportunities for diverse species. In addition, these waters arguably offer the best of the limited opportunities in Maryland's Chesapeake for wading or small boat fishermen.

For ease of organization, we shall deal with the Narrows and Chester River in one section and Eastern Bay and Wye River as another, but, in fact, these—and even the Bay Bridge—are connected and related fisheries.

Fishing at Kent Narrows and Chester River begins in early June and, like the Bay Bridge, can continue through to nearly the end of the year. The difference is that these waters offer more of a year-round shallow water fishery. The same migrating and post-spawn fish arrive in this area in May, but as of this writing, the Chester River, as a recognized striper spawning ground, is off limits for all fishing, even catch-and-release fishing, until June 1.

Six ramps on Kent Island, as well as several private ramps on the eastern side of Kent Narrows, provide access to Kent Narrows.

A good spot to fish is on the south end of Kent Narrows on an outgoing tide.

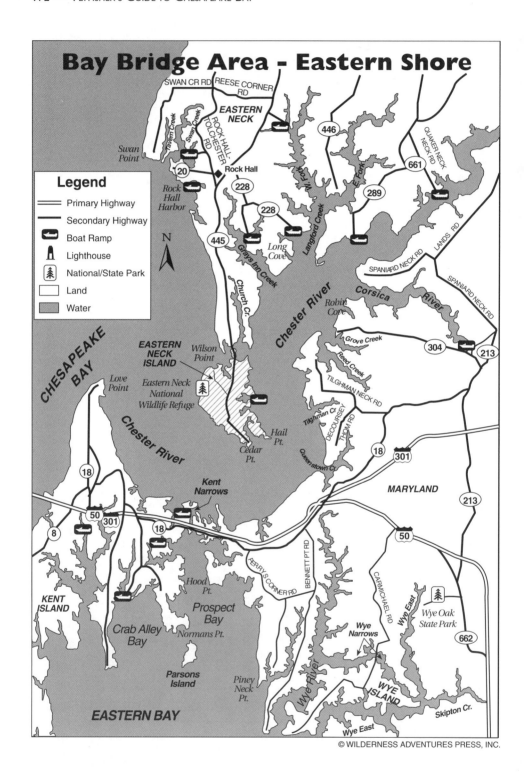

Bay Bridge Area - Eastern Shore

For those who know the area well, there are also some good wading possibilities, but most still require a boat for access to these areas, and there are some treacherous drop-offs.

Some of the best fishing is found at Kent Narrows, the roughly 100-yard wide channel between the Chester River on the north and Prospect Bay, a subsection of Eastern Bay, directly to the south. With strong currents and the resulting humps, holes, and ledges, this is a dependable fishery from May through the end of the year, even in the heat of summer. The best time is usually early morning, when boat traffic is light, and tides are not running too fast. It's also a terrific night fishery in the summer through late fall.

There are two downsides: Everybody knows about this fishery, and boat traffic through this channel is intense at times. But there are a number of rips and edges in water from 3 to 20 feet. If you can beat the crowds, with early morning, evening, or weekday fishing, this area can be counted on for good fishing. Like much of the Eastern Bay area, there's a lot of cover and the fish move. Sometimes they'll be along the channel edges, sometimes relating to the bridge pilings, on the bottom, suspended near the top, and so on. You need to watch the depthfinder and explore the water by fan casting until you find the fish.

The classic way to fish the Narrows is to work the edges with streamer flies on sinking lines or with bucktails or jigs and plastics on conventional tackle. With two bridges and lots of channel edges, holes, bars and lumps, one could easily spend a half-day working the immediate Kent Narrows waters.

This is another area where a good, bow-mounted electric motor can be invaluable for positioning and holding the boat.

Once clear of the Narrows, and beginning June 1, you can work northwest along the shoreline and drop-offs of Kent Island all the way to the mouth of the Chester River at Love Point, the northern tip of Kent Island. Then you could work out to Chester River Light, a big rock pile at the mouth of the river that is an early season stop-off point for big, spawning stripers working their way out of Chester River or down the Bay from Susquehanna Flats.

At this point you can cross the river and work your way back along the shoreline and rock piles of Eastern Neck Island, home of Eastern Neck Island National Wildlife Refuge. There are plenty of drop-offs and shelves along both of these shorelines, with shallower drop-offs along the Eastern Neck Island side. Eastern Neck Island can also be accessed by land from the north, and this is an excellent and safe wading area, offering good fishing in spring and fall and during low-light periods in summer.

Or you could turn northeast, fishing both sides of the river all the way up the east side to the Corsica River, which also offers largemouth bass and some pickerel in addition to the saltwater species, and all the way up the west side including the small bays and creeks such as Grays and Langfords Creeks.

The primary species in these waters are stripers and white perch. You can also expect some bluefish, croaker, and spot in summer and gray trout in late September through mid-November. Most of these latter species will be incidental catches. Breaking fish are common in this area from midsummer on and can be expected most days in the fall.

While Bay-standard boats and tackle will work in Kent Narrows and Chester River, you can get by with a lot less. Boats of 14 to 16 feet with motors of 10 to 30 horsepower, preferably with bow-mounted electric motors, are fine for the area immediately around Kent Narrows on both the Chester and Eastern Bay sides and for the upper (eastern) areas of the Chester above the Hells Delight area. Fly rods as light as 7-weight may be used (although they are not a good idea for poppers), and medium casting or spinning tackle with 10- and 12-pound test lines will suffice.

While the central channel of the Chester is over 60 feet deep at points, much of the Chester offers shallow water fishing in the 3- to 6-foot range, dropping to depths of 20 feet. Our recommended 9-foot, 9-weight fly rod is fine here, with poppers on a floating line and a 300- to 350-grain fast-sinking line. Because of the shallow shelf fishing possibilities, sink-tip lines and/or intermediate sinking lines may be good choices, too.

The standard flies to match the prevalent baits, such as Bay Anchovy, Silverside, and Glass Minnow patterns and Clouser and Deceiver patterns in 2- to 6-inch lengths and shrimp patterns are the best choices. Eel patterns may be considered from midsummer on. Again, spinner flies are good choices for abundant white perch and will also attract stripers.

For conventional tackle, bucktails, jighead and plastic combinations, poppers and swimmers are the best choices. The guide favorites, 4- and 5-inch Bass Assassins fished on ¼-, ³/₈-, and ½-ounce jigheads are probably the prime lures for these waters. Safety pin spinners attached to small jig and grub combinations are perch killers and will also take stripers.

If you care for baitfishing this area, the same medium casting or spinning tackle is the choice. Eeling and livelining can be very effective at times, especially toward dusk. Chunking with cut menhaden, spot, and bluefish can be effective. You can also fish various bottom rigs baited with shrimp, squid, or bloodworms for abundant white perch throughout the season and for spot and croaker in midsummer. Some regulars target white perch and spot on bloodworms then use these fish on liveline rigs to target big stripers in some of the deep holes and drop-off areas.

Like so many places on the Bay, the best times are in mid-August. Guide Richie Gaines advises that the rip at Love Point "can be counted on" as long as there is a hard running tide. If you have a big enough boat, he recommends the following circle route: Start fishing at Kent Narrows, then hit the Eastern Neck rock piles, then fish the Love Point-Chester River Light area, then work the Bay Bridge pilings, then the Thomas Point rock piles, then the Bloody Point rock piles, then swing up into Eastern Bay to fish the humps and channel edges and return to Kent Narrows. Of course, he adds, you'll undoubtedly encounter schools of breaking fish along this route, and you ought to fish those, as well.

Kent Island Loop

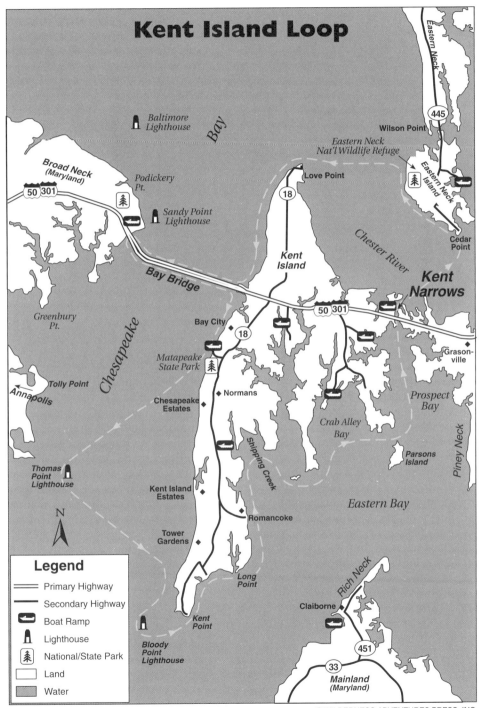

Baltimore Lighthouse

Bay

Eastern Neck

445

Wilson Point

Eastern Neck Nat'l Wildlife Refuge

Broad Neck
(Maryland)

Podickery Pt.

Love Point

Eastern Neck Island

50 301

18

Cedar Point

Sandy Point Lighthouse

Chester River

Kent Narrows

Bay Bridge

Kent Island

Greenbury Pt.

50 301

Chesapeake

Bay City

18

Grason-ville

Matapeake State Park

Normans

Prospect Bay

Annapolis
Tolly Point

Chesapeake Estates

Crab Alley Bay

Parsons Island

Piney Neck

Thomas Point Lighthouse

Shipping Creek

Kent Island Estates

Eastern Bay

N

Romancoke

Tower Gardens

Rich Neck

Legend

Long Point

Claiborne

━━━ Primary Highway

━━━ Secondary Highway

Boat Ramp

Lighthouse

National/State Park

Land

Water

Kent Point

451

Bloody Point Lighthouse

33

Mainland (Maryland)

© WILDERNESS ADVENTURES PRESS, INC.

A nice striper with a typical outfit and flies. Note—for stripers, the expensive reel shown is overkill. Stripers fight hard, but don't run far.

EASTERN BAY AND WYE RIVER

From May through the end of the year, Eastern Bay offers some of the finest fly and light-tackle fishing for a wide variety of species on the Chesapeake. This 30-square-mile area of water provides a diverse environment—grass beds, points, humps, bars, and inlets of three major rivers—Chester, Wye, and Miles—and several minor ones, plus such artificial structures as sunken boats, pilings, sunken reefs, breakwaters.

Good fishing begins in May, with stripers migrating up and down the Bay and white perch just behind them. These fish will be in Eastern Bay until the end of the year during most years. As the waters warm in June and July, blues, spot, hardhead, and flounder arrive and will usually remain until late October. Gray trout fishing becomes consistent by mid-September, peaks in October and November, then tapers off as the fish depart with dropping water temperatures.

These are the home waters of fly and light-tackle guide Richie Gaines. His advice on fishing these waters applies to many areas of the Bay: "Eastern Bay is one of those spots where it would do an angler good to sit down with a chart and mark it before he or she goes out. What you see on the chart that looks like it should be good, will be good—prominent points that stick way out and have some tide flow on them, islands, rock piles, drop-offs, edges, underwater points that are obvious on the charts but not obvious when you're out there, they all hold fish. I love points that have current going across them. If I pull up see bait dimpling the surface, I know I'm going to catch a lot of fish there. If I pull up and I don't see bait, I still fish it, because it can hold fish."

We also agree with his statement that some of the older maps can actually be better at showing and naming structure. For example, Marsh Island is no longer an island but an underwater hump, and the depth should be adjusted accordingly, but it's easier to find this spot on an older map that still shows it as an island.

Tides are moderate, usually in the range of one foot. There are a number of protected areas that provide opportunities to small boats, and there are some wading areas, as well. On the other hand, pleasure boat traffic is often heavy, especially on summer weekends, and open areas are often subject to significant winds.

Eastern Bay offers a chance to dip into your whole bag of tricks, from the shallow water and weed bed approaches of the Susquehanna Flats and Upper Bay rivers to the deep jigging techniques of the Upper Bay lumps. But it offers a wider variety of species, and, since the waters are generally less than 30 feet, most of it is suitable for fly fishing (wind and waves permitting).

Two breakwaters are located a few hundred yards south of the Kent Narrows Bridges, one a concrete wall, the other a rock jetty. A rip forms around both ends of the concrete wall, washing into a hole about 17 feet deep on the east side and about 11 feet on the west side. Fishing can be good on both tides, and, not surprisingly, the deeper hole is more reliable. Gaines likes to fish this area on an outgoing tide by holding in the eddy of the south side and casting flies or lures upcurrent and letting them swing through holes (much like the upcurrent casts to Bay Bridge pilings). The rock jetty is best fished on an incoming tide by retrieving the flies or lures parallel to the wall and working them through the gaps in the jetty. This water is only a few feet deep, and in low-light conditions is prime popper territory.

While you're in the area, a point in front of the townhouse development on the eastern side forms a rip that's worth exploring with a few casts, especially early in the morning.

This general area is known as Prospect Bay. From here south, fly fishing for hardheads can be outstanding from Mother's Day through the third week of June when the waters begin to warm, and the fish head deeper. The early season fishing throughout Eastern Bay offers shallow water opportunities for stripers and white perch in waters from 3 to 12 feet deep, such as around Bodkin Island and Bloody Point Light.

Continuing south you'll encounter a series of holes and ledges, including lower Prospect Bay and Bald Eagle below Parson Island and Sawmill and Mill Hill near the mouth of Greenwood Creek on the east. Three long north and south running points of land offer good fishing at their tips and both sides.

Cox's Neck on Kent Island has Bodkin Island, a nearly sunken island, off the southern tip. To the east lies Crab Alley and Crab Alley Creek; to the west lies the shoal of sunken Long Marsh Island and a series of holes in Cox's Creek and Shipping Creek.

Rich Neck, jutting up from the south of the mainland, is bordered by a series of stair-step shelves (bordering on Bodkin Island and Bodkin Shoal) on the west, a tapering bar off Tilghman Point to the north, and the long Bugby Bar, which meets the mouths of the Wye and Miles Rivers to the east.

Best of all is Kent Point, the very southern tip of Kent Island, with an artificial reef in the Bay to the east and Holaga Snood above that, Bloody Point Light to the southwest in the Chesapeake, and the bars off Kent and Bloody Points to the west, also in the main Chesapeake.

That's an awful lot of geography. Fortunately, Richie Gaines offers the following tips: At Bodkin Island, fish the southwest and eastern edges, working down the flats to 26 feet of water in both places. If birds are sitting on the water, redouble your efforts. At Greenwood Creek, work the 9-foot hole next to the sandy point on the south side of the creek entrance and the log-littered flats to the south at high tide. Also fish the riprap along the north point, especially on an outgoing tide. The underwater hump of Long Marsh Island offers a series of flats that can be very productive in the fall. The artificial reef (remnants of an old, concrete bridge in 5 to 17 feet of water) is a magnet for all game species. The flats and channel edges of the small bay to the north of this shoal are particularly good in the fall.

Off Kent Point, Bloody Point Light marks the tip of the long, flat point where it drops into the main channel. The light is surrounded by a narrow rock pile in about eight feet of water. Fish typically hold tight to the rocks, so casts need to be right up against the light. This is another good spot for poppers in low-light situations and a great fall spot for stripers and bluefish.

The surrounding flats between the light and the shoreline are another good shallow water area. To the west and north, the main Bay outside the light along Kent Island is a good place for schools of breaking fish in the fall.

To the south and west of Bloody Point Light lies a long flat that tapers down and then drops into a 110-foot trough. This area offers terrific fly fishing for flounder. The technique is to get upwind or uptide and cast Clouser minnow patterns on fast-sinking lines and then drag them along bottom using a "strip, strip, strip, then fall back" retrieve. Flounder will hit on the drop. A similar flounder flat can be found on the eastern side of Eastern Bay in the 10- to 40-foot shelf between Wades Point and Tilghman Point.

Two significant rivers enter Eastern Bay from the mainland on the east, the Wye and the Miles Rivers. Both areas are famous historic and tourist areas, and the Wye is justly renowned for producing enormous blue crabs. Though somewhat diminished in recent years due to the loss of grasses, both still offer excellent small boat fishing and wading for school-sized stripers and big white perch, and there are occasional incidental catches of croakers, blues, and flounder, especially as the waters enter Eastern Bay. The Wye is our long-time favorite.

In the upper parts of these waters, we like to use medium tackle, 6- and 7-weight fly rods casting small Clouser flies and spinner flies on sinking lines and medium spinning rods casting safety pin spinners with $1/8$-ounce jig and grub combinations. As you approach the main body of the Chesapeake, standard Bay fly and conventional tackle is more appropriate.

Since each river has only one public ramp, it pays to know where crabbing is allowed or prohibited. During the height of crabbing season, the line at the Wye ramp can be literally more than a mile. The smart move is to go on days when crabbing is not allowed or to go in mid-afternoon of crabbing days when crowds are thinned. (As of this writing, the rules on crabbing are in flux due to the over-harvesting of crabs throughout the Chesapeake.)

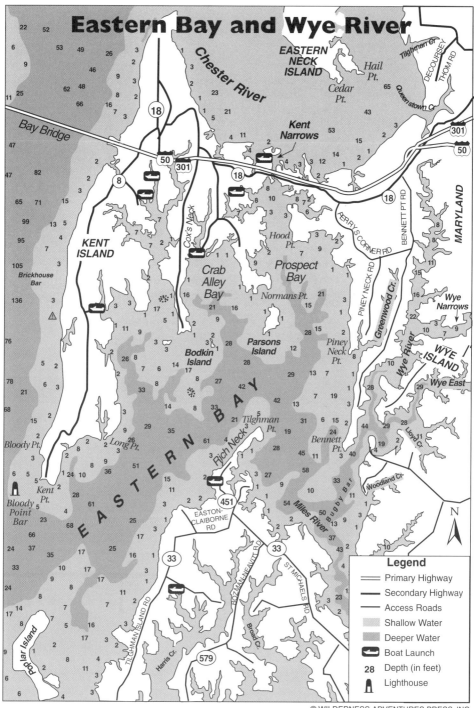

Eastern Bay and Wye River

Ed Russell's 22-foot Edgewater center console is an excellent boat for the open waters of the Bay.

This pickerel slammed a fly in the Magothy River near the Bay Bridge.

Hub Cities for Bay Bridge Area Rivers Eastern Shore

Kent Island
Chester, Population—3,723
Grasonville, Population—2,193
Stevensville, Population—5,880
Queenstown, Population—600

ACCOMMODATIONS

Comfort Inn Kent Narrows, 3101 Main Street, Grasonville; 800-828-3361

Pintail Point Resort (offering hunting, fishing, sporting clays and other activities), 511 Pintail Point Farm Lane, Queenstown; 410-827-7029

Chesapeake Motel and Conference Center, 107 Hissey Road, Grasonville; 800-822-7272

Hillside Hotel, Route 213, 2 miles north of Route 301, 2630 Centreville Road, Centreville; 888-305-2270

Holiday Inn Express, 1020 Kent Narrows Road, Grasonville; 888-877-4454

Holly's Motel, Route 50 and Jackson Creek Road, Grasonville; 410-827-8711

Sleep Inn, 105 VFW Avenue, Grasonville; 410-827-5555

Kent Manor Inn, 500 Kent Manor Drive, Stevensville; 410-643-5757

CAMPGROUNDS AND STATE PARKS

Martinak State Park, 137 Deep Shore Road, Denton; 410-479-1619; call 888-432-CAMP (2267) for reservations

Holiday Park Campground, Drapers Mill Road, P. O. Box 277, Greensboro; 410-482-6797 or 800-992-6691

Tuckahoe State Park, 13070 Crouse Mill Road, Queen Anne; 410-820-1668

RESTAURANTS

Anglers Restaurant & Marina (open for breakfast, lunch, dinner with fried oysters to die for), 3015 Kent Narrows Way South, Grasonville; 410-827-6717

Annie's Paramount Steak & Seafood House, 500 Kent Narrows Way North, Grasonville; 410-827-7103

Chesapeake Chicken & Rickin' Ribs, Rt. 50, Hissey Road, Exit 45A (West) Exit 45B (East), Grasonville; 410-827-0030

Fisherman's Crab Deck, 3036 Kent Narrows Way S., Grasonville; 410-827-6666

Fisherman's Inn, 3116 Kent Narrows Way S., Grasonville; 410-827-8807

Harris' Crab House, 433 Kent Narrows Way North, Grasonville; 410-827-9500

Hemingway's Restaurant, Bay Bridge Marina, Pier 1 Road, Stevensville; 410-643-CRAB

Hillside Steak & Crabhouse, 2640 Centreville Road, Centerville; 410-758-1300

RESTAURANTS, CONTINUED

Holly's, Rt. 50 & Jackson Creek Rd., Exits 43A & 43B, Grasonville; 410-827-8711

Kent Manor Inn & Restaurant, 500 Kent Manor Dr., Stevensville; 410-643-5757

Kentmorr Restaurant & Crab House, 910 Kentmore Rd., Stevensville; 410-643-2263

Lola's Tropical Bar & Grill, Pier 1 Rd., Stevensville; 410-643-CRAB

The Jetty Restaurant, 201 Wells Cove Rd., Grasonville; 410-827-8225

Sunflowers, 401 Love Point Rd., Stevensville; 410-643-9069

Tavern On The Bay, Chesapeake Bay Beach Club, 500 Marina Club Rd., Stevensville; 410-604-2188

Verna's Island Inn, 800 Main St., Stevensville; 410-643-2466

FLY SHOPS, TACKLE STORES, AND SPORTING GOODS

Angler's Sports Center Ltd, 1456 Whitehail Rd., Annapolis; 410-757-3442

Chesapeake Outdoors, 1707 Main Street, Chester; 410-604-2500

Island Fishing & Hunting, 115 South Piney Creek Rd.; Chester, 410-643-4224

Pintail Point, 511 Pintail Point Lane, Queenstown; 410-827-7029

Winchester Creek Outfitters, 313 Winchester Creek Rd., Grasonville; 410-827-7000

FLY AND LIGHT-TACKLE GUIDES

Richie Gaines, 410-827-7210

Gary Neitzey, 410-557-8801

Mark Galasso, 410-827-5635

Bruce Foster, 410-827-6933

MARINAS AND BOAT REPAIR

Bay Bridge Marina, Pier One Road, Stevensville; 410-643-3162

Castle Harbor Marina, Castle Marina Rd., Chester; 410-643-5599

Crab Alley Marina, Rt. 1 Box 286, Chester; 410-643-5588

Island View Marina, 1814 Crab Alley Dr., Chester; 410-643-2842

Kentmorr Harbor Marina, 910 Kentmorr Rd., Stevensville; 410-643-0029

Lippincott Marine, 3420 Main St., Grasonville; 410-827-9300

Mears Point Marina, 428 Kent Narrows Way, Grasonville; 410-827-8888

Pier One Marina, Pier 1 Marina Rd., Stevensville; 410-643-3162

Scott Marine Service, 3212 Main St., Grasonville; 410-827-8150

Skipjack Landing Marine Center, 1804 Crab Alley Dr., Chester; 410-643-2694

Queen Anne Marina, 412 Congressional Dr., Stevensville; 410-643-2021

LAUNCH RAMPS/RAMP PERMITS

Queen Anne's County

There are six public ramps on Kent Island. Matapeake is on the western shore of the island and faces the main stem of Chesapeake Bay, providing excellent access to the Chesapeake Bay Bridge. No stamp is required, but there is a daily use fee. The other five are all on the eastern shore of Kent Island providing access to Kent Narrows, Chester River, and Eastern Bay. All five require a Queen Anne's County launch permit. Probably the most convenient ramp is the double ramp at Piney Narrows, Exit 41 off Rts. 50/301.

RAMP PERMITS, CONTINUED

Queen Anne's County ramp permits may be purchased at:

Island Hunting and Fishing, in Chester on Kent Island, Exit 40A off Rts 50/301; 410-643-4224

Boaters World in Stevensville, off Rts. 50/301; 410-604-2613

Anglers, near Annapolis on the Western Shore, Exit 30 off Rt. 50; 410-974-4013, Talbot County (Wye Landing Access)

Wye Landing is a double ramp providing access well up the river to good striper and white perch fishing. In the upper reaches small boats may be used. Ice, bait and other necessities (but not fuel) are available at the ramp. Wye Landing also features a boat rental, with 50 wooden 16-foot skiffs, with or without 6-horse-power motors. (You can row to a lot of good fishing and crabbing waters.) The boats are available from Memorial Day through the end of October. Call 410-827-7663. From the north, take Rt. 50 to Rt. 213 south, to Rt. 662 south, to Wye Landing Road to the end. From the south, take Rt. 662 to Wye Landing Rd.

Talbot County ramp permits can be purchased at:

Island Hunting and Fishing, in Chester on Kent Island, exit 40A off Rts 50/301; 410-643-4224

Shore Sportsman in Easton; 410-820-5599

AUTO REPAIR

Ace Allen Auto Services, 106 Pier 1 Rd., Stevensville; 410-643-2886

Champion Auto Repair, 2130 Didonato Drive, 1561 Postal Rd., Chester; 410-643-8008

Farber's Service Center, 28701 Queen Anne Hwy, Wye Mills; 410-822-0728

HOSPITALS

Kent and Queen Anne's Hospital, 100 Brown St., Chestertown; 410-778-3300, Ext. 2505

OTHER ATTRACTIONS

Eastern Neck National Wildlife Refuge, 1730 Eastern Neck Road, Rock Hall; 410-639-7056 or 410-639-7100 or 410-639-7017 for boat rental; offers 2,285 acres of hiking, waterfowl and songbird watching

Terrapin Beach Nature Park, Exit 37 off 50/301; 410-827-7577 or 410-643-8170; a mile-long nature trail, pond, walkway to the Chesapeake, bird blinds, great bird watching

The Wildlife Trust of North America at Horsehead Wetlands Center, Perry Corner Rd. off Rts. 50/301; 410-827-6694; WTNA@shore.Internet.com; 500-acre sanctuary hosting a variety of waterfowl and other birds

FOR FURTHER INFORMATION

Queen Anne's County Department of Business & Tourism, 425 Piney Narrows Road, Suite 3, Chester, MD 21619; **888-400-RSVP;** tourism@qac.org

Kent County Office of Tourism, 100 North Cross St., Chestertown, MD 21620; 410-778-0416; webmaster@chestertown.com

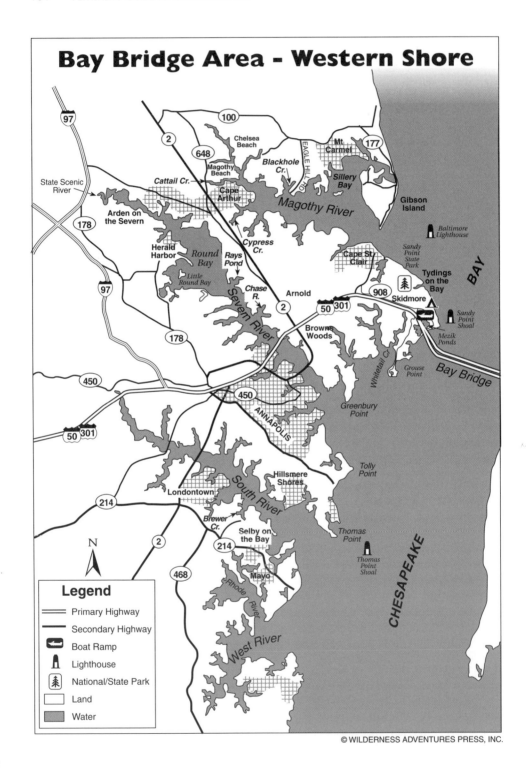

Bay Bridge Area - Western Shore

Fly shop owner Joe Bruce with a typical pickerel from the rivers near the Bay Bridge.

Bay Bridge Area Rivers, Western Shore

We fish the rivers on the west side of the Bay Bridge near Annapolis mostly in cold weather, when the frenetic swimming, sailing, water-skiing, and other boating activity declines, and the fishing improves. White perch and yellow perch are present in good numbers and so are stripers at times, especially in the Magothy. But the star attraction in cold weather is pickerel, and the "good old days" have returned. (As of publication, the season for pickerel is closed from March 15 through April 30 in all Maryland tidal waters. Also, yellow perch may not be taken from the Western Shore Rivers including the Magothy, Severn, South, and West Rivers.)

Cold weather used to signal good pickerel fishing in this area on the Magothy, Severn, and to a lesser degree, South Rivers from early fall through late spring of the following year. About 20 years ago, this fishing declined dramatically. But in the last few years the aquatic grasses have returned to these waters and so have the pickerel—with a vengeance. These rivers not only provide good numbers of pickerel but also good-sized specimens. Most pickerel are in the 1½- to 3-pound range, and fish of 5 pounds are caught every year.

Guide Gary Neitzey, who specializes in pickerel fishing, says pickerel can be taken year-round, but he targets the colder months. "The bite starts to get good in October, but the best time of the year is February and March, right up until the season closes. I like it best when the water temperature drops into the 50s. We can really catch them well as it drops all the way down into the 40s or so. Two years ago we were fishing a creek and casting our flies up onto skim ice. As we pulled our flies off the ice, the pickerel knocked the daylights out of them as they sank. Once the temperature drops below 40, the fish seem to get sluggish and this will slow down the bite considerably."

These rivers are small enough that you can get by with a boat as small as 14 feet with a 5-horsepower motor—if you launch at a spot close to the fishing grounds. (The private ramps and Truxtun Heights, listed at the end of the chapter, all provide close access to good fishing.) Larger boats and bigger motors, of course, provide safety and access to more of these waters. On any boat, an electric trolling motor, preferably bow-mounted, offers better boat control and maneuverability in some of the small coves and among the piers you'll want to work. (We also caution against running a boat in icy water, no matter how thin the ice.)

Pickerel are not tackle busters, comparing poorly pound-for-pound with stripers or bass, so medium conventional or fly tackle is the ideal choice. That means a 6- to 7-foot medium weight spinning or casting rod, reel spooled with 8-pound test monofilament, with a 2-foot "bite leader" of 15- to 20-pound test. The leader helps cope with pickerel teeth and barnacles on pilings, but it may have to be scaled back to 12-pound test in clear water conditions. (Some guides just spool with 12-pound monofilament and forego any bite leader.)

Ideal fly tackle is a 6- or 7-weight rod, with a 10-foot sink-tip line and a 3- to 4-foot leader of 15- to 17-pound test. The "problem" with this tackle is that stripers also move into these rivers, and you may find your fish-fighting skills challenged. One solution this is to carry along an extra 9-weight fly outfit and a full array of lines and a medium-heavy conventional rig in case stripers are encountered. Stray white perch and yellow perch should present no problems.

Fly fishermen will succeed with bright 2- to 4-inch streamer patterns tied on size 4, 2, or 1/0 long-shanked hooks, with bucktail and/or feathers of yellow, white, touches of red, and lots of flash material. Styles that keep the barbless hook riding up, like bendback or Clouser minnow patterns, work better among weeds and woody cover. A bendback style Lefty's Red-and-White fly and Joe Bruce's two Clouser Pickerel Fly patterns are good choices.

We also like the spinner fly rigs we use for perch (standard Clouser patterns such as Bruce's Pickerel Flies tied on jig hooks with small, inline or "safety pin" spinners attached to the hook eye). The recommended weight of the Clouser eyes is at least $\frac{1}{36}$-ounce and maybe as heavy as $\frac{1}{24}$. The strip-pause-strip retrieve is generally best. The strips may be comparatively short, but a long pause with the Clouser flies produces a jigging action that is the key to triggering strikes from pickerel (and often other species) in the opinion of Gary Neitzey, Joe Bruce, and other experts we've interviewed.

With conventional tackle our favorite lures are single hook models, preferably with the barbs mashed down for catch-and-release. The 4-inch Fin-S-Fish in alewife color or other, similar soft jerkbait, rigged with the hook partially buried according to the weed level, is the deadliest lure. The safety pin spinner and 3-inch white grub, small spinnerbait, and weedless spoon with pork rind or lip-hooked minnow are other good single hook lures. Among treble hook lures, the Tiny Torpedo in any natural finish is a good surface lure, and the 4-inch floating/diving Rapala, and #2 or #3 gold Mepps spinner are other good bets.

Spinner type lures are often best fished on a steady retrieve; use a twitch-pause-twitch with the others. Neitzey's favorite conventional lure is a white or chartreuse, 4-inch Kalin Grub on a ¼-ounce plain jighead, retrieved slowly.

The best natural bait is the classic 3- to 4-inch "bull minnow," lip-hooked on an open or weedless hook, with or without a splitshot and float. Pickerel often gently inhale a bait and suspend, so you need to be alert to the very subtlest motion of the line or bobber, which may indicate a take. Pause, wait for a second subtle movement, then set the hook. We've landed pickerel up to 5½ pounds this way, and sometimes the take is indicated only by a slight dip then slide of the small float.

Lure and bait combinations are a proven, effective approach and seem to be particularly effective as water temperatures drop. Lip-hook a 2- to 3-inch minnow on a small, weedless spoon so that the hook rides up and walk it over and through weed beds. Or lip-hook a minnow on a small jig or shad dart (1 or 2), with or without a float, and retrieve it steadily over and through weed beds.

Pickerel are ambush feeders that relate to cover, often at the edge of shallow water. However, they appear to cruise a lot, so the best tactic is usually working potential cover to find the fish. As Joe Bruce observes, sometimes the cover is weeds, sometimes it's wood such as fallen trees and docks. Sometimes it's both. Find this cover over a breakline and work your lure, bait or fly over and along the breakline. The edges of weeds or boat slips along a dock often indicate the slight change of depth of a breakline.

Bruce also targets back eddies created by tides at the bend of these rivers. A collection of floating leaves often indicates such an eddy. Creek mouths are another prime target.

Look for bays and points with such cover. Some specific locations are: Sillery Bay, Blackhole Creek, Cypress Creek, and Cattail Creek in the Magothy; and Rays Pond, Brewer Creek, and Chase Creek in the Severn. Chase Creek provides a drop-off into a 10-foot channel and is always worth a check for stripers; sometimes they are present in good numbers.

Cold weather pickerel fishing has a charm of its own. The rivers have little boat traffic and few other anglers are out except an occasional heron or loon, with the quiet only interrupted by flocks of migrating ducks, geese, and swans.

The best pickerel fishing runs from mid-September through the following March, with October to December the most pleasant months and January through mid-March (or until ice up) the prime months. Access to these rivers is limited.

Hub City for Bay Bridge, Western Shore

Annapolis
Population—33,200

Founded in 1649, the first U.S. peacetime capital, the capital of Maryland, the home of U.S. Naval Academy, with 418 miles of shoreline, and billing itself as "the sailing capital of America," Annapolis is a worthy destination featuring historic tours, outdoor activities, sports, arts, shopping, dining, and a host of other activities.

ACCOMMODATIONS
Annapolis-Days Inn, 2520 Riva Road; 410-224-2800 or 800-DAYS-INN
Annapolis Marriott Waterfront, 80 Compromise Street; 800-288-9290
College House Suites, One College Avenue; 410-263-6124
Lowes Annapolis Hotel, 126 West Street; 800-23-LOWES
Pirates Cove Restaurant & Marina, 4817 Riverside Drive, Galesville; 410-867-2300

CAMPGROUNDS AND STATE PARKS
Capital KOA Campground, a complete campground, provides shuttles to transportation to Baltimore and Annapolis; contact Capital KOA Campground, 768 Cecil Avenue, Millersville; 410-923-2771
Hart-Miller Island State Park, an island accessible only by boat, provides campsite; contact Hart-Miller Island State Park, c/o Gunpowder Falls State Park, 2813 Jerusalem Rd., P.O. Box 480, Kingsville; 410-592-2897

RESTAURANTS
Armadillo's, City Dock; 410-268-6680
Buddy's Crabs & Ribs, 100 Main Street; 410-626-1100
Cafe Northwest, 18 Market Space; 410-269-0969
Caliente, 50 West Street; 410-268-8548
Fran O'Briens, 113 Main Street; 410-268-6288
Griffin's, 18 Market Square; 410-268-2576
Harbour House Restaurant, City Dock; 410-268-0771
Harry Browne's, 66 State Circle; 410-263-4332
King Of France Tavern, Main Street at Maryland Inn; 410-263-2641
La Piccola Roma, 200 Main Street; 410-268-7898
Maria's Sicilian Ristorante, 12 Market Space; 410-268-2112
Maryland Inn, Church Circle; 410-263-2641
McGarvey's Saloon, 8 Market Space; 410-263-5700
Middleton's Tavern, City Dock at Randall Street; 410-263-3323
Mum's, City Dock; 410-263-3353
O'Brien's, 113 Main Street; 410-268-6288
Riordan's Saloon, City Dock; 410-263-5449
Treaty of Paris, Main Street at Maryland Inn; 410-263-2641

Fly Shops, Tackle Stores, and Sporting Goods
Great Feathers, 151 Main Street; 410-472-6799
Bass Pro Shops Outdoor World, 7000 Arundel Mills Circle, Hanover; 410-689-2500
Angler's Sports Center Ltd, 1456 Whitehail Road; 410-757-3442
Hudson Trail Outfitters, 149 Annapolis Mall; 410-266-8390
Beachys Hardware, 165 Main Street; 301-895-5208
Bart's Sport World, 6814 Ritchie Hwy., Glen Burnie; 301-761-8686
Dick's Sporting Goods, 6711 Ritchie Hwy., Glen Burnie; 410-760-3933
The Sports Authority, 595 East Ordnance Rd., Glen Burnie; 410-761-1151
The Sports Authority, 4520 Mitchellville Rd., Bowie; 301-352-5690
The Sports Authority, 3335 Corridor Marketplace, Laurel; 301-483-0062

Fly and Light-Tackle Guides
Gary Neitzey (entire area and especially the Annapolis rivers), 410-557-8801
Norm Bartlett, 410-679-8790
Richie Gaines, 410-827-7210

Marinas and Boat Repair
Port Annapolis Marina, Inc., 7074 Bembe Beach Road; 410-269-1990
Annapolis Harbor Boatyard, 326 First Street; 410-267-9050
Annapolis City Dock, 1 Dock Street; 410-263-7973
Annapolis Waterfront Hotel & Marina, 80 Compromise Street; 410-268-7555
Annapolis Landing Marina, 980 Awald Drive; 410-263-0090
Annapolis Yacht Basin, 2 Compromise Street; 410-263-3544
Arnold C. Gay Yacht Yard, 1 Shipwright Street; 410-263-9277
Back Creek Marina, 950 Awald Drive; 410-280-6417
Bay View Marina, 514 Deale Rd.; 410-798-6060
Chesapeake Harbour Marina, Inc., 2030 Chesapeake Harbour Drive; 410-268-1969
Fairwinds Marina, 1000 Fairwinds Rd.; 410-974-0758
Harbor Side Marine, 319 Sixth Street; 410-267-9700
Petrini Yacht Yard, 1 Walton Lane; 410-263-4278
Podickory Point Yacht & Beach Club, 2116 Bay Front Terrace; 410-757-8000
Sarles Boat & Engine Shop, 808 1/2 Boucher Avenue; 410-263-3661
Whitehall Yacht Yard, 1656 Homewood Landing Road; 410-757-4819
The Yacht Basin Company, 2 Compromise Street; 410-263-3544

Recommended Launch Ramps
Access is the big problem on these rivers. We recommend calling private ramps first to check for directions, fees, hours of operation, and in really cold weather, for ice conditions.

RECOMMENDED LAUNCH RAMPS, CONTINUED

Magothy River: Accessed from the Fairwinds Marina or Ferry Point Marina. Both ramps are private and charge a fee. Sandy Point State Park is public and charges a fee.

Fairwinds Marina, 1000 Fairwinds Road; 410-974-0758

Ferry Point Marina & Yacht Yard, 700 Mill Creek Road, Arnold; 410-544-6368

Sandy Point State Park, 22 ramps, also provides a longer run into the Magothy; take Rt. 50, Exit #32 north to park entrance; 410-974-2149

The Severn River: Accessed from Smith's Boat Yard, which is private and charges a fee, and from Truxtun Heights Park on Spa Creek, which is public and charges a fee.

Smith Marina, 529 Ridgely Rd., Crownsville; 410-923-344

Truxtun Heights Park, take Exit 22 off Rt. 50 to Rt. 655 east to Hilltop Lane east to Primrose Rd. north; park entrance is on the left; 410-263-7958

AIRPORTS

See Baltimore.

AUTO REPAIR

Annapolis Car Care, 1401 Forest Drive; 410-263-5433

Dunn's Auto Repairs, 149 Gibralter Avenue; 410-268-4000

Jack's Garage, 300 Chinquapin Round Road; 410-267-7909

Maryland Auto Care, 1814 George Avenue; 410-280-0098

HOSPITALS

Anne Arundel Medical Center, 64 Franklin Street; 443-481-1000

OTHER OUTDOOR OPPORTUNITIES

Thomas Point Park, 3890 Thomas Point Rd. off Maryland Rt.2 at Annapolis, features wildlife refuge and park for hiking, biking birding; 410-222-1969

Quiet Waters Park, 610 Quiet Waters Park Rd., Annapolis, features wildlife and marsh, plus hiking, biking, birding, and seasonal activities, including an outdoor ice rink

FOR FURTHER INFORMATION

If you're visiting the area, we recommend you request a free *Annapolis and Anne Arundel County Visitor's Guide* published by Annapolis and Anne Arundel County Conference And Visitor's Bureau, 26 West St., Annapolis, MD 21401; 410-280-0445; www.visit-annapolis.org

Bill May with a striper taken in the rips near the Kent Narrows Bridge.

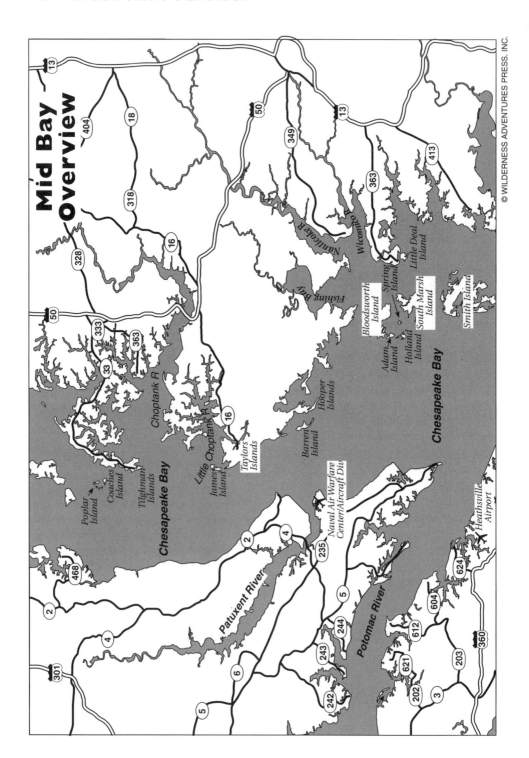

Mid Bay
Overview

Mid-Bay, Eastern Shore

POPLAR ISLAND

Less than five miles due south of Bloody Point, at the mouth of Eastern Bay, lies Poplar Island. It's not much of an island really; years of erosion have taken their toll washing away most of the original landmass, leaving behind several small islets instead of the original larger single island. Although little land remains, there are lots of stumps, downed timber and brush piles.

Years ago, this was a hotspot for bluefish, but this species is seldom found this far up in the Bay anymore. Striped bass, however, are another story. The cluttered remains of the island offer just the type of habitat that stripers like, making this an excellent choice for an angler using weedless flies or lures or top-water offerings.

As is typical with much of the Bay, spring and fall offer the best opportunities, but during the summer, early and late in the day can also produce. Besides stripers, flounder frequent these environs in late summer, and although most fishermen associate flounder fishing with bottom rigs and live minnows, the fact is that flounder are

Lefty Kreh, Joe Bruce, Bob Clouser, and guide Mike Murphy aboard Mike's boat.

active sight feeders and a fly or lure fished near the bottom can trigger a strike. Sometimes it's unexpected. Once, while targeting stripers, we caught several good-sized flounder on small bucktails. It was fall, and we were fishing one of the shallow flats between two of the "islands" and we could see the flounder follow the bucktail before striking.

If you look at a chart of the area, you will notice that the entire group of islands is surrounded by shallow water. Almost anywhere you try may be good, but we've usually had the best luck on the west side where most of the structure is located.

Often, there are grasses growing just below the surface of the deeper portions of the flats. A favorite technique then is to fish a lure like Bill Lewis's Slap-Stick. This lure floats vertically, with just the head above water. Initiating a retrieve causes the lure to move to the surface and then wobble erratically, much like an injured baitfish; pause, and the lure returns to vertical. This is a quiet, but provoking retrieve that is well suited to shallow areas like this one.

Whether for better or worse, this area is slated to change. A Corps of Engineers project is underway to restore the island to its configuration as of 1847. As part of a 20-year project to widen and deepen the Bay's shipping channel, the enlarged island will be created from spoil material dredged from the Bay's bottom. The intent is to not only to rebuild the island, but to recreate an 800-acre shallow cove that is expected to allow for the re-colonization of submerged aquatic vegetation. Whether the final result will be good or bad is open to conjecture, but for now, the stumps and flats of Poplar Island remains a good spot to fish.

Guide Mike Murphy with a nice croaker.

TILGHMAN ISLAND AND THE MOUTH OF THE CHOPTANK

Knapps Narrows is what makes Tilghman Island an island. This cut through the peninsula formed by the Chesapeake on the west and Harris Creek on the east is a great aid to fishing a lot of really productive water because it enables you to easily go from one side of the peninsula to the other, saving what would otherwise be an eight-mile run.

Both sides of the peninsula offer many fishing possibilities. Poplar Island Narrows, an expanse of deep water between the shallow shoreline of the mainland and that of Poplar Island is a good place to start.

Work the edges on either side and you may find striped bass, weakfish, or speckled trout. In recent years, an expanding population of croakers has made for good fishing for this species here in late summer.

Blackwalnut Point, at the southern tip of the peninsula, forms the northern end of the mouth of the Choptank. The point has historically been a hotspot for stripers and bluefish. Years ago, mixed schools of blues and rock (the local name for stripers) were pretty much a sure bet any morning or late afternoon in late summer and fall. The bluefish can still be found, but they're usually fairly small, and not as numerous as the stripers. Like many spots, an outgoing tide is best, as the waters of Harris Creek, Broad Creek and the Choptank River all combine to wash baitfish past this point.

Due west of the point, the state has created an artificial reef. There are lots of humps, lumps, and bumps that attract all manner of fish. You can locate the reef by motoring due west and watching your depthfinder.

Spanish mackerel usually show up in late summer and remain till the waters start to cool. These speedsters often break the surface in a feeding frenzy that is amazing. Unlike stripers or blues, which usually just break the surface, when Spanish mackerel drive bait to the surface they frequently come totally out of the water in their attempt to gobble baitfish. Spanish seldom venture into any of the rivers, preferring the more open waters of the Bay, so you'll usually find these fish outside the mouth of the Choptank. Any tidal rip is worth investigating.

Moving around Blackwalnut Point, you'll see Nelson Point about 4 miles to the northeast. Nelson Point forms the western mouth of Broad Creek. It is quite shallow right near shore, but Broad Creek itself is fairly deep, and an outgoing tide creates an excellent tide rip along the tip of the island. Cast a streamer or small spinning lure uptide. Retrieve just fast enough to keep the offering moving with the current. You want to imitate a helpless baitfish being swept along by the tidal flow. Depending on the season, you might pick up a striper, a croaker, or a speckled trout. Also, check out the edges of the deeper water around little Nelson Island about a mile off the point. This is one good spot to look for croakers in shallow water early in the spring. If you look at a chart, you will notice lots of structure in this area in the form of shallow points and bars. All are potentially productive. Just use caution, some have submerged stumps or rocks. Mostly, though, you'll just have to watch your depth.

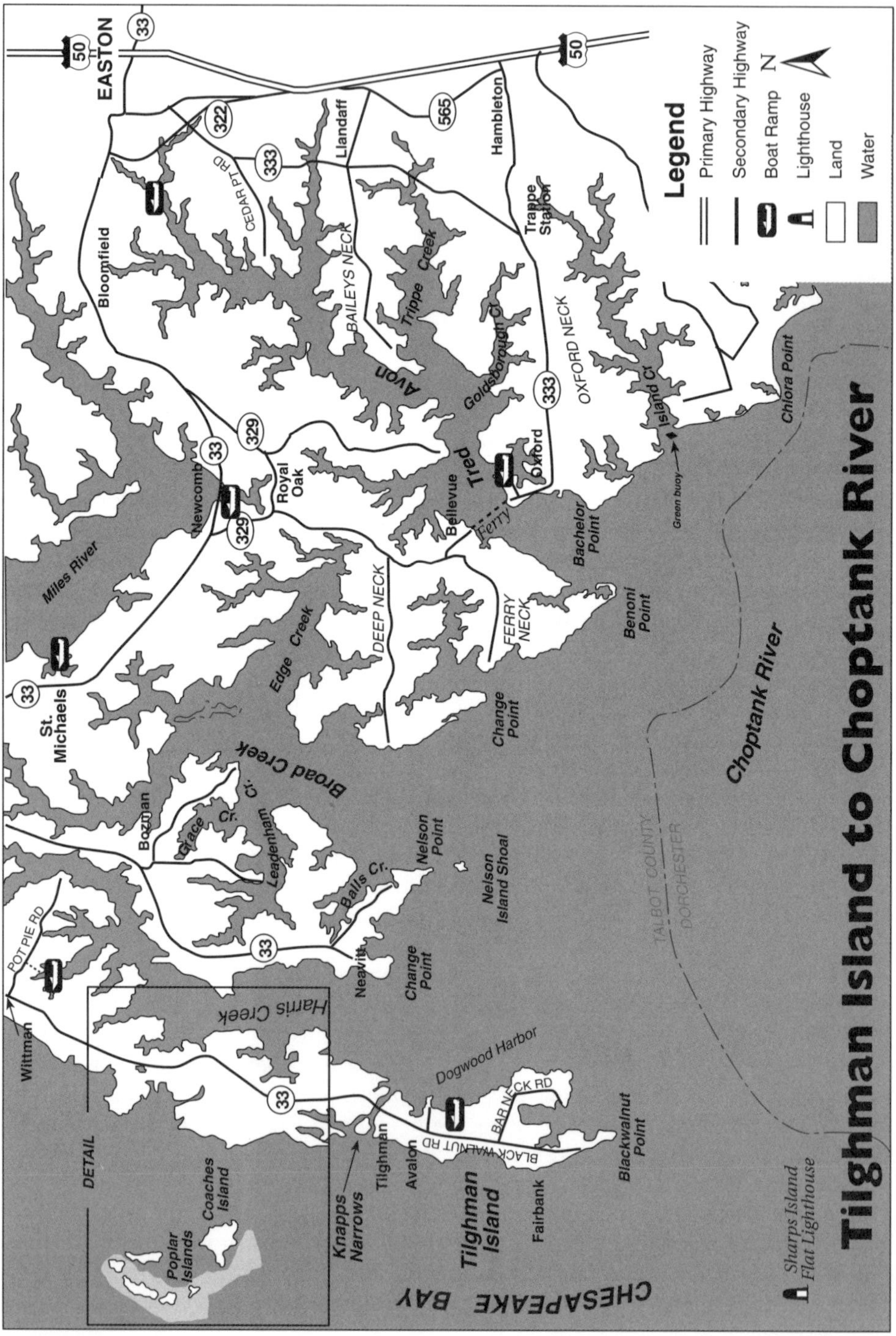

Tilghman Island to Choptank River
Legend
Primary Highway
Secondary Highway
Boat Ramp
Lighthouse
Land
Water
N
EASTON
50
33
322
333
565
329
CEDAR PT RD
Llandaff
Hambleton
Trappe Station
Bloomfield
BAILEYS NECK
Trippe Creek
Goldsborough Cr.
OXFORD NECK
Island Cr.
Chlora Point
Avon
Tred
Oxford
Royal Oak
Newcomb
Bellevue
Ferry
Bachelor Point
Green buoy
Miles River
DEEP NECK
FERRY NECK
Benoni Point
Edge Creek
St. Michaels
Change Point
Choptank River
Broad Creek
Bozman
Grace Cr.
Leadenham Cr.
Balls Cr.
Nelson Point
Nelson Island Shoal
TALBOT COUNTY
DORCHESTER
POT PIE RD
Neavitt
Harris Creek
Wittman
Dogwood Harbor
BAR NECK RD
BLACK WALNUT RD
Blackwalnut Point
DETAIL
Coaches Island
Poplar Islands
Knapps Narrows
Tilghman
Avalon
Tilghman Island
Fairbank
CHESAPEAKE BAY
Sharps Island Flat Lighthouse

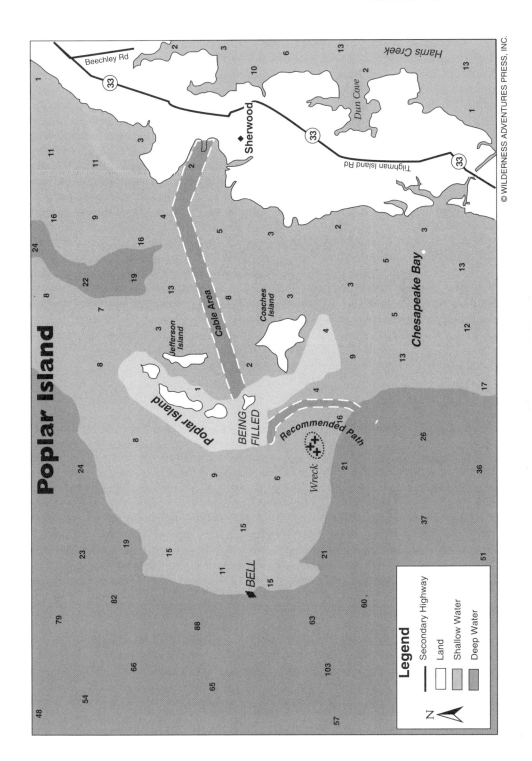

Poplar Island

Beechley Rd

Sherwood

Harris Creek

Dun Cove

Tilghman Island Rd

Chesapeake Bay

Poplar Island

Jefferson Island

Cable Area

Coaches Island

BEING FILLED

Recommended Path

Wreck

BELL

Legend

Secondary Highway

Land

Shallow Water

Deep Water

N

Due east of Nelson Point there's a red #2 channel marker. There is a significant depth change, going from about 19 feet to 9. This edge is a hotspot for rock, trout, and flounder. The shoreline from the mouth of Bells Creek to the mouth of Leadenham Creek is all riprap with lots of grass beds. This is a good spot for both stripers and perch. Fall is the best time of year, and the first two hours of the outgoing tide the best time. Couple that with low-light levels and you have perfect conditions. Farther up Broad Creek, the deeper water near the red #4 buoy is a good spot to find white perch in the fall.

Moving out of Broad Creek, following the eastern shoreline for about 4 miles south east of the #2 buoy, you'll come upon Benoni Point at the mouth of the Tred Avon River. This is a good area, but be careful, the bottom near shore is rock-covered and can be dangerous. Just out from the point towards the middle of the Choptank's mouth is a series of stair-step drop-offs. In the fall, this is a really good spot for specks. Mike Murphy (probably the most knowledgeable guide that fishes this area) always tries to spend some time here.

Bachelor Point, on the east side of the Tred Avon just below the town of Oxford, is another good spot. A little to the southeast, at the mouth of Island Creek, look for the #1 green buoy. There is a 15-foot deep hole near the buoy, right amid some shallow water. It usually holds a lot of fish.

In the net, a nice croaker taken on a bucktail jig.

The shoreline between Island Creek and Chlora Point is covered with riprap, and usually holds both stripers and white perch.

Directly west of Island Creek stands the Choptank River Light. This is a "spider" structure that is surrounded by fairly deep water with lots of bottom structure, including a stone pile that was most likely ballast dumped by a sailing ship several hundred years ago. This stone pile rises up about 10 feet from the surrounding 20-foot depths and almost always holds one species or another. You'll have to search for the stone pile using your depthfinder. Actually, even if you can't find the stone pile, it doesn't matter a whole lot. You can fish all around the light with the expectation of finding stripers, speckled trout, and white perch. This is another spot that anyone fishing the area should try.

Todds Point, west of the light, is the next stop. There are several rock jetties parallel to shore that are not always visible above the waterline. They offer a good hiding spot for several species, but they also present the opportunity to damage a propeller. Use caution.

Cook Point, due west from Todds Point, forms the southeast entrance to the Choptank. This spot is considered by many to be the best spot in the river. On an outgoing flow, enormous tide rips form here. You may find stripers, speckled trout, and even Spanish mackerel. Usually the mackerel won't show up until about August. The waters between red buoys #10 and #12, directly north of the point, are good for flounder.

Due west of the mouth of the Choptank is Sharps Island Flat. It's marked by a lighthouse that is tilted to one side and is one of the most easily recognized spots on the Bay. Extensive shallow water flats surround the light, making it a top spot for breaking stripers in the fall. Sometimes small bluefish will be mixed with the stripers, and often, speckled trout will be lurking beneath the breakers. If the breaking fish are too small for your liking, go deep. You may be surprised.

Getting There

Tilghman Island, Poplar Island and Harris Creek can be reached by taking Maryland Route 33 from Easton. This road runs the entire length of the peninsula ending up near Blackwalnut Point. One of the reasons for the good fishing is the fact that it's out of the way. From Easton, it's about 25 miles to the launch ramp below Knapps Narrows.

Launch Ramps

The only public ramp on the lower portion of the peninsula is at Dogwood Harbor. Take Route 33 across Knapps Narrows to Dogwood Road. The ramp is to the left on Harris Creek. This ramp, located as it is right near Knapps Narrows, is your best choice if you want to fish the Poplar Island area and points south.

Another ramp, Cummings Creek Landing, is near the town of Wittman on the north end of the peninsula. Take Route 33 to Pot Pie Road East to Howeth Road South. The ramp is on Cummings Creek.

Balls Creek Landing accesses Harris Creek and the Choptank from the east side of Harris Creek. To get there take Route 33 out of St. Michaels to Route 579, Broad Creek Road. Follow that to the ramp at the end of the road.

Local Services

There's not a whole lot on the entire peninsula. Harrison's Chesapeake House at Dogwood Harbor, not far from the ramp, has overnight accommodations and a moderately priced, surprisingly good restaurant. Call 410-886-2121 for information. The Tilghman Island Inn on Coopertown Road (800-866-2141), is a more upscale—and expensive—restaurant.

While you are in the area, try to make time to see the Maritime Museum in St. Michael's. It's fascinating, and it even includes an actual Chesapeake Bay lighthouse.

St. Michaels, by the way, is a very popular tourist spot. There are loads of hotels and restaurants. If you want to sample Maryland seafood at it's finest, be sure to go to The Crab Claw Restaurant (410-745-2900). It's at Navy Point right in town and is excellent. If you would like to stay at a really fine place, look no farther than The Inn at Perry Cabin. It's been rated as the fifth best Resort Hotel in the country. Be sure to bring your credit cards—it's expensive. Call 410-745-2200.

One other worthwhile side trip is to the town of Oxford. This sleepy little town on the banks of the Tred Avon River is noted for its slow pace of life.

Overlooked for many years, many wealthy people have now built homes there. It too is "touristy" in that there are quite a few bed and breakfasts, restaurants, and gift shops, and you can rent bicycles to tour the town. Despite its newfound popularity, it's worth seeing. Fall is a wonderful time to visit. Oxford is on Route 333, eight miles southwest of Easton.

CHOPTANK SOUTH TO TAYLORS ISLAND

Coming out of the Choptank and moving south, the next good spot is the area around Hills Point and Hills Point Cove. There's a little wishbone-shaped island out from the point that can be good for specks.

Ragged Point on the north side of the Little Choptank is a very good early spring spot. Often, the shallow water in this area will be clear enough to sight fish. If conditions are right you may be able to cast to striped bass or speckled trout that you can see. Obviously, this fishing is fairly short-lived since the water clarity will disappear as soon as the water warms. A shallow-draft boat and a stealthy approach is a help.

James Island is a couple of miles west of Ragged Point and is one of the best spots in the Mid-Bay region for several species. Depending on the time of year, you can catch stripers, specks, croaker, flounder, and Spanish mackerel around or near the island.

The northeast end of the island is loaded with downed timber and underwater stumps. This is one of Mike Murphy's favorite spots for casting surface lures. A weedless fly rod popper is deadly here; in fact, there is so much underwater structure that a surface lure is almost the only way to fish this area.

The middle of the island is the place to look for speckled trout from mid-May until about the end of June when they will retreat to deeper water. The shallow nearshore areas pick up again in the fall.

An interesting and important fact to remember is that in the spring the water temperature around James Island can vary as much as eight degrees with a tide

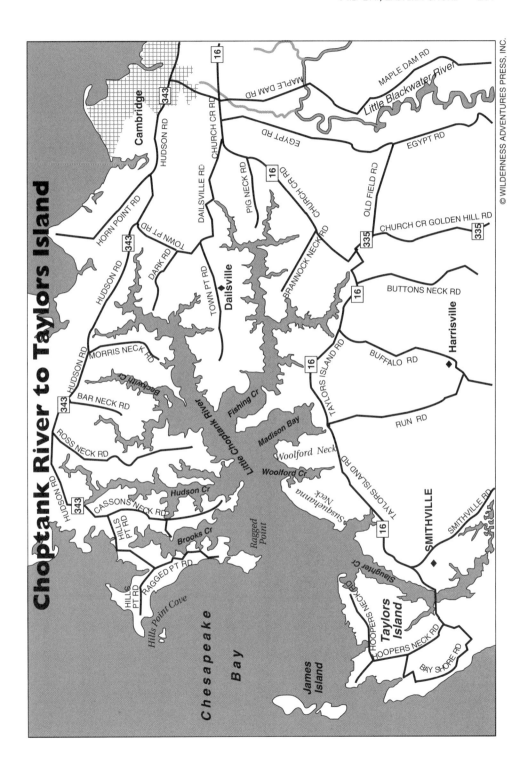

Choptank River to Taylors Island

Joe Bruce with his best-ever striper taken on a fly. This fish, which was estimated to be about 40 pounds, was taken in early December near Hooper Island.

Joe with a croaker taken on a Clouser off Hooper Island.

change. This is due to the temperature disparity between the shallower, warmer waters of the Little Choptank and the deeper cooler waters of the main Bay. On an outgoing tide, the water from the Little Choptank will raise the water temperature around the island, often triggering a feeding spree.

Although the west and north sides of James Island are usually best, the west side is surrounded by a shallow flat that can be quite productive at times. Try fishing these flats near the high tide point. As the tide begins to fall, move off to the edge of deeper water. Often game fish will prowl this edge looking for baitfish moving off the flat as the water recedes.

TAYLORS ISLAND

Oyster Cove, just south of James Island, at the top of Taylors Island, presents another shallow water opportunity. Work into the cove on high water and work the points on either side as the tide flows out.

There is a tiny island on the western side of Oyster Cove that is home to a lot of water birds. It's a good shallow water spot for striped bass, but be careful. To the southwest of this little island is an unmarked rock pile just under the surface. It's a good spot to cast to, but you want to avoid finding it with your propeller.

The next several miles of shoreline along Taylors Island are unexceptional, but fishing may be good at times, and it is worth a shot. The best spot along this area is at the mouth of Punch Island Creek, about midway down the shoreline. The mouth and about 100 to 200 yards inside the creek are good on an outgoing tide. Early spring is best, though fall can be productive, as well.

HOOPER ISLAND

Hooper Island begins where Taylors Island ends, at a cut between the Honga River and the main Bay called Fishing Creek. This is the beginning for some of the Bay's finest fishing areas. Route 335 crosses the bridge and runs the length of Hooper Island. The bridge itself is an excellent spot for striped bass pretty much year-round and supports a good flounder fishery during the summer months.

Since the Fishing Creek cut is quite narrow, tide changes create strong currents— ideal for rockfish. Work a lure as close as possible to the bridge pilings and allow your offering to move naturally with the flow. Some anglers prefer to position themselves downtide and cast up and retrieve with the current. Others prefer fishing from an uptide position, letting their fly or lure drift downcurrent. We feel that whichever way works best for you is the way to go, although a position off to the side may be best of all. This positioning allows a quartering upcurrent cast, which in turn allows easy control of the lure or fly as it sweeps past the bridge abutment and allows you to release line as the artificial moves downcurrent.

The currents under the Fishing Bay Bridge can be confusing, often moving in different directions simultaneously. We've had someone attempt to explain this phenomenon, but we still don't understand it. Just take our word for the fact that during an outgoing tide, for example, the current at the north end of the bridge may be moving west, while at the south it may be moving east. It's weird, but it makes for some interesting fishing.

This bridge, like several others in the Chesapeake region, is a good bet for night fishing for stripers. Since the roadway is illuminated, the light spills over to the water and the roadway blocks the light, creating a definitive shadow line. Stripers hold just back from the edge of the shadow line, facing uptide and waiting for baitfish to be swept into easy striking range. They use the shadow line the way a brown trout uses an undercut bank.

You can fish this two ways. The first is to position your boat under the bridge facing uptide. Cast up and out—into the light. What you want to do is get your offering to land in the illuminated water, where the fish will spot it, and then drift into the shadows, preferably right around an abutment.

The other way is to anchor uptide from the bridge, cast quartering downtide and let your fly or lure be carried into the shadows. Strikes usually occur right at the shadow's edge. Either way works. The one advantage to fishing from under the bridge is that you can actually see the fish you are targeting. The disadvantage is that you will often be fishing in close quarters and you must be careful not to break a rod.

Due west of Fishing Creek is Barren Island. The west side of this island has a sand flat that drops off to four feet of water the length of the island. It's a good spot to fish at the beginning of a falling tide. The east side of the island is shallow and tricky. It's best avoided.

A mile or so farther down the island, there is another cut through to the main Honga River. Be advised that this is marked with only a single green marker, and that marker is misplaced. According to the "rules of the road" a green marker should be on your left as you move "in from the sea"—in this case from the Bay to the river. However, this particular marker is on the wrong side of the channel. You must go to the north of the marker to enter and safely traverse this narrow cut. There are usually branches sticking up as a makeshift indicator of the deeper water. Pay attention to these indicators and you shouldn't have any trouble. Or you can simply follow the previously mentioned, well-marked channel through the island at Fishing Creek. This is a safer bet.

MOUTH OF THE HONGA RIVER

Moving south along the shore, don't pass up Hooper Island light. In the fall, especially, you will often find schools of breaking stripers, and sometimes bluefish, patrolling these waters. The rocks and substructure around the light is always worth fishing. You can find both stripers and speckled trout amid the rocks. This is also an excellent spot to find Spanish mackerel. Look for them during a strong tidal flow from late summer through mid-fall.

As you move around the end of Hooper Island, be aware that the water close to shore is shallow, and in some places right near the tip, it's very shallow and hard. Stay well out from shore as you make the turn and you shouldn't have any trouble. As an aside, be sure you have a current chart of the area. It is foolish in the extreme to venture into most of the Chesapeake's waters without such a chart. Our favorites are the

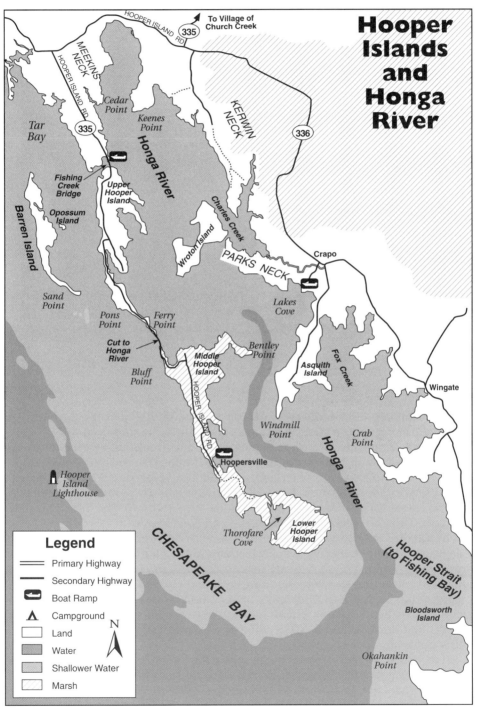

Hooper Islands and Honga River

To Village of Church Creek

335 HOOPER ISLAND RD

MEEKINS NECK

HOOPER ISLAND RD

Cedar Point

Keenes Point

KERWIN NECK

336

Tar Bay

335

Honga River

Fishing Creek Bridge

Upper Hooper Island

Opossum Island

Charles Creek

Wroton Island

Barren Island

Sand Point

Pons Point

Ferry Point

Cut to Honga River

PARKS NECK

Crapo

Lakes Cove

Bentley Point

Middle Hooper Island

Bluff Point

HOOPER ISLAND RD

Asquith Island

Fox Creek

Wingate

Windmill Point

Crab Point

Honga River

Hooper Island Lighthouse

Hoopersville

Thorofare Cove

Lower Hooper Island

Hooper Strait (to Fishing Bay)

CHESAPEAKE BAY

Bloodsworth Island

Okahankin Point

Legend

═══ Primary Highway
─── Secondary Highway
⬗ Boat Ramp
▲ Campground
☐ Land
▨ Water
▨ Shallower Water
▨ Marsh

N

A striper comes to the net. Notice that the net is made of rubber.
This greatly reduces injuries to fish that are released.

charts and chart books produced by ADC in Alexandria, Virginia (703-750-0510). In addition to being very detailed, their charts are printed on waterproof stock.

Once you round the turn into the Honga, you are faced with several choices, all good. The mouths of the Wicomico River, the Nanticoke, and the Honga come together at this point. All offer excellent opportunities. If you look at a chart, you will quickly see that the three rivers have deep channels that shelve rather abruptly into shallow water. These edges are some of the best spots to find fish. You may encounter stripers, speckled trout, bluefish, and flounder.

Inside the Honga, there are several particular spots to fish. Just north of the Hoopersville Ramp there are several wrecks indicated on the chart. Never fish this area without working these. Directly across from the ramp is Windmill Point. There are shallow flats that shelve rather abruptly into 20 to 30 feet of water. This is an excellent spot for speckled trout and stripers. North of the ramp and marked by #5 green buoy is Bentley Point. This is an excellent spot to find breaking stripers in October and November. In fact, the entire area around Bentley Point, Bentley Cove, and Asquith Island is very productive water.

If there is a more overlooked fishing spot in the Chesapeake Bay region than this area at the mouth of the Honga, we don't know what it is. This is undoubtedly one of the most productive areas north of the Chesapeake Bay Bridge Tunnel.

With the exception of Mike Murphy, who regularly runs guided trips on his 25-foot Parker, few Chesapeake Bay light-tackle guys bother with the area. Why? We're not at all sure, but it may have to do with driving distances and lack of facilities. It's a tad remote. If you are coming form the east, Salisbury is about the same distance from Crisfield as it is from Hooper Island. From the west, Deal Island is closer than Hooper Island, and although Crisfield is farther, the roads are much better, so driving time to either location is similar. And Crisfield has a number of fine restaurants and good motels as well as available camping in a state park, hence its greater popularity.

Hooper Island, by contrast, has no motels or restaurants worthy of the name, but the remoteness of the area lends itself to an overnighter. The nearest facilities are in Cambridge, but I'm told that Easton, another 20 minutes farther away, has far better accommodations and eating establishments. However, these disadvantages translate into some advantages in that there is little fishing pressure, and there are at least four launch ramps that have easy access to the area.

The best of these ramps is at the very end of Hooper Island Road in the village of Hoopersville. This is an excellent concrete ramp that can accommodate several sizeable boats simultaneously, and it features good solid piers and deep water. It's also free. The other area ramps are best suited to boats under 19 feet.

Launching at the Hoopersville Ramp puts you very near the mouth of the river in protected waters, and the fishing can be excellent just minutes from the ramp. We've fished there in the fall and found excellent action for breaking stripers all over

Ed Russell casting to the American Mariner. This rusted hulk is in the middle of the Bay about midway between Point Lookout and the mouth of the Honga River.

Pipe insulation cable tied to a boat rail makes a great place to temporarily store flies and lures.

the area. Once, the action in late afternoon was awesome in an area between Asquith Island and Bentley Cove, less than five minutes run upriver from the ramp. Small pods of striped bass were breaking all over the area, and it wasn't even necessary to do the usual gun-and-run procedure normally associated with working breaking fish. When an active pod sounded, we would either drift or await another to surface (which was never long in coming) or motor slowly a short distance to another active school. We didn't even have to depend on gulls, although there were hundreds of these feeding birds all over. There were so many breaking fish that frequently the birds would be working one school of fish while we worked another. Normally, the breaking fish will be smallish, with a 5-pounder a good catch, but there will usually be no lack of numbers.

Although the breaking stripers may be modest in size, larger versions can be found. As fall progresses and the water cools, bigger stripers move into the deeper parts of the river. November and early December are the best times to find the larger fish. Check out the channels, holes, and drop-offs. A good chart of the area, coupled with a quality depthfinder can help you locate fish.

If you want to target larger fish, there's another option; the waters of the open Bay are quite near, and you're not far from the Middle Grounds—one of the most popular Mid-Bay hotspots. This is likely the most popular area of the Bay for chumming, and breaking fish are usually an everyday occurrence.

In addition to striped bass, seatrout have been quite abundant in the region in recent years. Again, check out the deeper lies in the Honga proper and near the river's mouth and in the Mid-Bay deep spots. A 1-ounce Bass Assassin in limetreuse, or a 1-ounce Stingsilver are especially good choices. Just make sure you allow your lure to get to the bottom; that's where you'll generally find seatrout.

If you wish to use bait for seatrout, nothing beats a piece of soft crab, but that bait will likely be hard to find this time of year. However, there's an alternative that has gained wide popularity—a fresh strip of chicken breast. We've not tried this as yet, since we infrequently use bait, but all reports indicate that white chicken meat is almost as productive as crab, and it's a hell of a lot cheaper.

If you can't find fish, you might be able to get them to come to you. Mike Murphy always carries a couple of bags of frozen chum, and if things get tough, he anchors up and drops the bag of frozen menhaden over the side on a line. An occasional jiggle of the bag will create a small chum line, and you should be able to pick up some stripers or blues using small bay anchovy or silverside imitations on a fly rod. Use an intermediate sinking line for best results. Cast out and retrieve with short twitches followed by longer pauses. In this instance, you are not trying to imitate cut up menhaden (as with a chum fly) but rather the prevalent baitfish that are attracted to the chum. Stripers and blues both target the baitfish, and since you are mimicking an active critter, you won't have much worry about deep hooking the stripers.

For spinning or casting tackle, a small suspending minnow-shaped lure is an excellent choice. The Yo-Zuri Pin Minnow, or Rebel's Ghost Minnow are good examples that work quite well. A ¼-ounce jighead with a small glittery soft plastic tail (like Bass Assassin's Opening Night model) a Hopkins Spoon or a Stingsilver, is another good bet, and, since these go deeper than the plugs, they may dredge up some larger fish. One piece of advice—it's best to replace any treble hooks with single hooks for this fishing, or at least bend down the barbs on the existing hooks. One trick that we frequently employ, in addition to crushing the barbs, is to cut off the lower of the hooks on each treble. This doesn't seem to reduce the hooking ability, and it makes removing a hook much easier. Try it. You'll be pleasantly surprised. In any case, bend down the hook barb.

Another advantage to this area is the fact that you can usually get out of the wind if it's blowing hard. Except for the open mouth of the river, the rest of the Honga is guarded by landmass, so you can get shelter in any but a southeast blow, and even then, there are several islands that you can duck behind.

If you can't find fish in the Honga, there is yet another option. You can run out the river's mouth, through Hooper Strait, and then go north into the mouth of Fishing Bay, or go a little farther east and run up into the Nanticoke where you can almost certainly find sheltered waters and good fishing.

All in all, this area is well worth investigating. Fishing pressure is normally light, and unless the weather is unusually cold, November and early December are great times to find both striped bass and seatrout in the Honga River area.

If you're a newcomer to the area, we'd strongly suggest hiring a guide. One we can recommend is Mike Murphy. Mike runs Tide Runner Charters featuring a very comfortable 25-foot Parker. He specializes in light-tackle fishing and knows the waters in and around the Honga River quite well. Call him at 410-820-8087 for information. I personally feel that hiring a guide when fishing new waters for the first time pays big dividends. You'll learn more in a day with a competent guide than you will on your own in a month.

Getting There

As mentioned, this area is fairly remote (for an Eastern Seaboard location, that is). Taylors Island is reachable by taking Route 16 out of Cambridge, which will bring you right to a launch ramp on Slaughter Creek. You can follow Smithville Road south to Route 335 (Hooper Island Road) to reach Hooper Island and the mouth of the Honga. To bypass Taylors Island and go directly to Hooper Island, again take Route 16 from Cambridge, but pick up Route 335 (Church Creek Road) at the village of Church Creek. Follow that to Hooper Island Road (still Route 335). This road runs the entire length of the island.

Launch Ramps

Several ramps serve this area. Taylors Island Ramp is on the north end of Taylors Island. To reach it, take Route 16 from Cambridge to Taylors Landing on the north side of road (just before Slaughter Creek). Best suited to smaller boats.

Hooper Island has two ramps. The first (Tyler Cove) is right by the Route 335 Bridge over Fishing Creek. Suited to small boats. The second (and best) one is at Hoopersville near the end of Hooper Island. It's an excellent concrete ramp with deep water and can handle two boats simultaneously. The ramp is right on Route 335 by a fish-packing house.

Local Services

There isn't much. The nearest accommodations are in Cambridge. Restaurant choices on the islands are quite limited. Taylor's Island has the Taylors Island General Store (410-221-2911) right on Route 16. They do a brisk lunch business. It's quite inexpensive and the food is good.

Hooper Island features the Old Salty Restaurant (sometimes); its hours of operation are a little vague: usually, they're open quite early for breakfast, and they do a brisk lunch business. Whether dinner is offered tends to be sporadic. When it's open, it has good, inexpensive food. Call 410-397-3752 for more information.

In Cambridge, try Snapper's Waterfront Café (410-228-0112). It has a wide choice of menu items and is moderately priced.

Tackle and Techniques

Everything previously said about suitable tackle for the Bay still applies; however, there are a few new twists. A favorite local fly is a so-called Crab Clouser. Developed by Baltimore fly shop owner Joe Bruce, From the top down, this fly has a layer of olive bucktail, a thick layer of copper Flashabou, a layer of tan bucktail, a few strands of gold Krystal Flash, and a bottom layer of white bucktail. I have no idea why this combination is so effective, but it is.

For spinning or casting tackle, try a ¼- or ½-ounce jighead with a chartreuse or pearl soft plastic body. We favor 4- or 5-inch Bass Assassin Split Tail Shad. For a crankbait, it's hard to beat a ½-ounce Rat-L-Trap. Of all the noise-producing lures, this one is our favorite. Two colors that have worked well are silver with a blue back or fire tiger.

To catch Spanish macks, you'll need small flashy flies or lures. Two-inch streamers with plenty of flash material tied in will draw strikes. One problem with fishing for Spanish with a fly rod is the fact that these fish like a very fast retrieve—something that is possible to do with a fly rod, but very tiring. A fast-retrieve spinning reel works a lot easier.

One thing worth mentioning: for a lot of this fishing, especially when targeting stripers that have a 2-per-day limit, barbless hooks are the way to go. They are much easier to remove from the mouth of a fish that is to be released than one with a barb. They come out of your arm better too, if you are unlucky enough to find out.

Rat-L-Trap lures in ¼- and ½-ounce sizes are now available with barbless, Teflon-coated treble hooks. However, Ken Chaumont, of Bill Lewis Lures, the makers of the Rat-L-Traps, tells me that it's difficult to persuade the rank and file fisherman of the advantages of barbless hooks. Most feel that fish more easily throw a barbless hook than one with a barb. Our experience, and that of many expert guides, including those who fish for tarpon (a fish with a notoriously tough mouth), indicates that the reverse is true. A barbless hook simply penetrates more easily, and if the hook design is right, will generally go completely through the jaw of most fish. The slippery Teflon coating on the Eagle Claw hooks that Rat-L-Traps employ enhance this characteristic. If you plan to release any fish, and if you fish for stripers, barbless hooks make a lot of sense. Although we'd still prefer a lure with a single hook, most anglers resist this concept even more than barbless trebles, so at least the new barbless Teflon-coated hooks are a step in the right direction.

One other trick that you can try is to cut off the lower hook of all trebles. This makes hook removal easier, decreases the lure's tendency to pick up grass, and as far as we can tell, has no effect on the lure's hooking ability.

A Cordell Red Fin is a good choice for open water.

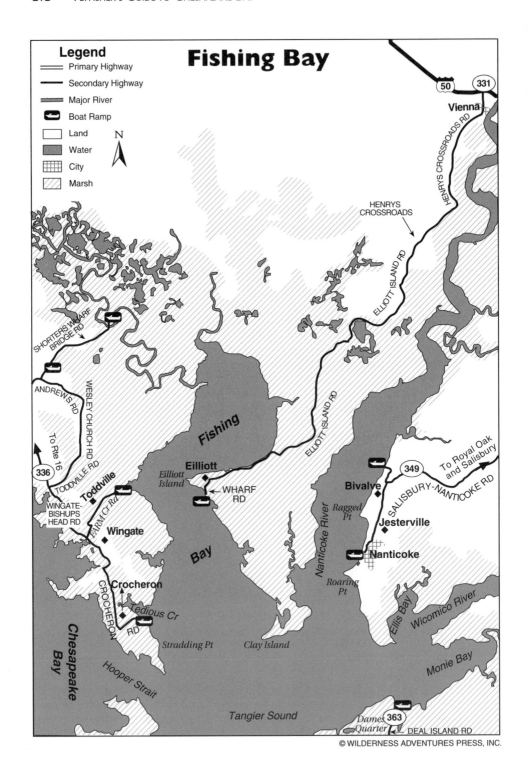

Fishing Bay

Legend
- Primary Highway
- Secondary Highway
- Major River
- Boat Ramp
- Land
- Water
- City
- Marsh

N

© WILDERNESS ADVENTURES PRESS, INC.

FISHING BAY, NANTICOKE RIVER, AND WICOMICO RIVER

There's not a whole lot to say that's different than what's already been mentioned about the Honga. These three rivers are quite similar to the Honga and share many of the same characteristics. Each river has a deep channel that shelves abruptly to shallow water, but the deep water in the Honga tends to be narrower, and thus concentrates the fish more. Underwater grasses, sandy points, and tidal rips abound, however, and anywhere a tide washes across a bar is a good bet.

When the waters are muddied after a period of heavy rain, the grassy spots will be clearer and more attractive to fish; actually, this premise holds true throughout the Bay. Anytime you can find clean water amid turbid, this will be a hotspot. Sometimes the dirty water can be the result of stingrays foraging in the shallows. If too many rays are present, the entire area will get murky; however, when only a few rays are active, many predator fish will follow the rays looking to pick-off any stray baitfish they dislodge. A fly or lure cast in front and to the side of a ray may bring a strike from a striper or bluefish. It pays to check.

In Fishing Bay, two good spots are the two points that define the mouth of the river. The inside of Stradling Point on the west side of the river is best on an outgoing tide. Clay Island (actually part of the point) on the east side works best on incoming, although either tide may be productive. Stripers can be found here most of the year. Speckled trout and/or gray trout (weakfish) may also be there. The shallows are good for the two trout species from early May to mid-June. After that, the shallows will get too warm and they'll move to deeper, cooler water. When trout are the target early on, any of the flies and lures already mentioned can be productive. If the fish get "picky" try tipping your lure with a piece of peeler crab. It's the best bait of all for trout. In a pinch, you can use a strip of squid, or, do as Mike Murphy does and purchase some of the frozen shrimp that are being sold exclusively as bait. It's available in many sporting goods stores and is cheaper than what's sold for human consumption. we suspect that this is shrimp that has gotten "a little past its prime."

The Nanticoke River is just to the east of Fishing Bay. Smaller than the previous two, with not as many "nooks and crannies," there are still a couple of good spots. On the western side of the mouth of the river, there is a grassy flat called Sandy Island. This is a good spot to visit near the top of the tide. When the water is deep enough for predator fish to work these flats, fishing can be quite good.

On the eastern side, two significant points, Ragged Point and Roaring Point, intrude into an otherwise featureless shoreline. Either would be good on an incoming or outgoing tide, but Roaring Point, nearest the mouth, creates the best tide rips because it is quite pronounced, and it usually offers the best fishing.

Much of the shoreline in this area is deceptive. What appears to be quite shallow actually may be several feet deep. The soil at the shoreline is soft and tidal action undercuts the banks, providing an ideal hiding spot for several fish species. Depending on water temperature, you may find stripers, flounder, or seatrout working these undercut banks. If the water is a couple of feet deep, with grass on the bottom, you might want to try a floater/diver offering. Often, the action of a fly or lure that floats then dives beneath the surface when retrieved proves irresistible to game fish. Try a Clouser Floating Minnow on a fly rod. This fly is exceptionally easy to construct and deadly in operation. Cast it, let it sit briefly, then give a pull, and it dives a little beneath the surface. Although developed by Bob Clouser for use on small-mouth bass, it works equally well in shallow saltwater applications.

For a lure, consider a Bill Lewis Slap-Stick. This minnow-shaped lure floats near vertical, but when retrieved, moves up then dives just below the surface. It's great for working over subsurface grasses because its running depth can be controlled by the speed of your retrieve. Work it slow and it stays just under the surface. A faster retrieve will take it down about a foot. Stripers and both species of trout love it.

Around the corner from the Nanticoke is the Wicomico River. Much the smallest of the other rivers mentioned in this section, it has a narrow channel and much less water flow. An incoming tide will produce more flow than outgoing and will usually fish best. Nanticoke Point marks the western mouth of the river and Wingate Point the eastern side, and both are key spots in the river. There are submerged pilings right off the tip of Nanticoke Point, which are both a good spot to fish and a place for caution. The upriver side of both points should be most productive with incoming water. Monie Bay, to the east side of the river's mouth, is an excellent spot on a rising tide. Just as the flood tide begins to turn, try working the mouths of the three creeks that empty into Monie Bay. A receding tide will bring lots of baitfish with it that had moved up into these shallow areas to feed and escape predators.

Launch Ramps

Fishing Bay is served by several boat ramps. The best three are Elliot Island Ramp about midway on the east side of the river, Toddville Farm Creek Ramp midway on the west side, and Crocheron near the end of the peninsula on the west side.

To get to the Toddville Ramp, follow Route 16 from Cambridge to Church Creek. Then follow Route 335 to the "T" at Route 336. Take 336 south to Farm Creek Road. Follow that to the ramp.

To reach the ramp at Crocheron, follow the above directions, but do not turn at Farm Creek. Stay on Route 336 to the town of Crocheron. The ramp is near the road's end on the left at Tedious Creek.

To reach Elliott Island, follow Route 50 to the town of Vienna—about midway between Cambridge and Salisbury. Go south on Henry's Crossroads Road (which is at the junction of Routes 50 and 331) past Henry's Crossroads. The road becomes Elliott Island Road, which you will follow all the way to the end. The ramp is by McCready Creek.

The Nanticoke River is served by two ramps: Cedar Hill Park and Nanticoke Park. Both are on the eastern side of the river. To reach Cedar Hill, follow Route 349 west from Salisbury. You will pass Royal Oak then Cox's Corner heading towards Bivalve (Virginia had first dibs on Oyster). The ramp is in Cedar Hill Park. The second ramp, at Nanticoke Park, is several miles farther downriver on the same road at Nanticoke.

The Wicomico has only one nearby ramp, and that is the Deal island Ramp on the northern end of Deal Island. Follow the Route 13 bypass around Salisbury to Route 13 south. Take Route 13 south to Princess Anne. At Princess Anne, take Route 363 to Dames Quarter. The ramp is on the right.

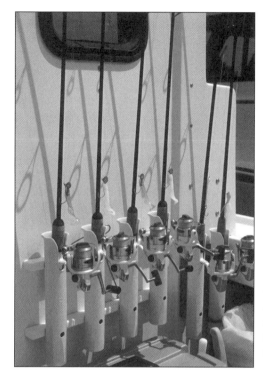

Guide Mike Murphy keeps many rods rigged and ready for his clients.

DEAL ISLAND AND BLOODSWORTH ISLAND

Deal Island lies between Tangier Sound and the Manokin River. For the most part, the island itself is of little interest as far as fishing goes. One exception is the rocky jetties that form the entrance to the harbor and launch ramp at the south end of the island. On a moving tide, these rocky structures are excellent spots to seek striped bass and sometimes speckled trout. Typically, the best side to fish will vary with the tide, but it will almost always be the side that pushes your boat towards the rocks. Since you pass these structures whenever you launch or retrieve your boat when you use this ramp, always take the time to make at least a few casts. A streamer or a swimming lure is the best bet. Cast uptide and let the current wash your offering along the edges of the rocks. Where the water swirls around the tip of the jetty is a prime spot. This is a good spot to fish a soft plastic lure on a jighead. A red head and a green body is a very popular combination for trout, and chartreuse and/or pearl are top colors for stripers.

Deal Island is a good "jumping off" spot to fish the open waters of Tangier Sound to the south, the mouth of the Manokin River to the east, and

Bloodsworth Island and South Marsh Island due west. This entire area can offer good fishing for several species depending on the time of year.

From about mid-May to mid-June, large Atlantic croaker populate the shallow grassy areas throughout this entire region pretty much from the mouth of the Honga

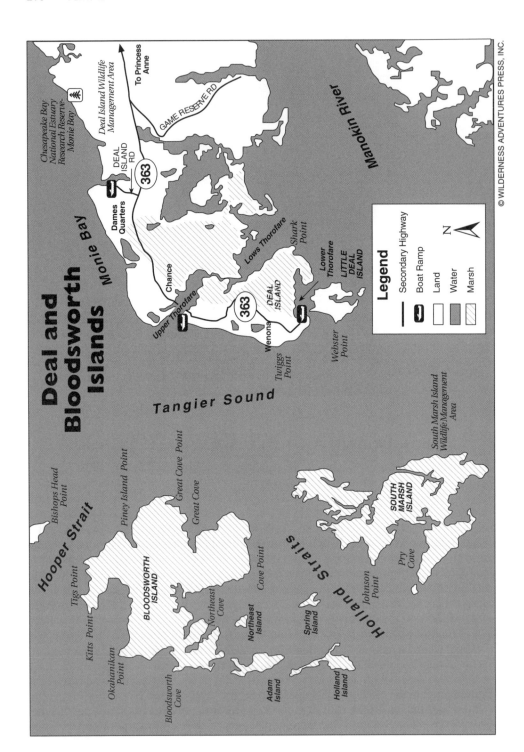

Deal and Bloodsworth Islands

River south. Typically, these hard fighting fish will be found mixed among weakfish and/or speckled trout. During this period, a fly rod equipped with a slow-sinking line and a small flashy streamer (Clousers are perfect) will take its share of croakers. Of course, anglers favoring spinning or casting gear can score with smaller soft plastics on ¼-ounce jigheads. Chartreuse bodies with red heads are very popular. As the water warms, both the trout and croakers will move to deeper waters where many anglers fish for them with bottom rigs. Interestingly, anglers employing jigging spoons often do as well or better than those using bait.

It's possible to take croakers from these deeper lairs with fly gear as well, but fishing a 450-grain, fast-sinking line will be called for, and since the fish may be in depths of 40 feet or more, it takes an extremely patient fly fisherman to score.

Late summer and early fall will find large schools of Spanish mackerel frequenting the deeper water nearby, especially any spots where there is a good tide rip. Spanish prefer deeper, moving water. When you find schools of these fellows breaking, it can be pandemonium. Almost any small silvery offering will bring a strike, but the retrieve must be quite fast. Spanish mackerel are fast-moving fish and will generally ignore a slowly retrieved lure. This is one reason why trolling for this species is popular, you can troll at a good clip and present a fast-moving lure. However, about the only way you can tell that you've hooked a fish with this method is that the rod may be bent a little. We've done it, and trolling does put fish in the cooler, but as a sport, dominoes is more exciting.

This area is also a prime location to find breaking fish from late summer until mid-November. Sometimes the number of schools of breaking fish is just mind-boggling. It is no trick to hook up with 50 or more fish during an outing. It really can be quite amazing. On a good afternoon, you may literally see acre upon acre of breaking fish strung out for miles.

However, there are a few tricks to success. First and foremost, it is critical to avoid spooking the fish. This is easy to accomplish. Simply approach the breaking schools slowly from uptide or upwind and cut the engine just before you are into casting range. Done properly, you can find yourself with fish breaking all around the boat. When it's like this, the fishing is almost too good.

Match the lure or fly to the size and color of the baitfish. Believe it or not, this can be critical. The breaking fish, which can be either striped bass or bluefish (or both), will be feeding on bay anchovies or silversides. Both of these critters are small—usually no more than three inches and sometimes as small as an inch. We have seen countless examples where one angler was fishing a small surface popper and getting three times as many strikes an another angler fishing a lure just a little larger. Color can be important, as well. Our two favorite colors for these breaking fish are all silver or all white. A two-inch semi-transparent Clouser Minnow with a gray or olive back or a small, white pencil popper or crease fly are excellent choices. For a surface lure, a Super Pop-R, a Striper Strike, or a Spit-Fire in small sizes are perfect.

Typically, the breaking fish won't be too large; however, larger specimens are almost always lurking below the surface-feeding fish. Try dropping a Stingsilver, or a ½-ounce jig with a soft plastic tail over the side. Often, it won't even reach bottom. Usually, the fish you catch will be bigger and may also be a different species—usually

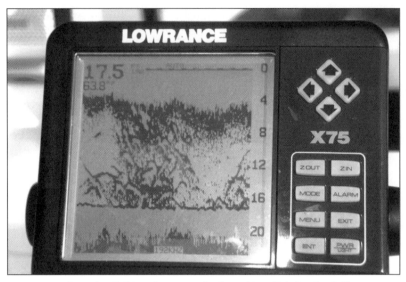

When the fishing heats up for breaking fish in the fall, a depthfinder can look like this.

weakfish or speckled trout. The only thing, of course, is that a surface strike is so much more exciting than a subsurface one.

It is not always roses, though. Problems arise when other unknowing or uncaring anglers run their boats directly into the breaking schools of fish in their haste to get in on the bonanza, causing the fish to sound and ruining the action completely. Or trollers may go directly through the school with similar results. Sadly, there seems to be no cure for stupidity or rudeness. You can either move on or wait for the fish to resurface. Fortunately, the fish usually don't stay down too long.

When the fish aren't breaking, it's a good time to explore the north end of Bloodsworth Island. If you look at a chart, you'll see that the shallow shoreline of the island drops off abruptly into much deeper water right near shore. This is probably the very best spot on the whole island. The western shore of the island is also good, and there is a fairly abrupt drop-off from 3 or 4 feet to about 14 feet. This drop-off is well worth fishing. The waters around the rest of the island are quite shallow and hazardous.

Speaking of hazards, it's well to note that Bloodsworth Island belongs to the U.S. Navy and is used for target practice. It is not at all uncommon to be buzzed by an A10 (those ungainly but effective tank-killers affectionately called the Warthog). If one of those guys comes blasting overhead—leave.

About midway between the north ends of Bloodsworth and Deal Islands is Shark Fin Shoal. Marked by a lighthouse, this can be a very productive spot. Late summer and early fall, it's a good spot for Spanish mackerel. Just off the north end of the light is a submerged wreck that is worth investigating.

Launch Ramps

Two launch ramps on the west side of Deal Island offer access to this area. The first is at the Upper Thoroughfare and the second (the best) is at the Lower Thoroughfare. Follow Route 13 from Salisbury to Princess Anne. Then take Route 363 past the ramp at Dames Quarters. When you cross the bridge to Deal Island, the first ramp is to the right. This ramp is suitable for boats to 22 feet. The second ramp is at the end of Route 363 at the town of Wenona. It is a good ramp (if a little smelly due to commercial crabbing and fishing activity) with a well-protected harbor. Also, the channel out to the sound is well marked and there are the previously mentioned rock jetties to check out. This is definitely the best launch ramp in the area.

Local Services

To say that the area we are covering in this section is a little remote doesn't quite convey the message. It's a step back in time. This is not a touristy area, it's well off the beaten path to virtually anywhere. The closest lodging to be had is in the towns of Cambridge, Princess Anne, and Salisbury. Cambridge is closest from the west side of Fishing Bay. From Deal Island, Princess Anne is closest followed by Salisbury. For the rest of the area, Salisbury is probably the best bet.

Salisbury has many restaurants as well as a host of fast food/carry-out spots. If you like seafood, try Waterman's Cove (410-546-1400). This is a local favorite. The Red Roost on Clara Road, Whitehaven (800-953-5443) features a huge all-you-can-eat menu that includes such items as snow crabs, ribs, and steamed shrimp, as well as more traditional fare. Or try Crab World, 507 west Salisbury Parkway (410-742-2028). All kinds of crabs are on the menu as well as oysters, clams, and lobster.

Captain Mike Murphy with a gray trout taken in the Honga River.

Hub Cities for the Mid-Bay Eastern Shore

Easton

Population—10,000

Rated one of the "Top Ten Small Towns in America," Easton offers the culture and amenities of a metropolitan area in a friendly, small town setting. The community prides itself on maintaining the historic character of its eighteenth century past while at the same time offering modern conveniences.

ACCOMMODATIONS
Atlantic Budget Inn, 8058 Ocean Gateway; 410-822-2200; shelym@goeaston.net
Comfort Inn, 8523 Ocean Gateway; 410-820-8333 or 800-221-2222
Econo Lodge, 8175 Ocean Gateway; 410-820-5555 or 800-55-ECONO; sitaram@crosslink.com
The Tidewater Inn & Conference Center, 101 East Dover Street; 410-822-1300 or 800-237-8775; info@tidewaterinn.com

RESTAURANTS
Denny's, 8394 Ocean Gateway; 410-820-9718
Golden Coral Family Steak House, 8451 Ocean Gateway; 410-822-9030
H & G Restaurant, 8163 Ocean Gateway; 410-822-1085
China Buffet, 8223 Elliott Road, Shoppes at Easton
The Inn at Easton, 28 South Harrison Street; 410-822-4910; inquiries@theinnateaston.com
Mason's, 22 South Harrison Street; 410-822-3204; masons@dmv.com
Rustic Inn, 200 North Harrison Street, Talbottown Shopping Center; 410-820-8212
Washington Street Pub, 20 North Washington Street; 410-822-9011; fax 410-822-9031; mstevens@expresshost.com.
Tom's Tavern & Steak House, 106 North West Street; 410-770-3710

FLY SHOPS, TACKLE STORES, AND SPORTING GOODS
Shore Sportsman Hunting & Fishing Unlimited, 8232 Ocean Gateway; 410-820-5599
G & H Bait Sales, 8749 Ocean Gateway; 410-819-8169
Winchester Creek Outfitters, 313 Winchester Creek Road, Grasonville; 410-827-7000

LAUNCH RAMPS AND MARINAS
Oak Creek Public Landing, Route 50 to Route 322 west to Route 33 west to Back Street south—look to the left
Easton Point Landing, Route 50 To Route 322 West To Port Street west
Wye Landing, Route 50 to Route 213 south to Route 662 south to Wye Landing Lane

BOAT EQUIPMENT AND REPAIR
Fred Quimby's Marine Service, 202 Bank Street; 410-822-8107
Mid-Shore Marine Service, 9202 Goldsborough Neck; 410-819-6561

AUTO REPAIR
Bay Street Garage, 28264 Saint Michaels Road; 410-822-5995
Bob Smith Automotive Group, 7677 Ocean Gateway; 410-822-1010

HOSPITALS
Easton Memorial Hospital, 219 S. Washington Street; 410-820-8444

FOR FURTHER INFORMATION
Talbot County Chamber of Commerce, 410-822-4653;
info@talbotchamber.org

*Guide Richie Gaines and client with a
school striper.*

St. Michaels

Population—1,193

St. Michaels is located in Talbot County, 10 miles west of Easton, between McDaniel and Newcomb along Highway 33. It is the home of Chesapeake Bay Maritime Museum.

ACCOMMODATIONS

St. Michaels Harbour Inn & Marina, 101 N Harbor Road; 410-745-9001 or 800-955-9001; www.harbourinn.com

Lowes Wharf Marina Inn, 21651 Lowes Wharf Road, Sherwood; 410-745-6684 or 888-484-9267; www.loweswharf.com; info@loweswharf.com

Best Western St. Michaels Motor Inn, 1228 S. Talbot Street; 410-745-3333; www.bestwestern.com/stmichaelsmotorinn

RESTAURANTS

Town Dock Restaurant, 125 Mulberry Street; 410-745-5577; www.town-dock.com

Tavern on Talbot, 409 Talbot Street; 410-745-9343

The Crab Claw Restaurant Navy Point; 410-745-2900; www.thecrabclaw.com

St. Michaels Crab House & Restaurant, 305 Mulberry Street; 410-745-3737; www.stmichaelscrabhouse.com

Bistro St. Michaels, 403 S. Talbot Street; 410-745-9111

208 Talbot Restaurant, 208 N. Talbot, Street; 410-745-3838; www.208talbot.com

FLY SHOPS, TACKLE STORES, AND SPORTING GOODS

Keepers of St Michaels, 105 S Talbot Street; 800-549-1872

LAUNCH RAMPS AND MARINAS

Balls Creek Landing, Balls Creek at end of Bozman-Neavitt Road in Neavitt, from Route 33 to Route 579 south and go to end; 410-822-2955

Bellevue Landing, Tred Avon River, end of Bellevue Road, Route 50 to Route 22 west to Route 33 west to Route 329 south to Bellevue Road south and go to end; 410-770-8050

Oak Creek Public Landing, Oak Creek at Oak Creek Bridge in village of Newcomb; Route 50 to Route 322 west to Route 33 west to Back St. south, look to the left; 410-770-8050

West Harbor Road, Miles River, Route 33 to town of St. Michaels to Chesapeake Ave. North to West Harbor Road; 410- 745-9535

St. Michaels Marina, 305 Mulberry Street, 410-745-2400, 800-678-8980; info@stmichaelsmarina.com; www.stmichaelsmarina.com

Higgins Yacht Yard, Inc, 203-205 Carpenter Street; 410-745-9303

End of the Harbor Docks, 217 East Chestnut Street; 410-745-0107; abbycampi@yahoo.com

BOAT REPAIR

St. Michaels Outboard and Mower Sales and Service, 1118 Talbot Street; 410-745-5557; stmichaelsom@aol.com; www.stmichaelsmd.org/members/smom

Tidewater Honda Marine Center, 1114 S. Talbot Street; 410-745-5678 or 800-300-2540; www.tidewaterboats.com

AUTO REPAIR

Bay Hundred Automotive, 1021 S Talbot St # B; 410-745-0071

St. Michaels Automotive Center, 906 S Talbot Street; 410-745-2848

HOSPITALS

Memorial Hospital at Easton, 219 South Washington St., Easton; 410-822-1000

FOR FURTHER INFORMATION

Talbot County Office of Tourism, 410-770-8000 St. Michaels Business Association, P.O. Box 1221, St. Michaels, MD 21663; 800-808-SMBA(7622); info@stmichaelsmd.org

Tilghman Island

Population—970

Tilghman Island is situated close St. Michaels, Oxford, and Easton. Tilghman is home to the skipjacks, the last commercial sailing fleet in North America.

ACCOMMODATIONS

Wades Point Inn, On the bay; 410-745-2500 or 888-923-3466

The Oaks Inn, Route 329 at Acorn Lane, Royal Oak; 410-745-5053; www.the-oaks.com/

Black Walnut Point Bed and Breakfast Inn, Black Walnut Road; 410-886-2452 www.tilghmanisland.com/blackwalnut/

Sinclair House Bed and Breakfast, 5718 Black Walnut Point; 410-886-2147 or 888-859-2147; www.tilghmanisland.com/sinclair/

RESTAURANTS

The Tilghman Island Inn, 410-886-2141 or 800-866-2141, Bay Hundred, 6178 Tilghman Island Road; 410-886-2126

The Bridge Restaurant, 6136 Tilghman Road; 410-886-2330

Harrison's Chesapeake House, 21551 Chesapeake House Dr.; 410-886-2121

FLY SHOPS, TACKLE STORES, AND SPORTING GOODS

See St. Michaels, Maryland.

LAUNCH RAMPS AND MARINAS

Dogwood Harbor, Harris Creek, Route 33 to Tilghman Island to Dogwood Harbor Road East; 410-770-8050

Eastern Bay Landing, Eastern Bay at Claiborne, Route 33 To Route 451 West to Claiborne Landing Road West; 410-770-8050

Cummings Creek Landing, Cummings Creek in Wittman, Route 33 To Pot Pie Road, east to end of Howeth Road South; 410-770-8050

Knapps Narrows Marina, 6176 Tilghman Island Road; 410-886-2720

Tilghman Island Marina, 5 Bayshore Drive; 410-886-2500

BOAT REPAIR

Colliers Marine Repair Service, 410-886-2522

Severn Marine Services, 410-886-2159

AUTO REPAIR

Covington Garage & Supply, 6066 Tilghman Island Road; 410-886-2282

Island Automotive, 5801 Tilghman Island Road; 410-886-2900

HOSPITALS

See Easton, Maryland.

FOR FURTHER INFORMATION

Talbot County Office of Tourism, 11 North Washington Street, Easton, MD 21601; 410-770-8010

Oxford

Population—970

Oxford is one of the oldest towns in Maryland, officially founded in 1683. Today, Oxford is enjoying a new resurgence based on tourism and leisure activities.

ACCOMMODATIONS

Combsberry, 4837 Evergreen Road; 410-226-5353; www.combsberry.com

The Nichols House, 217 S. Morris Street; 410-226-5799; nicholshouse@bluecrab.org

Oxford Inn, 504 S. Morris Street; 410-226-5220; oxfordinn@friendly.net; www.oxfordmd.com/oxfordinn

The Robert Morris Inn, 314 N. Morris St. & The Strand; 410-226-5111; www.robertmorrisinn.com

The 1876 House, 110 N. Morris Street; 410-226-5496; bb1876house.yahoo.com; www.oxfordmd.com/1876house

RESTAURANTS

Latitude 38° Bistro & Spirits, 26342 Oxford Road; 410-226-5303

Mathilda's Restaurant, 103 Mill Street; 410-226-0056

Mill Street Grill, 101 Mill Street; 410-226-0400

Oxford Market & Deli, 203 S. Morris Street; 410-226-0015

Pier Street Restaurant and Marina, West Pier Street; 410-226-5171

Schooner's Landing Waterfront Restaurant, foot of Tilghman Street; 410-226-0160

FLY SHOPS, TACKLE STORES, AND SPORTING GOODS

See St. Michaels, Maryland.

LAUNCH RAMPS AND MARINA

Oxford Landing Launch Ramp, Tred Avon River, end Of Tilghman Street; 410-226-5122

Town Creek Marina, 313 South Morris Street; 410-226-0207

Crockett Bros. Boatyard, 202 Banks Street; 410-226-5113

BOAT REPAIR

Oxford Boat Yard, 402 East Strand; 410-226-5101

Oxford Marine Services, 109 Third Street; 410-226-0223,

Oxford Boatyard, 402 E. Strand; 410-226-5101

Campbell's Town Creek Boatyard, 109 Myrtle Avenue; 410-226-0213; Campbells@Goeaston.Net

Bates Marine, 106 Richardson Street; 410-226-5105

FOR FURTHER INFORMATION

The Oxford Business Association, P.O. Box 544, Oxford, MD 21654-0544; 410-226-5730

Talbot County Chamber of Commerce, 410-822-4653; email:info@talbotchamber.org

Cambridge

Population—10,911

The seat of Dorchester County, Cambridge is one of the earliest settlements in Maryland. Its position on the Choptank River and its proximity to the Chesapeake Bay explain the array of work and pleasure boats that fill the harbor.

ACCOMMODATIONS

Commodores Cottage Bed & Breakfast, 210 Talbot Ave.; 410-228-1245
Holiday Inn Express, 2715 Ocean Gateway; 866-287-3140
Glasgow Inn, 1500 Hambrooks Boulevard; 410-228-0575, 800-373-7890
Cambridge House Bed And Breakfast, 112 High Street; 410-221-7700

CAMPGROUNDS

Madison Bay Campground and Marina, on Little Choptank River; 410-221-8005
Taylor's Island Family Campground, on the Chesapeake Bay, Box 156, Taylor's Island, MD 21669; 410-397-3275

RESTAURANTS

Carols Eastside Kitchen, Aireys Rd & Cordtown; 410-228-3830
The Cator House, 411 Muse Street; 410-221-7517
English's Family Restaurants, 410-228-4344
Ironwood Inn Restaurant, 410-221-0800

FLY SHOPS, TACKLE STORES, AND SPORTING GOODS

Shore Sportsman Hunting & Fishing Unlimited, 8232 Ocean Gateway, Easton; 410-820-5599

LAUNCH RAMPS AND MARINAS

Great Marsh Launch Ramp, Choptank River, Route 50 to Route 343 west to Leonards Lane north to Glasgow St. west to Somerset; 410-228-1955
Franklin Street Launch Ramp, Choptank River, Route 50 to Route 343 west to Leonards Lane North to Glasgow St. west to Somerset Ave. north; 410-228-1955
Trenton Street Launch Ramp, Cambridge Creek, Route 50 to Maryland Ave. west to Trenton St south, look on west side of street; 410-228-7291
Secretary Launch Ramp, Warwick River, Secretary, MD, Route 50 to Route 16 north to Route 14 north to town of Secretary to Temple St. south

BOAT REPAIR

Baycraft Marine, 6062 Todds Point Road; 410-228-9432
Mid-Shore Marine Service, 9202 Goldsborough Neck, Easton; 410-819-6561

AUTO REPAIR

Hubcap's Automotive, 421 Academy Street; 410-228-5040
Jimmy's Automotive, 2955 Ocean Gateway; 410-228-0550

Hospitals
Dorchester General Hospital, 300 Byrn Street; 410-228-5511

For Further Information
Dorchester County Tourism, 2 Rose Hill Place, Cambridge, Maryland 21613; 410-228-1000 or 800-522-TOUR; www.tourdorchester.org; info@tourdorchester.org

*Gary Diamond with a good-sized
striper taken on fly tackle.*

Gary Diamond with a big croaker. They're present in large numbers in the summer.

Salisbury

Population—23,743

Salisbury is located at the headwaters of the Wicomico River and is the county seat of Wicomico County. The city boasts the second largest water port in Maryland and the second largest airport (the only one on the Eastern Shore offering commercial airline service).

ACCOMMODATIONS

Best Budget Inn, 804 N Salisbury Blvd.; 410-546-2238
Economy Inn, 1500 N Salisbury Blvd.; 410-749-6178
Ramada Inn, 300 S Salisbury Blvd.; 410-546-4400
Sleep Inn, 406 Punkin Ct.; 410-572-5516
Super 8 Motel, 2615 N Salisbury Blvd.; 410-749-5131

RESTAURANTS

Applebee's, 2703 N. Salisbury Blvd.; 410-546-0997
Crab World, 507 W. Salisbury Pkwy.; 410-742-2211
La Tolteca Mexican Restaurant, 110 Truitt Street; 410-749-8663
Mulligan's, 1309 S. Salisbury Blvd.; 410-742-6400

FLY SHOPS, TACKLE STORES, AND SPORTING GOODS

Keepers #2, 909 S Shumaker Drive; 410-742-4988
Salisbury Fly Shop, 325 Snow Hill Road; 410-543-8359

LAUNCH RAMPS AND MARINAS

Port Salisbury Launch Ramp, Wicomico River, Route 50 to Small St. south to Main St. west, look on south side of road; 410- 548-3170
Wetipquin Boat Ramp, Nanticoke River, take Rt. 50 to Rt. 349 west and turn right on Wetipquin Road north, look for park by southwest corner of bridge; 410-548-4900
Cedar Hill Park Marina, Nantocoke River, Route 50 to Route 349 west to Cedar Hill Pkwy. west to Harbor View Road; 410-548-4900
Nanticoke Harbor, Nanticoke River, on Nanticoke Road off Rt. 349, Rt. 50 to Rt. 349 west, to town of Nanticoke to Harbor Rd. west; 410-548-4900

BOAT REPAIR

Mobile Marine, 6035 Hammond School Road; 410-546-4472

AUTO REPAIR

A & L Service Center, (Wrecker Service) 519 Burton Street; 410-543-8160

HOSPITALS

Peninsula Regional Medical Center, 100 E Carroll Street; 410-546-6400

FOR FURTHER INFORMATION

Wicomico Co. Convention & Visitors Bureau, 8480 Ocean Highway, Delmar, MD 21875; 800-332-TOUR, 410-548-4914

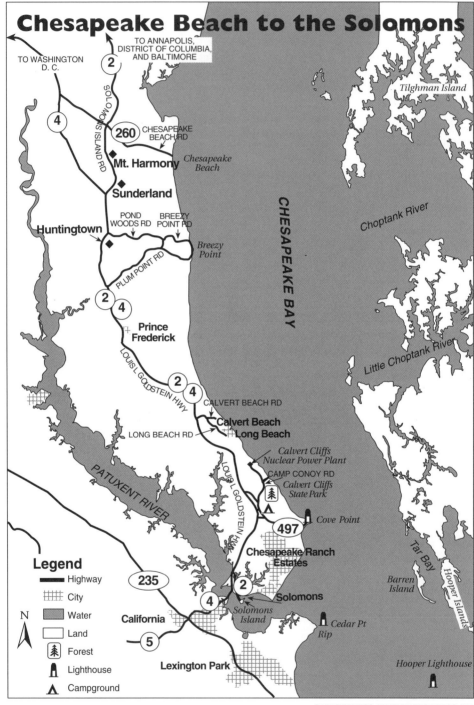

Chesapeake Beach to the Solomons

TO WASHINGTON D.C.

TO ANNAPOLIS, DISTRICT OF COLUMBIA, AND BALTIMORE

2

4

SOLOMONS ISLAND RD

260 CHESAPEAKE BEACH RD

◆ **Mt. Harmony**

Chesapeake Beach

◆ **Sunderland**

POND WOODS RD

BREEZY POINT RD

Huntingtown ◆

Breezy Point

PLUM POINT RD

2
4

⊹ **Prince Frederick**

LOUIS L GOLDSTEIN HWY

2
4

CALVERT BEACH RD

Calvert Beach

LONG BEACH RD — ⊞**Long Beach**

Calvert Cliffs Nuclear Power Plant

CAMP CONOY RD

🌲 *Calvert Cliffs State Park*

⚑

497 ⚑ *Cove Point*

Chesapeake Ranch Estates

CHESAPEAKE BAY

Tilghman Island

Choptank River

Little Choptank River

Tar Bay

Barren Island

Hooper Islands

PATUXENT RIVER

LOUIS L GOLDSTEIN HWY

235

2

4

California

Solomons Island

Solomons

⚑ *Cedar Pt Rip*

5

Lexington Park

Hooper Lighthouse

⚑

Legend

━━ Highway
⊞ City
N ⬆
▲
▓ Water
☐ Land
🌲 Forest
⚑ Lighthouse
⛺ Campground

© WILDERNESS ADVENTURES PRESS, INC.

Mid-Bay, Western Shore

This 50-mile stretch of shoreline features three of the most famous areas of Chesapeake Bay fishing—Chesapeake Beach, Solomons, and Point Lookout.

CHESAPEAKE BEACH

Fishing in the Chesapeake Beach area is typically trolling, chumming, and bottom fishing, not standard fly and light-tackle fishing. However, let us hasten to add, there are over 50 charter boats and head boats operating out of Breezy Point Charters (410-760-8242), Chesapeake Beach Fishing Charters (301-855-4665) and Rod-N-Reel Charters (301-855-8450 or 800-233-2080 in Maryland), and some of the canniest and most accommodating captains on the Bay are based here. There are a host of other attractions in the area, including public parks and beaches, waterfront restaurants, four major marinas, Calvert Cliffs State Park (famous for its fossil finds), a marine museum, water park, fishing and crabbing piers, nature parks, Chesapeake Biological Laboratory and even daily bingo.

Chesapeake Beach is only 30 minutes from Annapolis and the District of Columbia and about an hour from Baltimore. So we suggest that a call to one of the above charters may lead to connection with a captain willing to entertain fishermen wanting a fly and light-tackle approach.

We strongly suggest you contact the active tourist department:

Calvert County Department of Economic Development Courthouse
Prince Frederick, MD 20678
800-331-9771 or 800-735-2258
http://www.co.cal.md.us/ccedcced@co.cal.md.us

Gulls and breaking fish are common at Solomons.

SOLOMONS

At the southern shore of Calvert County lies Solomons, also known as the Patuxent River (the mouth) or Calvert Cliffs (a prominent feature to the north). Solomons is a recognized mecca for light tackle and saltwater fly fishing and is arguably the best spot in the Bay. As evidence, these are the home waters for pioneering Chesapeake fly fishing guide Brady Bounds, as well as Bo Toepfer. Mike Murphy, based in Hooper Island, also crosses the Bay to this area when the western shore side is hot, and many of the guides who cover wide areas of the Bay, such as Gary Neitzey and Norm Bartlet are regulars at Solomons.

Solomons has it all—terrific numbers of fish, good facilities to get to them from both the eastern and western shores, and lots of discrete cover, as well as schools of breaking fish. From late March through December stripers are abundant in the area,

Guide Brady Bounds holds his boat among the Cedar Point rocks so his clients can work this fish-holding structure thoroughly. He may get wet, but his boat remains unscathed.

and a warmwater discharge fishery exists for stripers through most of the winter; gray trout generally arrive in May and depart by early November; bluefish usually arrive shortly after the trout and leave about a month before. Spanish mackerel and hardheads are reliable summer fare.

All fly and light-tackle techniques can be employed in this area, including shallow water fishing, poppers and other surface lures, deep jigging, and chumming.

Prime time is October and November. We have been out on the middle of the Bay out of Solomons in late October and witnessed schools of breaking fish in every direction as far as the eye could see. And often schools of trout were stacked under the breaking schools, which were stripers, often with some blues or trout mixed in.

But fishermen with enough boat, say 18 feet with a 50-horsepower motor and larger rigs, can do well on their own. The three prime fish-holding areas are well known and clearly visible—the foundation of the old Cedar Point Light, the old gas docks, and the walls and pipes of Calvert Cliffs Nuclear Power Plant.

But there can be too much of a good thing. In the last few years hordes of chummers have descended on the gas dock area to the point where some of the above guides and many fly fishermen avoid it at times. The situation at the gas dock may very well change now that it is being reactivated. It is expected that some or all of this area will be off limits to fishermen. But we'll have to see how this situation unfolds with this facility and how anglers react.

Whether or not all or part of this facility is available to fishermen, there are still plenty of fish and a number of good alternatives for fly and light-tackle fishermen—if you are flexible and have a good depthfinder.

Standard Chesapeake Bay fly and light tackle will do, but there is some advantage in leaning toward the heavy end of the usual range. For fly tackle, a 10-weight is the choice both for casting poppers on a floating line and for bombing a fly to the depths with a 500-grain, fast-sinking line. Leaders should have 16-pound tippets for open areas and 20-pound test for the dock area. You'll need at least two fly lines or shooting heads, possibly three or four. A floating line with a tapered 8- to 9-foot leader and a fast-sinking line, with a 3- to 5-foot level leader are musts. An even faster sinking line, 450 to 500 grains or more, with a 3- to 5-foot leader is the choice for the deep areas described below, and an intermediate sinking line can sometimes be useful for fish working the sandbars and other shallow areas.

You don't need a variety of patterns, but you do need a variety of sizes. Stripers can be obsessive about certain sized baitfish at times, particularly in this area, and the other species mentioned, even bluefish, can play this game, too.

When bay anchovies or silversides are the predominant bait, we recommend 2- to 3-inch Clouser patterns on sizes 2 to 1/0 hooks, with $\frac{1}{24}$- or $\frac{1}{36}$-ounce eyes, tied with bucktail or Ultrahair in the colors olive over smoke (the Albieclouser) or chartreuse over white. Joe Bruce's Bay Anchovy, Silversides, and Spoon Flies, and Goddard's Glass Minnow are other good patterns.

Recommended standard streamer patterns, 2 to 6 inches on size 2 to 2/0 hooks tied with lots of flash materials, include Clouser, Deceiver, or Half-and-Half flies in chartreuse over white, all white, blue over white, and blue over pink over white; Rob Jepson's Thunder Bunny in chartreuse over white, blue over white, or all white; and Bruce's Crab-Colored Clouser.

Poppers and sliders work on top. Size is not nearly as critical, and 3- to 4-inch models cast well and provide plenty of disturbance.

Conventional tackle should be medium weight or—for yanking fish from some of the structures or working some areas of great depth or fast current—medium heavy. Monofilament lines should be 12- to 15-pound tests, and braided lines can be heavier. Lures should include the usual variety of poppers, swimmers, jigs, grubs, and plastics, and especially feature metal jigs and deep jigging rigs in the 2- to 4-ounce range. (This is the area where we learned of the Bunky Conners trout rig.)

Cedar Point Light

Fish the stone pile around the old lighthouse foundation with noisy poppers on moving tides and, preferably, in low-light conditions. This spot produces some big rockfish. The bar jutting out from the lighthouse often holds mixed schools of breaking fish throughout the day. Fish these with smaller Clouser patterns on sinking or intermediate lines. If you see bunker flying or rock feeding on smaller blues or Spanish mackerel, switch to larger flies.

With conventional tackle, poppers and jig and plastic combinations are the ticket.

A very productive but lesser known spot is the vertical drop from about 13 to 40 feet along the roughly southwest to northeast line from the lighthouse foundation to the traffic buoy. Fish this with sinking lines and streamers or jigs and jigheads and plastics.

The Calvert Cliffs Power Plant and "The River"

The south wall in front of the plant and the first outlet pipe are prime spots for poppers on floating lines or Clouser or Deceiver patterns on sinking lines. One favorite technique in this area is to have one angler using conventional casting or spinning tackle work a large, noisy popper, with or without hooks, with a fast retrieve to excite the stripers, then have a fly fisher drop a popper behind the conventional one to take the fish.

Poppers and various popper rigs, swimming plugs, jigs, and jighead and plastic combinations can be used as well.

Other prime areas are the northern outlet pipe and "the river," a powerful current and series of back eddies produced by an outlet pipe about a quarter-mile offshore. The pipe itself is a structure like a sandbar and fish often stage downcurrent of it. Use the same flies and lures here, but those that work deep are the best choice.

The winter fishing is mainly in the area of the river, drifting or very slow trolling along the edges of current lines and temperature gradient lines. Since tides and water flow from the Calvert Cliff Power Plant vary, this fishing takes some searching to find productive areas. But when you do, fish tend to concentrate in pods and sometimes these pods can hold double-digit stripers.

Fly fishing with heavy, deep sinking lines and flies is possible at times, but deep jigging techniques with 2- to 4-ounce rigs on medium-heavy tackle is a far more practical approach.

The Old Gas Docks

This is a several acre complex of pumping platforms supported by a forest of pilings that provides an abundance of structure and cover for baitfish and rockfish. Use your depthfinder to determine where the fish are holding. You'll want to use heavier fly and conventional tackle and lures and flies that work deep as you try to swim these naturally to fish holding against the pilings. Use the heavy rod tackle to winch your quarry out away from the barnacle-encrusted pilings as soon as you get a strike.

This area may be too crowded with chummers to make any fishing enjoyable, let alone fly and light-tackle fishing. However, Captain Bo Toepfer advises that you may want to explore it on a slack tide. Chumming becomes far less effective, and sometimes the stripers move close to the top searching for food, allowing you to sight cast to them.

Joe Bruce plays a large striper at the gas docks.

A secondary and often productive piece of structure is the boulder-covered pipe running along bottom from the gas docks to the storage tanks onshore. We've taken some big stripers suspended over this structure on fast-sinking lines and flies and with bucktail and pork rind combinations.

Again, bear in mind that some of this advice might be academic by the time this publication hits the market if the gas docks are reactivated and become off limits to fishermen.

Breaking Fish

Since breaking schools of fish are common at Solomons, either at the places already mentioned or others, it pays to keep an eye on the horizon. Once again, sinking lines and Clousers, Deceivers, or anchovy patterns and sinking lures on conventional tackle, not poppers, are the tools of choice. Often the bigger game fish are beneath the breaking fish, so get down quickly into their strike zone.

Fishing Farther Out From Solomons

There are plenty of good areas south and east of Solomons. To the east of Cedar Point lies Cedar Point Rip, a favorite fall spot. Going farther east, towards Hooper Island, the depths of the main channel drop from 50 to 60 feet on the western side to well over 100 feet, then rise up to 23 to 30 feet on the eastern side. This change of depth on the eastern side is so pronounced that some refer to this area as "the wall." From summer through late fall seatrout often hold over these channel edges, and it is not uncommon to take them deep jigging in waters 70 to 80 feet deep. Again, since small baits often predominate, feather your jig rigs and Stingsilver rigs with a small lure or fly above.

South of Cedar Point, all the way to Point Lookout, is a tapering shoreline and a series of holes including Cedar Point Hollow, Fish Hawk, and the Butler's Rock area, and we have caught fish all along here.

POINT LOOKOUT

Point Lookout is at the southern end of the peninsula of St. Mary's County where the Potomac enters the Chesapeake. This area is the widest portion—about 25 miles—of Maryland's Chesapeake. Like Chesapeake Beach, there are a host of charter boats and head boats operating out of ports northwest of Point Lookout along the shores of the Potomac River, and the primary methods of fishing are trolling, chumming, and bottom fishing. The Northwest and Southwest Middle Grounds, especially the latter, are nearly synonymous with chumming.

However, in recent years, more and more fly and light-tackle approaches have been used in this area. These approaches usually involve chumming and casting to breaking fish.

Fishing begins as early as the third week of April and can extend into early December in the Virginia waters south of Point Lookout. The early fishing tends to be

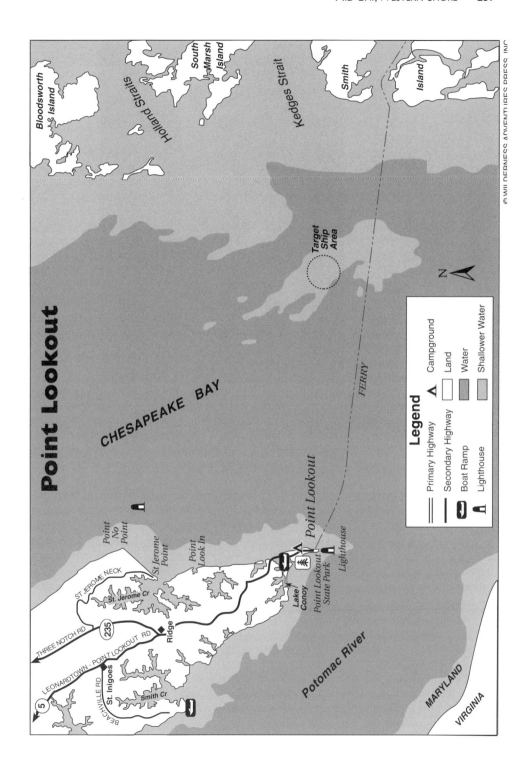

The western shores of the Mid-Bay Region hold some nice stripers.

trolling for trophy stripers. By late May, casting and chumming for stripers, trout, and hardhead is underway. By late June, the Spanish mackerel arrive and schools of breaking stripers and blues are a daily event. Several charters offer night trips during June, July, and August; this is usually bait fishing and chumming for hardheads and stripers.

The Spanish begin to depart by mid-September, the blues a month later. But stripers and trout are bigger and collect more in schools and this fishing is hot until after Thanksgiving.

Point Lookout also offers some small boat opportunities. The Point Lookout State Park Ramp is back in a protected bay, known as Lake Conoy. Once you emerge between the stone jetties into the Potomac, you're in fishing waters. We have taken numerous bluefish and stripers in the area of the jetties and west of Point Lookout in the areas known as Job's Rock and Cornfield Harbor. These areas also provide good fishing for perch, hardhead, and flounder by bottom fishing and deep jigging. However, there are two caveats: The rocky bottom eats lures and rigs, and there are tremendous concentrations of blowfish all around Point Lookout. These fish hit jigs and flies as well as baits.

The waters just offshore north of Point Lookout on the Chesapeake side provide similarly fine fishing, including a pretty reliable flounder bite. This area is particularly good for stripers and blues in the evening—as the hordes of fishermen armed with surf rods along the jetty wall will attest.

Once you clear the area immediately around Point Lookout, you're in big water calling for a big boat, at least 18 feet and preferably 20 or more, with a high horse-power motor to match.

With Patuxent Naval Air Station located at the south shore of the Patuxent on the northern end of the same peninsula as Point Lookout, the military is a big factor in this area. A look at nautical maps confirms this, with such annotations as "The Targets," "Restricted Area," "Prohibited Area," and the champ: "Bombing Area." Watching the planes in the Solomons and Point Lookout areas adds to the interest, and some of their targets add to the fishing. But you must realize they have first priority when they want to use these targets.

The shell-riddled target ship *American Mariner*—when not in use as a military target—is a prime target for fly and light-tackle fishermen, as is the sunken ship the *Old Hannibel* to the south. The usual technique is casting bucktails or jig and grub combinations on medium-heavy conventional tackle or casting streamers on Bay-standard fly tackle using streamer flies that match the bait as described under the Solomons section above.

These ships have been hit or miss in our experience. But northwest of these ships, from the Northwest Middle Grounds to an area known as "Deep Hole" (marked by buoy #72), is a series of humps, holes, and channel edges that has proven "money in the bank," or, at least, fish on the line. Add deep jigging techniques to the same jig fishing and fly fishing techniques described above to fish this area.

South of the target ships lies the Southwest Middle Grounds, another series of humps, edges, and holes. It may be fished as above. Breaking fish are also frequently seen in the area and those techniques can be employed here. You will frequently see dozens of private boats and charter boats in this area, all chumming. This technique is very effective, but be aware that infringing on someone else's chum line is taken very seriously in this area.

As mentioned above with Chesapeake Beach, there are a number of charter boats in the area, and some may be amenable to fly and light-tackle techniques, especially casting to breaking fish and chumming. The ground has been broken by Lefty Kreh, Boyd Pfeiffer, and others who began fly fishing in chum lines in the early 1980s with Captain Bruce Scheible, whose family has been operating charters out of these waters since 1946.

On one memorable occasion about five years ago, we were among the four fly fishermen chumming from a Captain Bruce Scheible charter boat who outfished twelve other outdoor writers fishing with conventional tackle during a writers' trip. (Having Boyd Pfeiffer and Captain Sarah Gardner as part of our "team" was a big help.)

From Point Lookout, you can also venture southeast into another series of structures just below the Maryland-Virginia line, north towards Solomons and the Hooper Island area, or northwest up the Potomac River. There is plenty of good fishing in all directions. We have listed above some of the prime areas for fly and light-tackle approaches, but there is almost unlimited room to explore here.

Hub Cities for Mid-Bay Western Shore

Chesapeake Beach, Population—3,180
Solomons, Population—1,536
Ridge, Population—947
Lexington Park, Population—11,021
California, Population—6,139

Mid-Bay Western Shore combines history with natural attractions, Patuxent Naval Air Station and arguably the best fishing in Maryland's Chesapeake.

ACCOMMODATIONS

Comfort Inn Beacon Marina, 255 Lore Rd., Solomons; 410-326-6303
Holiday Inn, 155 Holiday Drive, Solomons; 800-356-2009
Island Manor Motel, 77 Charles Street, Solomons; 410-326-3700
Scheible's Fishing Center, 48342 Wynne Road, Ridge; 301-872-5185
Super 8 Motel, 22801 Three Notch Road, California; 301-862-9822
Swann's Resort, 17220 Piney Point Road, Piney Point; 301-994-0774

CAMPGROUNDS AND STATE PARKS

Point Lookout State Park, P.O. Box 48, Scotland, MD 20687; 301-872-5688 or 888-432-CAMP(2267) for reservations
Southern Maryland Recreational Complex, Cedarville State Forest, 10201 Bee Oak Road, Brandywine, MD 20613; 301-888-1410 or 888-432-CAMP (2267) for reservations
Dennis Point Marina, 46555 Dennis Point Way; 301 994-2288, 800-974-2288

RESTAURANTS

Gatsby's Dockside Galley, Oyster House Rd., Broomes Island; 410-586-2437
Stoney's Seafood House, Osyter House Rd., Broomes Island; 410-586-1888
Abner's Seaside Crab House, 3748 Harbor Road, Chesapeake Beach; 410-257-3689
Rod & Reel Restaurant, Rt. 261 & Mears Ave., Chesapeake Beach; 410-257-2735
Captains Table, 275 Lore St., Solomons; 410-326-2772
Lighthouse Inn Restaurant, 14640 Solomons Island Rd., Solomons; 410-326-2444
Solomons Pier Restaurant & Lounge, Solomons; 410-326-2424
Spinnakers at Point Lookout Marina, Ridge; 301-872-4340
Scheible's Restaurant, Wynne Rd., Ridge; 301-872-5185

FLY SHOPS, TACKLE STORES, AND SPORTING GOODS

MacLellan's Fly Shop, P.O. Box 747, Hughesville; 301-274-5833
The Tackle Box, 22035 Three Notch Rd, Lexington Park; 301-863-8151
Bay Trading Post, P.O. Box 396, St. Leonard; 410-586-1992
Fred's Sport Shop, 2895 Crain Hwy., Waldorf; 301-645-5694
Island Creek Outfitters, 40 Honeysuckle Lane, Owings; 410-386-0950

FLY SHOPS, TACKLE STORES, AND SPORTING GOODS, CONTINUED
The Sports Authority, 3326 Crain Highway, Waldorf; 301-645-2767
Fred's Sport Shop, 2895 Crain Hwy., Waldorf; 301-645-5694

FLY AND LIGHT TACKLE GUIDES
Brady Bounds, 301-862-3166
Bo Toepfer, 410-535-9440 or 800-303-4950
Gary Neitzey, 410-557-8801
Norm Bartlett, 410-679-8790

MARINAS
(This is a partial listing; there are dozens in the area.)
Town Center Marina, 255 A St., Solomons Island; 410-326-2401
Point Lookout Marina, 16244 Miller's Wharf Road, Ridge; 301-872-5000
Arnold C. Gay Yacht Yard, 1 Main St., Solomons; 410-326-2011
Breezy Point Marina, 5230 Breezy Point Road, Chesapeake Beach; 301-855-9894
Broomes Island Marina, 3952 Oyster House Rd., Broomes Island; 410-586-0304
Calvert Marina, Dowell Rd., Solomons; 410-326-4251
Beacon Marina at Comfort Inn, Lore Road, Solomons; 410-326-3807
Harbor Island Marina, 105 Charles Street, Solomons Island; 410-326-3441
Kellam's Marina & Boat Yard, 8020 Bayside Rd., Chesapeake Beach; 410-855-8968
Rod & Reel, Rt. 261 & Mears Ave., Chesapeake Beach; 301-855-8450
Buzz's Marina, Rt. 5, Ridge; 301-872-5887
Cape St. Mary's Marina, 2050 Holly Ln., Mechanicsville; 301-373-2001
Colton's Point Marina, Colton Point Rd., Colton's Point; 301-769-3121
Scheilbe Fishing Center, P.O. Box 23, Ridge; 301-872-5185
Tall Timbers Marina, P.O. Box 9, Tall Timbers; 301-994-1508

BOAT EQUIPMENT AND REPAIR
Dennis Point Marina, 46555 Dennis Point Way, Drayden; 301-994-2288
Feldman's Marine Railways, 18042 Cherryfield Road, Drayden; 301-994-2629 or 301-994-0586
Reliable Marine, 23420 South Patuxent Beach Road, California; 301-862-2768
Tall Timbers Vacation Club & Marina, Tall Timbers; 301-994-1508

CHARTERS AND BOAT RENTALS
Solomons Boat Rental offers 20-foot boats for fishing (410-326-4060). More than 40 guides belong to the Solomons Charter Captains Association (410-326-2670), and a call might lead you to one willing to cater to fly and light tackle needs. One possibility is the knowledgeable and accommodating Sonney Forrest, Jr. (800-831-2702).

LAUNCH RAMPS
Public Ramp—Solomons
There are public ramps at Hallowing Point, well up the Patuxent on Route 231, and at the bridge between Calvert and St. Mary's Counties. We recommend the latter ramp. Take Maryland Rts. 2/4 and take the ramp exit near the bridge on the Calvert County side. There are four ramps, and restrooms are present. There is a fee.

Public Ramp—Point Lookout

There is a state ramp at Forest Landing on the Chesapeake and a series of ramps on the northern shore of the Potomac River at Wicomoco Shores, Chaptico Landing, Bushwood Landing, Abell's Wharf, Piney Point Recreation Area, St. Inigoes Landing, and Point Lookout State Park. We recommend the latter.

Take Maryland Rt. 5 south toward Point Lookout State Park, then follow the signs. There are four ramps and there is a launch fee. This ramp also features restrooms and a fish cleaning station, and there is a nearby store selling fuel, ice, bait, and tackle. This facility is nicely protected in Conoy Bay, facilitating launching and pickup even in difficult conditions. Call 301-872-5688.

AUTO REPAIR

Lexington Park Exxon, Great Mills Road, Lexington Park; 301-863-5300
Tommy's Auto Clinic, 15005 Old Marlboro Pike, Upper Marlboro; 301-627-4100
B & B Automotive Repair, 22664 Mercedes Dr., California; 301-737-0077

HOSPITALS

Calvert Memorial Hospital, 100 Hospital Road, Prince Frederick; 301-475-5250
St. Mary's Hospital, 25500 Point Lookout Road, Leonardtown; 301-475-8981

OTHER ATTRACTIONS

Historic St. Mary's City, an 800-acre, self-guided outdoor museum showing Colonial Maryland in the 17th century as well as an American Indian hamlet; 301-862-0990
Point Lookout State Park, Nature Center and Civil War Museum features fishing, hiking, camping, a site of a Civil War prisoner of war camp; 301-872-5688
Patuxent River Naval Air Museum, shows the history of naval aviation testing and development from 1911 to the present; 301-863-7218
St. Mary's River State Park, offers excellent fresh water fishing in a 250-acre lake, hunting, hiking, biking, horseback riding, playground, and picnic areas; 301-872-5688

FOR FURTHER INFORMATION

Calvert County Department of Economic Development, Courthouse, Prince Frederick, MD 20678; 800-331-9771, 800-735-2258; www.co.cal.md.us/cced
St. Mary's County Division of Tourism, P.O. Box 653, Leonardtown, MD 20650; 301-475-4405; stmedecd@mail.ameritel.net; www.somd.lib.md/US/STMA/Government?stmcdecd.html

Typical flies for school stripers, speckled trout, and croakers.

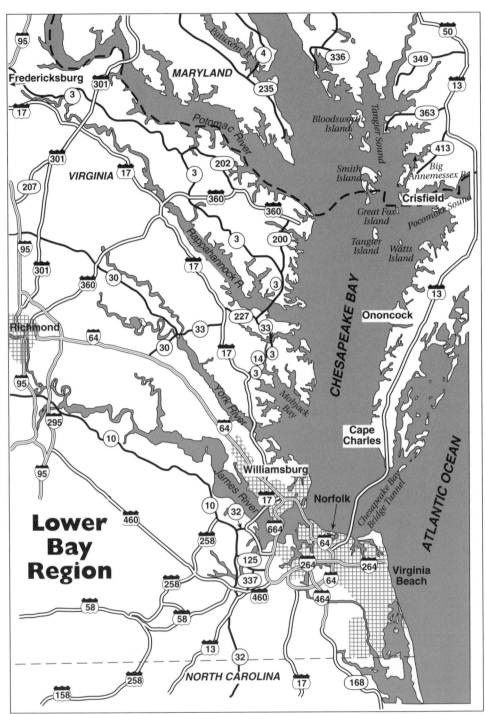

Lower Bay Region

© WILDERNESS ADVENTURES PRESS, INC.

An Introduction to Virginia Waters

There's more to fly and light-tackle fishing in Virginia than the Chesapeake Bay Bridge Tunnel. There's even more than the Chesapeake Bay Bridge Tunnel (CBBT) and Cape Charles. It's true; there really is.

In exploring Virginia waters, and after interviewing a number of veteran fishermen of these waters, we found great similarities with the Maryland portion of the Chesapeake in species, waters, tackle, and techniques. One major difference is the greater variety of species in the southern part of the Bay—far more trout, especially speck-led trout, for much of the year; likewise, more red and black drum, cobia and Spanish mackerel; more and bigger flounder; plus spadefish and some tarpon and false albacore, all of which are extremely rare in the Upper Chesapeake Bay.

One on the rod and one in the net near the Smith Island wrecks.

Except for the heavyweight species and the big water conditions of the CBBT, there are far more similarities than differences. The same tackle, lures, flies, and techniques recommended in earlier chapters are, with a few exceptions, still the choices. On both the Eastern and Western Shores of Virginia, we found the same kind of desirable structures as in the Upper Bay—sandbars, mud flats, lumps, channel edges, sunken or target ships, bridges, lighted bridges and piers, patchy grass beds and those seemingly magic 15- to 20-foot shelves that are such fish magnets.

It's even more specific than that: Much of what we wrote about the Susquehanna applies to the Rappahannock, with its runs of such anadromous species as white perch, stripers, and white and hickory shad. (Of course, the Rappahannock's blue catfish could eat the Susquehanna's channel catfish for lunch.) The York and the James also feature shad runs; and the James, like the Susquehanna, is also a renowned smallmouth stream upriver. Likewise, both shores have areas of structure similar to Crisfield, Eastern Bay, and the Upper Bay lumps and channels.

Perhaps the best general summary of Virginia waters can be provided in the words of fly and light-tackle guide Captain Lynn Pauls of Poquoson, Virginia:

"I have lived and fished around these waters all of my life, and so has my family. I come from generations of watermen who fished and made a living from these waters. I have seen the fishing change over the past 35 years. In the late '60s we fished the marshy points with peeler crabs, trying to catch 12-pound stripers only to be annoyed by catching 6- to 8-pound puppy drum. In the '70s a 10- to 12-pound bluefish would take any lure that you put in its path. In the '80s there were a lot of light-tackle fishermen using lead-headed jigs and plastic tails to catch speckled trout. Today the bigger fish are not as plentiful, and more fishermen are carrying fly rods, and releasing their catch."

The following advice applies to shallow water areas on both shores of Virginia's Chesapeake plus Lynnhaven and Rudee: "In this area light tackle and fly fishermen have the perfect opportunity to catch stripers, croaker, flounder, bluefish, speckled trout, and puppy drum. This can be done by fishing many of the drop-offs, shellfish beds, marshy points, mottled patches of sandy bottom, and submerged aquatic vegetation beds (some of the richest in the Chesapeake Bay) abundant in the area.

"The best time to fish the area is from mid-April to mid-November, when the water temperature goes above 53 degrees. As the temperature rises into the 60s fishing gets even better. If the wind is blowing from the east or northeast it will be too rough to fish in the Bay, but you can usually fish in the Poquoson River or Back River. (This applies to most of the rivers and inlets along the eastern and western shores, as well.) If the wind is blowing from the west fishing is always the best.

"If you are fishing for speckled trout, try a gloomy day with overcast skies, after a light rain, or after a weather front has gone through the area. For any kind of fishing you want to do it is a good idea to pick up a Tide Chart at any local bait and tackle store, because fishing is always the best between two hours before high tide, and two hours after high tide.

"One of the most important tactics for catching fish here is to fish with the tide. This is because many fish feed with their nose into the tide. Another tactic is to look for baitfish jumping because larger fish are feeding on them." (Note: We, and the experts we spoke with, consistently favor an outgoing tide in most situations throughout the Chesapeake.)

"Phases of the moon seem to play a big part in the size of the fish you catch. Several days before a full moon until several days past the last quarter is the time to catch the biggest fish. The best time to fish is very early or late in the day, and the best places are in shallow water and around marshy points."

We have fished Virginia waters since the early '70s and have noted through the years a certain hierarchy among many fishermen: There are good fishermen, above that there are great fishermen, above that there are great trout fishermen, and at the pinnacle are great speckled trout fishermen. More recently spadefish have become the hot item, which, incredibly to most Maryland fishermen, are greeted by some Virginia anglers with as much, if not more, interest than the return of the stripers.

A small spadefish in the net. In June, 10-pounders are common in the lower reaches of the Bay.

Preferences aside, Virginia waters have benefited in the last few years from the boom in croaker (hardhead) and gray trout (also known as weakfish or yellowfin), as well as striped bass. They have likewise suffered from the loss of double-digit bluefish, which, other than for a period in late fall and perhaps a week in the spring, seem to holding offshore and not entering the Bay in significant numbers, although one- to five-pound bluefish are common. Black and red drum populations, both of which seem to fluctuate, have generally also been on the rise in numbers and size in recent years.

Like their counterparts in such Upper Bay spots as Eastern Bay, Crisfield, and Hooper Island, Virginia fishermen have discovered that two- to three-pound croakers are terrific fly-rod and light-tackle fish when they first arrive in shallow water in the spring. In Virginia the prime time for this fishing is early May. But as early as late March or at least by mid-April the croakers will move into shallow mud flats in two to three feet of water, often late in the day inside Lynnhaven Inlet, James River, the Cherry Point areas and the remainder of Gwynn's Island, and the small creeks feeding into the mouth of the Piankatank River. The key is water temperature; the croaker are on the mud flats because they are seeking warmth and food. The ideal situation is to find this kind of structure on north-facing banks and creeks with south winds blowing into the banks.

You can catch these croakers fishing from the bank, or better yet, casting from a drifting boat. Sometimes they'll only take bait, but often they'll hit standard Clouser Minnows from 2½ to 4 inches long. Elly Robinson, an IGFA record-holder for several

species and member of the Virginia Angler's Club, likes to scout for active croaker by casting white or chartreuse Berkley Power Grubs before switching to flies.

These same approaches also work at these same times for both species of trout and puppy drum in Rudee Inlet and Lynnhaven Inlet.

And the croaker fishing isn't just restricted to these areas. Croakers have a tendency to migrate up the river systems, so by April you can expect croakers at the mouth of the York, and the tide lines in the James and Rappahannock.

Gary Diamond with a nice tautog pulled from beneath the hull of one of the concrete ships just out from Kiptopeake State Park.

SEASONAL FISHING CHART
FOR VIRGINIA'S LOWER BAY

The following seasonal fishing chart was developed by Captain Pauls, and it is available on his excellent website, www.tideflyer.com. We've added a few additional species to match the scope of this guidebook.

RATINGS:	E = Excellent	G = Good	F = Fair	N = Not Available

	JAN	FEB	MAR	APR	MAY	JUN	JUL	AUG	SEP	OCT	NOV	DEC
Bluefish	N	N	N	E	E	G	F	F	F	G	G	G
Cobia	N	N	N	N	G	E	G	G	F	N	N	N
Croaker	N	N	N	F	E	E	E	E	E	F	N	N
Flounder	N	N	N	F	G	E	E	E	E	G	F	N
Puppy Drum	N	N	N	N	E	E	E	E	E	E	N	N
Spanish Mackerel	N	N	N	N	F	G	E	E	G	F	N	N
Speckled Trout	N	N	N	G	E	E	E	E	E	E	G	N
Striper	N	N	N	E	E	E	E	E	E	E	E	E

	OUR ADDITIONS											
Hickory Shad	N	F	E	E	G	N	N	N	N	N	N	N
White Shad	N	N	F	E	E	G	N	N	N	N	N	N
White Perch	N	N	F	E	E	E	F	F	F	G	G	G
Gray Trout	N	N	N	G	E	E	E	G	E	E	F	N
Spadefish	N	N	N	N	G	E	E	G	G	F	N	N
Spot	N	N	N	N	N	G	E	E	E	G	N	N
Tautog	G	F	G	G	G	G	F	F	F	E	E	E

Virginia Ramps

As of this writing, the state of Virginia does not have an Internet guide to public boat ramps like Maryland has, although they have hopes of developing a similar site. The excellent fishing guide *Virginia Saltwater Angler's Guide* has an extensive list of ramps but: (1) It does not contain directions on how to get there. (2) Some of these "ramps" are narrow, single lane roads leading to a sandy beach permitting parking for only a few cars and launching for only cartop boats, canoes, or kayaks. Likewise, there are maps published by state agencies and a number of private companies showing ramps; these maps are also unreliable. Compounding matters, many ramps have local names that bear little resemblance to their official names.

To date the best publication on boat ramps is the brochure *On the Waters of Virginia's Chesapeake Bay*, which covers only the Northern Neck and Middle Peninsula. (Call 877-285-4593 for a copy.) It is accurate and lists all public ramps, dividing them into full boat launch ramps versus cartop ramps and large versus limited parking facilities. This brochure lists other amenities of the ramps, such as restrooms, bank fishing, etc. It also lists all marinas in these areas, again listing whether ramps are present. But it does not give directions to the ramps, and the phone numbers listed for the public facilities are often county maintenance shops.

So we have listed ramps we have used or at least visited or that have been recommended by several local sources. If you're in doubt about a ramp not listed here, check first or use the nearest commercial facility. Otherwise, you may find you have towed your 20-foot boat down a country lane that dead-ends at a waterfront beach.

Author Ed Russell with a good striper from the Lower Bay.

Lower Bay, Eastern Shore

CRISFIELD TO TANGIER ISLAND

The sun was just above the horizon as we left the slip at Janes Island State Park. It was mid-November and last night's weather report promised a fall day that you dream about—temperature in the sixties, little wind, and low humidity. We were fishing with Captain Kevin Josenhans of Crisfield, Maryland. Although we were hitting the tail end of the fall migration of striped bass, our hopes were high. Warm fall weather had kept the Bay water temperature up and the fish active.

As we rounded the northern tip of the island, and headed toward the open waters of the Chesapeake Bay, we began to see the birds; several mixed flocks of gulls and terns were wheeling and diving as they worked breaking schools of baitfish. Under the bait, and the reason they were on top, were marauding schools of striped bass.

Going upwind of the nearest activity and drifting into the breaking fish brought immediate action. White Lefty's Deceivers attached to fast-sinking shooting heads cast into the melee brought us each an immediate hookup. Not big fish, as stripers go, just about 18 inches, but strong fighters for their size and an auspicious start.

When the school sounded, Kevin fired up the Yamaha and headed to the next flock of gulls. This time, before the first cast could be made, all activity ceased. This pattern was repeated all day. Sometimes, just as we made a cast the fish would sound, and except that the depthfinder showed huge numbers of fish below us, the water appeared barren. Other times, hookups came as soon as the flies hit the water.

Although the stripers were feeding on baitfish that were attempting to fly in their desperate struggle to avoid becoming a meal, we fished primarily with sinking lines and streamer patterns. Surface poppers took their share of fish, but they were not nearly as effective as streamers. Perhaps the poppers simply did not stand out in the commotion created by the terrified baitfish.

Another reason for the subsurface offerings was the knowledge that the larger fish are often below the main school, feeding on the fallout, so to speak, as well as their smaller cousins. This wasn't the case this day, however, as all the fish seemed to be formed from the same mold; still, it was exciting fishing.

Kevin gradually moved south into Virginia waters in search of larger fish, but to no avail. The largest striper taken that day was 21 inches. It was a little late in the year for the big fish, although chummers across the Bay were still drawing up larger fish from deeper water.

We each caught and released more than 30 stripers. A more enjoyable day would be hard to imagine.

Although many anglers think of stripers as open-water school fish, the fact is that they, like freshwater bass, often like to hide and feed in structure. The stump-filled shorelines around some of the islands in this region provide an excellent habitat and are prime spots to fish. Two weeks prior to the above-mentioned trip, Joe Bruce and Bill May worked these spots guided by Josenhans. Fishing entirely in two to four feet

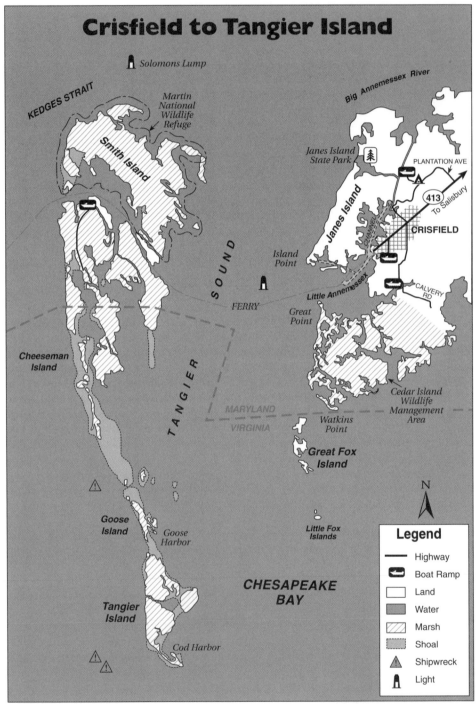

Crisfield to Tangier Island

Solomons Lump

KEDGES STRAIT

Martin National Wildlife Refuge

Smith Island

Big Annemessex River

Janes Island State Park

PLANTATION AVE

413
To Salisbury

CRISFIELD

Island Point

SOUND

CHANNEL

Janes Island

Little Annemessex

CALVERY RD

FERRY

Great Point

Cheeseman Island

TANGIER

Cedar Island Wildlife Management Area

MARYLAND

VIRGINIA

Watkins Point

Great Fox Island

Goose Island

Goose Harbor

Little Fox Islands

CHESAPEAKE BAY

Tangier Island

Cod Harbor

N

Legend

———	Highway
	Boat Ramp
☐	Land
	Water
	Marsh
	Shoal
⚠	Shipwreck
	Light

Chuck Edghill casting to the shoreline south of Crisfield.

of water, and using both streamers and surface poppers, each angler caught and released more than 40 stripers in the course of the day—and the fish were a lot bigger, a few topping 12 pounds. This is outstanding fishing by anyone's measure.

While fall is the season for breaking rock (stripers), spring is the time for spotted seatrout (locally called specks) and croakers in shallow water. From late April through June, depending on water temperatures, fly and light-tackle anglers can find both species in two to four feet of water. While drifting along the numerous grass beds or fishing in stump-filled shallows, a properly presented offering can draw a strike at any time.

A size 2 to 2/0 Closer Minnow in chartreuse and white is an excellent choice, as is a shrimp or crab imitation. For this type of fishing, a slow-sinking line is the right choice. we recently tried one of Scientific Anglers' Monocore lines that sinks at about one foot per second and found it ideal for the shallows. It also casts like a bullet.

Anglers using spinning or light casting gear may choose from a wealth of shallow-running, minnow-shaped lures.

This is more like flats fishing than almost anything else north of the Carolinas. Your boat must be capable of floating in two feet of water, and a push pole or an electric motor is required equipment. Silence is a must as these fish are easily spooked. Should you have to start the outboard to avoid running aground, chances are that spot is ruined for a while.

A view of the crab pots on Tangier Island.

The first speckled trout that you land will impress you with its beauty. These are handsome creatures with bright iridescent colors. They inhabit shallow water in the spring and are made to order for a fly rod. They are not known as spectacular fighters, but they take a fly willingly and are excellent table fare. A word of caution, specs sport some oversized canine teeth. While they will not try to bite you, as with bluefish, putting a finger in their mouth is not advisable.

Both trout and croakers like grass beds and rocky outcroppings. They will prowl the shallows looking for baitfish or shrimp or take up residence by some structure and wait for the tide to bring them a meal. Striped bass also frequent many of the same areas at the same time. You may be expecting a 4-pound spec and encounter a double-digit striper.

Just this situation occurred recently. We were in my (Ed Russell's) boat, while Lefty Kreh and Joe Bruce were with Kevin Josenhans. We were fishing a rock pile to prospect for trout. It was midday and things were a little slow. Since Kevin was then relatively new to fly fishing, Lefty offered to help him with his casting technique. As luck would have it, Kevin hooked what was to be the best fish of the day, a 12-pound striper. Talk about a comedy act. Kevin was doing his best not to lose the fish in the rocks while Joe and Lefty attempted to buoy the anchor and free the boat to follow the fish—all this while everyone was attempting to get a picture. It all worked out, and Kevin landed and released the unexpected fish.

While casting to breaking fish and working the shallows are lots of fun and generally effective, sometimes the fish do not cooperate and other measures are called for. Chumming has long been a popular method in this region, and while usually associated with bait fishermen, it is gaining popularity with flyrodders.

The technique is a little messy—actually it's a lot messy—but it's an astonishingly effective way to take large fish on a fly. Ground menhaden is ladled over the stern from an anchored boat, forming an oily slick. A moving tide is a must. The oily chum will spread out downtide and will draw stripers and other species literally to the transom. To be effective, the chum line must not be interrupted, nor should it contain too many large pieces of the ground bait. The trick is to entice not feed. Bait fishermen will impale a strip of menhaden and drift it with the chum, but a Chum Fly, consisting of nothing more than a tan rabbit strip palmered around a hook shank and topped with a couple of turns of red marabou, looks remarkably like a bit of fish and works just as well.

Cast this out with a sinking line of the appropriate sink rate to stay with the drifting chum and you will be amazed at the size and number of fish that you can take. It's a good idea to have fly lines of various sink rates with you, as tidal flow will influence the sink rate, and it is imperative that the fly stays at the same level as the drifting chum.

The area being discussed here is vast, encompassing Tangier Sound and extending into Chesapeake Bay proper, both in Maryland and Virginia. Shallow water flats edging salt marshes and low-lying islands abound. Some of the islands are just remnants of their former self, most of the land having been eroded by wind and wave. Some of these islands were timbered, and as the water encroached, the trees were harvested. The tree stumps that were left are now underwater—posing a potential hazard to propellers yet providing great fish habitat.

This is big water, not far from where the Bay joins the ocean. Venturing out without the proper equipment and knowledge is foolhardy. On calm days, small boats are okay, but since calm days can turn bad with little warning, an 18-foot craft is considered the minimum. Make no mistake; the Chesapeake can be very nasty.

Current charts and a good compass are necessities, and a GPS is desirable. Despite its size, much of the area is shallow, and there are flats in the darndest places. It is easy to run aground and easy to get lost, especially in a fog, but it's a fascinating area to fish.

Throughout the Bay, you will need a Chesapeake Bay fishing license, but in this area, since Maryland and Virginia have reciprocal agreements, a license from either state is valid.

Although spring and fall are the best times, summer fishing can also be good. Look for speckled trout and croaker around structure in deeper water, usually 6 to 12 feet. Stripers will also be present, though not in numbers like the fall. Use a fast-sinking line; floating lines are generally of little value during this period. Scientific Anglers, Teeny, and Courtland all make full lines and shooting heads that have a sink rate of more than five feet per second, and this is what you need.

When the tide goes slack, so does the fishing, but fortunately, this area offers other activities. There is much to be seen in the way of wildlife. Waterfowl abounds;

in fact, many of the islands have signs warning that they are nesting areas for shore-birds. You can see gulls of every description: terns, plovers, Canada geese, loons, and pelicans to name but a few. The bird population is incredible, especially in the spring and fall when migrating species swell the ranks of year-rounders.

About midway across the Bay is Tangier Island and Smith Island. The flats around both offer excellent spots to fish, and the breakwaters guarding the harbor entrances are especially good on an outgoing tide. They are also a good place to go if you want to take a midday lunch break or if you just want to play tourist.

The channels into the harbors are well marked, and there are many places to tie up your boat while visiting one of the eating establishments for lunch. If you want to take the time, walking around either island is quite interesting. A visit here is like a step back in time. Everything is slower and the islanders even have a unique dialect unlike anything else. It is like a combination of Deep South drawl combined with Elizabethan English from the islands' British heritage.

The islanders maintain a lifestyle apart from that of the mainland. Most of the inhabitants have made their living as watermen on the Bay for generations. Many of the Smith Island women earn extra income cleaning crabs in summer and shucking oysters in winter. It is notable that there are no schools past eighth grade on Smith Island. High school students attend school on the mainland, and catch the school boat rather than the bus.

Smith Island is interesting enough that there is a tour boat from Crisfield that goes there daily. Tangier Island sports motorized golf carts that visitors can rent for a small fee, and many locals will offer their services as a guide. Either island is well worth some time to visit. After all, fishing isn't just about catching fish. Learning something about the people and places that you visit is a large part of the experience.

The first time that we fished these waters was more than 30 years ago. Several members of a fledgling fishing club were guided by a young fellow named Doug Carson. The weather was poor—cold and windy—and we had little success. Doug was attempting to build a business guiding light-tackle fishermen, with special emphasis on fly fishing. Unfortunately, Doug was ahead of his time and never became successful. The mentality of most fishermen back then was to head for the open waters of the Bay and troll for striped bass, a method we don't like. Saltwater fly and light-tackle fishing was in its infancy.

Today, this has changed dramatically. Since the decline of striped bass, followed by their resurgence after a long moratorium, more sport fishermen are concentrating on the pleasurable aspects of catching these gamesters on light tackle and releasing all or most of their catch. There are still only a few light-tackle guides, and these are usually booked well in advance, but if you would like to fish these waters, we would suggest you contact one, at least for your first trip. Kevin Josenhans, about whom we have already spoken, is first rate. He lives on Janes Island and is intimately familiar with the local waters. He guides light-tackle fishermen exclusively and claims that more and more of his customers choose to fly fish. Matt Tawes, who also lives in this area, is another excellent choice.

Another light-tackle guide with whom we have had personal experience is Norm Bartlett of Joppa, Maryland. Norm fishes the entire Bay and will trailer his boat to where the action is best. He is an extremely accomplished fly fisherman and holds

Guide Kevin Josenhans of Crisfield with a nice seatrout.

the world record for seatrout (14 lbs., 4 oz.) on 4-pound test tippet.

Any of the above gentlemen will do their best to ensure you a good time and put you on fish as well as provide much knowledge about the local waters. For a new-comer to the area, the money spent for a day or two of guided fishing would be well spent. For more information, check the listing of light-tackle guides elsewhere in this book.

JANES ISLAND

The best fishing around the island is on the north and west side and in the deeper water near the south end. There's not much in particular to key on, and the usual method is to simply drift the shoreline while casting towards shore. In addition to the aforementioned species, you may pick up a flounder or two. Generally speaking, the area just south of Janes Island, including Little Annemessex River isn't much bothered with since it is quite shallow and difficult to fish.

GREAT FOX ISLAND

This little island, located about 9 miles south of Crisfield, is one of our favorite spots. The shoreline all along the southwest side and around the southern tip of the island is dotted with underwater stumps. The island has eroded and gotten smaller over time, and as the Bay waters intruded, the white pine trees were logged off, leaving what are now underwater stump fields.

Occurring in water depths of about three to eight feet, these stumps offer an excellent opportunity to fish structure frequented by striped bass and speckled trout and also pose a threat to the unwary boater who ventures too close. Be aware that you can't always see these stumps because they are completely submerged, and when the water is murky (as is often the case) they are difficult to spot. Because of the nature of pine, and because they are completely underwater, they do not rot but remain hard. The sound that a fiberglass hull makes as a wave lifts and then drops it onto a stump is one best left unheard.

Despite this caution, these stump fields offer excellent angling. They are favorite hangouts for both striped bass and speckled trout in spring and fall, and large Atlantic croaker also frequent them and the nearby grassy shallows in early summer.

SMITH AND TANGIER ISLANDS

To the west of the Foxes lie the large islands of Smith and Tangier. These are also excellent striper hangouts with lots of structure. The south side of Smith Island has stump fields similar to the ones at Great Fox. The rocky breakwaters guarding the entrances to the harbor on the northwest corner of Smith Island are another great location, especially on an outgoing tide. Depending on the velocity of the tide, you can drift along the edge of the rocks or anchor just outside the tip of the jetty. Cast your fly or lure uptide and let it drift along the edge of the breakwater. Most strikes seem to come as the offering sweeps past the end of the jetty. When the tide is running well, you will need a fast-sinking line to get a fly deep enough to be noticed. A Teeny 350 or 450 or equivalent is ideal. Bend-back or other weedless flies, or jug heads with soft plastic bodies rigged to be weedless, are recommended to avoid losing a lot of tackle to hang-ups in the rocks.

A word of caution regarding these rock jetties—they extend farther out than they appear; the rocks do not end at the exposed tip. Approach with caution.

Don't overlook the many cuts and channels that weave their way through the island's interior. Although we haven't experienced this, we're told that croakers up to 18 inches readily take Clousers in these shallow cuts.

Directly to the north of Smith Island is the Martin's Wildlife Refuge. All along this shoreline are undercut banks, exposed rocks, and grassy pockets that may harbor both stripers and speckled trout. Cast right up against the shoreline, literally, and retrieve rapidly. It seems that stripers will often hit flies that approach as if they were coming off the shoreline and ignore flies that are thrown five feet from the bank. It's really similar to fishing structure for largemouths, but the fish will be bigger.

Tangier Island lies to the south of Smith Island. Conditions are very similar, with one exception. These are Virginia waters, and Virginia seasons and regulations apply. The Virginia fall striper season usually differs from Maryland's, so don't make the mistake of thinking you can catch and keep what would be a legal fish in Maryland when Virginia's season is closed. Virginia marine police are very observant.

A couple of miles to the west of the island are several wrecks that are good spots for weakfish and sometimes stripers. These wrecks once were old World War II

Liberty Ships, but they are no longer recognizable as such. Because they have been used for target practice by Navy aircraft, all that remains above water are a few rusted pieces. There is plenty of structure below the surface, however, and this creates a good hiding place for game fish—and also poses problems for a boat. Approach carefully. The best fishing seems to be off the southern end of the wreck on an out-going tide. You'll need a fast-sinking fly line or 1-ounce lead-head jigs to get down quickly enough to score.

Getting There

To reach Crisfield from the Baltimore area, take Route 50 across the Bay Bridge all the way to Salisbury, where you will pick up Route 13 south. Follow that to Route 413 south to Crisfield. It's about a 3-hour drive from Baltimore. From points south, you will have to cross the Bay via the Chesapeake Bay Bridge Tunnel from Norfolk Virginia to Cape Charles. From there follow Route 13 north through Pocomoke City to Route 413 and proceed as above.

The town of Crisfield, located at the southern extremity of Maryland's Eastern Shore, is the jumping off spot for fishing Tangier Sound. Largely overlooked by progress since it is not on the route to anywhere, Crisfield remains much as it has since we first visited. It is, however, rapidly becoming known as a "place to go"

Guide Kevin Josenhans is releasing a fish while his clients work the water near Great Fox Island in Tangier Sound.

among knowledgeable light-tackle anglers. The changes that have occurred to the town are all for the good. Since this area is off the beaten path, fishing pressure is relatively light. Yes, you will see other boats, but usually in the distance. Because of its nearness to the ocean, you may see creatures not normally encountered, such as rays, dolphins, and the occasional shark. The fishing is excellent, the locale interesting, and the wildlife abundant. Altogether a very worthwhile place to fish.

Launch Ramps

There is an excellent state-run marina (Somers Cove) with rental slips and a concrete ramp that can handle four boats simultaneously. Restrooms and ice are available. Somers Cove is reached by taking Route 413 to Somerset Avenue. Follow Somerset Avenue to the end.

Janes Island State Park also has a good ramp, and you can keep your boat in a slip overnight if you are camping there. The ramp is in Janes Island State Park. Follow Route 413 south to Plantation Avenue. Go west to Jacksonville Road, then south to Alfred Lawson Road.

If camping is not on your agenda, the ramp at Somers Cove is a better choice.

Guides

If you are new to the area or don't have a suitable boat—18 feet is about the absolute minimum—we'd strongly suggest hiring a guide. This is big water and can get very nasty if a storm arises. Also, the best fishing spots are much less numerous than poor ones, and a day or so with a guide can mean the difference between an enjoyable experience and a bad one. We highly recommend Kevin Josenhans. Kevin is a long-time resident of Crisfield and a park ranger at Janes Island State Park. He knows the area intimately, and specializes in light-tackle fishing. He's a nice guy to boot. You can reach him at:

Captain Kevin Josenhans
26265 Alfred Lawson Drive
Crisfield, MD 21817
410-968-3579

Kevin used to be the only light-tackle guide in the area, but now there are some others. For several years now, Matt Tawes has been working basically the same waters as Kevin. Although we've not fished with Matt personally, he comes highly recommended by two of his fellow guides—Kevin Josenhans and Richie Gaines. Since we have firsthand knowledge of the first two we feel that if both of them have a high regard for Matt, we won't hesitate to recommend him. You can reach him at:

Captain Matt Tawes
26952 Holly Avenue
Crisfield, MD 21817
410-968-3286 or 443-235-5925 (mobile)
www.ChesapeakeAngling.com

Local Services for the Crisfield Area

The Pines Motel (410-968-0900), located off Somerset Avenue, is quite reasonable, with clean spacious rooms and, for those that desire it, a pool. More importantly, they cater to fishermen and have designated a large parking area specifically for trailered boats.

The Paddle Wheel, 701 W. Main (410-968-2220), has also been recommended, and there is a bed and breakfast by the name of My Fair Lady, 38 Main St. (410-968-3514), that, we are told, is excellent.

For those interested in camping, Janes Island State Park, just west of town, has 104 campsites. Forty have electricity, although none have individual water hookups, but ample supplies of fresh water are available. There are also four cabins that may be rented year-round; the campsites are available only from May through October. Campers may also rent boat slips for only a dollar or two per day at the launch ramp. It's free to campers and only $5 to the general public. There is, however, a downside to camping here—mosquitoes. They are large and plentiful. Bring plenty of repellent.

You can get an early breakfast at the Circle One (410-968-1969). It's right on Main Street (Route 413) as you come into Crisfield. They open at 5:30. Actually, most of the businesses are located on this street (curiously enough called Main Street). It's a small town; go too far in most directions and you reach water.

The Captain's Galley, 701 W. Main (410-968-2220) and The Waterman's Inn, 9th & Main (410-968-2119), are two restaurants at which we've eaten, and both are excellent, with heavy emphasis on seafood as you might expect. Prices are quite reasonable.

There are many other eating establishments, including pizza parlors and some fast food places, but you'll be hard pressed to find better than The Captain's Galley or the Waterman's Inn.

Ed Russell hoists his catch, while Bill May checks the scale.

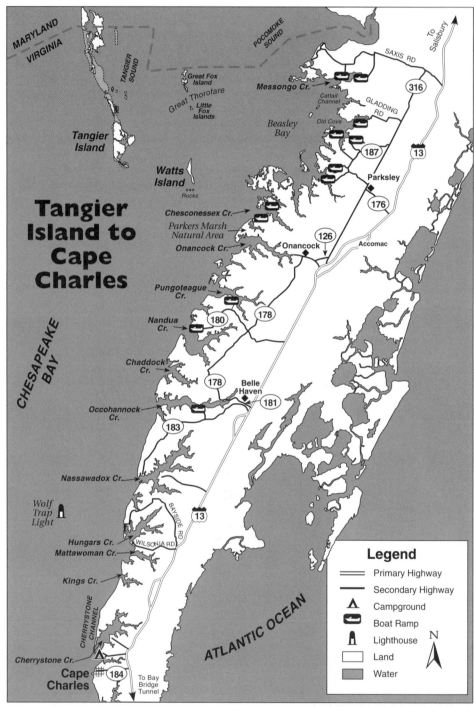

Tangier
Island to
Cape
Charles

Legend

═══	Primary Highway
────	Secondary Highway
⛺	Campground
⛴	Boat Ramp
🏮	Lighthouse
☐	Land
▨	Water

N

© WILDERNESS ADVENTURES PRESS, INC.

TANGIER ISLAND TO CAPE CHARLES

From a spot due east of Tangier Island southward to the town of Cape Charles is a distance of about 35 miles. Fishing opportunities abound along this shoreline; access points, however, do not. These are some of the least fished areas of the entire Bay. The only settlements of any size on the Bay side of the peninsula between Crisfield and Cape Charles are Belle Haven and Onancock, and neither is exactly a teeming metropolis. Further, virtually all of the charter captains who ply these waters specialize in bottom fishing, (predominantly for seatrout, flounder, or croaker), chum for striped bass, or troll for stripers or Spanish mackerel. Light-tackle fishing, except as practiced by some local anglers, is largely nonexistent. What this means, of course, is that although the fishing can be exceptional, you'll need a boat, and even then, there are only a few launch ramps. Some of the upper portions of the area are reachable from Crisfield, but it's a long run and there is a lot of good water in between to divert an angler.

WATTS ISLAND

The first spot to check out is Watts Island. Located about 7 miles south of Great Fox Island, Watts Island is reachable from Crisfield by either of two routes. You can go out into Tangier Sound and run due south, or you can take the "back way" and run down the Broad Creek channel and go south in Pocomoke Sound. One advantage to the first route is that you can first fish the areas around Fox Island, then move south to Watts Island. The second route limits your choices, but it is a good bet if it's windy. As you can see by looking at a chart, some very shallow water separates Tangier Sound

The channel through Tangier Island.

Doubled up! Lefty Kreh and Joe Bruce, with guide Kevin Josenhans, are hooked simultaneously to speckled trout.

and Pocomoke Sound. There is a cut between the two below Fox Island called the Great Thoroughfare. It's ill named. It's unmarked, difficult to locate, and offers excellent opportunities to run aground. We've done just that. The Tangier Sound route is best unless it's windy.

Shallow grass beds, reachable principally on a flood tide, surround Watts Island. In the spring, it's an excellent spot for speckled trout and croaker. The north end of the island is likely the best spot.

Directly south of the island is a rock pile called Watts Island Rocks (how original). When the waters are cool in spring and fall this is a very good, and little known, spot to fish for tautog. Although strictly a bottom feeder, and thus a little out of the purview of this book, tautog are worthy of mention principally because they are so good to eat. They feed almost exclusively on crustaceans, so pieces of hard crabs or sand fleas are the best bait. A standard bottom rig, with a sinker on the end of the line and a hook about a foot above it, is all that is necessary.

The difficulty in catching tautog is threefold. One problem is that they live right among the rocks, so your bait has to be dropped right in where it is most likely to hang up. Two, tautog are extremely strong and vigorously resist being removed from their rocky lair. Three, they take the bait very gently and a strike is hard to detect. However, if you like to eat fish at all, it's worth some time trying to catch a couple of these palate pleasers. Most folks who've tried tautog usually rate them as the best tasting fish in the Chesapeake.

Besides tautog, this is a very good spot to drift a fly on a slow sinking line for speckled trout and weakfish. Guide Matt Tawes frequents this spot in the spring. His favorite fly choice is either a yellow and white or chartreuse and white Clouser on about a size 2 hook. One significant advantage of the fly rod in this location is its ability to get your offering down and keep it in the strike zone without hanging up in the rocks. A lead-head jig fished with standard gear will get down quicker, but it will hang up more frequently.

Onancock Area

Southeast of Watts Island, on the Virginia shore at the end of Onancock Creek, is the town of Onancock. Some excellent water lies between it and Watts Island. Look at a chart, and you'll quickly see that the shoreline is mostly one big shallow flat interspersed with deeper narrow channels. These channel edges are always good spots for trout and stripers, and the sloping flats adjacent to them are excellent locations to find flounder.

The mouth of Onancock Creek is also a good area, as is the shoreline all around Parkers Marsh Wildlife Refuge. When the tide gets to flood stage, the predators, in this case possibly stripers, speckled trout, weakfish, or flounder, will move into the shallows in search of baitfish. When a high tide and low-light levels of early morning or evening coincide, conditions are at their peak. As the tide begins to recede, move to the deeper water just off the edge of the flats. Needing deeper water, the larger predators move off the flats first, then stage in the closest deeper water waiting for the tide to bring them a meal. As always, use caution when fishing these flats. The water is shallow and it's easy to go aground. If you get stuck on a falling tide, you're looking at a 6-hour wait—at least.

If you do get stuck, chances are you'll have to get out and push. Not an easy task. Sometimes rocking the boat from side to side will help, and if there are several anglers in the party, put all except the pusher up on the bow. This additional weight up front may be enough to free the stern.

South of Parkers Marsh, there is lots of very similar water—shallow flats that extend well out from shore shelving into deeper water. Since the water close to shore is so shallow and tricky, the best way to fish it is to approach from the deeper water to the west, fish an area, then move back out to deeper water before moving farther north or south.

Getting There

Onancock is 50 miles or so south of Salisbury, just off Route 13. Go past the town of Accomac and turn west (towards the Bay) on Route 126. It's just a short distance from that point, and the ramp is right in town.

Launch Ramps

The best ramp in the area is right in Onancock. It's a privately owned ramp with a launch fee. There are some other ramps in the area, but they are mostly shallow oyster shell ramps suited to small boats. Onancock is the best bet.

Local Services

The bulk of the places to stay and/or eat are in the Chincoteague area about 25 miles north, but there is at least one place to stay in Onancock—The Colonial Manor Inn at 84 Market Street (757-787-2105).

There are some eating establishments in Onancock, but we have no first-hand knowledge regarding them. Nearby Wachapreague has the Island House Restaurant, 15 Atlantic Avenue (757-787-4242), featuring fresh seafood. It's popular with locals—always a good sign.

About 12 miles south, right on Route 13 at Exmore, is Trawler Restaurant and Dinner Theater (757-442-2029). The last time we ate there, there was no theater, but the food was excellent.

Belle Haven to Nassawadox Creek

The next stop moving south towards Cape Charles is the town of Belle Haven. Located on Occohannock Creek, it offers good access to some excellent and little-fished waters. There's a marine supply store on the north side of the creek and a launch ramp on the south. The channel out to the Bay is well marked but narrow, and pay particular attention when you exit the mouth of the creek. The channel goes south, and so should you. There's some very shallow water directly out from the mouth. Besides, the best fishing spots are between there and Nassawadox Creek. There is lots of underwater structure, and the mouth of Nassawadox Creek is exceptionally interesting, with lots of grass beds that speckled trout love. Many of these grass beds are just off the channel and thus accessible. It's exceptionally tricky water, though, so make sure you have an up-to-date chart, and proceed very cautiously. A shallow-draft boat will shine in these waters.

A happy flyfisher displays her fine seatrout.

Tackle and Techniques

To fish these grass beds effectively, you will need a shallow-running offering. For a fly rod, your best bet is either a floating line or a sink-tip in about a size 8. In either case, an unweighted fly is desirable. A yellow and white Deceiver or Clouser will work quite well as will a couple of local favorites—the Crab-Colored Clouser, a chartreuse and white Crystal Bugger, or a flashy gold Spoon Fly.

Often, a surface offering will work well. A quiet fly, like slider or a crease fly will often out-fish a loud popper in these shallow waters.

For casting or spinning tackle, a lure that comes down softly, floats at rest, and runs only about a foot deep when retrieved is ideal. Good choices include Bill Lewis's Slap-Stik, and Excalibur's Saltwater Swim'n Image. Both are proven fish producers, as are many similar offerings from other manufacturers. Just be sure to buy saltwater versions with rust-resistant hooks and hardware.

If a shallow runner doesn't produce, try a surface plug. Usually (but not always), a quiet plug will be more effective in these shallow waters than will a noisy popper. Excalibur's Spit'n Image or Bomber's ⅜-ounce Floating Mullet are fine choices. Or you might try a popper fished slowly with not much commotion. This has an advantage in that, if the quiet retrieve doesn't work, you can kick up a fuss without changing lures. An all-time favorite is the Pop-R. Now made in saltwater versions, it and the similar Spit-Fire from Bill Lewis are top choices.

A deadly combination is to rig soft plastic jerkbait, like a Bass Assassin split-tail shad, or a Zoom Fluke, by attaching the hook to the very front of the lure using a hitchhiker (a small wire coil with a loop). The hook point goes through the loop and the coil is then screwed into the soft plastic. You fish the rig by casting it out and allowing the lure to slowly sink. Twitching the rod tip while slowly cranking the reel will move the lure towards the surface in a very erratic manner. Pause and it sinks again. The retrieve is simply a repetition of this sequence. It works incredibly well on all manner of fish.

Lately, we've been using some of the Daiichi Bleeding Bait Hooks with the soft plastics. This bright red hook is said to resemble the flash of a baitfish's gills and act as a strike trigger. This may or may not be the case, but the combination certainly works.

NASSAWADOX CREEK TO THE CONFLUENCE OF HUNGARS CREEK AND MATTAWOMAN CREEK

We now come to one of the most productive five-mile stretches of water on the eastern side of the Bay. The shoreline between Nassawadox and Hungars is shallow but accessible and filled with grass beds. It's fertile water and home to many of the Bay's species. If you are targeting speckled trout, there's probably no better spot north of the Carolinas. In fact, the area produced a 16-pound monster that is the current Virginia state record, and was the world record until an even bigger specimen of well over 17 pounds was caught in Florida in 1995. Although the Virginia fish was caught bottom fishing with a piece of peeler crab (undoubtedly the best bait you can use for specks), anglers using flies or lures take many large fish. In spring, especially, the numerous grass beds are hotspots. As the waters warm, the fish will retreat to deeper, cooler locations, and the nearby waters abound with such deep holes and channels.

If the area along the shoreline is good, the water just inside the confluence of the two creeks is outstanding. With the amount of grass beds, submerged pilings, and other structure you could fish this areas for hours and not move a half-mile. Be advised, however, that like much of the area already described, these waters require a shallow-draft boat. Even then, you must watch the tides to avoid becoming stranded.

Flounder are also abundant here, and this is one of the better spots to try for one on a fly or lure. Remember, although flounder do not search out their prey, preferring to lie hidden on the bottom and wait for a potential meal to swim by, they are nevertheless active predators that feed principally by sight. More and more anglers are finding out that flounder actually can be caught on artificials.

Bluefish also show up in this area, and they are usually abundant from mid-summer till mid-fall. Unfortunately, the large 10-pound-plus specimens that we used to see seldom come into the Bay anymore, but there are lots of blues ranging from little guys that scarcely stretch eight inches long up to about five or six pounds. Usually, though, the blues will be found chasing baitfish farther out in the Bay. Spanish mackerel also ply these waters, but like the blues, they will usually be found farther from shore in deeper water that has a fast tidal flow.

THE CELL

About five miles due west from the mouth of Hungars Creek is a large artificial reef called the Cell. Well marked on most charts and identified by a Coast Guard obstruction buoy numbered WT2, this artificial reef is a real fish magnet. Created in part from the remains of the Wolf Trap Degaussing Station, this is a large irregular structure with many parts near the surface. Be careful, especially at low tide. At the Cell, you can catch many of the species that frequent the Lower Bay waters and it's a very productive spot for spadefish.

Spades look a little like angelfish seen in aquariums, but they have prominent dorsal and anal fins and are much bigger. Two- to four-pound fish are common all season long, and in May and June, 10-pounders are not uncommon. In fact, Virginia gives out more citations for spadefish in June than any other month.

Ten years ago, fishing for spadefish was virtually unknown. Today, they're a hot item. They are very strong for their size, excellent on the table, and not really difficult to catch (on bait) once you've learned the basic technique.

Spadefish have probably been in the Lower Bay every summer for a long time, but either no one knew how to catch them, or anglers were unaware of their presence. Now that that's been figured out, spades are very popular with anglers who like to anchor up and fish.

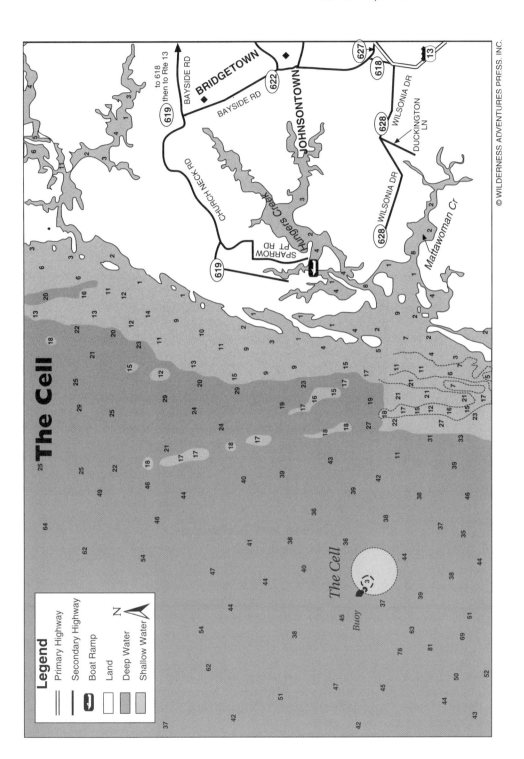

© WILDERNESS ADVENTURES PRESS, INC.

*Author Bill May with a spadefish taken near the
third island of the Chesapeake Bay Bridge Tunnel.*

Tackle and Techniques

Since spadefish feed principally on jellyfish, finding a way to attract these fish posed
several problems. Obviously, jellyfish are difficult to handle, and even more difficult
to put on and keep on a hook. A few local guides used the "cannonball jellyfish"
prevalent in the area as bait. This particular species has no stinging tentacles, is
round (hence the name cannonball) and fairly tough (as jellyfish go), and has a
strong, circular mouth.

The technique employed was to net several and tie a piece of mono to the mouth
with a sinker attached several feet below the creature, with another longer piece of
mono also tied to the mouth, so that the jellyfish could be lowered several feet down
and tied off. Additional jellyfish were broken up into small pieces and used as chum.
The angler would impale a small piece of jellyfish on a hook, and allow it to drift back
among the chum.

The spadefish would be attracted by the chum and would discover the tethered jellyfish and begin feeding on it as well as the drifting bits of chum. In theory, this sounds fine. The difficulty arises in keeping the bits of jellyfish on the hook—not an easy feat.

More recently, anglers have found that clams work just as well as jellyfish, can be readily purchased locally, and bits of clam (the foot at least) stay on a hook very well. Large ocean clams, in case you've never tried eating them, remind one of erasers dipped in garlic butter.

Typically, clams are crushed and thrown overboard shell and all to form the chum line. The usual technique is to tie the main line to a bobber. Then tie 3 to 6 feet of 20-pound test clear leader to the bobber. Run the end of the leader through an egg sinker and tie on a swivel. Then tie another 2 or 3 feet of leader to the swivel and affix about a size-1 circle hook. The egg sinker gets the bait down, and the bobber keeps the hook from going too deep and hanging up in the rocks. When the bobber goes under, you should have a spadefish.

There are only a couple of requirements for success. You need a moving tide, and you generally need underwater structure. The Cell provides both and is a hotspot, but there are other places too, which we'll cover in the following sections.

Can spadefish be caught on flies? Yes, but it certainly isn't easy. As far as we know, most people taking spadefish on flies have done so by using cottony materials tied in an amorphous glob that is first dipped in clam juice before being drifted back in the chum line. Although effective, it's not legal as far as the International Game Fish Association (IGFA) is concerned. Of course, if you aren't concerned about a record—so what?

If you want to try to catch a spadefish "legitimately" on a fly, the best time to do so is in May and early June when the spades first make their appearance. Then, they are hungry, and normally there will be a dearth of jellyfish so they won't be as particular about what they eat. Also, that's when the biggest fish are present, and all the spadefish tend to be fairly concentrated. Find the fish (which means scouting suitable structure) and set up a clam chum line. Using an intermediate sinking line, drift a fly that looks like a bit of clam (about as simple a fly as you could tie—just a bit of reddish brown wool lumped around a hook) back with the chum and you may well connect.

Although difficult to take with legitimate fly fishing methods, spadefish nevertheless provide a lot of action and great eating for anyone willing to use bait. Personally, we like to catch fish, and if bait is the only practical way, then bait it will be.

Launch Ramp

Hungars Creek is accessed from Route 13 going south towards Cape Charles. Turn right (west) on Route 618 just south of Exmore. Follow that to Route 619 to Hungars Creek. The ramp is at Chesapeake Marine.

CAPE CHARLES

And now, we come to the end of the line (literally). Cape Charles is the last town on the Eastern Shore of Virginia. A few miles south, Route 13 exits the peninsula by going into the eastern end of the Chesapeake Bay Bridge Tunnel (CBBT) on the way to Norfolk. The CBBT more or less marks the southern terminus of the Bay.

The nearby waters offer what is possibly the best and most varied fishing in the entire Bay. Depending on the time of year, every species of game fish that is present in the Bay can be caught here; often, in greater numbers and larger sizes than anywhere else.

As is typical throughout the Bay, spring and fall are best, but summer is also productive for some species, and even winter can be good. In fact, if the weather remains reasonable, large stripers can be caught around the islands of the CBBT into January.

Just north of town is Cherrystone Creek. The creek is long, narrow, and shallow, but the channel is fairly deep. A good way to fish this area is to start at one end or the other, depending on the tide, and drift along the channel casting into the shallow flats on either side. Target species will be flounder and speckled trout. Chartreuse and white Clousers are a good choice. For spin or casting gear, soft plastics like the Bass Assassin, Zoom Lures, or similar offerings in various colors produce. Favorite colors are chartreuse with a red head or pearl with a red or green head. If they don't produce, try pink. A weird color, I'll admit, but sometimes very productive. Also, MirrOlures are a local favorite.

OLD PLANTATION LIGHT AND
OLD PLANTATION CREEK

Southwest of Cherrystone is Old Plantation Light. The flats in that area can be a good spot to try for flounder and trout. The bottom on the east side of the flats shoals gradually, while the west side drops abruptly from about 10 feet to more than 70. Fish will cruise the eastern side and stack up right along the edge of the drop-off on the west side. On a falling tide, the north end will be best.

Plantation Light itself no longer exists. Some time ago, the lighthouse was blown up, and all that remains is a marker. All, that is, except all the rubble from the lighthouse, which, as you might expect, is a great holding spot for several species.

Early spring and late fall, when the water is cold, the rocks hold a good population of tautog. Also called blackfish, tautog live right amid the rocks. As mentioned earlier, fishing for tautog means fishing with bait. Period. Not only that, very specific bait. Since tautog feed almost exclusively on crustaceans, the bait of choice is a piece of hard crab or a couple of "sand fleas." It's simple fishing, really, but proper tackle is essential for success. You need a strong hook but a light sinker—just enough to get the bait to the bottom. A heavy sinker impedes your ability to detect a strike.

As to tackle, a stout, sensitive graphite casting rod and a quality reel coupled with no-stretch line like Berkley's Fireline is the best combination. Tautog are incredibly strong fish, but they take a bait very delicately and the take is difficult to detect. Once the fish is hooked, you must immediately put as much pressure on him as possible.

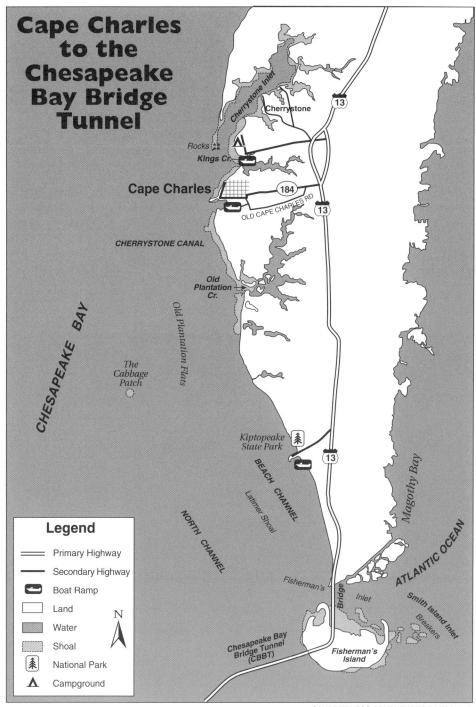

Cape Charles to the Chesapeake Bay Bridge Tunnel

Cherrystone Inlet

Cherrystone

13

Rocks ☆☆

Kings Cr.

Cape Charles

184

OLD CAPE CHARLES RD

13

CHERRYSTONE CANAL

Old Plantation Cr.

CHESAPEAKE BAY

Old Plantation Flats

The Cabbage Patch

Kiptopeake State Park

13

BEACH CHANNEL

Latimer Shoal

NORTH CHANNEL

Magothy Bay

ATLANTIC OCEAN

Fisherman's

Bridge

Inlet

Smith Island Inlet

Breakers

Chesapeake Bay Bridge Tunnel (CBBT)

Fisherman's Island

Legend

═══ Primary Highway

─── Secondary Highway

▭ Boat Ramp

▢ Land

▨ Water

▨ Shoal

⛺ National Park

▲ Campground

N

© WILDERNESS ADVENTURES PRESS, INC.

Once he feels the hook, he'll dive right for the rocks and if he makes it—he wins. Bring lots of sinkers and hooks. If you don't lose a lot, you aren't fishing where the fish are.

Plantation Light is also another good spot for spadefish from early June till late September. Sometimes, redfish (locally called puppy drum) frequent these rocks and you can actually cast to visible fish.

Redfish, by the way, are a target species in the waters of the Lower Bay, and there are a number of spots where they can be caught. However, there presence is unpredictable and most are caught incidentally while seeking other species. Locals, especially some of the light-tackle guides, are usually aware of their presence, and if you would like to try your luck for this species, we'd strongly suggest hiring a guide. Since just about all of the guides who fish this area live on the Western Shore, you'll find information on them in the section dealing with the Western Shore of the Lower Bay.

The shoreline south of Cape Charles is shallow and grassy. It's a good spot to try for speckled trout. The mouth of Old Plantation Creek can be especially good. You can get inside the creek's mouth and access some very productive grass flats. The trouble is that it's difficult to negotiate. A boat with a shallow draft is a must, and you had best keep a watchful eye on the tide. The best time would be the last hour of the incoming tide and the first hour or two of the outgoing. As the tide falls, the deeper water just outside the creek's mouth is the place to be.

A small redfish.

THE CABBAGE PATCH

Moving down the coast, about four miles southwest of Old Plantation Creek is an area called the Cabbage Patch. This is a new reef that was constructed with the aid of the Eastern Shore Chapter of the Coastal Conservation Association of Virginia and was funded with money from saltwater license revenues.

The reef consists of three distinct rows of "T" beams that run east to west. It's marked with a yellow artificial reef buoy. This structure and "The Cell" are two of the better spots in the Lower Bay for many species.

The water along the edge of the Cabbage Patch is fairly turbulent during a good tide and is a hotspot for Spanish mackerel from midsummer to early fall. Usually, the eastern side is best for these guys because the bottom is shallower and much "lumpier" than the western side, resulting in much greater turbulence.

By the way, several times we've mentioned fast, turbulent tidal flows and Spanish mackerel together. The reason is that Spanish mackerel almost invariably feed at or near the surface when tidal flows are strong since large schools of baitfish are swept along with the flow, and the fish can rip through them, feeding as they go.

The Cabbage Patch is another hotspot for spadefish. Other species can also be caught here. Tautog are here when the waters are cold enough, and croaker may be here from May till late summer. Speckled trout are available from May until about mid-November.

KIPTOPEAKE AND LATIMER SHOAL

Due east from the Cabbage Patch is Kiptopeake State Park. About a half-mile from shore are several concrete ships that have been scuttled and rest on the bottom, forming a breakwater for the state park. Yes, they are made from concrete. These are old World War II Liberty Ships. Although steel hulls were more common, some of the Liberty Ships had hulls made from Ferro-Concrete. Basically, this is a specialized hull-building technique that employs layers of interwoven steel reinforcing rods encapsulated in concrete. Although this may seem bizarre, the method works quite well, and even today some America's Cup-class racing sailboats are built with this method.

All that aside, what concerns us is this is a good spot to fish for tautog. Since these hulls have rounded bottoms, there's a gap all along the edge of the hull that extends well under it, where the bottom of the hull meets the bottom of the Bay. Of course, tautog, liking dark, well-protected environs, live here. To target these fish, anchor your boat as close as possible to the hull and drop your bait straight down. As mentioned before, avoid light tackle.

Occasionally, flounder and speckled trout can be caught here, as well, but there are better locations.

Just south of the concrete ships is Latimer Shoal. This is a good spot to find breaking stripers and bluefish in late summer and fall. It's also frequently good for Spanish mackerel. Looking at a chart, you can see that the mainland shoreline to the east of the shoal drops abruptly from 3 or 4 feet to as deep as 30 then rises more gradually to about a 15-foot average. The way the topography is, this side forms a natural funnel, and on an outgoing tide especially, this would be the place to be. This natural channel is a good spot to fish for speckled trout and weakfish. You'll need a fast-sinking fly line to get to the trout at this spot. For casting or spinning gear, the usual lead-head jigs or jigging spoons (Stingsilvers are the overwhelming favorite) are best.

If Spanish mackerel are your target, a slim flashy streamer no more than three inches long is about right, and for spinning or casting it's hard to beat a Stingsilver or a Gotcha Plug. Spanish have lots of small sharp teeth, so we'd suggest flies made from tough synthetic fibers. Avoid feathers, they shred quickly. Also, for the same reasons, don't use soft plastic lures for these guys.

It's important to realize that, along with the shoreline fishing, the whole expanse of the Bay in this region can provide excellent fishing for breaking fish. In late summer through the end of November schools of breaking striped bass are common. It's no trick to catch 50 a day. Many will be fairly small, but there will be some nice ones mixed in. Surface feeding bluefish may also be on the menu. Sometimes you will find schools of stripers and blues mixed together, so anytime you are working breaking fish, unless you know for certain that they are just stripers, use a short wire bite tippet on the end of your leader. You only need a length of about four inches. Longer wire leaders, so common in tackle shops, are designed for bait fisherman. There's absolutely no need for a long wire tippet on a fly or lure. Blue Water Designs in Connecticut (860-582-0623) markets wire leaders ideally suited to flyrodders. They weigh little and come with small snaps and pre-formed loops ready to attach to a leader.

Spanish mackerel will also be available at this time. Just look for good tidal action. Any type of bottom structure (artificial reefs, shoals, underwater lumps) will cause an upwelling of water with a moving tide. These forces sweep the schools of bait to the surface where they are easy prey. All the predators that surface feed in the area will focus on this, so you may well encounter stripers, blues, or Spanish mackerel.

Also, you should be aware, as mentioned elsewhere in this book, that speckled trout and seatrout, which predominately feed near the bottom, will often be beneath the surface feeders, targeting the "fallout." Larger specimens of striped bass, which are much less inclined to feed at the surface than their smaller brethren, may be there as well. So if you are into breaking stripers and they are too small for your liking, go deep. Countless times, we've been in this situation. By switching to a high density sinking line or changing to spinning or casting tackle with a lead-head jig or a jigging spoon, we'd immediately start picking up substantially larger fish. One thing to consider, though, is that if the surface action is "frenzied," as it often is, conventional tackle may be much more effective than fly gear for this particular endeavor. The fastest sinking line doesn't begin to get down as quickly as a lead jig and may not sink rapidly enough to get through the smaller fish. It's a nice dilemma, though.

A Spanish mackerel whose eyes were bigger than his stomach. Although small flashy flies or small silver spoons are the norm, when a school of mackerel is really "busting bait" they'll hit most anything.

FISHERMAN'S ISLAND

Fisherman's Island lies just below Latimer Shoal and is at the end of the Virginia peninsula. There's good fishing all around the island. There's a channel between the north end of the island and the mainland that offers access to some good spots. On the south side of the channel right under the bridge there is a large underwater rock pile. The water at the backside of the rock pile is nearly 20 feet deep and is a prime spot for seatrout. It's also a good spot for stripers.

Cast large surface plugs or swimming plugs right at the rocks. We favor two lures especially for this activity. Storm Lures' Rattlin' Chug Bug is our first choice for a surface lure for plugging the rocks. It's noisy, creates a big splash, and floats. The latter feature is very desirable when casting to rock piles. If you cast a little too far and hang up in the rocks, just let the line go slack. Unless you have missed your mark by a wide margin, the next wave will lift the lure free. For a swimming plug, we favor the Rebel Windcheater with a white belly and a blue back. Stripers and blues seem to love this lure, and they are among the most durable plug of this type on the market; an important consideration when you consider how often you are going to smash one into the rocks. Our second choice would be one of the magnum Rat-L-Traps.

Big streamers on slow sinking lines or large durable poppers are the right stuff for the fly rod. Just make sure the poppers are durable. Cork and some foam popper bodies will break up rather easily when bounced off the rocks. You might want to try some of the Mr. Bob's popping bugs. They're made from very durable foam. They're a little heavy, but they are really tough. Another good choice would be one from Edgewater. They're not quite as durable as Mr. Bob's, but they're lighter.

Just past the island is a large expanse of grassy shallows that is a good spot for speckled trout. A little farther around the end of the peninsula you enter Magothy Bay. This is very productive water, although difficult to navigate. In June, in addition to the normal species, you may have the opportunity to sight cast to cruising redfish or cobia. Both of these species may be present in fishable numbers, but it's a crapshoot for the most part. Consider them targets of opportunity. We'd not suggest a trip here to fish for either of these species specifically. However, the thought of catching either adds a lot of spice to a trip here for other fish.

Both redfish and cobia are strong, determined fighters. If a redfish were a running back, a cobia would be the biggest, strongest lineman ever. A cobia will test tackle to the utmost, and if put in the boat too quickly, they will definitely break things. Be careful with these fish. Should you hook one, make sure that it is thoroughly beaten before you attempt to land it.

Getting There

The town of Cape Charles is reached by following Route 13 south about 90 miles from Salisbury to Route 184. A right turn on 184 will take you directly into town.

Launch Ramps

Two launch ramps serve the area. The first is at the Old Coast Guard Station near what used to be the Cape Charles Fishing Center (which no longer exists). If you want to fish Cherrystone Creek, the Cape Charles Reef or Old Plantation Light, this ramp is a good choice.

The second ramp is about six miles farther south at Kiptopeake State Park. This ramp is far superior to the one in town and offers the closest access to the better fishing spots. If you are interested, Kiptopeake offers complete camping facilities and primitive camping, as well. For more information, call 757-331-2267.

Hub Cities for the Lower Bay, Eastern Shore

Crisfield, Maryland

Population—2,880

Lying at the end of a peninsula in Somerset County, Crisfield is the southernmost city in Maryland. Smith and Tangier Islands are nearby and daily excursion boats offer trips. Other attractions include Assateague Island National Seashore and Chincoteague National Wildlife Refuge in Virginia, home of the world famous wild ponies.

ACCOMMODATIONS
Paddlewheel Motel, 701 W Main Street; 410-968-2220
Pines Motel, 127 N Somerset Avenue; 410-968-0900
Somers Cove Motel, 700 Norris Drive; 410-968-1900

CAMPGROUNDS AND STATE PARKS
Janes Island State Park, 26280 Alfred Lawson Drive; 410-968-1565 (office); PARK-JANES-ISLAND@Dnr.State.Md.Us; 888-432-CAMP(2267) or reservations

RESTAURANTS
Dockside Restaurant, 1003 W. Main Street; 410-968-3464
Side Street Seafood Market & Restaurant, 204 South Tenth St; 410-968-2442
Tropical Chesapeake, 712 Broadway Street; 410-968-3622
Watermen's Inn, 901 W. Main Street; 410-968-2119

FLY SHOPS, TACKLE STORES, AND SPORTING GOODS Closest are:
Darcy's Sport Shops, 17.54 miles, 7 Dunne Rd., Parksley, VA; 757-665-4927
Bennett Street Sporting Goods, 17.60 miles, 24312 Bennett St., Parksley, VA; 757-665-5013

LAUNCH RAMPS AND MARINAS
Janes Island State Park Ramp, Annemessex Canal on Janes Island, Route 13 to Route 413 south to Plantation Ave. west to Jacksonville Rd. south to Alfred Lawson Drive West
Crisfield Ramp, Annemessex Canal, Route 13 to Route 413 south to Crisfield, once in town go right on Brick Kiln Road; 410-651-0320
Jenkins Creek Ramp, Jenkins Creek, Junction of Calvery Road and Sackertown Road, Route 13 to Route 413 south to Crisfield to Somerset Ave. south to Calvery Rd. south, look on north side of bridge for ramp; 410-651-0320
Somers Cove Marina, Little Annemessex River, Route 13 to Route 413 south, take Route 413 to Crisfield, turn left on Somerset and follow to ramp; 410-968-0925

BOAT REPAIR

Crisfield Propeller-Sea Mark, 855 W Main Street; 410-968-0800
Evan's Boat Construction & Repair, 4335 Crisfield Hwy.; 410-968-3396
Logan's Marine, 10th Street; 410-968-2330

AUTO REPAIR

Mariner Auto Repair, 4462 Crisfield Hwy.; 410-968-2010
Sam's Auto Center, 4019 Crisfield Hwy.; 410-968-1375

HOSPITALS

E. W. McCready Memorial Hospital, 201 Hall Hwy.; 410-968-1200

FOR FURTHER INFORMATION

Somerset County Tourism, P.O. Box 243, Princess Anne, MD 21853; 410-651-2968, 800-521-9189; somtour@dmv.com

Everything is on the water at Tangier Island.

Pocomoke City, MD

Population—4,098

Settled in the 1600s on the banks of the Pocomoke River, the town of Pocomoke City was formed in 1878.

ACCOMMODATIONS

Days Inn, 1540 Ocean Hwy.; 410-957-3000
Holiday Inn, 125 Newtown Blvd.; 410-957-6444
Pocomoke Inn, 912 Ocean Hwy.; 410-957-1029
Quality Inn, 825 Ocean Hwy.; 410-957-1300

RESTAURANTS

Don's Seafood, 344 Ocean Hwy.; 410-957-0177
Friendly's Restaurant, 2112 Old Snow Hill Road; 410-957-6500
Kenny's Place, US Highway 13 S; 410-957-2213
Trader's Fried Chicken, 123 Ames Plaza; 410-957-1682

FLY SHOPS, TACKLE STORES, AND SPORTING GOODS Closest are:

Oyster Bay Outfitters, 13.14 miles, 6332 Maddox Blvd, Chincoteague, VA; 757-336-0070
Pioneer Sports, 18.46 miles, 104 N Fruitland Blvd, Fruitland, MD; 410-546-9599
Whitetail Outpost, 18.52 miles, 6516 Bowden Road, Newark, MD;410-632-0313

LAUNCH RAMPS AND MARINAS

Pocomoke City Park Ramp, Pocomoke River, Route 13 to Route 371 to Cedar Hall Wharf Road south; 410-757-1334
Winter Quarters Ramp, Pocomoke River, Pocomoke City, Route 13 to Pocomoke City to Winter Quarters Road north; 410-757-1334
Cedar Hall Wharf, Pocomoke River, Pocomoke City, end of Cedar Hall Road, Route 13 to Route 371 to Cedar Hall Wharf Road south; 410-632-5623

BOAT EQUIPMENT AND REPAIR

Ford's Outboard Service, 101 Vine Street; 410-957-0066

AUTO REPAIR

Hensler's Auto Center, 1612 Market St Ext.; 410-957-0560
Pocomoke Car & Truck, 428 Bank Street; 410-957-0457

HOSPITALS Closest is:

E. W. McCready Memorial Hospital, 17.41 miles, 201 Hall Hwy., Crisfield, MD; 410-968-1200

FOR FURTHER INFORMATION

Worcester County Tourism Office, 113 Franklin Street, Unit 1, Snow Hill, MD 21863; 410-632-3110, 800-852-0335

Princess Anne, Mayrland

Population—2,313

This quaint Maryland town dates back to the 1600s and is listed in the National Register of Historic Places.

ACCOMMODATIONS

Econo Lodge Princess Anne, 10936 Market Lane, US 13; 866-226-9330
Travelers Budget Inn, 30359 Mount Vernon Rd.; 410-651-4075
Washington Hotel Inn, 11784 Somerset Ave.; 410-651-2526

CAMPGROUNDS AND STATE PARKS

Princess Anne Campground, 12370 Brittingham Lane; 410-651-1520

RESTAURANTS

Independence Hall, 31 N Somerset Ave.; 410-651-1976
Peaky's Restaurant, 30361 Mount Vernon Road; 410-651-1950
Spikes Pub & Subs, 30264 Mount Vernon Plaza; 410-651-9124
Washington Hotel Inn, 11784 Somerset Avenue; 410-651-2526

FLY SHOPS, TACKLE STORES, AND SPORTING GOODS

Closest are:
Pioneer Sports, 9.28 miles, 104 N Fruitland Blvd, Fruitland, MD; 410-546-9599
Dave's Sport Shop, 10.96 miles, 23701 Nanticoke Rd. Quantico, MD; 410-742-2454
Strikers, 10.97 miles, 1318 S Salisbury Blvd, Salisbury, MD; 410-749-8914

LAUNCH RAMPS AND MARINAS

Websters Cove Marina, Wicomico River, Route 13 to Route 362 west (north side of Princess Anne) to Mt Vernon, turn north on Dorsey Ave. and go to end; Dept, of Public Works, 410-651-0320
Dames Quarter Public Launch Ramp, Dames Quarter Creek, Route 13 to Princess Anne to Route 363 west to Long Point Rd. north, then take first right turn; Dept. of Public Works, 410-651-1930
St. Peters Creek Launch Ramp, St. Peters Creek, Route 13 to Princess Anne to Route 363 west to Route 627 south to Champ Rd. south to Champ Wharf Rd. west; Dept. of Public Works, 410-651-0320
Wenona Launch Ramp, Lower Thorofare, Wenona, Route 13 to Princess Anne to Route 363 west, follow to end and look to north side of road; Dept. of Public Works, 410-651-0320
Deal Island, Upper Thorofare, Deal Island, Route 13 to Princess Anne to Route 363 west to Deal Island, take second right once on island; Dept. of Public Works, 410-651-0320

BOAT EQUIPMENT AND REPAIR

See Pocomoke City or Crisfield.

AUTO REPAIR
Advantage Auto Repair, 12450 Loretta Road; 410-651-1900
Somerset Automotive, 12471 Somerset Avenue; 410-651-0900

HOSPITALS
See Easton or Salisbury.

FOR FURTHER INFORMATION
Somerset County Office of Tourism, P.O. Box 243, Princess Anne, MD 21853;
410-651-2968

A fish-eye view of the Chesapeake Bay Bridge Tunnel.

Onancock, Virginia

Population—1,450

Founded in 1680, Onancock is one of the largest towns on Virginia's Eastern Shore peninsula. Several museums and Victorian architecture contribute to the town's charm.

ACCOMMODATIONS Nearest are:
Comfort Inn, 1.84 miles, 25297 Lankford Hwy, Onley, VA; 757-787-7787
Best Value Inn, 1.94 miles, 25597 Coastal Blvd, Onley, VA; 757-787-8000
Captain's Quarters Motel, 3.99 miles, 29136 US Route 13, Melfa; 757-787-4545

CAMPGROUNDS AND STATE PARKS
Sandpiper Cove Camping Resort, 757-787-7781

RESTAURANTS
Backfins, 47 Market Street; 757-787-2906
Flounders Restaurant, 145 Market Street; 757-787-2233
Hopkins & Brothers Restaurant, 2 Market Street; 757-787-3100
Peppers Market & Deli, 151 Market Street; 757-787-3457
Stella's, 13 North Street; 757-789-7770

LAUNCH RAMPS AND MARINAS
Saxis Landing, Pocomoke Sound, Route 13 north from Onancock, left on route 695 to end
Onancock Town Landing, Onancock Creek, Route 13 to Route 179 to ramp
Schooner Bay Ramp, mouth of Chessonessex Creek, Route 657 to 656 to end
Morley's Warf, Occohannock Creek, south of Onancock about midway to Cape Charles, Route 13 south to Route 183 to right on 606

BOAT EQUIPMENT AND REPAIR Nearest are:
Sea Side Marine, 12.79 miles, 13323 Heath Lane Exmore, VA; 757-442-5995
Melson Marine, 12.96 miles, 11498 Davis Wharf Dr. Belle Haven, VA; 757-442-9242

AUTO REPAIR
Carey's Car Care, 116 Market Street; 757-787-9254
Certified Auto, 161 Market Street; 757-787-3686

HOSPITALS Closest are:
Shore Memorial Hospital, 17.47 miles, 9507 Hospital Ave Nassawadox, VA; 757-414-8000
E. W. McCready Memorial Hospital, 20.62 miles, 201 Hall Hwy, Crisfield, MD; 410-968-1200

FOR FURTHER INFORMATION
Eastern Shore of Virginia Tourism, Post Office Box 460, US Route 13 South, Melfa, VA 23410; 757-787-2460; info@esvatourism.org

Cape Charles, Virginia

Population—12,900

Established in 1884, Cape Charles was placed on the National Register of Historic Places. The town boasts one of the largest concentrations of late-Victorian and turn-of-the-century buildings on the East Coast.

ACCOMMODATIONS
Best Western Inn, 32246 Lankford Hwy.; 757-331-1776
Cape Motel, 26460 Lankford Hwy.; 757-331-2461
Days Inn, 29106 Lankford Hwy.; 757-331-1000
Sunset Beach Inn, 32246 Lankford Hwy.; 757-331-1776

CAMPGROUNDS AND STATE PARKS
Cherrystone Family Camping, 1511 Townfield Drive; 757-331-3063
Sunset Beach RV Resorts, 32246 Lankford Hwy.; 757-331-1776
Kiptopeake State Park, 3540 Kiptopeake Drive; 757-331-2267

RESTAURANTS
Bailey's Drive-In, 757-331-2159
Harbor Grille, 203 Mason Avenue; 757-331-3005
Pelican Bay Pub, 32246 Lankford Hwy.; 757-331-4229
Rebecca's Restaurant, 7 Strawberry Street; 757-331-3879
Sting-Ray's, 26507 Lankford Hwy.; 757-331-2505

FLY SHOPS, TACKLE STORES, AND SPORTING GOODS
South of Pocomoke City, tackle shops that cater to light-tackle enthusiasts are few and far between, and the farther down the peninsula you go, the fewer there are.

Bailey's Bait & Tackle, 327 Mason Avenue; 757-331-1982

LAUNCH RAMPS AND MARINAS
Cape Charles Boat Ramp, Chesapeake Bay, take Route 184 from Route 13 and follow to end Kiptopeake State Park Boat Ramp, mouth of Chesapeake Bay, Route 13 south to end at state park

BOAT EQUIPMENT AND REPAIR
Closest are:
Sea Side Marine, 21.35 miles, 13323 Heath Lane Exmore, VA; 757-442-5995
Melson Marine, 20.99 miles, 11498 Davis Wharf Dr., Belle Haven, VA; 757-442-9242

AUTO REPAIR
Eastern Shore Auto Care, 29140 Lankford Hwy.; 757-331-0011

HOSPITALS

Closest is:

Shore Memorial Hospital, 16.39 miles, 9507 Hospital Ave., Nassawadox, VA; 757-414-8000

FOR FURTHER INFORMATION

Cape Charles/Northampton County Chamber of Commerce, P.O. Box 87, Cape Charles, VA 23310; 757-331-2304

The Chesapeake Bay Bridge Tunnel—the largest artificial reef in the world.

THE CHESAPEAKE BAY BRIDGE TUNNEL

With a length of 17½ miles, the Chesapeake Bay Bridge Tunnel is the longest artificial reef in the world. It's also the longest bridge-tunnel complex in the world, as well as one of the costliest to traverse. It will cost you $10 to cross one way. If you are towing a boat, add several dollars for each additional axel. Pricey? Maybe, but consider that the only other option to go between Cape Charles and Norfolk on Virginia's Western Shore is to go north to the Bay Bridge (the only other crossing) cross the Bay and then go south to Norfolk, a distance of almost two hundred miles and close to five hours driving time. The toll seems cheap when you consider that.

Built at a total cost of 450 million dollars the CBBT is actually two separate parallel tunnels. The original tunnel was opened in 1964, and the second was completed in 1999. The crossing consists of a series of low-level trestles interrupted by two approximately one-mile-long tunnels beneath Thimble Shoals and Chesapeake navigation channels. The man-made islands, each approximately 10 acres in size, are located at each end of the two tunnels. There are also high-level bridges over two other navigation channels: North Channel Bridge and Fisherman Inlet Bridge. Finally, between North Channel and Fisherman Inlet, the facility crosses at-grade over Fisherman Island, a barrier island which includes the Fisherman Island National Wildlife Refuge administered by the U.S. Fish and Wildlife Service.

What this means for us fishermen is that the CBBT is the best fish-attracting structure in the Chesapeake Bay, maybe along the entire East Coast. At some time of the year, the CBBT attracts virtually every species of fish in the Bay, and you can catch something literally 24 hours a day.

Let's start with night fishing for stripers. Since the bridge is illuminated, the lights for the highway also fall on the waters below, while the bridges cast a dark shadow on the water. Striped bass collect in these shadows, like a trout will hide under an undercut bank, and feed on baitfish as they are swept along with the tide. Fishing for them is easy. You can approach the fish from two directions. One way is to carefully position your boat in the shadow of the bridge facing uptide. You want to be the length of an easy cast from the shadow's edge. You will actually be able to see stripers lying just under the surface inside the shadow's edge near the bridge supports. Usually, they will be actively feeding. Cast a small streamer above the fish in such a manner that it sweeps past the bridge abutments as you retrieve. You will likely get at least a follow on every cast.

This is exciting fishing because you can see the fish hit. A downside, however, is the difficulty in keeping the boat positioned correctly without banging into the bridge supports. Also, it's pretty easy to damage a rod on the structure if you aren't careful with your casting.

The other option is to anchor your boat uptide from the shadow line, a cast length away. With this positioning, you won't be able to see the fish, but casting is much easier, and you can make a good presentation much more easily by casting quartering downtide and allowing your fly to sweep past the bridge pilings. We feel this is much the better method, but it does lack the appeal of actually seeing the fish.

In either case, the best offering is normally a streamer from 2 to 4 inches long, depending on the size of the baitfish. Because the predominant bait will be silver-

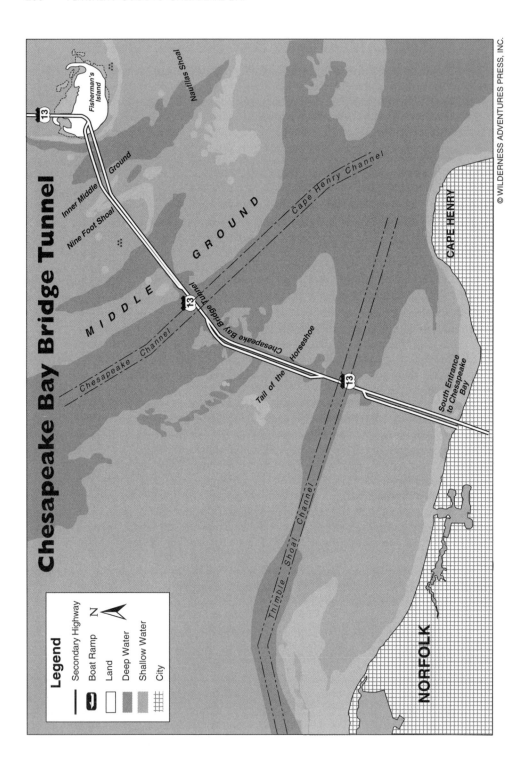

© WILDERNESS ADVENTURES PRESS, INC.

Chesapeake Bay Bridge Tunnel

Fisherman's Island

Nautilus Shoal

Inner Middle Ground

Nine Foot Shoal

MIDDLE GROUND

Cape Henry Channel

Chesapeake Channel

Chesapeake Bay Bridge Tunnel

Tail of the Horseshoe

CAPE HENRY

South Entrance to Chesapeake Bay

Thimble Shoal Channel

NORFOLK

Legend

Secondary Highway
N
Boat Ramp
Land
Deep Water
Shallow Water
City

sides or bay anchovies, smaller is better. For the spin fisherman, a small minnow-shaped, shallow-running plug without too much action is usually best. Any of the smaller Rebel, Bomber, Rapala or Yo-Zuri plugs with this configuration should work, as will small MirrOlures. However, this is one situation where a fly rod is definitely the best bet. This fishing can be done throughout much of the year, and when the season on stripers is closed, the single-hooked fly makes releasing fish much easier. Further, you can better control the presentation and drift with a fly rod.

The fish will usually be just under the surface, but sometimes you may need to get a little deeper. Still, you'll almost never need more than a slow sinking line.

You are probably thinking, "If the fish are holding that near the surface, why not try poppers?" Well, they don't seem to be nearly as effective as a subsurface offering. We've tried poppers with only limited success. In one instance, anchored in the shadow and casting to visible fish, we observed a few fish turning on the popper but not taking and others that shied away from the fly. One possibility would be to utilize a so-called crease fly. This fly is made by simply gluing some folded flat foam, which has been trimmed to roughly a minnow shape, over a hook with a tail previously affixed. The result is very light and drops on the water quite gently. It makes little disturbance and looks much like a dead or dying minnow lying on its side. Although we haven't tried this fly, other anglers are very enthusiastic about it. Try them if you like. Perhaps you'll have success. For our money, we'll fish streamers.

Fishing the shadow line as just described is a blast, but there are many more opportunities at the CBBT. The man-made islands offer excellent fishing. The best times are the first two or three hours of light and the last two in the evening. If you happen upon dreary overcast weather, fishing can be good all day long.

The rocks around the man-made islands can provide spectacular fishing. In late fall and early winter, you can catch some big stripers. This is one time that you will need pretty stout tackle if you hope to land one of these big guys. You must move the fish away from the rocks immediately to have any chance of landing it. Forget your multi-tapered leader—a 4-foot length of 16- to 20-pound test leader is commonly used. You don't need finesse, you need strength.

All of the islands offer good fishing, but the favorites seem to be the third and fourth (counting from the Western Shore). The third island, in particular, is excellent. There are lots of rocks around this island, and those extending towards the east are exceptional. However, here's a word of caution. The rocks slope downward toward the eastern shore then disappear underwater. But 50 feet farther on there is another series of rocks visible at low tide but just under the surface at high tide that have crunched many a hull. Called the "rogue rocks," they are to be avoided.

Whatever the time of year, the fishing technique remains the same. Throw your fly or lure right up against the rocks. The closer you come, the better your chances of a strike.

Both stripers and bluefish hang out around these rocks. Typically, stripers won't move far from their security zone. If a striper is going to eat your offering, it will do so within the first several feet of your retrieve. Bluefish, however, may strike right by the rocks or may follow your offering almost to the boat before striking.

Some years, medium-sized black drum will feed along the edges of the islands.

A selection of a rattle flies designed by Ed Russell. Named "The Incorporator," they feature a weighted head, a rattle enclosed in the body, a baitfish profile, flash materials, and prominent eyes.

When they do, you can often see the fish, making for some exciting sight fishing. However, don't plan on finding these fish. It's purely a hit or miss proposition. Some years fishing can be quite good; some years you won't find any.

When you first fish the CBBT, you may be overwhelmed by the amount of structure, but like any bridge anywhere, some spots seem to hold more fish than others. Maybe it's the way the current flows or the underwater structure. In any case, any of the pilings can be good, but the rocky third and fourth islands are consistently the most productive.

As mentioned, you need accurate casts right up against the rocks. Placement is essential. Stripers, in particular, will not hit an offering more than a few feet from the sanctuary of the rocks. Almost without exception, a cast that lands five feet short of the rocks will fail to yield a strike, especially from a striped bass.

For flyrodders, big streamers like Lefty's Deceivers or Whistlers or poppers made from durable foam are the ticket. For those using spinning or casting gear, use the same things mention previously for casting into the rocks.

Other species are available at the CBBT. Spanish mackerel are there in good numbers from midsummer to fall. The best place to look for these speedsters is between the islands directly over the tubes. Here, the water on either side of the tubes may be as deep as 70 feet, while over the tubes it's about 30. During a moving tide, this disparity causes quite a bit of surface disturbance, and baitfish that are swept along with the tide are forced to the surface by the water hydraulics. Spanish will feed heavily during these tidal flows, and when conditions are right, you could find yourself amid a real feeding frenzy, with fish and gulls competing for baitfish. Pretty much any small flashy fly will take fish. The only trick is to retrieve as fast as you can. Mackerel like their food moving quickly. Spinning tackle sometimes has an edge here, since a high retrieve ratio spinning reel can really move a lure along. The most popular spinning lure is a small Stingsilver, followed by a Gotcha Plug. Of course, sometimes nothing works and other times almost anything will take fish. We once had such a day, with the tide ripping, the wind blowing, and mackerel taking just about anything. We actually caught several on a 4-inch Blue Windcheater quite a bit larger than the bait. But because it was moving fast, the mackerel hit it with abandon.

If you would like to try for some really big flounder, this is the place. The standard procedure is to drift across the tunnels using about six ounces of lead and a big strip of squid. Strong, stiff tackle is called for, and you'll lose a lot of terminal tackle. Of course, you may also catch a flounder pushing 10 pounds. It's not exactly light-tackle fishing, but if you are in the area, you might want to give it a try.

We've mentioned spadefish in other areas, and those spots are generally better than around the CBBT, but spades can be caught here, as well. Just anchor uptide from a tidal flow that moves around rocky structure and use the methods described earlier. You should almost always catch fish.

Bluefish used to be a big deal at the tunnel, especially in early spring when schools of blues over 15 pounds would move in to feed on the large Atlantic menhaden that moved into the Bay. In the '60s and '70s it was no trick to catch 10 or more of these monsters on surface poppers or plugs in the course of a day. Sadly, these big fish haven't been making an appearance for quite a while. Perhaps one of these springs, they will return. Until then, you will have to content yourself with blues in the 5-pound range. Actually, that's not too bad when you consider how well these fish fight. Blues will be available around the rocks of the CBBT from mid-April until October. Streamers, poppers, spoons, or wobbling plugs all work. When bluefish are actively feeding, you could probably catch them on a file handle.

Cobia also cruise the waters near the CBBT. These fish will test your tackle (and you) to the utmost. Although more cobia are probably taken on cut bait than any other way, they do present an opportunity for sight casting to fish cruising just under the surface in June near the tunnel or into the ocean proper. These fish like surface structure and will be found most often near lighthouses or buoys. It's another iffy proposition, but if you can find them, throw a streamer, a popper, or a surface plug in front of them. If one strikes, set the hook and hang on.

Other species are present in the nearby waters. Seatrout and speckled trout are available in the deeper waters near the tunnel once the shallows get too warm for their liking, usually in early June, and remain there until fall. In recent years, most of the Lower Bay has had a very heavy population of croakers. These fish move in about the same time as the trout, but exit sooner, and are generally gone by later August or early September.

All in all, the CBBT represents a fish haven during most of the year. If you were to fish only one location in the Bay, the Bridge Tunnel area would be hard to beat.

Getting There

US Route 13 takes you to the CBBT from either shore. Charles City provides the clos-est services from Virginia's Eastern Shore (see the Hub Cities in the previous section). The sprawling Hampton Roads area on the west shoreline has everything a traveling angler could want, starting right in Norfolk near the CBBT. (See the hub cities in the "Tidewater" section.)

Launch Ramps

The middle of the CBBT is about equidistant from the ramp at Kiptopeake on the Eastern Shore or ones at Lynnhaven Inlet or Little Creek on the west side.

A typical Virginia boat ramp.

Lower Bay, Western Shore
The Northern Neck

The Mouth of the Potomac at
Smith Point to the Mouth of the Rapphannock River

In the area of Smith Point, the first attraction is the end of the jetty out of the Little Wicomico River, where a 20-foot hole stacks with flounder and provides especially good fishing on an ebb tide. This hole attracts puppy drum, stripers, both species of trout, and most of the other game fish of the Bay. Likewise, the shelf from the mouth of the Little Wicomico all the way past Great Wicomico River Light to the mouth of the Great Wicomico River and south all the way to the Dameron Marsh area provides ideal fish-holding structure with water dropping from 2- to 3-foot shallows to the prime 15- to 20-foot depths. This is the kind of structure best explored by drifting, casting fast-sinking lines, and dragging Clousers, Half-and-Halfs, and Jiggy patterns on fly tackle or using conventional tackle to cast bucktails, jigheads and plastics, Stingsilvers and other metal lures or sinking lures like MirrOlures or Rat-L-Traps.

As Derrick Armstrong of Smith Point Marina observes regarding the inshore fishery, "This place is flounder, trout, and croaker heaven, and everybody bottom fishes. But I go out in the morning and evening with fly tackle and have a ball with these fish, plus stripers and blues. All you need are some poppers and Clousers."

Moving offshore, work Smith Point Bar to Smith Point Light the same way. Smith Point Light is particularly good for gray trout at night using the same techniques, flies, and lures as above. To the east and south of the light lie three wrecks in waters roughly from 50 to 65 feet—the target ships—*City of Annapolis*, the *Dorothy* and the *Brazilia*. Directly east of the light is the series of lumps known as the Cabbage Patch (discussed earlier). All these structures can be worked with deep jigging techniques.

Smith Point Jetty, Smith Point Light, and the target ships are all gathering points for gray trout in the fall (late September and early October) as the fish prepare to push down the Bay to the CBBT.

At the mouth of the Great Wicomico River, the whole area of Ingraham Bay to the Great Wicomico River Light is a consistent hotspot for stripers and trout, particularly for gray trout at night. Directly to the east lies Davidson Wreck, a renowned cobia spot, and farther south are Tangier Lumps, the Old Texas, and San Marcos Wreck. Again, all four spots may be worked with deep jigging techniques, but the latter two might be better skipped or at least fished with great care due to their proximity to an area restricted because of unexploded ordnance.

A good light-tackle area is the series of grass beds in the Dameron Marsh area and the waters at the mouth of Dividing Creek. This is a particularly good area for Spanish mackerel during the summer.

At the northern mouth of the Rappahannock River lies Fleets Island, and the entire "shelf" from Windmill Point up to Little Bay is another ideal game fish-holding area. The Fleets Island shelf is good for croaker and is a proven area for winter stripers.

Angler Dick Roethel with a redfish. Note the kayak. Guide Kevin Du Bois specializes in taking clients into very shallow waters, such as around this grassbed.

Windmill Point, the southern tip of Fleets Island, and the whole area from this point out past Windmill Point Light is also a recognized hotspot for all species of game fish. The 30-foot waters around the light are another Spanish mackerel hotspot in the summer.

THE RAPPAHANNOCK RIVER

The Rappahannock River is a major fishery, and much like the Susquehanna or Potomac, worthy of a book in itself.

The "Rap" offers a wealth of fishing. Largemouth bass, smallmouth bass, pickerel, bluegills and sunfish, channel catfish and blue catfish are residents in the upper reaches. From March through May—some years you can often extend that range another month in either direction—the river is invaded by such desirable anadromous species as white and hickory shad, herring, white perch, and stripers. These fish work all the way up to the "fall line" in Fredericksburg, also described as "more or less the Route 1 Bridge." Croakers will also be part of this early migration.

Although the other anadromous species depart at the end of spring, stripers and white perch will remain throughout the length of the river, at least through the fall. Just about the time the shad and herring are leaving, the gray trout, followed by speckled trout, begin arriving, and these species may move upstream at least as far as the Route 360 Bridge at Tappahannock and remain in the river through November.

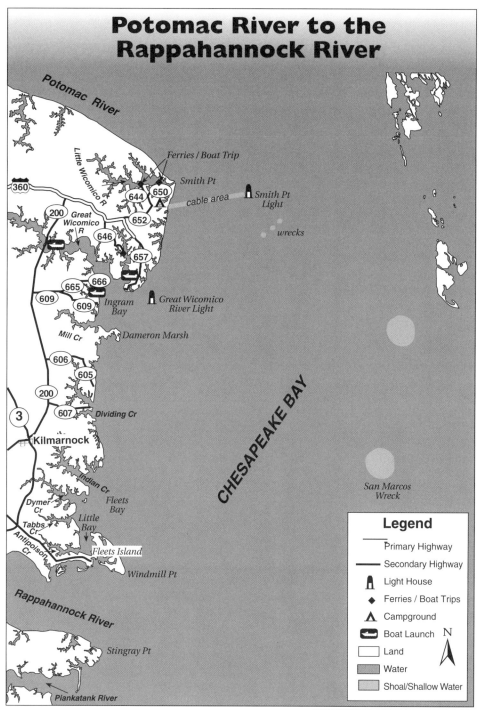

Potomac River to the Rappahannock River

Potomac River

Little Wicomico R

360

200 Great Wicomico R

644 650 Ferries / Boat Trip

Smith Pt

cable area

Smith Pt Light

652

646

657

wrecks

665 666

609 609 Ingram Bay

Great Wicomico River Light

Mill Cr

Dameron Marsh

606

605

200

3

607 Dividing Cr

Kilmarnock

Indian Cr

CHESAPEAKE BAY

Dymer Cr

Tabbs Cr

Antipoison Cr

Fleets Bay

Little Bay

Fleets Island

Windmill Pt

San Marcos Wreck

Rappahannock River

Stingray Pt

Piankatank River

Legend

Primary Highway

Secondary Highway

A Light House

◆ Ferries / Boat Trips

▲ Campground

Boat Launch N

☐ Land

Water

Shoal/Shallow Water

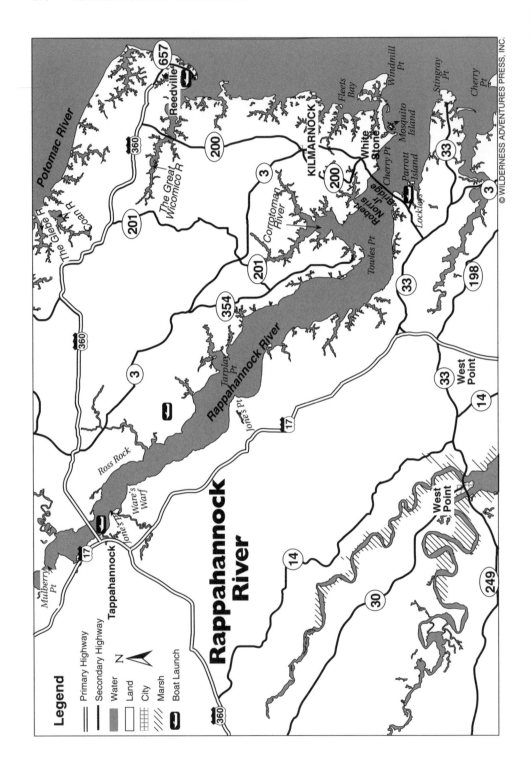

© WILDERNESS ADVENTURES PRESS, INC.

Rappahannock River

Legend

Primary Highway
Secondary Highway
Water
Land
City
Marsh
Boat Launch

Again, croakers arrive earlier but will inhabit the same range as the trout and depart about the same time.

Gordon Holloway, the ebullient owner of The Fall Line Fly Shop in Fredericksburg, lists some of the upriver hotspots for the typical saltwater species, working downriver from the fall line:

Stripers can be taken at the fall line in the spring and around the pilings of the Rt. 301 Bridge through most of the year, but the latter area is particularly good in the fall. Hunter's Marsh is another good striper area.

The area around the Rt. 360 Bridge in Tappahannock is another hotspot for stripers, as well as gray trout, which are often found under layers of stripers. Look for 15- to 17-foot ledges. The Mulberry Point area above the bridge and the shelf waters all the way to the Ross's Rock area two miles below the bridge are all good areas for stripers and both species of trout, as well as hardheads and spot.

Farther downriver, the Ware's Wharf area offers a hard bottom and good structure for casting to trout and stripers. While most fishermen approach the Bowler's Rock Light area by trolling, the lump there provides good fishing for fly and light-tackle casting.

Guide Kevin Du Bois with a redfish that was caught in Lynnhaven Bay.

Jones Point is a proven early spring spot for casting Clouser Minnow patterns and small jigs for croakers in early spring, and Tarpley Point on the other side provides good casting for trout and stripers on an outgoing tide.

The mouth of Ware's Creek, and just about every feeder creek into the Rappahannock, offers good fishing for most river species.

Continuing downriver, Holloway recommends the Towles Point Bar area, another big trolling ground, as a good spot for casting for stripers. Across the river, the Cherry Point area near White Stone, above and especially below the Rt. 3 Bridge, offers good fly and light-tackle fishing for flounder, stripers, croaker, and both species of trout.

The area around Lockleys, below Parrott Island, is a proven speckled trout hotspot. Across the river and downriver, Mosquito Point, with its mud flats and channels, features stripers, trout, and flounder.

Butler's Hole, below Butler's Rock, is a popular area for head boats and is another good speckled trout area, as is Windmill Point from the marina to the point. Stingray Point at the southern tip of the mouth of the Rappahannock and Stingray Point Light offshore are proven spots for school-sized stripers and blues, and this is an area where breaking schools are frequent.

A nice speckled trout taken on a Clouser.

Hub City for
Virginia's Northern Neck
Reedville, Population—2,037
Kilmarnock, Population—1,107
White Stone

Natural beauty in the most rural of the three peninsulas, birthplace of George Washington and Robert E. Lee, the Civil War battlegrounds of Fredericksburg and Spotsylvania, hunting (for deer, turkey and waterfowl), outstanding fishing in fresh to brackish to salt water.

Accommodations

Bay Motel, Rt. 360, Reedville; 804-453-5171

Best Western Warsaw, 4522 Richmond Road (Route 360 East), Warsaw; 800-780-7234 or 804-333-1700

Northumberland Motel, P.O. Box 211, Callao; 804-529-6370

Holiday Inn Express, 5334 Mary Ball Road (Rt. 3), Kilmarnock; 800-844-0124

Whispering Pines Motel, Methodist Church Road (Route 3), White Stone; 804-435-1101

The Tides Inn, 480 King Carter Drive, Irvington; 800-843-3746

Windmill Point Marine Resort & Conference Center, P.O. Box 368, White Stone; 804-435-1166

Campgrounds and State Parks

Belle Island State Park, features a ramp on the Rappahannock among other amenities, Rt. 3, Lancaster; 804-462-5030

Chesapeake Bay/Smith Island KOA, in Reedville, waterfront, marina, boat slips, boat ramp, pier, pool, cabins; 804-453-3430

Heritage Park Resort, on Menokin Bay includes boat rentals; 804-333-4038

Naylor's Beach Campground, on the Rapphannock near Warsaw; 804-333-3951

URBANNA area:

Bethpage Camp Resort, on Robinson Creek, 804-758-4349

Bush Park Campground, on Bush Park Creek; 804-776-6750

Dublfun, on the Rappahannock River; 804-758-5432

Cross Rip Campground, Deltaville; 804-776-9324

Gray's Point Camp Resort, on the Rappahannock, Topping; 804-758-2485

New Point Campground, New Point; 804-725-5120

Restaurants

Chesapeake Café, Rt. 3 north, Kilmarnock; 804-435-3250

Horn Harbor House, on the Great Wicomico, Burgess; 804-453-3351

Elijah's Restaurant, 729 Main Street, Reedville; 804-453-3621

Sandpiper Restaurant, Rt. 3, White Stone; 804-435-6176

Tripp's, Reedville; 804-453-5359
The Crazy Crab, Reedville; 804-453-6789
Village Green, Callao; 804-529-9440

FLY SHOPS, TACKLE STORES, AND SPORTING GOODS
Port Royal Landing, at the ramp in Port Royal; 804-742-5834
R. W.'s Sport Shop, 1494 Northumberland Hwy, Callao; 804-529-5634
Jett's Hardware, Route 1, Reedville; 804-453-5325
Queen's Creek Co, Intersection of 3 & 198, Cobbs Creek; 804-725-3889
Chesley's Tackle, P.O. Box 176, Fredericksburg; 540-373-1051
Rapphannock Angler & Outdoor Adventures, 4721 Plank Rd., Fredericksburg;
    540-786-3334
The Fall Line, 520 William St., Fredericksburg; 540-373-1812
The Sports Authority, 1461 Carl D Silver Parkway, Fredericksburg; 540-785-8071
Pride of Virginia Seafood Products, Reedville; 804-453-6191
Chesapeake Bait, 567 Seaboard Drive, Reedville; 804-453-5003
Regensburg Marine, Severn; 804-642-9112
Pride of Virginia Bait & Oyster, 3031 Little Bay Road, White Stone; 804-435-6740

FLY AND LIGHT-TACKLE GUIDES (Also, see Middle Peninsula.)
Ferrell McLain, Reedville/Smith Point area; 703-691-1758
    Note: This is another area where there is a lot of fishing, but fly and light-tackle
    approaches aren't emphasized. There are about 50 charter captains working
    here. The best listing we have found is the Virginia Charter Boat Association
    (VCBA) website at www.fishvs.org/Northernneck.html. Contacting some of
    these members could turn up one able to take you out for light-tackle fishing.

MARINAS AND BOAT EQUIPMENT AND REPAIR
Buzzard's Point Marina, Rt. 1, Box 1332, Reedville; 804-453-3545
Chesapeake Bay/Smith Island KOA, Reedville; 804-453-3430
Chesapeake Boat Basin, on Indian Creek, Kilmarnock; 804-435-3110
Fairport Marina, Rt. 1, Box 1115, Reedville; 804-453-5002
Ingrham Bay Marina, on Towles Creek, Wicomico Church; 804-580-7292
Pittman's Marina, on Cockrell's Creek, Reedville; 804-453-3643
Smith Point Marina, on Little Wicomico River, Smith Point; 804-453-4077
Reedville Marina, on Cockrells, Creek, Reedville; 804-453-6789
Windmill Point Marina, Windmill Point; 804-435-1166

LAUNCH RAMPS
SMITH POINT/LITTLE WICOMICO
    The only reliable ramp (other than the Chesapeake Bay/Smith Island KOA
    listed below) is at Smith's Point Marina. Take Rt. 360 toward Reedville to Rt. 652
    northwest to the marina.

LAUNCH RAMPS, CONTINUED
GREAT WICOMICO

Cedar Point Launch, in Reedville, take Rt. 360 to Rt. 639 south

Glebe Point Landing, in Reedville, off Rt. 200

Shell Landing, at Fleeton, take Rt. 360 to Rt. 657 south

RAPPAHANNOCK RIVER, from Rt. 301 to the Mouth—North Shore

Point Royal Landing, at Port Royal off Rt. 301

Totusky Creek Landing, southeast of Warsaw, off Rt. 3 at Totusky Creek

Simonson Landing, near Downing, take Rt. 3 south to Rt. 608 to Rt. 606 south at Morattico Creek

Belle Isle State Park, near Somers, take Rt. 3 to Rt. 354 to Rt. 683 west

Greenvale Creek Landing, near Mollusk, take Rt. 3 to Rt. 201 southwest to Rt. 354 south

Upper Mill Creek Landing, near Parrott Island, take Rt. 3 to Rt. 623 north, to Rt. 626 north

RAPPAHANNOCK RIVER, from Rt. 301 to the Mouth—South Shore

Tappahannock Dock St., off Rt. 17 right in downtown Tappahannock. (Just up the street is a commercial marina with a ramp, June Parker (804-443-2121)

Prince Street Landing, near Tappahannock, on south shore near Rt. 360 Bridge

Ware's Wharf, near Dunnsville, take Rt. 17 to Rt. 611 northeast

Canoe House Landing, near Jamaico, take Rt. 17 to Rt. 605 north

Mill Stone Landing, in Water View, take Rt. 17 to Rt. 640 to Rt. 608

Oaks/Saluda Landing, near Saluda on Urbanna Creek, take Rt. 17 to Rt. 618 northeast

AUTO REPAIR
Randy's Dunn Rite Automotive, 10522 Jessie Dupont Memorial Hwy, Kilmarnock; 703-366-3866

Scott's Quality Automotive, 63 N Main St., Kilmarnock; 804-435-1753

HOSPITALS
Rappahannock General Hospital, Box 1449, Kilmarnock; 757-435-8000

OTHER ATTRACTIONS
Reedville features the Reedville Fisherman's Museum (804-453-6529) and a historic walking tour. It is also the departure point for cruises to Tangier Island and Smith Island, two working watermen's communities that offer a glimpse of the Chesapeake Bay of yesteryear.

Some natural attractions include the 1100-acre Rappahannock River National Wildlife Refuge (804-333-5189) near Warsaw, the Voorhees Nature Preserve and Westmoreland Berry Farm (804-224-9171) at Oak Grove, Beaverdam Park

(804-693-2107) with its 635-acre freshwater lake and boat rentals near Gloucester Courthouse, and Hughlett Point Natural Area (804-684-7577) near Kilmarnock, which features species-rich beach and marsh areas.

FOR FURTHER INFORMATION

Northern Neck Tourism Council, P.O. Box 1707, Warsaw, VA 22572; 800-393-6180, www.northernneck.org

Virginia's Chesapeake Bay, P.O. Box 149, Saluda, VA 23149; 800-336-3078

*A soft green plastic body with a red lead head
is a very popular combination for trout.*

Fredericksburg

Population—19,000

Some of the area attractions include George Washington's boyhood home, Civil War Battle of Fredericksburg in 1862, historic scenic Route US 17 following the Rappahannock River, and James Monroe Museum.

ACCOMMODATIONS

Best Western-Fredericksburg, 2205 William Street; 540-371-5050, 800-373-3177

Comfort Inn-Southpoint, 5422 Jefferson Davis Hwy.; 540-898-5550, 800-373-1776

Days Inn, Fredericksburg North, 14 Simpson Road; 703-373-5340; pet-friendly accommodation

Holiday Inn South, 5324 Jefferson Davis Highway; 703-898-1102

Super 8 Motel, 5319 Jefferson Davis Hwy.; 540-898-7100 / 800-373-1776

CAMPGROUNDS AND STATE PARKS

Fredericksburg KOA Campground, 7400 Brookside Lane; 540-898-7252, 800-443-7887; located conveniently to historic Fredericksburg, battlefields, and Washington DC; 115 sites and 7 cabins

RESTAURANTS

Chele's Restaurant and Lounge, 5044 Plank Road; 540-786-1134; country cooking specializing in barbecue ribs

Dragon Inn, 3567 Plank Road; 540-786-8624; Chinese restaurant

El Charro Authentic Mexican Restaurant, 5203 Jefferson Davis Hwy.; 540-891-8685

Otani Japanese Steak & Seafood Restaurant, 12131 Amos Lane; 540-548-3888

Villa Capri Restaurant, 4407 Plank Road; 540-786-4997; authentic southern Italian cuisine

Bistro 309, 2312 Plank Road; 540-371-9999; American food with a southern flair

Claiborne's Chophouse, 200 Lafayette Blvd.; 540-371-7080

FLY SHOPS, TACKLE STORES, AND SPORTING GOODS

Fall Line Fly Shop, 520 Williams Street; 540-377-1812

Rappahannock Angler, Fall Hill Avenue; 877-752-9822

Corky's, 921 Caroline Street; 540-371-7932

The Sports Authority, 1461 Carl D Silver Parkway; 540-785-8071

AUTO REPAIR

Bryant's Garage, 817 Mountain View Road; 540-659-2359

Burton's Automotive Service, 1443 Warrenton Road; 540-752-5761

HOSPITALS

Mary Washington Hospital, 1001 Sam Perry Blvd.; 540-899-1100

FOR FURTHER INFORMATION

Fredericksburg, Virginia Regional Chamber of Commerce, P.O. Box 7476, Fredericksburg, VA 22404; 540-373-9400, Fax: 540-373-9570; www.fredericksburgchamber.org

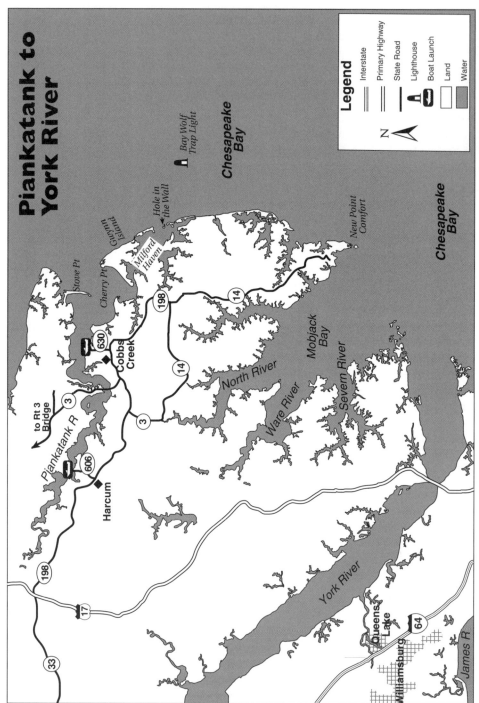

Piankatank to York River

Legend

Interstate

Primary Highway

State Road

Lighthouse

Boat Launch

Land

Water

N

© WILDERNESS ADVENTURES PRESS, INC.

Chesapeake Bay

Bay Wolf Trap Light

New Point Comfort

Chesapeake Bay

Hole in the Wall

Gwynn Island

Stove Pt

Cherry Pt

Milford Haven

Cobbs Creek

Mobjack Bay

Severn River

North River

Ware River

to Rt 3 Bridge

Piankatank R

Harcum

York River

Queens Lake

Williamsburg

James R

630

198

14

14

3

3

606

198

17

33

64

THE MIDDLE PENINSULA

The Mouth of Piankatank River to the Mouth of the York River

As mentioned earlier, the Piankatank River is a magnet for early season croakers. Upstream of the Rt. 3 Bridge, Ferry Creek is a feeder with good fishing at its mouth for stripers, trout, and puppy drum. On the north shore, the large horseshoe bend and island at the ramp off Rt. 630 near Stampers is a natural holding area for blues, trout, and stripers from summer though fall.

The mouth of the Piankatank also provides terrific speckled trout fishing in April and May. The peak is the first full moon in May. The key structure is shallow-water grass beds, as the specs move up to look for spawning grounds and to feed on crabs. Sometimes bluefish will be mixed in with the specs during this period.

The pilings of the Route 3 Bridge offer more fish-holding structure, particularly for trout and stripers, and fishing is good along both shores all the way to the mouth of the Piankatank. Gordon Holloway cites the Cobbs Creek area as particularly good.

Stove Point, a mile-long peninsula running north and south on the north shore of the Piankatank provides a sandy bottom plus pilings to attract all species of fish and is a good spot for early season croaker.

Cherry Point (there's more than one in this area) at the tip of the southern shore of the Piankatank is a renowned trout hotspot, as well as providing early season croaker fishing. Offshore, Deep Rock is a good trout hole.

The whole bayside edge of Gwynn Island provides fish-holding shelf structure. This is a good area for night fishing for trout during June and July, as the fish move into water as shallow as two to three feet to feed. Again, weighted flies like Clousers on fly tackle and Power Grubs and Sassy Shads on conventional tackle are the ticket.

Inside the southern tip of the island, the grass beds in Milford Haven harbor trout. Farther offshore, off the southern tip, there is a state reef and south of that the Hole in the Wall. Both spots are good for flounder, trout, blues, Spanish mackerel, and a variety of the other species. Farther south in the Bay Wolf Trap Light and the surrounding channels and humps harbor the same species. Wolf Trap Light can also harbor spadefish after mid-June.

The top of Mobjack Bay, at the junction of the North and Ware Rivers on Ware Point, also has great speckled trout fishing in April and May on grass beds, much like those found on the Piankatank. Besides the usual speckled trout lures, such as Clouser Minnow flies, grubs, MirrOlures, local fishermen have recently taken to trapping native minnows and fishing them beneath floats for outstanding catches.

New Point Comfort and the surrounding sandbars, humps, sloughs, and the grass beds at the mouth of Mobjack Bay offer stripers, blues, trout, flounder, and cobia, and Bluefish Rock is known for citation-size cobia and, in summer, spadefish. New Point Comfort Shoal is a red drum hangout in the fall.

The York River also has a March through May run of shad, with hickory shad coming in first and American shad (white shad) arriving in mid-April and staying later into May.

Hub Cities for
Virginia's Middle Peninsula

Tappahannock, Population—1,629
Deltaville, Population—800
Gloucester Point
Urbanna, Population—564

History, natural beauty, and fresh and saltwater fishing attract tourists
and anglers to this region.

ACCOMMODATIONS

Dockside Inn, Route 33 E, Deltaville; 804-776-9224
Islander Motel, Gwynn's Island; 804-725-2151
The Gloucester Inn and Motel, Rt.17, Gloucester; 757-642-3337
Tidewater Motel, Gloucester Point; 804-642-2155
Days Inn, Tappahannock Blvd., Tappahannock; 804-443-9200
Super 8, Highway 17, Tappahannock; 804-443-3888
Saluda Motor Court, Route 17, Saluda; 804-758-2782

CAMPGROUNDS AND STATE PARKS

Gwynn's Island Camper's Haven (This is Gordon Holloway's favorite, providing
access to the Bay, the Piankatank, the Rappahannock.); 804-725-5700
New Point Campground, at New Point on the Bay; 804-725-5120
Gloucester Point Campground, on the Severn River; 804-642-4316
Rainbow Acres Campground, on the Mattaponi; 804-785-9441

RESTAURANTS

Lowery's Seafood Restaurant, good dining since 1938, 528 Church Lane,
Tapphannock; 804-443-2800
Taylor's Restaurant, all the locals eat here—and for good reason, Deltaville;
804-776-9611
Galley Restaurant, Deltaville, 804-776-6040; for seafood
Cobb's Creek Market and Deli, Cobb's Creek; 804-725-4635
Virginia Street Café, Virginia and Cross Sts., Urbanna; 804-758-3798
Eckhard's, Rt 3, Topping; 804-758-4060
River's Inn Restaurant and Crab Deck, 8109 Yacht Haven Drive, Gloucester Point;
804-642-9942
Seabreeze Restaurant, Gwynn's Island; 804-725-4000

FLY SHOPS, TACKLE STORES, AND SPORTING GOODS

J & W Seafood, Deltaville, great seafood and lots of tackle; 804-776-9778
Queen's Creek Company, a new and comprehensive tackle shop, intersection of
Rt. 3 and Rt. 198, Cobb's Creek; 804-725-3889
A & S Feed Supplies & Sporting Goods, Gloucester Point; 804-642-4940

FLY SHOPS, TACKLE STORES, AND SPORTING GOODS, CONTINUED
Old Hooker Bait & Tackle, 1802 George Washington, Gloucester Point; 804-642-4665
Regensburg Marine, Severn; 804-642-9112

FLY AND LIGHT-TACKLE GUIDES
Harvey Cuje, Gwynn's Island; 804-520-2900
Mark Horner, Deltaville; 804-741-4680
Hank Norton, Deltaville; 804-776-6807

MARINAS AND BOAT EQUIPMENT AND REPAIR
There are a number of marinas with ramps in the area, including:
Deltaville Marina, Rt. 683 P.O. Box 962, Deltaville; 888-741-9812
Norview Marina, Rt.33 Broad Creek, Deltaville; 804-776-6463
J & M Marina, Rt. 1112, Deltaville; 804-776-9860
Dozier's Regatta Point Yachting Center, 137 Neptune Lane, Deltaville; 804-776-6711
Fishing Bay Harbor Marina, Rt. 1104, Deltaville; 804-776-6800
Norton's Yacht Sales & Marina, Marina Rd., Deltaville; 804-776-9211
Stingray Harbor, P.O. Box 527, Deltaville; 804-776-7272
York River Yacht Haven, 8109 Yacht Haven Rd., Gloucester Pt.; 804-642-2156
Severn River Marina, 3398 Stonewall Rd., Hayes; 804-642-6969

LAUNCH RAMPS
PIANKATANK RIVER
Deep Point Landing, near Harcum, take Rt. 17 to Rt. 198 southeast, to Rt. 606 northeast
Ginney Point Marina, Cobb's Creek is a complete commercial facility; 804-725-7407

GWYNN ISLAND AREA
Milford Haven, near Cricket Mill, take Rt. 3 to 198 east to 626 east Gloucester, take Business 17 in downtown Gloucester to Rt. 621 east (Warehouse Road)

MOBJACK BAY
Town Point, off Rt. 14 between Mathews and Harbour Town York River—North Shore
West Point/Glass Island, take Rt. 33 to Rt. 605 northwest to the west side of the river
Chain Ferry Landing, take Rt. 33 to Rt. 605 northwest to east side of the river
Tanyard Landing, near Signpine on the Poropotank River, take Rt. 17 to Rt. 610 south to Rt. 617 northwest
Capahosie Landing, at Almondsville, take Rt. 17 and 14 to Rt. 606 south to Rt. 614 east, to Rt. 618 south
Gloucester Point Beach Park, take Rt.17/14 to Rt.1206 and follow the signs to the Virginia Institute of Marine Science, then follow signs to park

AUTO REPAIR

Neds Marine & Auto Center, 2115 George Washington Highway, Yorktown; 757-873-1333

Clarkes Auto Service, 232 Lagrange Industrial Dr., Tappahannock; 804-443-1434

HOSPITALS

Riverside Tappahannock Hospital, 618 Hospital Road, Tappahannock; 804-443-3311

OTHER ATTRACTIONS

The Middle Peninsula is rich in natural resources and history. The Nature Conservancy has dubbed the upper part "the heart of the most pristine freshwater complex on the Atlantic Coast."

The Mattaponi, Pamunkey, and Piankatank (known as Dragon Run in the upper section) Rivers provide fine freshwater fishing for sunfish, largemouth, pickerel, several species of catfish, plus terrific spring runs of white perch and some migrating stripers. These are good kayak, canoe, and small boat waters with abundant and diverse wildlife to provide a rich day in the outdoors. Numerous access points, offer float trip possibilities.

Two American Indian reservations are available for visiting on special occasions; you may call before visiting the Mattaponi Reservation (804-769-2229) and Pamunkey Reservation (804-843-4740). Both tribes also have museums open to the public. Again, please call in advance to the Pamunkey Indian Museum (804-843-4792) and the Mattaponi Indian Museum (804-769-2229). Narrated river cruises of the Mattaponi and Pamunkey Rivers are also available from the Pamunkey Reservation (804-769-0841).

There are also a number of walking tours featuring the English history of the area, including Gloucester, Tapphannock, West Point, Saluda, Urbanna, and other towns.

Finally, we recommend two wonderful nature preserves near the town of Mathews: New Point Comfort Nature Preserve and Lighthouse (804-295-6106) and Bethel Beach Natural Area Preserve (804-684-7577).

FOR FURTHER INFORMATION

Middle Peninsula Travel Council, P.O. Box 386, Saluda, VA 23149; 800-217-8912. Make sure to ask for, among other things, two pamphlets which cover the Northern Neck and Middle Peninsula: *Virginia's Chesapeake Bay* includes a detailed map of campgrounds, parks, boat rentals, marinas, etc. and *On the Waters of Virginia's Chesapeake Bay* provides the most accurate directory of ramps (cartop versus large boat), marinas, hotspots, etc.

A nice redfish taken on a Rat-L-Trap.

THE LOWER PENINSULA

The Mouth of the York River to the Mouth of the James

Guide Lynn Pauls states that for angling purposes the peninsula can be divided into two sections. The first section runs from the Goodwin Islands to the Grandview Nature Preserve, and it includes the Back and Poquoson Rivers. Any of the points in Back River will produce strikes from local species. Going out of the mouth of the river to the north, around Plumtree Point, will carry you to Drum Island Flats and Poquoson Flats. Adjacent to this is Plumtree Island National Wildlife Refuge, 3,400 acres of marsh closed to the public.

The Grandview Fishing Pier is in the Grandview area. About a half-mile south of the pier is a rock jetty. Fishing next to and parallel with the jetty with streamers, jigs, and swimming lures produces stripers and trout. Fishing back up the beach towards the pier along sandbars that parallel the beach will net you flounder. In past years, in early fall, false albacore could be seen in this area. To the north side of Beach Road is the Grandview Nature Preserve. This is about two miles long and ends at Northend Point, or Factory Point, as the locals call it. This preserve is open to the public and you can fish anywhere on it. This is the only spot that is good for wading in the area. You can expect to catch any species that is native to the region.

The second section runs from Grandview Nature Preserve to Old Point Comfort

You need to use a big offering to interest a striper of this size.

at Fort Monroe. This area covers about seven miles. The piers located to the left and right of the Chamberlin Hotel are good for light-tackle fishing, casting, leadhead jigs, and bucktails. The best times for this kind of fishing are nighttime and high tide. Expect to catch striped bass, croaker, and gray and speckled trout. The area north of Fort Monroe to the salt ponds at Buckroe Beach is by turns heavily populated or part of a military reservation and not the best place to fish.

The whole area of the peninsula, particularly the upper part, as Captain Pauls notes, is a terrific fly and light-tackle area.

Captain Richard Bartlett recommends working the shallows of the Goodwin Island area (just south of the mouth of the York River) in early May for hardheads, blues, flounder, and speckled trout by casting flies, jigs and small swimming plugs along the bottom. Like other area experts, he recommends small, 1- to 2-inch flies and grubs "in every color of the rainbow" and recommends a "real, real, real slow" retrieve, just crawling the fly or lure along the bottom or "just picking it up and laying it down." He also will drift baits such as small hogfish, a speckled trout killer, beneath floats while fishing with artificials.

These fish move into deeper water by mid-June, but they will return to the shallows along with stripers in September and October.

Redfish up to 40 pounds can be taken at night in the spring in the Thoroughfare area by drifting half a peeler crab rubber-banded to a hook. The bar outside Poquoson Flats provides excellent cobia fishing from late May through July, again on

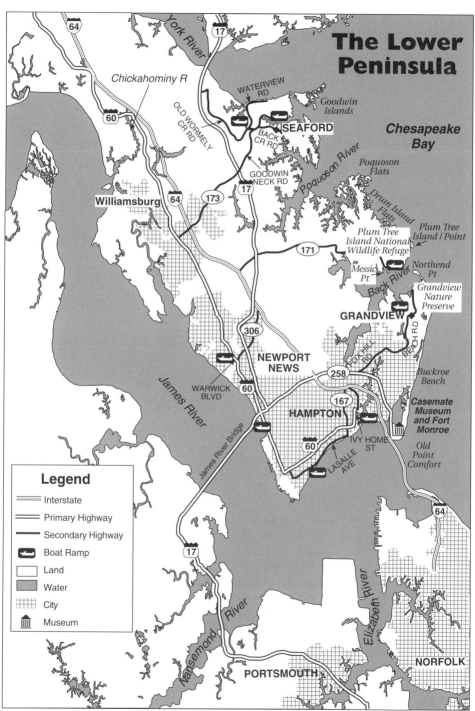

The Lower Peninsula

Chickahominy R

York River

WATERVIEW RD

Goodwin Islands

OLD WORMLEY CR RD

SEAFORD

BACK CR RD

Chesapeake Bay

GOODWIN NECK RD

Poquoson River

Poquoson Flats

Williamsburg

Drum Island Flats

Plum Tree Island / Point

Plum Tree Island National Wildlife Refuge

Messic Pt

Northend Pt

Back River

Grandview Nature Preserve

GRANDVIEW

BEACH RD

NEWPORT NEWS

FOX HILL RD

Buckroe Beach

WARWICK BLVD

James River

HAMPTON

Casemate Museum and Fort Monroe

IVY HOME ST

Old Point Comfort

James River Bridge

LASALLE AVE

Legend

- Interstate
- Primary Highway
- Secondary Highway
- Boat Ramp
- Land
- Water
- City
- Museum

Nansemond River

Elizabeth River

NORFOLK

PORTSMOUTH

© WILDERNESS ADVENTURES PRESS, INC.

live or cut baits, with a live eel the best bait. One good method is to take a smaller fish caught on light tackle and liveline it in this area; a 3- to 4-pound bluefish is tops for this, but croaker or trout also work.

Jeff Moss, of the Peninsula Salt Water Sport Fisherman's Association, Inc. (PSWSFA), has developed a method for taking 18- to 30-inch-plus red drum along the shallow marshes of Back River and Poquoson Flats, but as he points out, this method would work in any such area from Smith Point to the mouth of the Bay, in addition to the Eastern Shore and Lynnhaven and Rudee. He uses a medium weight, 7-foot spinning rod, matching reel, and 10-pound braided line, such as Fireline, with a short monofilament leader to cast a gold or silver Johnson Silver Minnow against the shallow banks. Using the electric bow-mounted motor on his 18-foot boat, he eases into shallows and feeder creeks so small he must back the boat out to exit. Once he hooks a redfish, he drops anchor and works the school.

He likes spinning over fly tackle because it lets him cast into the wind, and, more importantly, to cast farther. The big advantage with the long cast is that other fish in the school usually follow a hooked fish only a short distance out, so they are not spooked by the boat.

Often, a few stripers are mixed in with the reds. Most of the fish are taken by blind casting to likely shoreline structure. Moss rarely sees the reds in advance, although the noisier stripers will sometimes give away a school as they chase bait. This method works best on an outgoing tide and is effective from late April through October. Although he feels there are resident fish in all these areas, Moss describes typical redfish yearly movements this way: "Usually you'll hear about people catching them in Rudee in the spring. Then they catch them in Lynnhaven, and then they come up farther, up on Poquoson Flats, and then up towards the York. In the fall they'll go in reverse."

Cobia arrive "when the dogwoods bloom" near the end of May and arrive on the Western Shore first around Bluefish Rock and the whole area between the James and the York. They are usually found in 10 and 15 feet of water along ledges and bars. The best fly fishing opportunities are usually in late July and August in the open Bay, where you can see schools of fish in the 15- to 30-pound class and bigger around buoys. Often, they will take a streamer fly or a bucktail. And Ken Neil notes that they never turn down a live eel.

Tautog fishing can be quite good in the colder months, between October and May, at places like the Back River Reef, the new reef at York Spit Light, and at Chub Rock on the Poquoson River.

Like the Rappahannock and the York, the James also features a March through May run of hickory and white shad, with the hickories kicking off the action in March and the white shad coming in later and leaving later. The Hopewell area of the main river and the Chickahominy below Lexana and at Walker's Dam are proven hotspots.

Finally, like the well-known "Hot Ditch" on the Elizabeth River, a mini hot ditch is located along the York River between the coast guard station and the Amoco Refinery Pier. Since this ditch is barely more than a cast wide, this is a shoreline fishery. However, it is popular with locals, especially during the striper season from October through December, and some large stripers are taken here. It has also produced speckled trout up to 5 pounds and an occasional red drum up to 25 pounds.

Hub Cities for
the Lower Peninsula

Yorktown, Population—203
Poquoson, Population—11,800
Hampton, Population—146,430
Newport News, Population—180,150

History, freshwater and saltwater fishing, city attractions, museums.

ACCOMMODATIONS

Holiday Inn Hampton Hotel and Conference Center, 1815 W. Mercury Blvd., Hampton; 757-838-0200

Hampton Inn & Suites, 12251 Jefferson Avenue, Newport News; 757-249-0001; 800-426-7866

Omni Hotel, 1000 Omni Blvd., Newport News; 800-843-6664

Ramada Inn & Conference Center, 950 J. Clyde Morris Blvd., Newport News; 757-599-4460

Townplace Suites by Marriott, 200A-B Cybernetics Way, Newport News; 800-257-3000

Chamberlin Hotel, Fort Monroe, Hampton; 800-582-8975

Courtyard by Marriott, 1917 Coliseum Drive, Hampton; 800-321-2211

Holiday Inn Hampton Coliseum Hotel, 1815 W. Mercury Blvd., Hampton; 757-838-0200

CAMPGROUNDS AND STATE PARKS (Also see Williamsburg.)

Ed Allen's Chickahominy Recreational Park, 804-966-2582, Lanexa, provides cabins, campsite, fishing on the Chickahominy and easy access to the historical areas

Newport News Park Campsites, 757-888-3333

RESTAURANTS

Crab Shack, Mercury Blvd. and River Road at the James River Bridge, Newport News; 757-245-2722

Cracker Barrel Old Country Store, 12357 Hornsby Lane, Newport News; 757-249-3020

Japan Samurai Steak & Seafood, 12233 Jefferson Avenue, Newport News; 757-249-4400

Captain George's Seafood Restaurant, 2710 W. Mercury Blvd., Hampton; 757-826-1435

Olive Garden Italian Restaurant, 1049 W. Mercury Blvd., Hampton; 757-825-8874

Second Street Restaurant & Tavern, 132 E. Queen Street, Hampton; 757-727-9700

County Grill, 1215 George Washington Memorial Hwy., Yorktown; 757-591-0600

Duke of York Restaurant, 508 Water Street, Yorktown; 757-898-5270

Nick's Seafood Pavilion, Route 238 Water Street, Yorktown; 757-887-5269

Fly Shops, Tackle Stores, and Sporting Goods, continued

Bishop Fishing Supply, Hampton; 757-723-7343

Wallace's Bait & Tackle, 365 Dandy Point Road, Hampton; 757-851-5451 (Wallace's is adjacent to the Dandy Point Boat Ramp and a good place to get local information on where the fish are biting and on what.)

The Sports Authority, 2106 Coliseum Dr., Hampton; 757-826-5033

West Marine, 2121 West Mercury Boulevard, Hampton; 757-825-4900

The Bait Shop, 5828 Jefferson Ave., Newport News

Tidewater Police and Sport, 7328 Warwick Blvd., Newport News

Vanasse Bait and Tackle, 28 Dandy Point Rd., Hampton

B & B Bait & Tackle, 90 West Mercury Boulevard, Hampton; 757-722-0676

Buckroe Bait & Tackle & Seafood, 815 Buckroe Avenue, Hampton; 757-850-4166

King St. Bait & Tackle, 1709 North King Street, Hampton; 757-722-5437

Georges Bait & Tackle, 1909 Jefferson Avenue, Newport News; 757-245-0770

Performance Lures, Newport News; 757-877-8831

Sports Inc., 618 J. Clyde Morris Boulevard, Newport News; 757-595-9333

Wilcox Bait & Tackle, 9501 Jefferson Avenue, Newport News; 757-595-5537

Back River Market, 1250 Poquoson Avenue, Poquoson; 757-868-4130

The Weekender Boating Center, 105 Rens Road, Poquoson; 757-868-4072

Fly and Light-Tackle Guides

Captain Richard Bartlett, on the York River; 757-890-3003

Captain Lynn Pauls, in Poquoson, specializes in fly and light tackle fishing the Poquoson Flats area; 757-868-8356; www.tideflyer.com

Marinas and Boat Equipment and Repair

Bell Isle Marina, 2 Bells Island Rd., P.O. Box "N", Hampton; 757-850-0466

Dandy Haven Marina, 374 Dandy Haven Rd., Hampton; 757-851-1573

Downtown Public Piers, transient slips, Hampton; 757-727-1276

Salt Ponds Marina Resort, 1 Ivory Gull Crescent, Hampton; 757-850-4300

Sunset Yachting Center, 800 S. Armistead Ave., Hampton; 757-722-3325

Launch Ramps

YORK RIVER—SOUTH SHORE

York River SP/Croaker at James City, take I-64 to Exit 231, Rt. 607 (Croaker Rd.) northeast into park

Old Wormley Creek Landing, near Waterview, take Rt. 17 to Waterview Rd.

POQUOSON/BACK RIVER AREA

Back Creek Park, near Seaford, take Rt. 17 to back Creek Rd., turn right on Rt. 78

Messick Point, in Poquoson, take Exit 256B onto Victory Blvd. (Rt. 171 East) and follow it to the end

Dandy Point Boat Ramp, Grandview Area, take Exit 263 off of I-64 to Rt. 258 at (Mercury Blvd.) then left onto Fox Hill Rd. (Rt. 169 East), then left onto Beach Rd. and follow this road to the end

Poquoson Marina, a complete commercial facility recommended by Captain Lynn Pauls, provides direct access to the Poquoson River; 757-868-6171

Old Point Comfort, take Exit 263 off I-64 onto Rt. 258 East (Mercury Blvd), follow this to the end, until you get to Fort Monroe and the Chamberlin Hotel

Gosnolds Hope Park, take Rt. 258 North to King St. to Little Back Creek Rd. to Shelby Avenue

HAMPTON

Gosnold's Hope Ramp, (see Poquoson/Back River Area above)

Dandy Point, (see Poquoson/Back River Area above)

Sunset Boat Ramp, on Ivy Home St. off Rt. 60

NEWPORT NEWS

Anderson Park (Peterson Yacht Basin) open 24 hours and provides access to Hampton Roads Harbor, take I-64 east to Exit 265 to LaSalle Ave., right on Chesapeake Huntington Park Ramp, 9285 Warwick Blvd., also open 24 hours and gives access to James River, take I-64 to Exit 263A

Denbigh Park Boat Ramp, open dawn to dusk, provides access to York River via Warwick River, take Rt. 60 (Warwick Blvd.) to Rt. 173 west (Denbigh Blvd.)

JAMES RIVER—NORTH SHORE

Wilcox Wharf at Charles City, take Rt. 5 to Rt. 618 south

Fishing Piers

James River Fishing Pier, on James River Bridge; 757-247- 0364

Buckroe Beach Fishing Pier, in Hampton; 757-851-2811

Grandview Fishing Pier, in Hampton; 757-851-9146

Auto Repair

Economy Auto Service, 211 E Mercury Blvd., Hampton; 757-722-3513

Bellwood Automotive, 450 Bellwood Rd., Newport News; 757-595-5910

Denbigh Automotive, 14818 Warwick Blvd., Newport News; 757-874-4755

Hospitals

Mary Immaculate Hospital, 2 Bernadine Dr., Newport News; 757-886-6000

Sentara Hampton General Hospital, 3120 Victoria Blvd., Hampton; 757-727-7000

Other Attractions

Nearby Williamsburg, Jamestown, and Yorktown are major historical attractions.

Newport News Park (757-886-7912) features two freshwater lakes for boating and fishing (rentals available), two golf courses, miles of hiking and biking trails. The Mariner's Museum is in Newport News (800-581-SAIL).

For Further Information

Hampton Visitors Center, 710 Settlers Landing Rd., Hampton, VA 23669; 800-800-2202; www.hamptoncvb.com

Newport News Tourism Development Office, 2400 Washington Ave., 7th floor, Newport News, VA 23607; 888-493-7386; www.newport-news.org

Colonial Williamsburg Foundation Visitor Center, 800-246-2099
Jamestown Settlement Information Center, 757-253-4838
Yorktown Victory Center, 757-253-4838
Busch Gardens Information Center and Water Country USA, 800-343-7946

Bill May with a fly-caught croaker.

Cobia this large can be caught in the Lower Bay, but they're not common. Those that are taken usually run much smaller than this big guy, and they are most frequently taken outside the mouth of the Bay.

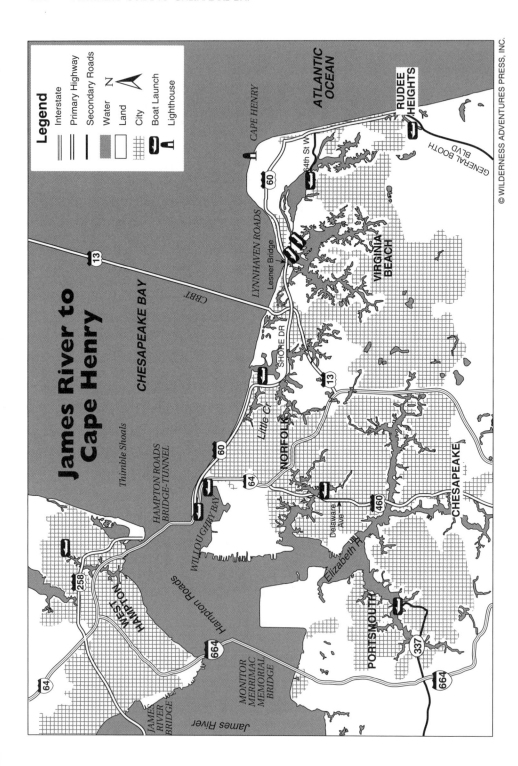

TIDEWATER

The Mouth of the James to Cape Henry and Beyond

The mouth of the James offers three bridges whose spans provide fish-holding structure for trout, stripers, and other species from May through December. In order (from upstream down to the Bay) these are the James River Bridge, the Monitor-Merrimac Bridge, and the Hampton Roads Bridge Tunnel. The pilings of the first two offer great structure for gray trout, stripers, croaker, and other species. The Hampton Roads Bridge offers additional structure in the form of islands and humps over the underwater tubes.

All three structures can be fished successfully by day from early May through December. But most locals find fishing even better by night, with gray trout providing the bulk of the action from May through October, and stripers providing the action from October through the end of the year.

These structures provide terrific fly and light-tackle opportunities for casting streamer flies on fast-sinking lines or leadheads and plastics or bucktails and letting the current swing them against the pilings. With the "light line" technique, the boat is usually anchored or tied off to a piling in the darkness, and the fly or lure is cast across the current and swung into the light where the bait are collecting and the game fish lurking. In fly fishing, either a floating or slow sinking (intermediate) or fast-sinking line may be used. (These are the same bridge fishing and night fishing

Guide Kevin Du Bois with a redfish caught near the Hampton Roads Bridge Tunnel, not far from Virginia Beach.

techniques used in such places as the CBBT and Baltimore Harbor.) Deep jigging techniques can be used by day or by night.

Often, you can see the fish lurking and striking. Swinging the fly or lure just under the surface provides fast action, sometimes with the additional appeal of a visual strike.

Hampton Bar just outside Hampton is a summer hotspot for flounder on flies, jigs, or baits.

The Elizabeth River, near the VEPCO power plant, has a warmwater discharge, known as the "Hot Ditch," where double-digit stripers and speckled trout may be taken during the depths of winter by casting or trolling MirrOlures or leadheads and plastics or cut bait. One good technique, related by Jeff Dail of PSWFSA, is anchoring up, tossing out one or more rods with cut bait or live bait beneath a float, then fan casting an area with fly or conventional tackle and slowing bumping the flies or lures along the bottom.

But as Lewis Gillingham of the Virginia Marine Resources Commission points out, just about all species of game fish native to the area—and some that are not— can be trapped by a thermal barrier during the winter months. Some of the more exotic and unexpected species taken there include ladyfish, Spanish mackerel, and even black drum up to 90 pounds.

Moving out into the Bay, Thimble Shoals is another formation that can hold many game species, including spadefish during the summer. Farther east, East Ocean View Reef (Old Dominion Reef) and the state reef just west of Little Creek offer the same benefits.

The whole Bay area along the shoreline from Willoughby Bay and Willoughby Spit to the CBBT and beyond to Cape Henry offers excellent fly and light-tackle opportunities, particularly from late April through October for speckled trout, hard-head, flounder, and bluefish. There are summer opportunities farther offshore in deeper waters, roughly 20 feet, which are littered with a series of lumps and obstructions, often at the seemingly magic 15-foot depth.

The Chick's Beach area on the south shore of the CBBT provides a good shoreline opportunity for both species of trout, flounder, and stripers. It can be fished from April through the end of the striper season. It is particularly good in the fall and at night for gray trout, and in early morning in October. Striper fishing is also good, especially at night from October through the end of the winter striper fishing. Best of all, weather conditions that make fishing miserable on open waters, such as strong winds from the north and northwest, actually improve the fishing here. It's easy to get to and easy to fish, but otherwise, it's not for the faint of heart.

With its firm, gently-sloping bottom, you can wade out as much as 100 yards at low tide. It's the waves that make things interesting. Some anglers go with full wet suits to fish this area in the fall, but neoprene waders, a waterproof belted jacket, and a waterproof hat will usually do. This is a popular spot and many anglers crowd into the area near the pilings, but experts feel that the best bet is the west (Bay) side of the CBBT, casting into the darkness and swinging the lure or fly into the light or even fishing in the full light. You can fly fish this area under ideal conditions, but the problem is that the winds that bring the fish in the closest also make fly fishing adventurous to impossible. The usual flies (Clousers, Deceivers, and so on) and lures (bucktails, jighead and grub combinations, metal jigs, and swimming lures) in dark colors are the choices.

Chick's Beach can be reached by taking Rt. 60 (Shore Drive) north to Pleasure House Road, then taking a left to Lookout Road then right to Bay Landing Drive to the end.

Cape Henry has Spanish mackerel all summer and cobia on the buoys in the spring and fall. Cape Henry Light is another cobia hotspot.

Two other Western Shore areas are worth mentioning, even though they are slightly beyond the scope of this book—Lynnhaven Inlet just east of the CBBT and Rudee Inlet off the Atlantic about two miles south of Cape Henry. Both offer great public ramps, terrific small boat fishing, wading on sandbars, and a fishing refuge from the Bay and ocean when the weather kicks up. In addition, both are terrific baitfish traps, and since their shallow waters and muddy banks warm early, the whole fishing calendar above can be moved up by as much as a month. Croakers may be taken in Rudee as early as March. Croaker and speckled trout are usually in Lynnhaven by mid-April. Bluefish, spot, and flounder (in addition to blue crabs) are other species found in these waters.

But the big attraction in both Rudee and Lynnhaven is red drum. Guide Kevin Du bois targets arriving red drum at Rudee from mid-March through April and works the shallows of Lynnhaven from June through September. This fishing depends on weather and temperature. The 18- to 30-inch-plus reds don't come into either inlet every year or necessarily at the same times. But when they do, it's a terrific shallow water fly fishing opportunity, particularly Lynnhaven, which offers flats-style fishing with as much fishing by wading as from the boat. (You still need a boat to get to most of the good spots.)

While stripers are usually not plentiful in either body, they are found just outside. The waters just outside Lynnhaven, from the Lesner Bridge into the Bay, are a proven striper hotspot at night in November; however, this borders on "combat fishing" or is at least extremely hectic. Stripers are also commonly taken by casting flies and lures against the rock jetties on either side of Rudee. Generally, the south jetty has been more productive. Both waters can offer good fly and light-tackle opportunities for working shorelines, bars, and holes when things aren't too busy.

Hub Cities for Tidewater Area
Norfolk
Population—234,403
Oceans, parks, beaches, maritime museums.

ACCOMMODATIONS
Norfolk Airport Hilton, 1500 North Military Highway; 757-466-8000
Holiday Inn Select, Norfolk Airport, 1570 North Military Highway; 800-465-4329
Norfolk Waterside Marriott, 235 Main Street; 757-627-4200
Sheraton Norfolk Waterside Hotel, 777 Waterside Drive; 757-622-6664
Tides Inn, 7950 Shore Drive; 800-284-3035

RESTAURANTS
Fisherman's Wharf, 1571 Bayville Street; 757-480-3113
Freemason Abbey, 209 West Freemason Street; 757-622-3966
Green Trees Café, 112 Bank Street; 757-625-7041
Ships Cabin, 4110 East Ocean View Avenue at Shore Drive; 757-362-4659
Wild Monkey, 1603 Colley Avenue; 757-627-6462

FLY SHOPS, TACKLE STORES, AND SPORTING GOODS
C Tackle, 1821 East Little Creek Road; 757-587-1003
Cobbs Marina Inc., 4524 Dunning Road; 757-588-5401
Fishin Stuff, 7434 Tidewater Drive; 757-480-2004
Harrison Boat House & Fishing Pier, 414 West Ocean View Avenue; 757-587-9630
Hopkins Fishing Co, 1130 Boissevain Avenue; 757-622-0977
Portco Lures Outlet Store, 7625 Shore Drive; 757-587-1755
Sandy Point Tackle & Marine, 5015 Colley Avenue; 757-440-7696
Screaming Eagle Charters and Sea Talon Lures, 820 West 21st Street; 757-627-2598
Taylors Landing Tackle Shop, 8180 Shore Drive; 757-587-5595
The Sports Authority, 5900 E. Virginia Beach Blvd; 757-466-8107
City Park Bait & Tackle, 5015 Portsmouth Boulevard, Portsmouth; 757-465-5399
Rawls Hunting & Fishing Supplies, 3247 Tyre Neck Road, Portsmouth; 757-686-3688

FLY AND LIGHT TACKLE GUIDES (See Virginia Beach.)

MARINAS AND BOAT EQUIPMENT AND REPAIR
Willoughby Bay Marina, 1651 Bayville St.; 757-588-2663
Willoughby Harbor Marina, 1525 Bayville St.; 757-583-4150
Clydes Marina, 4521 Pretty Lake Ave.; 757-362-5000
Cobbs Marina, 4524 Dunning Rd.; 757-588-5401
Bay Marine, 4621 Pretty Lake Ave.; 757-362-9502
Bay Point Marina, 4801 Pretty Lake Ave.; 757-362-8432

Little Creek Marina, 4801 Pretty Lake Ave.; 757-362-3600
Todd Marine Enterprises, 508 E Indian River Rd.; 757-494-0600
L & W Marine Service, 8172 Shore Dr.; 757-480-1608
Taylors Landing Marina, 8172 Shore Dr.; 757-587-3480
Ron Rob Marine, 850 W. 40th Street; 757-451-3429
Pilot Marine Corp., 904 Southampton Ave.; 757-623-4148

LAUNCH RAMPS
WILLOUGHBY BAY
Willoughby Bay Landing, Norfolk, take I-64 to Exit 272, to Bayville St. and 13th View
Willoughby Spit Marina (Willoughby Bay Marina), 757-588-2663, at the sameexit as above is a full service marina that also provides rental boats (16-foot fiberglass with 8-horsepower motors) and good access to the Hampton Roads Bridge Tunnel
Haven Creek, Norfolk, at the junction of Llewelyn Ave. and Delaware Ave., open-sunrise to sunset

PORTSMOUTH
Portsmouth City Park Boat Ramp, in Portsmouth, on the western branch of the **Elizabeth River**, 140 City Park Ave., take Rt. 337 (Nanesemond Parkway), also provides access to Hot Ditch

ELIZABETH RIVER—HOT DITCH
Deep Creek Locks Park, I-64 to Exit 296 Jordan River Branch (by toll booth);probably the closest ramp to the action is the commercial ramp at Chesapeake Yachts (757-487-9100), which is available 24 hours for a modest fee; take I-64 to Rt.104 (Dominion Blvd.), right on Cedar St., and 5 miles to Millville Rd.

FISHING PIERS
Harrison Boat House and Pier, 757-587-9630
Willoughby Bay Marina, 1651 Bayville Street; 757-588-2663

AIRPORTS
Norfolk International Airport, 2200 Norview Ave.; 757-857-3351, Fax 757-857-3265; www.norfolkairport.com

AUTO REPAIR
A-1 Automotive Repair, 1544 Early St.; 757-855-6362
D & M Automotive, 2400 E. Indian River Rd.; 757-545-8199
Family Auto Care, 7433 Sewells Point Rd.; 757-587-4881

HOSPITALS
Norfolk Community Hospital, 2539 Corprew Ave.; 757-628-1400
Sentara Norfolk General Hospital, 600 Gresham Dr.; 757-628-3000

OTHER ATTRACTIONS

Naval Station Norfolk provides a tour of the largest naval installation in the world and home of the Atlantic Fleet, 757-444-7955.

FOR FURTHER INFORMATION

Norfolk Convention and Visitors Bureau, 232 E. Main St., Norfolk, VA; 800-368-3097; www.norfolkcvb.com

Norfolk Visitor Information Centers, 1 Waterside Drive, Norfolk, VA 23510; 800-368-3097; www.norfolk.va.us/tourism

Don Benson with a cold-weather striper.

Virginia Beach

Population—393,100

Chesapeake Bay Bridge Tunnel, Virginia Marine Science Museum, Cape Henry Memorial.

ACCOMMODATIONS

Days Inn Oceanfront, 32nd Street and Atlantic Avenue; 800-292-3297

Econo Lodge at Bay Beach, 2968 Shore Drive; 800-553-2666

Ocean Holiday Hotel, 25th Street and Atlantic Avenue; 800-345-7263

Best Western Oceanfront, 1101 Atlantic Ave.; 800-631-5000

Comfort Inn-Little Creek, 5189 Shore Drive; 757-460-5566

Comfort Inn-Oceanfront, 2015 Atlantic Avenue; 757-425-8200

Hampton Inn, 5793 Greenwich Road; 757-490-9800

Holiday Inn Oceanside, 21st & Oceanfront; 757-491-1500

La Quinta Motor Inn, 192 Newtown Road; 757-497-6620, a pet-friendly accommodation

CAMPGROUNDS AND STATE PARKS

First Landing State Park, 2500 Shore Drive, 757-412-2300, housekeeping cabins, campsites, picnic areas, boat ramps and a bicycle trail

Holiday Trav-L-Park, a favorite in our younger days, 1075 General Booth Blvd.; 757-425-0249 or 800-548-0223

North Bay Shore Campground, 3257 Colchester Road; 757-426-7911

Outdoor Resorts Virginia Beach RV Resort, 3655 South Sandpiper Road; 800-333-7515

Virginia Beach KOA Campground, 1240 General Booth Boulevard; 800-562-4150

RESTAURANTS

Hot Tuna Bar & Grill, 2817 Shore Drive; 757-481-2888

Longbranch Steakhouse and Saloon, 4752 Virginia Beach Blvd; 757-499-4428

Rosie Rumpe's Regal Dumpe, 14th Street & Boardwalk, 1307 Atlantic Avenue #114; 757-428-5858

Alexander's on the Bay, 4536 Ocean View Avenue; 757-464-4999

Croc's Mighty Nice Grill, 19th Street and Cypress Avenue; 757-428-5444

The Happy Crab Restaurant and Oyster Shucking Bar, 550 Laskin Road; 757-437-9200

FLY SHOPS, TACKLE STORES, AND SPORTING GOODS

Tackle Shop, 313 Virginia Beach Boulevard; 757-428-1000

Skip's Sports Equipment, 521 Old Neck Road; 757-498-3635

The Sports Authority, 2720 North Mall Dr.; 757-498-3355

Chesapeake Gun Works, 6644 Indian River Road; 757-420-1712

West Marine, 2865 Lynnhaven Drive; 757-549-7020

Long Bay Pointe Bait & Tackle, 2109 W Great Neck Rd.; 757-481-7517

FLY SHOPS, TACKLE STORES, AND SPORTING GOODS, CONTINUED

Bait Barn, 5785 Northampton Boulevard; 757-464-6544

Bubba's Marina, 3323 Shore Drive; 757-481-3513

Fish Safari, 2029 Lynnhaven Parkway; 757-416-1600

J & B Rods, 2100 Marina Shores Drive; 757-496-2206

Lighthouse Tackle, 4461 Shore Drive; 757-318-3818

Lynnhaven Inlet Fishing Pier Corporation, 2350 Starfish Road; 757-481-7071

Mr. Wiffle Lures, 5180 Cleveland Street; 757-499-1007

Oceans East Tackle Shop, 309 Aragona Boulevard; 757-499-2277

Raugh Company, 1270 Diamond Springs Road; 757-363-8320

Sandbridge Station, 309 Sandbridge Road; 757-426-2400

FLY AND LIGHT-TACKLE GUIDES

Gary Watts, in Virginia Beach; 757-428-5573

Kevin Du Bois, in Virginia Beach; 757-486-6735

Mark Marcella, in Virginia Beach; 757-724-6453

Laurence Ritter, in Virginia Beach; 757-481-9200; www.inletcharter.com

Herb Gordon, in Virginia Beach; 757-464-3974

Pete Bregant, in Virginia Beach; 757-631-9793

On the Fly, in Virginia Beach; 757-426-3912

MARINAS AND BOAT EQUIPMENT AND REPAIR

Lynnhaven Marine Center, 2150 W. Great Neck Rd.; 757-481-0700

Marina Shores, 2100 Marina Shores Dr.; 757-496-7000

Birdneck Marine, 1288 Laskin Rd.; 757-428-3653

Marina Shores Marina, 2100 Marina Shores Dr.; 757-496-7000

Lynnhaven Waterway Marina, 2101 W. Great Neck Rd.; 757-481-7517

Bay Area Marine Service, 2103 W. Great Neck Rd.; 757-481-1883

Great Neck Marine Parts & Service, 2103 W. Great Neck Rd.; 757-496-6695

Lynnhaven Marine, 2150 W. Great Neck Rd.; 757-481-0700

Marine Services, 2216 W. Great neck Rd.; 757-481-1891

Duke's Dock, 3211 Lynnhaven Dr.; 757-481-7925

Rising Sun Yacht Repair, 3224 Barrington Dr.; 757-468-7018

Fisherman's Wharf Marina, 524 Winston Salem Ave.; 757-428-2111

Islander Boat Rentals, 524 Winston Salem Ave.; 757-428-8699

Performance Engine & Driveline, 593 S. Birdneck Rd.; 757-425-3533

Barcos Marine Railway, 948 Laskin Rd.; 757-425-6347

Rudee Inlet Station Marina, S. Ft. Ave.; 757-422-2999

LAUNCH RAMPS

VIRGINIA BEACH

Lynnhaven Boat and Beach, take I-64 to Rt.13, exit on Rt. 60 south (Shore Drive), just before the (north side) Lesner Bridge over Lynnhaven Inlet, turn west on E. Stratford to the ramps

Bubba's, a limited commercial ramp on the south side of the Lesner Bridge

Cobb's at Little Creek, is a full service commercial marina, take Rt. 60 to Dunning Rd. to end

First Landing Park, on Broad Bay, accesses Broad Bay to Lynnhaven, basically dawn to dusk hours, take Rt. 60 to 64th St. west

RUDEE INLET

Owl Creek Municipal Boat Ramp, take Rt. 60 (Shore Drive or Atlantic Ave.) to General Booth Blvd.

FISHING PIERS

Lynnhaven Fishing Pier, 2350 Starfish Rd.; 757-481-7071

Seagull Fishing Pier, on CBBT; 757-464-4641

Little Island Fishing Pier, in Sandbridge; 757426-7200

AUTO REPAIR

Firestone Tire & Auto, 1772 Virginia Beach Blvd.; 757-428-4622

Firestone Tire & Auto, 953 Chimney Hill Shopping Center; 757-498-1935

Lowes Auto Repair, 604 18th St.; 757-428-8285

HOSPITALS

Doctor's On Call Minor Emergency, 1368 N Great Neck Rd.; 757-481-0303

Doctors On Call, 1055 Kempsville Rd.; 757-495-5003

Sentara Bayside Hospital, 800 Independence Blvd.; 757-363-6100

Virginia Beach General Hospital, 1060 First Colonial Rd.; 757-488000

OTHER ATTRACTIONS

Virginia Beach offers wonderful beaches, a boardwalk, and the typical oceanfront tourist fare.

First Landing Park (formerly known as Seashore State Park) and a great personal favorite, offers bayside campgrounds, cypress swamps, nature trails, cabins, fishing, hiking, programs, swimming

The Virginia Marine Science Museum, near Rudee Inlet in Virginia Beach, offers a terrific aquarium, maritime displays, even a chance to sign up for winter whale watching trips; 757-425-FISH; www.vmsm.com

FOR FURTHER INFORMATION

Virginia Beach Chamber of Commerce, 420 Bank St., P.O. Box 327, Norfolk, VA 23501; 757-622-2312; www.hrccva.com

Virginia Beach Visitors Information Center, prefers phone or Internet inquiries; there is a visitor's centers for brochures and other information at 2100 Parks Ave. in Virginia Beach; 800-VA-BEACH; www.va-beach.com

Guide Bo Toepfer casting near an island in Chesapeake Bay.

The Future of the Chesapeake Bay

If one just reads the headlines, a mixed picture of the Chesapeake emerges. Striped bass, the premier species of Bay, have rebounded from the moratorium of the mid-1980s, and the "young of the year" indices of reproduction have generally been encouraging. The population and size of croakers (hardheads) has rebounded, with fish in the 18-inch range becoming more common. Gray trout have rebounded to a lesser degree in recent years and so have bluefish, although not to the large numbers and double-digit sizes of the early 1980s. Both hickory and white shad have rebounded, the latter because of harvesting bans, though not to levels of 50 years ago.

On the other hand, oysters and Bay grasses are barely holding steady at dramatically reduced levels, both despite heroic efforts by conservation agencies and private groups; blue crabs are in sharp decline, leading to reduced harvest regulations; menhaden, "the most important fish in the sea" (and Bay), have been decimated; and we've seen outbreaks of Pfisteria and micobacteriosis (in three flavors) and related "fish handler's disease" in humans in the last five years.

Okay, it's not that bad—yet. But in truth, there's good news and bad news on the Bay. There are significant threats due to over-harvesting and pollution, and there is dawning awareness and some organizations in place, both state and interstate conservation agencies and private organizations, that can lead to protection of the great treasure that is Chesapeake Bay—if we realize we're all in this together. We've tried blaming each other for Bay degradation for the last 100 years, probably the last 400 years. It hasn't worked.

Today, we're told that there are more stripers in the Bay than "ever before." (Any fisheries biologist will tell you: "Single species management is a fool's game.") If that's true, why do so many of our friends who guide light-tackle clients often have such difficulty putting their clients into quality fish? There may be lots of stripers, but they are mostly small fish. One friend, who guides extensively in the Crisfield/Tangier Sound area, told us recently that for each of the last five years, he has had to travel greater distances to find fish, and each year, the average size has diminished. That's a bad sign.

OVER-HARVESTING

The regulations imposed on commercial fishermen by Maryland appear over-generous, as are those of Virginia, which owns and controls the southern half of the Bay. We, and many other area outdoor writers, have been decrying the quotas allowed commercial fishermen. We still do, but there is another problem. As stated years ago in the cartoon strip *Pogo* (a thinly veiled political satire), "We have met the enemy and he is US." Us, in this case, is the recreational fishermen.

Since the lifting of the moratorium, the ranks of saltwater anglers seeking striped bass in the Chesapeake, has grown exponentially. Unfortunately, the resource has not. Both groups are going to have to face the unwelcome realization that we can't operate the way we used to 100 or 50 or even 10 years ago.

In many areas, the methods of fishing have changed. Where trolling used to be the predominant method for catching stripers (fe fly and light-tackle fishermen are well in the minority), chumming has now become *de rigueur* for much of the year. Many anglers are now "fly fishing" by drifting a baited hook back into a chum line of ground menhaden—not exactly what we would categorize as fly fishing. So many boats are setting out simultaneously chum lines in popular areas like the Middle Grounds, located in mid-Bay east of Point Lookout, that the stripers have become habituated to this "soup kitchen." Like Pavlov's dog, which salivated in expectation of food when a bell was rung, striped bass have been observed queuing up like pigs at a trough behind the stern of a boat as the boat sets its anchor, associating food with the action. Many anglers feel that this excessive dependence on the chum has resulted in the fish failing to search for normal food sources, thus concentrating the fish in a relatively small area. The same situation exists in the gas dock area northeast of Solomons.

Chumming has other undesirable implications. First, the use of menhaden contributes to the overall decline of this critical species (more on that in a bit) and some feel that the quantity of ground menhaden being released into the Bay is acting as a pollutant. Another factor is the number of fish killed. In Maryland, an angler is allowed two "keeper" striped bass per day. What constitutes a "keeper" changes several times a year, but basically, during the summer months, when the water temperatures in the Bay can top 80 degrees, two fish over 18 inches are allowed per day. Unfortunately, during the warmest months, there may be only one legal fish for every 20 caught. This means that out of 40 fish that are caught, 38 are thrown back supposedly to survive. Studies have shown, however, that there is almost 100 percent mortality in striped bass that are "released" in those kinds of water temperatures.

This brings up another important point. We all know that bait fishing tends to injure fish because the fish attempt to swallow the bait. Of course they do; it's actually food. Circle hooks help a great deal because if the fish does swallow the hook, it tends not to lodge in the intestines since the hook has to hit something hard (such as the fish jaw) in order to tip over and penetrate. However, those of us taking the moral high ground with our use of artificials are just about as culpable because, although we seldom have to deal with a fish swallowing the lure or fly, the fish still fights as hard for its freedom and is stressed just about as badly as one caught on bait. We tend to think of ourselves as being harmless when we practice catch-and-release. In reality, when water temperatures are high, we are just about as damaging as anyone else. Catch-and-release is more like "catch-and-release-to-die" when water temperatures are above 75 degrees.

Another bothersome "fish management" practice is Maryland's so-called "spring trophy striper season." This questionable practice allows the taking of 1 fish per day *over* 38 inches in May as they begin their journey out of the Bay to migrate up the coast. These are the most important striped bass that swim in the Chesapeake. Why on earth are anglers encouraged to target the very fish most responsible for sustaining the gene pool? As far as we can tell, this season is an attempt by our legislators to appease a small but politically powerful group of charter captains. (In Maryland the state legislature, not fisheries biologists, determine the fishing seasons.) This is a money making proposition for these captains, and we can understand their desire to cash in on this bonanza. Unfortunately, they are shooting themselves (and you and me) in the foot. Killing these big brood fish is reprehensible and should be curtailed.

But all this is just the proverbial tip of the iceberg. The aforementioned problems can be solved. With enlightened fisheries management professionals and decent state legislators, catch limits, both commercial and recreational, could be more effectively set, and seasons could be established in periods better suited to the survival of the species. The health and welfare of the Bay's game fish can be better controlled. However, the health of the Bay itself is also in grave danger.

POLLUTION

Pollution is the number one problem. Consider these facts:

Oysters, the most important filter feeder in the Bay, are all but extinct. At the turn of the century, the bay's waters were completely filtered every eight hours. Today, these same waters are filtered approximately once a year.

Menhaden, the primary remaining hope for cleansing the Bay, are at an all-time low due to over-harvesting.

We don't have fully accurate data on the number of sewage treatment plants that empty directly into the Bay, but estimates are over 150. This does not include all those

Anglers and tourists who enjoy spending time on the Bay all need to work to preserve this special place.

upstream on the Susquehanna. This river, which drains three states—New York, Pennsylvania and Maryland—is the primary source of fresh water entering the Bay. It's also a major source of pollution. Considering all the cities, towns, and villages along the Susquehanna, the amount of pollutants released by treatment plants dumping waste into the river is staggering. Most sewage plants discharging into the Bay, either directly or indirectly, are non-compliant. That is, they fail to meet federal standards for sewage disposal. In fact, many of these "treatment plants" do very little actual treatment.

The largest sewage treatment plant emptying into the Bay is located in Baltimore City. A recent TV news story named this plant as the largest single source of pollution on the bay. The good news is that the plant is scheduled for a 1.8 billion dollar upgrade.

In addition to the sewage, there are many other pollutants. Consider that the Susquehanna flows through farmland for almost its entire length. Most farmers rely heavily on fertilizers and pesticides, so every heavy rain causes runoff of these toxins into the river and, ultimately, the Bay. Chesapeake Bay Foundation estimates 40 percent of the nitrogen load in the Bay comes from Pennsylvania.

More chickens are raised on the lower Eastern Shore (actually the Delmarva Peninsula) than anywhere else in the country. The poultry industry contributes mightily to the pollution problem in two ways. First, chicken manure is disposed of mainly by spreading it on fields as fertilizer. This leads to both air and water pollution. Rainfall causes much of this to run off into nearby Bay tributaries, where it is responsible for greatly increased algae growth in the area, some of it toxic. This runoff has been blamed for "nutrient enrichment" of several Eastern Shore Bay tributaries that resulted in the outbreak of *Pfiesteria* (called "the cell from hell") that occurred in 1997. Second, the poultry industry is the major customer of the menhaden netters. Menhaden are ground and processed into food pellets used primarily as food for chickens. The sad thing about this is that soybeans can be utilized just as well, but are somewhat more costly, and no business is going to use a product that costs more, despite environmental consequences, unless forced to.

Suburban lawns and over-fertilized golf courses contribute heavily to the pollution. It is not gratuitous that storm drains in Baltimore and Howard Counties (both of which surround Baltimore City) are stenciled with signs reading "Chesapeake Bay Drainage."

Smoke emissions from power plants and industries burning fossil fuels in the Ohio and Tennessee Valley and even from Canada, carried by predominantly westerly winds, add to local power plants as significant sources of Bay pollution.

Then there are automobiles and urban and suburban sprawl. Although few people want to acknowledge it—it's easier to blame local governments, watermen, and farmers—an estimated one-third of nitrogen pollution is produced by cars. We had this reinforced during a day of catch-and-release fishing in Eastern Bay one bluebird day in May. About midmorning, we noticed a gray-brown linear cloud on the hori-

Striper.

zon, which we pointed out to guide Richie Gaines. "That's from traffic," Richie stated. "Forms every weekday about this time." As environmental writer Tom Horton pointed out in the July, 2002 edition of *Chesapeake Bay Magazine:* "Without significant reduction in air pollution and at least a stabilization of urban runoff, Bay advocates say it's unlikely that oxygen levels and aquatic grasses will rebound—even if more improvements are made in sewage treatment (which is likely) and agricultural practices (which is questionable)."

The Bay's subaquatic vegetation is not increasing from its current low levels despite heroic efforts by the Chesapeake Bay Foundation and others to re-establish this vegetation. (The Upper Bay is improving; the Middle Bay is declining, and the Lower Bay remains the same, for no net gain.) Basically, the problem is this: Underwater grasses are a wonderful filtering agent, but like all plant life, need adequate sunlight to flourish. When pollutants increase turbidity to a point where the plants no longer receive adequate sunlight they die, resulting in the loss of yet another filtering system, which in turn further increases turbidity.

Does all this sound depressing? It is. But there is hope. There's always hope. Most people don't realize that the overall health of the Bay has actually improved between the low point in 1983 and 2000. Last year, 2001, was the first year of a slight decline in pollution since '83, according to Chesapeake Bay Foundation's rating system.

A lot of the improvement cited was not due to purely natural forces but reflects the Bay's strong capacity for regeneration when sources of damage are limited. (Yeah, we know, many species are cyclical in their numbers. Unfortunately, this term is often misused to explain away declines until it's too late.) We mentioned earlier the rebound of striped bass and white shad due to regulation, some of it interstate. Chesapeake Bay Foundation is making progress in Pennsylvania farmlands by working with farmers to create buffers that protect local streams and the Bay downstream.

In similar fashion, that rebound of croakers and trout didn't just happen. There's good evidence that when regulations were put in place for the southeastern coast and Gulf shrimp netters to install "Turtle Escape Devices" to reduce the bycatch and killing of sea turtles, it also drastically reduced the bycatch of croakers and trout.

Let's look at the number one problem that *can* be corrected—namely, the over-harvesting of menhaden. With the oysters all but gone, menhaden are the only filtering agent of note in the Bay. Marine biologist Sara Gottlieb, quoted in an article entitled "The Most Important Fish in the Sea" in the September, 2001 issue of *Discovery* magazine, has likened menhaden to a person's liver in its function. You can't live without a liver, and over-harvesting menhaden is like removing the Bay's liver. And there is absolutely nothing in the Bay that is on a par with the menhaden.

Menhaden swim in dense schools with their open mouths sucking up vast amounts of plankton along with all sorts of detritus—like giant vacuum cleaners. This filter feeding helps clear the water by purging suspended particulate matter, thus decreasing turbidity, which encourages filtering grasses to grow. In addition, the menhaden's filter feeding greatly limits the spread of potentially deadly algae blooms responsible for oxygen-depleted "dead zones" and diseases. (Again, Tom Horton writes in *Chesapeake Bay Magazine*: "It's estimated that as much as a third of the Bay's water has less than healthy oxygen levels during summer months.") Had there been the normal number of menhaden in the Bay, the 1997 *Pfiesteria* outbreak probably would not have occurred.

They are also the most important food fish for striped bass that swim in the Bay. With the greatly reduced numbers of menhaden, stripers have turned to other food sources, primarily bay anchovies. Unfortunately, these little fish do not possess the nutritional value of the fat-rich menhaden. As a result, we are now seeing a lot of long, skinny stripers, many of which are covered with sores resulting from a mycobacterium infection. Healthy, well-nourished fish are able to fight off this infection.

So, it is apparent that the over-harvesting of menhaden must be stopped. In addition to the sorry state of the Atlantic menhaden, look at the sorry state of the Atlantic groundfish. Over-fishing the Grand Banks by U.S. fishermen, as well as those from a host of foreign ships, has reduced the catch to almost nothing, and the same thing is happening to our menhaden stocks, just not due to any foreign influences.

It's true that the Chesapeake menhaden fleet has gotten smaller, but that's simply because the schools of menhaden have been reduced to a point that not as many ships are needed to capture the smaller schools of fish. By the way, note that Maryland has banned menhaden netting in its portion of the Chesapeake; Virginia has not. They should. We note that Delaware and New Jersey have also banned this fishery.

The use of menhaden as chicken food should be stopped or sharply curtailed. Something also must be done to eliminate the pollution from chicken manure used as fertilizer. One viable solution is to incinerate the waste; this solves the problem almost entirely, but it adds to the cost of raising chickens. These added costs would undoubtedly be passed on to the consumer, but it's a price we should be willing to pay.

Possibly, chumming should be eliminated. This would remove one possible pollutant from the bay, and would kill fewer fish unnecessarily.

The warm weather striper seasons should be eliminated. Maryland did not have such seasons in the past, and Virginia, to their credit, does not now. Maryland should revert to more sensible seasons.

Whether you are chumming, trolling, fly fishing, or using lures with other light tackle, if you catch numerous stripers in overly warm waters, you ultimately kill most of those you release. Some anglers dispute this, claiming, "The fish I released were fine—I watched them swim away." The simple fact that a fish swims away means nothing. Because they don't die right in front of you does not mean they don't die minutes or hours later. You can help reduce this needless waste in several ways. First, obviously, avoid catch-and-release fishing when the Bay's waters are too warm— usually July to early September. When you are fishing and releasing fish at times when survival is likely, help ensure this survivability by doing several things. Avoid handling the fish if at all possible. Nets with rubber baskets, and devices like the Boga Grip help. (They'll also help protect the fisherman in the event of a diseased fish.) If you lift the fish from the water, get him back in as quickly as possible. You might try this technique: When you lift a fish from the water, hold your breath. When you begin to need to breathe, so does the fish. Put him back.

We probably need to stop targeting the big brood fish of Maryland's spring "trophy" season. We are targeting the very fish that most need protection. This season should be abolished. When we were growing up, it was illegal in Maryland to keep a striper over 15 pounds. We feel that this limitation should be re-imposed.

As far as pollution goes, there is little that we, as fishermen, can do; but as citizens, we can make our voices heard. Help elect environmentally concerned government officials, and call, write, or email your legislators to express your concerns.

But we need to work together. Some have proposed a fisherman's corollary to the National Rifle Association. Hunters and non-hunters alike have banned together to counter a common threat (i.e., the loss of their firearms). Fishermen don't face losing their tackle but instead face losing the resource and thus the sport in its entirety. Unfortunately, there are a number of organizations that attract fishermen to protect individual species or local waters, but there is no cohesive national front.

When you realize that Chesapeake Bay is a 6-state, 41-million-acre watershed and the primary nursery of the East Coast striped bass fishery, accounting for 65 percent of the stripers, it's easy to argue that it merits more than regional support by fishermen. But we think even broader, more powerful coalitions can be developed to protect the Bay. Air pollution is a major problem for the Bay; it's also a major health problem and may be a major factor in the growth of childhood asthma. We need allies for clean air.

The Chesapeake is also a major nursery for waterfowl and other birds. The decline in menhaden is believed to be adversely affecting osprey and loons, among other species. How about fuller partnerships with organizations like Ducks Unlimited and the National Audubon Society? (Some of this is going on now.)

The closest thing to a workable, multi-state group, and the best place to start, is probably the Coastal Conservation Association (CCA). Unfortunately, there's an ongoing conflict between recreational and commercial fishermen. There probably always will be, since each side thinks the other is taking fish from them. This can be sorted out, though. The fact is that both of these groups need to act as one in the battle to save the Bay and its fishes from complete destruction.

We also support The Chesapeake Bay Foundation (CBF), the principal organization fighting for the overall recovery of the Bay.

Together, these two organizations are leading the battle. Besides these and other organizations mentioned above, another player, an international organization with a slightly different emphasis, is The Nature Conservancy. They are also doing some great things in Bay country. These organizations need and deserve our support in money and time. If we are passive, the Bay is doomed. If we band together, we can turn things around.

A bluefish still hooked to a Rat-L-Trap.

Thoughts on Fishing and Boating on the Bay

To fish the Chesapeake successfully requires knowledge about many things. To catch fish, you need to know when and where to fish, as well as the appropriate fly or lure to for a particular species at any given time. Many factors come into play. You must know the tide stages for your chosen spot and whether an incoming or outgoing tide is best. On what are the fish feeding currently? Sure, you can throw out your favorite lure or fly, and perhaps you'll be successful, but as the old saying goes, luck favors the prepared. Therefore, the first things you need to find out are where and when the fish are feeding, and on what are they feeding most heavily. It doesn't make a whole lot of sense to prospect with a fly or lure that imitates a 6-inch baitfish when your quarry is homing in on 3-inch silversides, so observation and experimentation may be called for.

Often, especially during the warmer months, low-light levels can be the most productive time. If possible, try to time your fishing so that you are working the most productive spots early morning or early evening within a couple of hours of high tide. Usually, the best time to fish any saltwater spot is during the last two hours of an incoming tide or the first two of an outgoing. Occasionally, slack high tide can be productive, but slack low tide is rarely so.

One thing to keep in mind is that unlike their freshwater brethren saltwater bait-fish seldom remain stationary. Freshwater baitfish are unaffected by tidal movement and tend to congregate at particular locations that offer shelter and food. Saltwater bait does not have that luxury. Too small to fight a decent tidal movement, they typically move to and fro with the tide. Predator fish, of course, know this and will seek out feeding stations where they can take up a position out of the main current where they can still easily nab food as it is swept past them. This explains why one particular spot, such as a point of land or jetty, will be a hotspot on an incoming tide but poor on an outgoing one. It all depends on how the tide moves around the obstruction. Look to see how the current flows around an obstruction and where a predator fish might hold.

With this in mind, if you look carefully at a good marine chart, you can predict with some degree of success which side of any obstruction will fish best on any stage of a tide. Also, since fish are cold-blooded, water temperature can be quite important. Fish will seek out water temperature that suits them. Thus, during early spring, the water coming out of shallow Bay tributaries will normally be warmer than the deeper main body of the Bay, so the fish may favor the area influenced by this flow. During the summer, that same area may be too warm, and fish will favor deeper, cooler water.

A good example of this temperature preference is what occurs on the Susquehanna Flats during the early spring catch-and-release striper season. Typically, the temperature on most of the flats will be in the high 40s to maybe 52 degrees. However, the Northeast River on the upper eastern side will be several degrees warmer, and the best fishing will almost always be just south of where the river empties into the flats. Later in the season, as the water warms up all over, the stripers tend to spread out.

As you can see, there are many factors to consider when trying to locate fish. Hopefully, this book will be of some help in making informed choices. Consider wind effect, for instance. Few anglers consider the effects of wind, but a sustained wind from any direction tends to push baitfish towards the nearest opposite shore, so follow the bait. The predators do. One shallow cove that we like to fish is a good example of this phenomenon. With a high tide and a sustained north wind, both the bait and stripers will be concentrated along the south end of the cove, and fishing can be red hot.

During a low tide, a flat may be too shallow even for baitfish, but as the tide begins to rise, the little guys will move onto the shallows seeking both food and escape from predators. If the tide rises enough, game fish will move onto the flat seeking food as well, so during the last hour or so of the incoming tide, predator fish can be found all over the flat. If there are some deeper channels in the flats, check them especially well. As soon as the tide begins to ebb, the larger predators will move off into deeper water to take up positions that allow them to grab the hapless bait as they are forced off the flat. Find some deeper water adjacent to an expanse of shallows, and fish there at the beginning of the outgoing tide. Notice that we said the beginning of the tide. Once enough water has left the flat, moving most, if not all, baitfish with it, the predators will leave their positions, as well.

We mention the importance of structure throughout this book. Most fish, predator and prey alike, avoid open, featureless expanses of water. You can really draw a fair comparison between a body of water and a desert. In both, there will be large areas with little or no life, interspersed with oases full of life. In the desert, water is the key; in the Bay, it's food and shelter provided by various forms of structure.

Besides fishing knowledge, you had better have good boating skills and at least a rudimentary knowledge of weather patterns to safely fish the Bay. If you venture out without a compass, VHF radio, and good current charts, you are asking for trouble. The Chesapeake is big water, and the area is famous for thunderstorms. You must always be on guard against sudden squalls. An adequate boat is a must. Personally, we think 18 feet is about as small as you want to go, although there are a few quality 17-footers that are okay.

Although you can "get by" with only a radio and compass, you'll be much better off if you also invest in a depthfinder and a GPS. When a fog rolls in, which is quite common on the Bay, especially in spring and fall, you'll be disoriented and all but blind. A compass will tell you which way shore is, but that's all. A depthfinder helps pinpoint your location if you have a current chart showing bottom contours. A GPS, however, especially one with built-in charts, can tell you precisely where you are and the exact route home. Some anglers fail to see the need for a GPS, claiming they can find their way just fine with a chart and compass. And you can until you lose visibility in a fog or at night. Still, a quality GPS has many other benefits. You can traverse a tricky channel slowly the first time through, marking the critical direction changes as you go; then, any time you need to travel that route again, regardless of time of day or weather conditions, you can find your way. It's important to purchase a quality unit from a well-known manufacturer. We especially like units from Garmin and Lowrance. As of this writing, the charting information from Lowrance does not show depth contours, while that from Garmin does. We prefer the latter, but by the time you read this, Lowrance will most likely have caught up.

Another seldom thought of but extremely valuable feature is that many of the GPS units with map features allow you to leave a "trail" as you motor along. If bad weather greatly reduces your visibility, you can easily and safely backtrack to your starting point.

Speaking of navigating at night, some cautions are in order. First, things look totally different at night. You can't discern shoreline features, and the lights on shore are disconcerting the first time out. A couple of years ago, while fishing a particular spot at night for the first time, the GPS failed. It had never happened before and never happened again, but that night we really missed the unit. We were only a few miles from home base, but we had to travel a circuitous route around much shallow water. What normally took about 10 minutes to traverse took us well over an hour.

Another problem encountered when night fishing on the Bay is the overwhelming number of crab trap buoys in some areas. Often, it's difficult enough to get around during the day; at night, it's a nightmare. The best bet is to avoid areas with lots of crab traps, or if that is impossible, go slowly and have someone in the bow with a powerful spotlight. A red or green filter over the lens of the light will help preserve your night vision. Some lights come equipped with such filters, but if not, some colored plastic film and a big rubber band will accomplish the same purpose.

We're not going to go into the basic safety gear that every boater should carry. If you don't know what you need, contact the Coast Guard or a local Power Squadron. No one, and we mean no one, should venture out without at least the minimum required safety equipment. Your life could depend on it. Make no mistake, the Chesapeake Bay is big water, and the farther south you go, the bigger it gets. In the lower reaches, you can lose sight of land.

Storms can be fierce. During the construction of the Chesapeake Bay Bridge Tunnel, a hurricane came up the coast and ripped into the Chesapeake, stopping construction for a number of days. A huge piece of machinery was used to lay down the roadbed for the bridge. It spanned three sets of pilings and weighed an enormous amount. The hurricane's wind and accompanying waves lifted the device completely off the pilings and deposited it into the Bay proper. The machine was far too large to be recovered and another had to be built.

Okay, so much for the cautions; now for a few tips to make your day on the water more enjoyable and productive. In addition to the normal compliment of fishing tackle and lures we usually carry the following items:

- Raingear. Most of us fish from open boats, and rain gear protects us from spray on rougher days as well as rain.

- Sunblock. Both body cream and lip balm. Absolutely necessary. SPF 15 as a minimum. We prefer 30, and make sure it's waterproof. Gels that soak in quickly are generally preferable to creams that can be slippery.

- A hat. Although baseball style caps are most popular, a wide brimmed version is really better. It protects your ears and neck from sun and helps ward off errant hooks. Our favorite is the Tilley Endurable. Terrific hat. Comes with a neck strap so it won't blow off. Also, carry a spare hat of some sort. We've lost more than one hat on a windy day.

- Insect repellent. It seems that flies and biting insects can fly enormous distances to find your boat. Be careful of getting it on your palms; some varieties can damage fly lines.

- A fly swatter. Really.

- A net. The ones with a rubber basket are best if you plan to release fish unharmed.

- A Boga Grip or a Berkley Lip Gripper. Invaluable for handling species like bluefish, which can inflict a nasty bite. Also great for when you want to release your catch. The hook can be removed without ever touching the fish with your hands.

- Fingerless Gloves. Spring and fall, these are a welcome addition, especially if you are the one at the wheel. They keep your hands warm while allowing the use of your fingers. Our preference is for those made of fleece with a gripping surface on the palm. Fleece is great. If it gets wet, it's easy to wring out. A ski mask is a worthwhile addition if you run the boat in cold weather.

- A fleece hood or Balaclava with a long neck. These will keep your head and ears warm when it's cold and can be rolled down and used as just a neck warmer if desired. They can make an enormous difference in your comfort level on a cold day.

- A retrievable grapple-style anchor. Our favorite is called the Mighty Mite. It's unique in that the grapple hooks, which hold in anything, are aluminum. If the anchor becomes lodged a strong pull will bend the tine, allowing easy retrieval, and the tine can be re-bent to its original configuration. The shank of the anchor is encased in a lead-filled cylinder, which greatly aids getting the hook to hold bottom.

- A bag of rags. Hardly anyone thinks of this until they've handled a fish and have to wipe their hands on their pants.

- Waterless hand cleaner. Comes in small bottles and is invaluable.

- Lens cleaner. If you wear sunglasses, and just about every fisherman should, you'll need this. One tip: should your glasses need cleaning, you can always lick them to remove salt deposits, then wipe them clean. Old fisherman's trick.

- Good pliers with good cutters. An absolute necessity. Look for ones that are corrosion-proof, with good gripping jaws and hardened replaceable line cutters. Models with cutters on the outside are easier to use than those with inside cutters. There are many brands on the market, some quite expensive. Some of the expensive ones, particularly those made by Van Staal, are worth the money.

- A Baker "Hook-Out." Buy only the stainless version. Absolutely nothing beats this gadget for removing a hook lodged deep in a fish's mouth.

- A quality knife. We usually recommend one with a partly serrated blade. You'll need the serrated blade for heavy cutting chores like severing rope. Excellent models are made by Buck, Kershaw, Gerber and Schrade. They are reasonably priced, especially considering how good they are. Do not waste your money on models from China. They use very inferior steel.

- Bottled water. Some should always be on board.

- A decent first-aid kit in a waterproof container.

- Spare spark plugs and a few essential tools in a waterproof box.

- A trash bag. We'd advise against a plastic bag as they blow out too easily. A fine mesh net bag is a better choice. Ones designed to hold small laundry items are available in most supermarkets.

- And, lastly, toilet paper because you just never know.

Travel/Boating Checklist

This list could be used for any trip from one day to one month. Obviously, not all items would be checked for each trip.

Tackle

___Casting rod(s)

___Casting reel(s)

___Spinning rod(s)

___Spinning reel(s)

___Extra spools

___Mono/Fluorocarbon leader material

___Metal leaders/material for conventional tackle

___Fly rod(s)

___Fly reel(s)

___Extra spool(s)

___Extra head(s)

___Extra leader butts

___Spools of tippet material

___Two-foot sections of lead core

___Metal leader material

___Stripping basket

___Finger guards

___Boga Grip or Berkley Big Game Lip Gripper

___Long-nosed pliers

___Wire cutting pliers

___Line clippers

___Braid cutting scissors

___Tide charts

___Up-to-date navigational charts

___Appropriate saltwater and/or fresh-water licenses

___Booklet or sheet of local fishing/boating regulations

___Knot booklet

___Spray oil

___Spray electrical cleaner, e.g., CRC

___Small waterproof flashlight plus extra AA batteries

___Clip-on light using same batteries as above

___Hook hone(s) and/or file(s)

___A selection of plastic bags for flies, food, fish, covering gear, etc.

___Fish cleaning tools

___Ice chest for food and/or fish

___Extra glasses

Personal and Safety

____First-aid kit
____Prescription medications
____Cash
____Credit card(s)
____Traveler's checks
____Cell phone
____Portable VHS
____Portable GPS
____Portable weather radio
____Notebook, pocket-size and larger
____Pens and pencils
____Pocket tape recorder
____Sunblock, SPF 30
____Sun gloves
____Hat(s)

____Scarf
____Hand towel
____Small bottle of "Hand Sanitizer," e.g., Purell or Dial
____Insect repellent
____Good wraparound polarizing sunglasses with case
____Backup sunglasses or clip-ons with case
____Pocket packs of tissue paper
____Dramamine and/or manual anti-seasick cuffs
____Two quarts of bottled water

Clothing

____Suitable boat shoes
____Fishing pants
____Fishing shorts
____Underwear
____Socks
____Extra shoes
____Toilet articles
____Fishing shirts
____Good raingear
____Fleece (preferably) or sweater for layering

____Wading gear
____ Hip boots
____Chest waders
____Fleece wader liners
____Wading boots and cuffs
____Flats booties/sandals
____Wading shorts or bathing suit
____Wader patches
____Fishing vest or chest pack or fanny pack
____Shooting basket

Other

____Camera(s)
____Extra lenses
____Film (Slide and/or print)
____Digital camera
____Extra cards for digital
____Maps

____Camera batteries
____Tripod
____Filters
____Lens paper
____*Flyfisher's Guide to Chesapeake Bay—Includes Light Tackle* guide

Making Shooting Heads and Add-Ons

SHOOTING HEADS

Shooting heads have been around for years, but new materials available in the last few years have made do-it-yourself versions dramatically more effective. Some excellent commercial heads have also become available. With these new line materials, plus improved rods and casting techniques, relatively easy 70-foot casts are well within the capability of average fly casters; good casters can add another 20 feet, and some great casters throw over 100 feet regularly.

A shooting head is basically an extreme version of a weight-forward line. In a weight-forward fly line, the line has a balloon-like taper in the first 20 to 30 feet or so that accounts for all the rated weight of the line. Thus, the front taper of a WF-9-F (Weight Forward-9-Floating) line accounts for the 240 grains in weight (plus or minus 10 grains) of the 9-weight designation; the remaining 70 feet or so is a much thinner, lighter running line. A shooting head is an exaggeration of this profile—an even denser head and a thinner, or at least slicker, shooting line.

Generally, a shooting head is selected one line size heavier than the rated line weight of the rod. So for a rod rated for a 9-weight line, we would select a head rated at 10-weight. There are two ways to make such a head: One is to buy a weight-forward line, WF-10 in this example, cut off the first 40 feet and attach a running line. A better way is to buy a double tapered line, a DT-10, and cut it in mid-taper to produce two heads from 40 to 45 feet long.

For the average to good caster, a good rule of thumb is to cut the head to a length of 35 feet; an excellent caster may be able to handle 40 to 45 feet. The best bet is to start with the longer length and try casting with it, then cut it back until you're comfortable. You don't want to go below 30 feet, and again, 35 feet is probably ideal.

The running line and the way you attach it are critical. The best choice is a hollow braided line, the same material that end-of-fly-line loops are made of, made either by Cortland in 30-pound test or Elite in 35-pound test. These lines come with a special needle and instructions telling you how to form the end loop for the end of the line, but we have a couple of valuable tips.

First, despite what the instruction with the line say, there's a better way to form the loop—bring the end inside the main line for about ½ inch, then outside the main line, then back in again. Then add a drop of knot cement at the point where the butt of the line stops inside the main line. Then add a nail knot of 12-pound monofilament, or better yet, a pair of nail knots. We guarantee you this loop will not open.

You can make the loop at the end of the fly line small, perhaps ¼ inch in diameter. But you should make the loop in the end of the running line that attaches to the fly line about 5 inches in diameter. This way you can store an extra head on a reel spool, and when you want to change heads merely remove the old head, run the big loop of the running line through the head loop and over the spool holding it, and then wind it onto the reel. (See the top photo on the following page.)

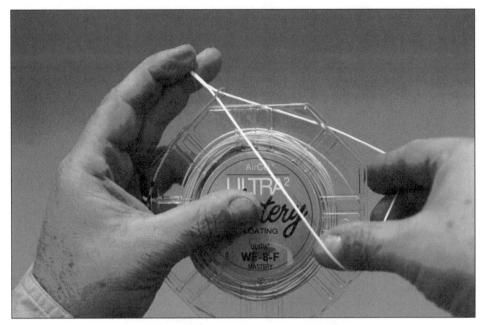

Changing heads.

Loop-to-loop method.

All connections between heads and running lines are made via the loop-to-loop method. (See the bottom photo on page 344.)

If you don't like braid, you can use thin running line instead. Scientific Anglers running line with AST finish, either the freshwater or saltwater version, is our choice. For the loop that attaches to the rear loop of the head, you can either make a small, whipped loop on the running line or use braid to make a small or large loop.

Typically, on our saltwater fly reel spools, we'll have 175 to 225 yards of 20- or 30-pound test running line, such as Cortland's Micron, then 50 to 75 feet of braided line attached to the running line via an Albright knot, then end the braid with a 5-inch diameter loop to attach to the shooting head via a loop-to-loop connection. We'll carry floating, intermediate-sinking, and fast-sinking heads.

An easier way, with the sacrifice of quick interchangeable heads, is to buy lines designed with head-like tapers and built-in braided running lines. The two major line companies make such lines—Cortland's XRL series comes in floating, interme-diate, and fast-sinking designs; Scientific Anglers' Striper lines are intermediate lines with a smooth coat over the braid. Again, we recommend one size heavier than the rod's rated line weight.

Casting with heads is similar to standard fly casting, simply work out about 30 feet of fly line, shoot back the head plus an extra 5 feet on the backcast and make your forward cast. Form a circle with the thumb and index finger of your line hand to serve as an extra stripping guide and to quickly grab the running line at the end of the cast. (We've caught many a striper and bass that struck as soon as the bug or fly hit the water with this technique.) A stripping basket is a big help in keeping the braided running line from tangling.

Shooting heads have some disadvantages: First, they're not quite as accurate. Second, you must retrieve the line all the way back to the head before you can pick up and cast again. Third, all the above lines except the Striper lines have a rough fin-ish, so you must use light gloves or tape the fingertips of your rod hand to protect your hands.

We don't use heads for trout fishing, since delicacy and line control are impor-tant and short casts are preferable. But for all-day, repetitive distance casting, such as in most saltwater, bass, steelhead, or shad fishing, shooting heads are the ideal solution.

ADD-ONS

Add-ons are typically used to make a floating line into a sink-tip line or to make a sinking line sink faster. A simple approach, used by outdoor writer Boyd Pfeiffer, is to employ one or more sections of fast-sinking line, like Cortland's LC-13 (a density of 13 grains per foot) or lead core line. Boyd makes up 2-foot sections using a whipped loop at each end. He uses one section or multiples to achieve sinking sections of 4, 6, or 8 feet or more. There are also commercially made add-ons available in differing lengths and densities; Orvis is one company that makes these.

We have encountered circumstances where one or more add-ons clipped to a sinking line produced much better results. On one memorable occasion stripers were stacked on a breakpoint along a sharply sloping bottom with a fairly strong current. Although we were all using similar fast-sinking lines, we noticed Boyd was outfishing us. Then we discovered his secret: A sink-tip between the line and leader presented his fly along the sloping bottom much more effectively. Not being proud when it comes to catching fish, we quickly followed his example.

Turning a floating line into a good casting, good fishing sink-tip is not that simple. Most add-ons create a hinge effect, which tends to translate into "helicopter" casts. Joe Bruce, proprietor of The Fisherman's Edge in Baltimore, has come up with a method that works well. Joe makes his sinking line portions in 5-foot and 10-foot lengths using 8-weight Cortland 333 Level, Type 6 (a sink rate of 6 inches per second), Salmon Trolling Line, again with a whipped loop at each end. With floating lines with an extreme front taper, such as Wulff Triangle Taper lines, Joe finds you can simply add either tip and get good casting and retrieving qualities. With most other weight-forward floating lines, you'll need to cut off a 4-foot tip section of the floater to provide good casting and retrieving with the sink-tips. The floating line with the last 4 feet removed continues to function well as a floating line as long as a heavy butt-tapered leader is used.

The stripping basket in action. The line is retrieved directly into a stripping basket. This approach allows for tangle-proof fly fishing, even under windy conditions.

The Indispensable Stripping Basket

Saltwater fly fishing is a specialized pursuit that typically demands long, repetitive casts of large, wind-resistant flies and bugs under breezy conditions. Specialized fly lines or shooting heads, featuring exaggerated, large front tapers and thin running lines, have been developed for this purpose.

If you've ever tried this kind of fishing, you know the problem—the 50 feet or more of fine, light running line, abetted by the breeze, wraps around everything and anything in the boat. So just when you're cranked up for that 80 foot cast to the tip of that promising rock pile, your line suddenly stops 40 feet short because the running line is: (a) under your foot (b) wrapped around another rod and reel in the boat—taking it overboard if you're having a really bad day (c) tied in a big wind knot that won't go through the guides or (d) all of the above plus a few other problems.

The answer to these problems is a shooting basket, a lightweight box that hangs from your waist into which you strip and store running line. Stripping baskets sell in tackle shops and catalogs for $25 to $40, but you can make your own custom basket for less than half that price. The text below tells how to do it, but you may want to look at stripping baskets in the stores to see what an ideal configuration is before you make one.

Here's one easy method. Get a plastic storage basket, with inside dimensions of roughly 15 inches long, 10 inches wide, and 9 inches deep, at a local discount store. Depth is particularly important; if the basket is not deep enough, the line can easily blow out. Most standard dishwashing tubs aren't suitable because they aren't deep enough. Ours, made by Rubbermaid, tapers in slightly on all sides and is made of clear plastic, both minor advantages.

You'll need some kind of vertical "fingers" or bumps or cones protruding a few inches from the bottom and spaced at regular intervals to keep the line from tangling. Cones can be purchased commercially to glue and screw into your basket at regular intervals.

Or you do it yourself. With the tapered sides, the bottom of our basket measures 13 inches long by 8 inches wide. Mark the outside bottom of the basket with a felt tip pen to indicate the insertion points. Mark an evenly spaced, straight row of 5 fingers along each long side about 1¼ inches in from the sides. Mark another straight row of 4 right down the middle. These too are evenly spaced, but also spaced at distances exactly in the middle of the marks of the two side rows of 5.

We use pieces of plastic electrical strapping to form the fingers. We cut each stem to a length of 2½ inches and form a tapered point to facilitate the line's sliding off each finger. We then make a 1/8-inch slit with the point of a knife at each mark and push in the strap, then add a drop of Goop or waterproof glue. Then we push in the strap until the butt of the strap is flush against the outside bottom of the basket and in the pool of Goop or glue.

Various other things, such as pieces of 100-pound test mono with an overhand knot at the end, can be used to form the fingers. But you may want to make the fingers out of some more rigid material. The advantage of this approach is simply saving space. When packing for a trip you could place such items as maps, fly boxes, etc. in your stripping basket without the risk of bending the flexible fingers. This is especially appealing if your basket, like ours, comes with a lid.

The final step is making the attachment for the basket. Usually, unless you're wading, you do not want to have the basket hang in front of you at waist level, even though some commercial units are made and displayed this way. The ideal location is mid-thigh or just above the knee of the leg on the same side as your stripping hand. The goal is to be able to strip the line directly into the basket.

Our basket, like most plastic baskets, has a fold-over plastic rim. Mark the center of the long side of the rim and drill two 3/16-inch holes near the edge of the rim and one inch on each side of the center point of length marked. Use a 19-inch bungee cord, hooked into each hole, with your belt running through the loop of the cord to hang the basket. The bungee cord is removable and can be stored in the basket when not in use. This is a good height for a one-handed line retrieve right into the basket. You can adjust the height of the basket upward or downward by making additional or fewer wraps of the cord around your belt.

A second bungee cord, about the same length, is used to hold the basket firmly in place along the side of the thigh. This cord is attached into a 3/16-inch hole drilled about one inch down from the rim and in from the outside edge of each end of the same long side holding the other bungee cord. Attach all bungees so the open hooks point in toward the body for the most secure attachment and the least snagging.

The stripping basket can be held in place anywhere along the side to the front of the thigh to adjust for the retrieve merely by pulling the basket to the desired spot. At times, we'll make extremely fast retrieves by placing our rods under our left arms after the cast and retrieving line quickly by alternate pulls with the left and right hand. Generally, we move the basket almost directly in front of the body and up near belt level with this retrieve, and the basket position is easily adjusted as described above.

You may feel, as we once did, that another piece of gear is the last thing you need. But we predict that once you use a stripping basket you'll never want to fly fish from a boat again without one.

This shows how one bungee is looped over the belt to adjust the height of the basket, and the second loops behind the thigh to hold the basket in position. Note the hooks on both bungee attachments are pointed downward and in toward the body to hold more securely and avoid catching the fly line and running line.

Making Deep Jigs

In recent years, homemade deep jigging lures have become the rage in the Chesapeake, especially in areas from the Solomons to the Honga River south to the Virginia line that are so hot from late October through mid-December. (The striper season usually runs later in Virginia, and seatrout are available later in the southern portion of the Bay.)

Several articles and a number of Internet reports have come out recently on how to make these jigs. Two common approaches involve beating the sinkers semi-flat, perhaps with a slight curve, and using powder paint in bright colors.

Besides being effective, these lures are cheap and easy to make. Here's how to do it:

Tools and materials that can be used include, (above, clockwise from the top), Everglow tubing, inline sinkers, metallic tape, split rings, hooks, grubs, bucktail or other tailing material, thread, paint, and a brush. Any paint may be used, but the powder paints, easily baked on by heating the body and dipping it into the power, provide a particularly bright, tough finish. Three tips on these paints: (1) Pour the paint powder into a shallow tub or dish (2) Stir the powder to a fluffy consistency (3) Heat the body of the jig with a propane soldering torch.

Spray paint is another option. Preferred paint colors are white, silver, yellow, chartreuse, combinations of blue and white, green and white, pink and white, and chartreuse and white. Preferred tail colors are white and chartreuse.

Here, we're creating a luminescent chartreuse body by slipping an Everglow sleeve over the sinker/body. A variety of sleeve materials are available in various colors at fly fishing shops. The ends of the sleeve are tied off with fly tying or rod wrapping thread and the windings sealed with lacquer. You can leave trailing fibers at one or both ends of the body for extra flash.

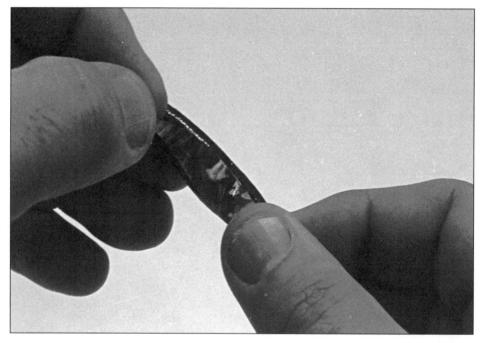

Here's another body enhancement: adding reflective tape. In this case, we took the optional step of flattening the sinker/body by hammering it flat on top of a vise. You can also flatten a sinker by simply cranking the vise on the sinker, perhaps adding a little "encouragement" with a hammer applied to the front of the vise. A slight curve can be added by placing the flattened sinker on top of the vise and then tapping the ends of the sinker. In all this manipulation, be careful not to weaken the ends of the sinkers where the loops are attached. Once any shaping is done, complete the body by painting and/or taping. Adding stick-on eyes is another option.

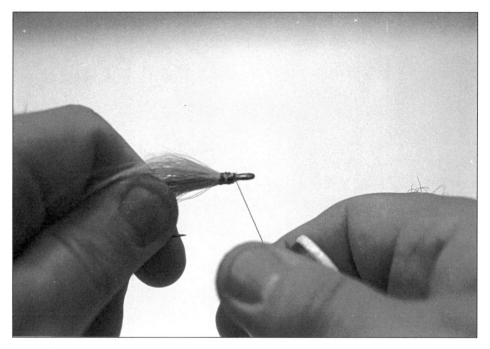

A fly tying vise is helpful but not necessary in adding a tail. Here, the hook and bucktail material is simply held in one hand while attaching it to the hook with rod wrapping thread with the other hand. Grubs and other plastics are other tail options that may be used alone or added to the bucktail. We prefer a strong, short-shanked single hook, preferably an oversized hook or double hook, but you could also use a treble.

Attach the hook to the body with a split ring. The ring is a critical link; make sure you use sufficiently strong rings, even if they may appear a bit oversized. You can also use a soft wire ringed hook for fishing heavy snags; if snagged, you will be able to pull the hook open, but the lure will be saved.

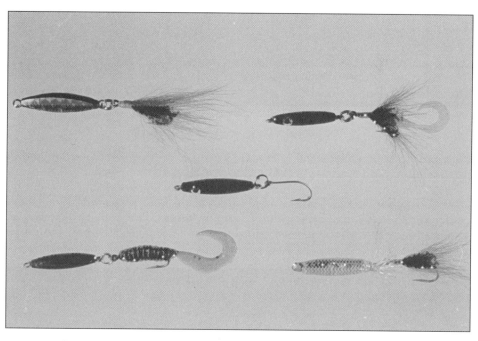

A collection of jigging lures showing some of the body and tail options discussed. Weights for these lures range from ¾ to 1¼ ounce, but that range may be extended in either direction. Some Mid- and Lower Bay anglers use 2- and 3-ounce jigs, and jigs as heavy as 6 to 8 ounces may be used at the Chesapeake Bay Bridge Tunnel (CBBT).

Resources

STATE INTERNET SITES

These websites are a great source of information for fishing regulations, licenses, ramp locations and other aspects related to fishing the Bay.

Maryland: www.dnr.state.md.us

Click on "Fisheries." Under this header you'll see along the left margin of the page such features as "Atlas of MD Boat Ramps," which provides locations, directions, and facilities at each ramp; "Fishing License Application," providing a form that can be filled out and mailed; and links to "Tide Information," "Maryland Weather," and "Maps & Directions." The first block to the right is "Fishing Report." Click on that for weekly updates from spring through the end of the year, including "Freshwater," "Chesapeake," and "Ocean" along with other information.

Take it from someone who knows something about websites and has seen hundreds: the Maryland DNR website is outstanding, packed with information, easy to navigate, and the envy of DNR agencies in many states.

Virginia: www.mrc.state.va.us

Click on "Recreational" on the menu along the top. This will get you the Virginia Marine Resources Commission (VMRC), with information on regulations, applying for a license, and so on. At the bottom of this page, you can bring up the electronic version of the *Virginia Saltwater Angler's Guide*, a terrific 70-page publication loaded with how-to information, fishing clubs, and much more. However, let us warn you, we have found the information on ramps unreliable. Some of the ramps listed are great facilities; others are dirt roads ending at the waterfront, suitable only for launching cartop boats.

Clicking on "Newsletters" along that same top bar takes you to weekly fishing reports for Chesapeake Bay and offshore.

GUIDES

CHESAPEAKE GUIDES ASSOCIATION (FLY AND LIGHT-TACKLE GUIDES)
www.chesapeakeguides.com or call 410-827-7210

UPPER BAY CHARTER CAPTAINS ASSOCIATION, INC.
www.baycaptains.com/index.htm
Virginia Chart Boats Association, www.fishva.org
CCA Maryland Guides, www.ccamd.org, then click on "Fishing Guides"
CCA Virginia Guides, www.ccavirginia.org, then click on "Charter Captains"

Other Recommended Internet Sites

Fishing

Delmarva Fishing
www.beach-net.com/Fishinghome.html
www.sandseekers.net/html/fishing.html
www.delmarvafishing.com/charterboats.html

Ocean City, Maryland
www.ocean-city.com/fishing/

Tidewater, Virginia
www.pswsfa.com.
> This is a terrific site from the Peninsula Salt Water Sport Fisherman's Association, Inc., a great club in a great fishing area. Their "how-to" articles are excellent.

Virginia Beach
www.vabeach.com/sun/fishing.htm; www.virginiafishing.com; www.sunnydayguide.com/vb/fishing.html

Fly Fisherman **Magazine**
www.flyshop.com is a premier fly fishing site.

Tidalfish
www.tidalfish.com
> Provides local fishing information and has an active bulletin board. As for the reliability of some of the information on the board, we leave that to the reader.

Game and Fish **Magazine**
www.gameandfish.about.com/library/weekly/b/va_index.htm

Weather and Tide Resources

www.marineweather.com
www.annapolisyc.org - Tides and currents, weather and more
www.baydreaming.com - Specifically features the Chesapeak Bay area
www.harbortides.com - Tide listings
www.saltwatertides.com - Eastern tide infromation
www.nws.noaa.com - National Weather Serives

Boat Towing Membership Organizations

TowBoat US - Annual Membership, 24 hour service
Phone: 703-461-2866
Website: www.boatUS.com

STATE MAPS AND OTHER PUBLICATIONS

These are usually available from the Maryland DNR at outdoor shows, or you can try calling the number listed below.

Public Access Guide: *Chesapeake Bay, Susquehanna River & Tidal Tributaries*—
published by VA, MD, PA, and D.C. The information on Virginia ramps gives some idea of the size of the ramps, but, still, some of this is suspect.

A Fisherman's Guide to Maryland Piers and Boat Ramps
Published by the Maryland DNR, call 800-688-FINS.

Maryland Guide to Freshwater Fishing
Published by the Maryland DNR, call 800-FINS or 410-974-3061.

COMMERCIAL MAPS

There are many maps available, but these four companies are outstanding. They have paper and CD formats and the maps are widely available in bookstores or you can order directly from the company.

ADC Maps: 800-232-MAPS or www.adcmap.com/.
We have their set of three Chesapeake Bay maps; Northern, Central, and Southern and highly recommend them, or you can purchase a wall map of the entire Bay.

DeLorme: 800-561-5105 or www.delorme.com.
These are state-specific maps and are extremely detailed. Maryland and Delaware are in one book and Virginia in another.

GMCO Maps: 888-420-6277 or www:gmcomaps.com/.
They produce maps of some key rivers, such as the York and James, as well as the Chesapeake itself.

Maptech Waterproof Charts and Embassy Guides: 888-839-5551 or
www.maptech.com
E-mail: marinesales@maptech.com
Aerial photos, navigation advice and over 500 marine facilities

FISHING AND CONSERVATION ORGANIZATIONS

These organizations promote conservation and/or fishing, feature regular meetings and outings, and most have publications ranging from newsletters to slick magazines.

Maryland Saltwater Sportsfishermen's
Association (MSSA)
410-255-5535 or www.MSSA.net

Maryland Coastal Conservation
Association (CCA)
101 Ridgely Ave., Suite 12A
Annapolis, MD 21400
888-758-6580 or www.ccamd.org

Virginia Coastal Conservation
Association (CCA)
2100 Marina Shores, Dr., Suite 108
Virginia Beach, VA 2451
757-481-1226 or www.ccavirginia.org

Maryland Fly Angler
www.geocities.com/CapitolHill/Senate/
2243/mfa

Federation of Fly Fishers
www.fedflyfishers.org (click on FFF
Clubs)

Free State Fly Fishers
(based in Annapolis)
410-796-3279 or 301-262-8292

Chesapeake Bay Foundation
(the preeminent Bay watchdog)
Phillip Merrill Environmental Center
6 Herndon Avenue
Annapolis, MD 21403
410-268-8816 or www.cbf.org

Alliance for the Chesapeake Bay
www.alliancechesbay.org/
As part of its conservation work this
organization features Bay and river
sojourns.

National Audubon Society
www.audubon.org
With a number of branches in Bay
country, they're working to protect a lot
more than birds.

Maryland Aquatic Resources
Coalition—a coalition working to protect all Maryland waters.
M.A.R.C.
P.O. Box 307
Maryland Line, MD 21105
717-235-7951

BOOKS AND VIDEOS BY LOCAL AUTHORS

The Fisherman's Edge's Striper Fly Pattern, by Joe Bruce

Fly Fishing for Striped Bass, by Joe Bruce

Fly Design Theory and Practice, by Joe Bruce

Lesson with Lefty, by Lefty Kreh (a terrific videotape on casting)

Masters of Fly Tying, Volumes 1 and 2, by Lefty Kreh and Bob Clouser

Saltwater Fly Patterns, by Lefty Kreh

Solving Casting Problems in Saltwater, by Lefty Kreh

Advanced Fly Fishing Techniques, by Lefty Kreh

Practical Fishing Knots, by Lefty Kreh and Mark Sosin

101 Fly Fishing Tips, by Lefty Kreh

The Complete Book of Tackle Making, by Boyd Pfeiffer

Shad Fishing, by Boyd Pfeiffer

Fly Fishing Saltwater Basics, by Boyd Pfeiffer

Flies of the Chesapeake, Volume 1 and Volume 2, by Virginia Coastal Fly Anglers
(Contains some wild but effective patterns. Contact the club at P.O. Box 2866,
Virginia Beach, VA 223452 or email them at VCFA@home.com.)

The Cast, by Ed Jaworoski

Note: The above titles and other fishing related books and videos are available
from Wilderness Adventures Sporting Books at 800-925-3339 or online at:
www.wildadv.com

PHONE NUMBERS FOR RIVER INFORMATION

Conowingo Dam Fisherman's Hotline: calling 410-457-4076 will give a recorded
message of the planned release of water through the dam. Four small gates is the
absolute maximum flow for any safe wading.

Susquehanna River at Harrisburg: 800-362-0335. A good wading/fishing level is 3.5
feet at Harrisburg. If you plan to fish the Susquehanna River or the flats, this is a
good number to monitor along with the Conowingo number above.

TOURIST INFORMATION

Tons of information is available free from state and county governments via phone, mail, the Internet, and tourist information centers along major highways. There are also numerous commercial sources in the forms of newspapers, magazines, radio programs, Internet sites, and travel guides available in bookstores or from AAA and other such sources.

However, for the Chesapeake Bay area, there's one source so outstanding it deserves special mention: *The Longstreet Highroad Guide to the Chesapeake Bay*, by Deane Winegar is available in bookstores and much of this information is also available on the Internet at http://sherpaguides.com/chesapeake_bay/.

Guide Kevin Josenhans nets one.

Marine Symbols

The Bay will attempt to kill you if you act foolishly in general: head out unprepared, drink lots of alcohol while boating, or fail to pay attention and think defensively.

Acquaint yourself with the symbols on the following pages or on any maps you may purchase and study your charts before a trip out onto the sea, or hire a seasoned professional guide that is familiar with the Bay.

Buoys and Beacons

#	Symbol	Description	#	Symbol	Description
1		Position of buoy	17	RB RB	Bifurcation buoy (RBHB)
2		Light buoy	18	RB RB	Junction buoy (RBHB)
3	BELL	Bell buoy	19	RB RB	Isolated danger buoy (RBHB)
3a	GONG	Gong buoy	20	RB G	Wreck buoy (RBHB or G)
4	WHIS	Whistle buoy	20a	RB G	Obstruction buoy (RBHB or G)
5	C	Can or Cylindrical buoy	21	Tel	Telegraph-cable buoy
6	N	Nun or Conical buoy	22		Mooring buoy (colors of mooring buoys never carried)
7	SP	Spherical buoy	22a		Mooring
8	S	Spar buoy	22b	Tel	Mooring buoy with telegraphic communications
†8a	P	Pillar or Spindle buoy	22c	T	Mooring buoy with telephonic communications
9		Buoy with topmark (ball) (see L-70)	23		Warping buoy
10		Barrel or Ton buoy	24	Y	Quarantine buoy
(La)		Color unknown	†24a		Practice area buoy
(Lb)	FLOAT	Float	25	Explos Anch	Explosive anchorage buoy
12	FLOAT	Lightfloat	25a	AERO	Aeronautical anchorage buoy
13		Outer or Landfall buoy	26	Deviation	Compass adjustment buoy
14	BW	Fairway buoy (BWVS)	27	BW	Fish trap (area) buoy (BWHB)
14a	BW	Mid-channel buoy (BWVS)	27a		Spoil ground buoy
†15	R "2" R "2"	Starboard-hand buoy (entering from seaward)	†28	W	Anchorage buoy (marks limits)
16	"1"	Port-hand buoy (entering from seaward)	†29	Priv maintd	Private aid to navigation (buoy) (maintained by private interests, use with caution)

AIDS TO NAVIGATION ON NAVIGABLE WATERWAYS
except Western Rivers and Intracoastal Waterway

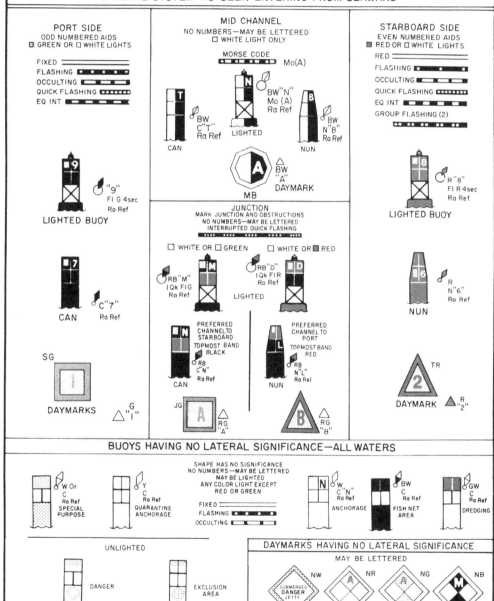

LATERAL SYSTEM AS SEEN ENTERING FROM SEAWARD

PORT SIDE
ODD NUMBERED AIDS
GREEN OR WHITE LIGHTS

FIXED
FLASHING
OCCULTING
QUICK FLASHING
EQ INT

"9" Fl G 4sec Ra Ref
LIGHTED BUOY

C"7" Ra Ref
CAN

SG
DAYMARKS

MID CHANNEL
NO NUMBERS—MAY BE LETTERED
WHITE LIGHT ONLY

MORSE CODE
Mo(A)

T
BW C"T" Ra Ref
CAN

N
BW"N" Mo(A) Ra Ref
LIGHTED

B
BW N"B" Ra Ref
NUN

A
BW "A" DAYMARK
MB

JUNCTION
MARK JUNCTION AND OBSTRUCTIONS
NO NUMBERS—MAY BE LETTERED
INTERRUPTED QUICK FLASHING

WHITE OR GREEN   WHITE OR RED

M
RB"M" IQk Fl G Ra Ref

D
RB"D" IQk Fl R Ra Ref
LIGHTED

N
PREFERRED CHANNEL TO STARBOARD TOPMOST BAND BLACK
RB C"N" Ra Ref
CAN

L
PREFERRED CHANNEL TO PORT TOPMOST BAND RED
RB N"L" Ra Ref
NUN

JG
A
RG "A"

B
RG "B"

STARBOARD SIDE
EVEN NUMBERED AIDS
RED OR WHITE LIGHTS

RED
FLASHING
OCCULTING
QUICK FLASHING
EQ INT
GROUP FLASHING (2)

8
R"8" Fl R 4sec Ra Ref
LIGHTED BUOY

6
R N"6" Ra Ref
NUN

2
TR
DAYMARK
R "2"

BUOYS HAVING NO LATERAL SIGNIFICANCE—ALL WATERS

W Or C Ra Ref
SPECIAL PURPOSE

Y C Ra Ref
QUARANTINE ANCHORAGE

SHAPE HAS NO SIGNIFICANCE
NO NUMBERS—MAY BE LETTERED
MAY BE LIGHTED
ANY COLOR LIGHT EXCEPT
RED OR GREEN
FIXED
FLASHING
OCCULTING

N
W C"N" Ra Ref
ANCHORAGE

BW C Ra Ref
FISH NET AREA

GW C Ra Ref
DREDGING

UNLIGHTED

DANGER

EXCLUSION AREA

DAYMARKS HAVING NO LATERAL SIGNIFICANCE
MAY BE LETTERED

NW
SUBMERGED DANGER JETTY
W Bn

NR
A
RW Bn

NG
A
GW Bn

NB
M
BW Bn

Dangers

1 Rock which does not cover (elevation above MHW) ♥ (25)	**11** Wreck showing any portion of hull or superstructure (above sounding datum)	(5½) Obstr **27** Obstruction
		28 Wreck (See O-11 to 16)
2 Rock which covers and uncovers, with height in feet above chart (sounding) datum *Uncov 2 ft ✿Uncov 2 ft ★(2) ✿(2)	**12** Wreck with only masts visible (above sounding datum) ⊹ Masts	Wreckage Wks **29** Wreckage
	13 Old symbols for wrecks	**29a** Wreck remains (dangerous only for anchoring)
3 Rock awash at the level of chart (sounding) datum ✳	**13a** Wreck always partially submerged	Subm piles **30** Submerged piling (See H-9, L-59)
When rock of O-2 or O-3 is considered a danger to navigation ✳ ✳	**†14** Sunken wreck dangerous to surface navigation (less than 11 fathoms over wreck) (See O-6a) ⊹	Snags Stumps **30a** Snags; Submerged stumps (See L-59)
†4 Sunken rock dangerous to surface navigation ⊡	**15** Wreck over which depth is known (5½) Wk	**31** Lesser depth possible
5 Shoal sounding on isolated rock (replaces symbol) (5) Rk	**†15a** Wreck with depth cleared by wire drag (2½) Wk	**32** Uncov Dries **33** Cov Covers (See O-2, 10) **34** Uncov Uncovers (See O-2, 10)
†6 Sunken rock not dangerous to surface navigation (more than 11 fathoms over rock) +	**16** Sunken wreck, not dangerous to surface navigation ⊹	(3) Rep (1958) Reported (with date)
6a Sunken danger with depth cleared by wire drag (in feet or fathoms) (2½) Rk (2½) Wk (2½) Obstr	**17** Foul ground Foul	Eagle Rk ✳ (rep 1958) **35** Reported (with name and date)
7 Reef of unknown extent Reef	**18** Overfalls or Tide rips Tide Rips [symbol] Symbol used only in small areas	**36** Discol Discolored (See O-9) **37** Isolated danger
8 Submarine volcano ⊙ Sub Vol	**19** Eddies Eddies ७ ७ ७ ७ Symbol used only in small areas	**†38** Limiting danger line
9 Discolored water ⊙ Discol Water	**20** Kelp, Seaweed Kelp ⋞ ⋞ ⋞ Symbol used only in small areas	rky **39** Limit of rocky area
	21 Bk Bank **22** Shl Shoal **23** Rf Reef **23a** Ridge **24** Le Ledge	**41** P A Position approximate **42** P D Position doubtful **43** E D Existence doubtful **44** P Pos Position **45** D Doubtful **†46** Unexamined
10 Coral reef, detached (uncovers at sounding datum) Coral Co Co	**25** Breakers (See A-12)	Subm Crib Crib (above water) **(Oa)** Crib
Coral or Rocky reef, covered at sounding datum (See A-11d, 11g) +Co 3 Reef Line	**26** Sunken rock (depth unknown) + When rock is considered a danger to navigation +	■ Platform (lighted) HORN **(Ob)** Offshore platform (unnamed) ■ Hazel (lighted) HORN **(Oc)** Offshore platform (named)

Light Symbols and Their Meanings		
Symbol	**Meaning**	**Description**
F	Fixed	A continuous, steady light.
F Fl	Fixed and flashing	A fixed light at regular intervals by a flash of greater brilliance.
F GP Fl	Fixed and group flashing	A fixed light varied at regular intervals by groups of 2 or more flashes of greater brilliance.
Fl	Flashing	A single flash showing at regular intervals, the duration of light always less than the duration of darkness.
Gp Fl	Group flashing	Groups of 2 or more flashes showing at regular intervals.
Qk Fl	Quick flashing	Shows not less than 60 flashes per minute.
I Qk Fl	Interrupted quick flashing	Shows quick flashes for about 5 seconds followed by a dark period of about 5 seconds.
E Int	Equal interval	Duration of light equal to that of darkness.
Occ	Occulting	A light totally eclipsed at regular intervals, the duration of light always equal to or greater than the duration of darkness.
Gp Occ	Group occulting	A light with a group of 2 or more eclipses at regular intervals.

Fly Shops
and Bait & Tackle Shops

MARYLAND	ADDRESS	PHONE
-A-		
Great Feathers	151 Main Street Annapolis, MD 21401	410-472-6799
Angler's Sports Center Ltd	1456 Whitehail Rd Annapolis, MD 21401	410-757-3442
Hudson Trail Outfitters Ltd	149 Annapolis Mall Annapolis, MD 21401	410-266-8390
Beachys Hardware	165 Main Street Annapolis, MD 21401	301-895-5208
-B-		
The Fishin' Shop	9026 C Pulaski Hwy Baltimore, MD 21220	410-391-0101
The Upstream Angler	9191 Baltimore National Pike Baltimore, MD 21042	
Clyde's Sport Shop	2307 Hammonds Ferry Rd. Baltimore, MD 21227	410-242-6108
Fisherman's Edge	1719-1/2 Edmondson Ave Baltimore, MD 21288	410-719-7999
Set's Sport Shop	509 York Rd Baltimore, MD 21204	410-823-1367
Tochterman's Fishing Tackle	1925 Eastern Ave Baltimore, MD 21231	410-327-6942
Gentleman Hunter	4829 Fairmont Ave Bethesda, MD 20814	301-907-4668
Dick's Sporting Goods	540 West PacPhail Rd Bel Air, MD 21014	410-638-7404
Dick's Sporting Goods	5220 Campbell Blvd Baltimore, MD 21236	410-933-0134
The Sports Authority	6510 Baltimore National Pike Baltimore,MD 21228	410-788-9650
Randy Day	11238 Adkins Rd Berlin, MD 21811	410-641-5029
The Sports Authority	4520 Mitchellville Rd Bowie, MD 20716	301-352-5690
S & S Bait & Tackle	1710 Eastern Avenue Baltimore, MD 21231	410-563-3243
The Hunting and Fishing Depot	810c Backriver Neck Rd. Baltimore, MD 21221	410-687-3300
-C -		
L.L. Bean	10300 Little Pawtucket Prk Columbia, MD 21044	410-715-7020
Tommy's Sporting Goods	300 Sunburst Hwy Cambridge, MD 21613	410-228-3658

Chesapeake Outdoors	1707 Main Street Chester, MD 21619	410-604-2500
Island Fishing & Hunting	115 South Piney Creek Rd Chester, MD 21619	410-643-4224
Dick's Sporting Goods	118 Shawan Rd Cockeysville, MD 21030	410-584-9050
Dick's Sporting Goods	6221 Columbia Crossing Circle Columbia, MD 21045	410-872-1100
Stemple Brothers	188 Conowingo Rd Conowingo, MD 21918	410-378-5594
-E-		
Shore Sportsman Hunting & Fishing Unlimited	8232 Ocean Gateway Easton, MD 21601	410-820-5599
-F-		
Hunting Creek Outfitters	29 N Market St Frederick, MD 21701	301-668-4333
Rod Rack	181 Thomas Johnson Dr Frederick, MD 21702	301-694-6143
The Sports Authority	5425 Urbana Pike Frederick, MD 21704	301-696-0252
-G-		
Galyan's	2 Grand Corner Ave Gaithersburg, MD 20878	301-947-0200
Winchester Creek Outfitters	313 Winchester Creek Rd Grasonville, MD 21638	410-827-7000
The Sports Authority	110 Odendhal Ave Gaithersburg, MD 20877	301-926-3445
Hudson Trail Outfitters	401 N Fredrick Ave Gaithersburg, MD 20879	301-948-2474
Bart's Sport World	6814 Ritchie Hwy Glen Burnie, MD 21061	301-761-8686
Dick's Sporting Goods	6711 Ritchie Hwy Glen Burnie, MD 21061	410-760-3933
The Sports Authority	595 East Ordnance Rd Glen Burnie, MD 21061	410-761-1151
The Sports Authority	6250 Greenbelt Rd Greenbelt, MD 20770	301-220-4120
H		
Broad Caster	19330 Leitersburg Pike Hagerstown, MD 21742	301-733-3474
Keystone Sporting Goods	13611 Pennsylvania Ave Hagerstown, MD 21742	301-733-0373
MacLellan's Fly Shop	P.O. Box 747 Hughesville, MD 20637-0747	301-274-5833
Bass Pro Shops Outdoor World	7000 Arundel Mills Circle Hanover, MD 21076	410-689-2500
Dick's Sporting Goods	17780 Garland Groh Blvd Hagerstown, MD 21740	240-420-0140
Penns Beach Marina	Foot of Lewis Street Havre De Grace, MD 21078	410-939-2060

	-K-	
Vonnies Sporting Goods	12503 Augustine Herman Hwy Kennedyville, MD 21645	410-778-5655
	-L-	
The Sports Authority	3335 Corridor Marketplace Laurel, MD 20724	301-483-0062
The Tackle Box	22035 Three Notch Rd Lexington Park, MD 20653	301-863-8151
Rod N Reel Hunting & Fishing Supplies	18161 3 Notch Road Lexington Park, MD 20653	301-872-5878
	-M-	
Backwater Angler	538 Monkton Rd Monkton, MD 21111	410-329-6821
On the Fly	538 Monkton Road Monkton, MD 21111	410-329-6821
Gunshack/Crosswind	P.O. Box 73 Mt. Airy, MD 21771	301-829-0122
Spring Creek Outfitters	P.O. Box 159 McHenry, MD 21541	301-387-2034
	-O-	
Backbone Mountain Sport Shop	4768 George Washington Hwy Oakland, MD 21550	301-334-5814
AKE Marine	12930 Sunset Ave Ocean City, MD 21842	410-213-0421
Island Creek Outfitters	40 Honeysuckle Ln Owings, MD 20736	301-812-1842 or 410-386-0950
	-P-	
Gunpowder Falls Outfitters	18827 Frederick Rd Parkton MD 21120	410-343-2328
Hanson's Hatchery	17675 Kohlhoss Rd Poolesville, MD 20837	
	-Q-	
Dave's Sport Shop	23701 Nanticoke Rd Quantico, MD 21856	410-742-2454
Pintail Point	511 Pintail Point Lane Queenstown, MD 21658	410-827-7029
	-R-	
Old Reistertown Bait & Tackle	16 Westminster Rd. Reistertown, MD 21136	410-526-6500
Ted Godfrey's Tackle	3509 Pleasant Plains Dr Reisterstown, MD 21136	410-239-8468
The Sports Authority	12055 Rockville Pike Rockville, MD 20852	301-231-8650
Hudson Trail Outfitters, Ltd	12085 Rockville Pike Rockville, MD 20852	301-881-4955

	-S-	
Keepers of St. Michaels	105 S Talbot St St Michaels, MD 21663	800-549-1872
Keepers #2	909 S Shumaker Dr Salisbury, MD 21804	410-742-4988
Salisbury Fly Shop	325 Snow Hill Rd Salisbury, MD 21804-5626	410-543-8359
Fly Emporium of Baltimore	8600 Foundry St Savage, MD 20763	410-792-0340
Great Feathers	14824 York Rd Sparks Glencoe, MD 21152	410-472-6799
LE Hitch & Son	1506 South Salisbury Blvd Salisbury, MD 21801	410-219-5887
Bay Trading Post	PO Box 396 St. Leonard, MD 20685-0396	410-586-1992
BJ's	11329 Savage River Rd Swanton, MD 21561	301-777-0001
	-T-	
Thurmont Sporting Goods	4 East Main Thurmont, MD 21788	301-271-7404
The Sports Authority	1238 Putty Hill Drive Towson, MD 21286	410-821-0210
Hudson Trail Outfitters	424 York Road Towson, MD 21204	410-583-0494
	-W-	
The Sports Authority	3326 Crain Highway Waldorf, MD 20601	301-645-2767
Fred's Sport Shop	2895 Crain Hwy Waldorf, MD 20601	301-645-5694
The Sports Authority	9987 Pulaski Highway White Marsh, MD 21220	410-916-3860
Angler's Hollow	34 W. Main St. Westminster, MD 21157	410-751-9349

VIRGINIA FLY SHOPS	ADDRESS	PHONE
-A-		
Neal's Handcrafted Lures	416 W Main St Abingdon, VA 24210-2608	540-628-4140
Virginia Creeper Fly Fish	17172 Jeb Stuart Hwy Abingdon, VA 24211	540-628-3826
Abingdon Outdoorsman	825 Cummings St Abingdon, VA 24211-3637	540-928-6249
Trout and About	3488 N Emerson St Arlington, VA 22201	703-536-7494
Angler's Lie	2165 N Glebe Rd Arlington, VA 22207	703-527-2524
The Sports Authority	3701 Jefferson Davis Highway Alexandria, VA 22314	703-684-3204
West Marine	601 South Patrick Street Alexandria, VA 22314	703-549-7020
Fishing World B&T	8796-1 Sacramento Drive Alexandria, VA 22309	703-781-4976
Hudson Trail Outfitters	1201 South Joyce Street Arlington, VA 22202	
-B-		
Dusty Wissmath's Fly Fishing	18116 Raven Rocks Rd Bluemont VA	
Mountain Sports Ltd	1021 Commonwealth Ave Bristol, VA 24201	540-466-8988
Blue Ridge Outdoors	125 North Main Street Blacksburg, VA 24060	540-552-9012
-C-		
Mountain River Outdoors	1301 Seminole Trail Charlottesville, VA 22901	804-978-7112
The Albemarle Angler	1129 Emmet St Barracks Rd Charlottesville, VA 22903	804-977-6882
PR Fly Fishing Inc	PO Box 669 Crozet, VA 22932	434-823-1937
Queen's Creek Co	Intersection of 3 & 198 Cobbs Creek, VA 23035	804-725-3889
Dances Sporting	570 Southpark Blvd Colonial Heights, VA 23834	804-526-8399
Pat's Sporting Goods	14812 Jefferson Davis Colonial, VA 23834	804-748-4165
The Bait Place	707 E Morris Hill Rd Covington, VA 24426	540-965-0633
Clarksville Sports Center	8200 Hwy 15 Clarksville, VA 23927	
-E-		
Murray's Fly Shop	121 Main Street Edinburg, VA 22824	540-984-4212

-F-		
Galyan's	12501 Fairlakes Circle Fairfax, VA 22033	703-803-0300
Anglers Lane	PO Box 1265 Forest, VA 24551	804-385-0200
Chesley's Tackle	PO Box 176 Fredericksburg, VA 22404	703-373-1051
Rapphannock Angler & Outdoor Adventures	4721 Plank Rd Fredericksburg, VA 22407	540-786-3334
The Fall Line	520 William St Fredericksburg, VA 22301	540-373-1812
The Sports Authority	12300 Price Club Plaza Fairfax, VA 22030	703-266-9283
Hudson Trails Outfitters	9488 Arlington Blvd Fairfax, VA 22030	703-591-2950
Hudson Trail Outfitters	11781 Lee Jackson Hwy Fairfax, VA	703-591-2950
Ed's Bait & Tackle	9766 Lee Highway Fairfax, VA 22031	703-273-1437
The Sports Authority	1461 Carl D Silver Parkway Fredericksburg, VA 22401	540-785-8071
Fisherman & Hunter's Den	115 Water St. Front Royal, VA 22360	540-636-3778
-G-		
Green Top Sporting Goods	10193 Washington Hwy Glen Allen, VA 23059	804-550-2188
Surber & Son	208 W Main Street Glad Spring, VA 24340	276-429-5383
Dick's Sporting Goods	9940 Brook Rd Glen Allen, VA 23059	434-261-1853
West Marine	10819 West Broad Street Glen Allen, VA 23060	434-346-9502
A & S Feed Supplies & Sporting Goods	Gloucester Point VA 23062	804-642-4940
Old Hooker Bait & Tackle	1802 George Washington Gloucester Point, VA 23062	804-642-4665
-H-		
Wallace's Bait & Tackle	365 Dandy Point Road Hampton, VA 23664	757-851-5451
Mossy Creek Fly Shop	2058 Autumn Lane Harrisonburg, VA 22801	800-646-2168
Blue Ridge Angler	1756 S Main St, Harrisonburg, VA 22801	540-574-3474
Hanover Flyfisher's Ltd.	PO Box 525 Hanover, VA 23069	804-537-5036
The Homestead Resort & Allegheny Outfitters	Rt 2 20 Main Street Hot Springs, VA	540-839-7760
Bishop Fishing Supply	Hampton, VA	757-723-7343

-H-		
The Sports Authority	2106 Coliseum Dr Hampton, VA 23666	757-826-5033
West Marine	2121 West Mercury Boulevard Hampton, VA 23666	757-825-4900
B & B Bait & Tackle	90 West Mercury Boulevard Hampton, VA 23669	757-722-0676
Buckroe Bait & Tackle & Seafood	815 Buckroe Avenue Hampton, VA 23664	757-850-4166
King St B & T	1709 North King Street Hampton, VA 23669	757-722-5437
Vanasse Bait & Tackle	28 Dandy Point Road Hampton, VA 23664	757-851-9732
-L-		
Reel Time Fly Fishing	23 W Washington St Lexington, VA 24450	540-462-6100
Timberlake Sporting Goods	10119 Timberlake Road Lynchburg, VA 24502	434-239-3474
Mountain View Gun Shop	1146 Shenk Hollow Road Luray, VA 22835	540-743-4028
The Shenandoah Lodge and Outfitters	100 Grand View Drive Luray, VA 22835	800-866-9958
Dick's Sporting Goods	4040 Wards Rd Lynchburg, VA 24502	804-832-5666
-M-		
L.L. Bean	8095 Tyson's Corner Ctr McLean, VA 22102	703-288-4466
Virginia Outdoorsman	679 Lake Ctr #B3 Moneta, VA 24121	540-721-4867
-N-		
Georges Bait & Tackle	1909 Jefferson Avenue Newport News, VA 23607	757-245-0770
Performance Lures	Newport News, VA 23602	757-877-8831
Robbins Military Surplus	17423 Warwick Boulevard Newport News, VA 23603	757-887-2516
Sports Inc.	618 J Clyde Morris Boulevard Newport News, VA 23601	757-595-9333
Wilcox Bait & Tackle	9501 Jefferson Avenue Newport News, VA 23605	757-595-5537
The Sports Authority	5900 E Virginia Beach Blvd Norfolk, VA 23502	757-466-8107
C Tackle	1821 East Little Creek Road Norfolk, VA 23518	757-587-1003
Cobbs Marina Inc.	4524 Dunning Road Norfolk, VA 23518	757-588-5401
Fishin Stuff	7434 Tidewater Drive Norfolk, VA 23505	757-480-2004

Harrison Boat House & Fishing Pier	414 West Ocean View Avenue Norfolk, VA 23503	757-587-9630
Hopkins Fishing	1130 Boissevain Avenue Norfolk, VA 23507	757-622-0977
Portco Lures Outlet Store	7625 Shore Drive Norfolk, VA 23518	757-587-1755
Sandy Point Tackle & Marine	5015 Colley Avenue Norfolk, VA 23508	757-440-7696
Screaming Eagle Charters and Sea Talon Lures	820 West 21st Street Norfolk, VA 23517	757-627-2598
Taylors Landing Tackle Shop	8180 Shore Drive Norfolk, VA 23518	757-587-5595
-O-		
P Bee Sports	Rt. 20 Orange, VA 22960	804-672-4542
-P-		
Back River Market Inc.	1250 Poquoson Avenue Poquoson, VA 23662	757-868-4130
The Weekender Boating Center	105 Rens Road Poquoson, VA 23662	
City Park Bait & Tackle	5015 Portsmouth Boulevard Portsmouth, VA 23701	757-465-5399
Rawls Hunting & Fishing Supplies	3247 Tyre Neck Road Portsmouth, VA 23703	757-686-3688
Flat Rock Sporting Goods	2515 Anderson Highway Powhatan, VA 23139	540-598-5466
-R-		
Chesapeake Bait	567 Seaboard Drive Reedville, VA 22539	804-453-5003
Pride of Virginia Seafood Products	Reedville, VA 22539	804-453-6191
Angler's Cove	9121 Staples Mill Rd Richmond, VA 23228	804-672-3474
The Complete Fly Fisher	5703-A Grove Ave Richmond, VA 23226	804-282-5527
Short Pump Outfitters	1362 Gaskins Rd Richmond, VA 23233	804-741-4562
Orvis Roanoke	1711 Blue Hills Drive Roanoke, VA 24022	540-345-3635
Blue Ridge Fly Fishers	5524 Williamson Rd Roanoke, VA 24012	540-563-1617
Fly Fish The World Inc.	5705 Grove Ave Richmond, VA 23226	804-282-5527
Minnow Pond	615 9th St SE Roanoke, VA 24013	540-342-5585
H & V Sporting Goods	102 Front Street Richlands, VA 24641	276-963-2415

-R-		
Angler's Lab Outfitters	1362 Gaskins Rd. Richmond, VA 23233	757-491-2988
Dick's Sporting Goods	1520 W Koger Center Blvd Richmond, VA 23235	804-897-5299
-S-		
Regensburg Marine	Severn, VA 23155	804-642-9112
Thornton River Fly Shop	29 Main Street Sperryville, VA 22740	540-987-9400
Dashiell's Half Round Showroom	1436 Holland Rd Suffolk, VA 23434	757-539-7854
Hudson Trails Outfitters	6701 Loisdale Rd Springfield, VA	703-922-0050
The Sports Authority	6658-B Springfield Mall Springfield, VA 22150	703-922-5600
Dick's Sporting Goods	45633 Dulles Eastern Plaza Sterling, VA 20166	800-690-7655
The Sports Authority	21070 Southbank Street Sterling, VA 20165	703-421-7010
-T-		
The Outdoorsman	3085 Burrland Lane The Plains, VA 20198	540-253-5545
Fletcher's Hardware & Sporting Goods	P.O. Box 29 Vansant, VA 24656	276-935-8332
-V-		
Orvis Tyson Corners	8334 Leesburg Pike 7-123 Vienna, VA 22182	703-556-8634
Angler's Lab Outfitters	1554 Laskin Rd #120 Virginia Beach, VA 23451	757-491-2988
Long Bay Pointe Bait & Tackle	2109 W Great Neck Rd Virginia Beach, VA 23451	757-481-7517
Chesapeake Gun Works	6644 Indian River Road Virginia Beach, VA 23464	757-420-1712
The Sports Authority	8355 Leesburg Pike Vienna, VA 22182	703-827-2206
The Sports Authority	2720 North Mall Dr Virginia Beach, VA 23452	757-498-3355
West Marine	2865 Lynnhaven Drive Virginia Beach, VA 23451	703-549-7020
Bubba's Marina and Crabhouse	3323 Shore Drive Virginia Beach, VA 23451	757-481-3513
Fish Safari	2029 Lynnhaven Parkway Virginia Beach, VA 23456	757-416-1600
J & B Rods	2100 Marina Shores Drive Virginia Beach, VA 23451	757-496-2206

Lighthouse Tackle	4461 Shore Drive Virginia Beach, VA 23455	757-318-3818
Lynnhaven Inlet Fishing Pier	2350 Starfish Road Virginia Beach, VA 23451	757-481-7071
Mr. Wiffle Lures	5180 Cleveland Street Virginia Beach, VA 23462	757-499-1007
Oceans East Tackle Shop	309 Aragona Boulevard Virginia Beach, VA 23462	757-499-2277
Raugh Company	1270 Diamond Springs Road Virginia Beach, VA 23455	757-363-8320
Sandbridge Station	309 Sandbridge Road Virginia Beach, VA 23456	757-426-2400
Tackle Shop	313 Virginia Beach Boulevard Virginia Beach, VA 23451	757-428-1000
-W-		
Rhodes Gift & Fly	P.O. Box 53 Warrenton, VA 20188	540-347-4161
Pride of Virginia Bait & Oyster	3031 Little Bay Road White Stone, VA 22578	804-435-6740
Feathered Hook Outfitters Inc	3035 Valley Ave Winchester, VA 22601	540-678-8999
Old Dominion Sports Center	370 Battle Ave Winchester, VA 22601	540-667-4867
Dawson's	14510 Jefferson Davis Hwy Woodbridge, VA 22191	703-490-3308
Hassett Gun Supply	1300 W Main Street Waynesboro, VA 22980	540-942-9581
The Sports Authority	2700 Potomac Mills Circle Woodbridge, VA 22192	703-491-0106
West Marine	13330 Gordon Boulevard Woodbridge, VA 22191	703-492-6225
Hudson Trail Outfitters	4530 Wisconsin Ave Washington, DC 20016	202-363-9810
-Y-		
Bishop Fishing Supply	1215 George Washington Mem. Hwy, Yorktown, VA 23693	757-591-9300
Catfish Unlimited	Yorktown, VA 23692	757-865-0854
Grafton Fishing Supply	5760 George Washington Yorktown, VA 23692	757-890-2100

*Writer Boyd Pfeiffer with a Delaware Bay
striper taken on spin tackle.*

Index

About the Artist

Duane Raver, Gamefish illustrations. A native of Iowa, Duane was educated in central Iowa schools and received a degree in Fisheries Management from Iowa State University in 1949. He was employed as a fishery biologist with the North Carolina Wildlife Resources Commission in 1950. In 1960, Duane transferred to the Education Division of the Wildlife Commission and was on the staff of *Wildlife in North Carolina* magazine. He was Managing Editor of the magazine until 1970, when he was appointed Editor.

Wildlife artwork has always been a major activity in his life, and Duane completed over 200 cover paintings for *Wildlife in North Carolina* during his 30 years with the Wildlife Commission. He retired in 1979 to do wildlife artwork full time.

Duane works primarily in acrylic and opaque watercolor. He does only wildlife subjects with emphasis on fish and gamebirds. He welcomes inquiries and visits at his home studio at 910 Washington Street, Cary, NC 27511. Duane can be reached at 919-467-9277.